THE
SKILLFUL
TEACHER

BUILDING YOUR TEACHING SKILLS

Jon Saphier
Robert Gower

Research for Better Teaching, Inc., 56 Bellows Hill Rd., Carlisle, Massachusetts 01741

To order copies of this book, or to request reprint permission, please contact Research for
Better Teaching, Inc., 56 Bellows Hill Road, Carlisle, Massachusetts, 01741.

10 9 8 7

CONTENTS

Preface

We have written this book to assist teachers in their efforts to build greater competence in teaching skills. Our values are obvious. We believe teachers and teaching are the heart of the educational enterprise. *The Skillful Teacher* views the teacher as the central figure in both the design and the implementation of classroom activity. We further believe that a teacher's skill makes a difference in the performance of students, not only in their achievement scores on tests (as important as that might be), but in their sense of fulfillment in school and their feelings of well-being. We do not mean to imply that being skillful substitutes for other human qualities; but we will argue that, whatever else teachers do, they perform in the classroom and their actions set the stage for students' experiences—therefore, only a skillful performance will do.

As the chapters of this book unfold, our exploration of teaching will be guided by three key concepts: comprehensiveness, repertoire, and matching.

> *Comprehensiveness* refers to our efforts to understand teaching as a whole. We are working toward the day when one might say, "These are the areas that make up teaching. Know how to handle these things and you have all the basic tools for the job."

> *Repertoire* represents the fact that there is more than one way for teachers to handle any basic area of teaching. Repertoire is a concept that challenges us to develop a variety of strategies and behaviors for dealing with teaching situations.

> *Matching* is an idea that directs us to think about what behavior to pick from our expanding repertoires in light of the situation, the group, or the characteristics of individual students.

The structure of this book will rotate through these three ideas again and again. As each new area of teaching is defined and described, we will take it through the range of options we have uncovered for handling it. And then we will address the issue of matching for that area and what is known about it.

We have built the framework of *The Skillful Teacher* upon a large number of very specific teaching behaviors and situations so that it can be immediately useful as a tool for self-improvement, staff development, supervision, and teacher evaluation.

The framework ties theory directly to practice. Examples are extensively provided to illustrate the teaching performances being discussed. It is our hope that in this way readers will be able to understand their own teaching (or the teaching of another) more fully and accurately; and, more importantly, will be able to control their own teaching so that it better serves their ends and the needs of their students.

Acknowledgements

We are grateful to the many teachers and administrators in Concord, Newton, Carlisle, and Brookline, Massachusetts, who cooperated with us in our observational studies over a three-year period. Our interviews and feedback sessions with them directly helped us refine the Parameters of Teaching.

Over a period of years Jinny Chalmers, Susan-Jo Russell, Suzanne Stuart, and Risa Whitehead held many intense and important discussions with the authors about teaching and opened their classrooms and their hearts with sincerity and generosity. They participated in more ways than they know in the development of our thinking.

Kim Marshall's detailed critique helped enormously in editing an earlier edition into more lucid, jargon-free prose. Roland Barth performed a similar and much appreciated task.

John Glade's fine editorial talents and Christine Glade's design wizardry helped move the book forward a quantum measure in quality and appearance.

A book that attempts to synthesize as much information as this one is obviously indebted to a host of authors and thinkers. The bibliography at the end of each chapter should indicate the range of people who have influenced our thinking.

About the Authors

Jon Saphier was a classroom teacher at both secondary and elementary levels for 10 years. He has served as a team leader, as a staff developer in a large urban school system, and as a university instructor and supervisor of student teachers. Since 1980 Dr. Saphier has been a full-time consultant and works in-depth with about a dozen school districts annually in long term projects for instructional improvement.

Bob Gower is presently a faculty member at the University of Lowell in Lowell, Massachusetts. He has been a public and private school teacher, a K-8 school principal, a manager of training for a large computer company, and a consultant for public schools. Dr. Gower is currently active in graduate level teacher education and school site staff development in public schools.

"How do we bring to a conscious level the fact that you and I are using them [teaching skills] daily? You can't transmit something that isn't conscious, that's simply intuitive. I know that when I used to train teachers directly I would say, 'Let me take that reluctant group. Now watch what I do and then you do it.' And I found that teacher picked up all my bad habits, and missed what really made that lesson go because I had not articulated it."

—Madeline Hunter, *Association for Supervision and Curriculum Development* National Conference, Houston, 1977

1

The Skillful Teacher: Introduction

THE SKILLFUL TEACHER: INTRODUCTION

I'd ask to know what I was walling in or walling out
—Robert Frost, "Mending Wall"

What is Skill in Teaching?

Teaching is one of the most complex human endeavors imaginable. Both as teachers ourselves and as students and researchers of teaching we have been awed by the immensity of the task of understanding teaching. We know that a good teacher is many things, among them a caring person. But a good teacher is also a skillful practitioner, meaning adept at certain specifiable, observable actions. Being skillful means you can *do* something that can be seen; it means different levels of skill may be displayed by different individuals; and it means, above all, that you can *learn how* to do it and can continue to improve at it.

Skillful teachers are made, not born. They have learned (though probably not at teachers' college) the skills they use, and we can look at what they are doing in the classroom and say what is skillful about it. Many skillful teachers do not have the terms or the concepts for describing what they already do. They just "know" what to do, and seem to do it effortlessly and naturally. . .intuitively, some might say. To us, this effortlessness is an unconscious, automatic kind of knowing— "tacit knowledge" Michael Polanyi (1966) calls it. The limitation of it is that this kind of knowing is acquired only by a few—not God-given at birth, we want to re-peat, but learned by them unpredictably over time in many different ways. And they can't pass it on to the rest of us because they can't say what they do.

There are some people, of course, who are not cut out to be teachers, just as some of us are not cut out to be race-car drivers. No amount of skill training is go-ing to make some of us able race-car drivers. But the great majority of us who are not born with a feel for the road in our fingertips can still be taught the skills of race-car driving; we can get very competent at it, and we can continue to improve.

Being skillful in teaching and our attitude about that is an important theme of this book. As we develop that theme we want to be clear that we are not "walling out" from our conception of teaching certain important things, like being a human being. We value teachers who can feel a hurt, who know how to laugh and how to love. Being skillful is not in competition with being a thinking, feeling being. But we are highlighting the skillful part of being a good teacher in this book. There is more to good teaching than skill, but there's no good teaching without it.

Our image of skillful teachers is of people who are aware of the complexity of the job, people who try to be *conscious and deliberate* about what they do. They don't do what they do just because that's the way it's always been done, or because that's the cultural expectation for how it shall be done. They do what they do because they've thought about it and it seems like the best thing to do. They make choices from a repertoire of options. They want to control and regulate their teaching to have a positive effect on students, so they are willing to monitor what they do, get feedback, and try different things.

Skillful teachers are *determined* that students will succeed. If students are not succeeding, they examine their programs, their curricula, and their own teaching to see if they must adjust.

In addition to being determined, skillful teachers are *clear*: clear about what is to be learned, clear about what achievement means, clear about what they are going to do to help students attain it. And if that doesn't work, they will make another plan that is also technically clear and well-thought out.

Finally, skillful teachers are *learners*—"always a student of teaching," as Joyce (1981) says. Skillful teachers, though confident and competent, constantly reach out to the world around, to the research, to colleagues, with an assertive curiosity that says, "I don't know it all. No one does or ever will, but I am always growing, adding to my knowledge and skills and effectiveness." To skillful teachers, that openness and reaching out is an important element of professionalism.

So what, then, are the skills of teaching and how will we address them?

Everything You Always Wanted to Know About Teaching

Are the following among the things you'd like to know?

1. How do I get students to pay attention and stay on-task? *(Attention)*
2. How do I keep the flow of events moving with smooth, rapid transitions? *(Momentum)*
3. How do I communicate to students what I expect of them, and are my expectations appropriate? *(Expectations)*
4. How do I build good personal relationships with students? *(Personal Relationship Building)*
5. How do I deal with very resistant students? *(Discipline)*
6. What does it take to explain things clearly? *(Clarity)*
7. How do I make lessons more efficient and effective? *(Principles of Learning)*

8. How do I get the most out of my space and furniture? *(Space)*
9. How do I time events and regulate schedules so that students get the most productive learning time? *(Time)*
10. What procedural routines are important, and how do I get maximum mileage out of them? *(Routines)*
11. How can I vary my teaching style? *(Models of Teaching)*
12. How can I adjust for students' learning styles? *(Learning Experiences)*
13. What is my hidden curriculum? *(Dimensionality)*
14. What should I teach, and how should I frame my objectives? *(Objectives)*
15. How do I know what students have really learned? *(Evaluation)*
16. How do I build/adjust curriculum for maximum effectiveness? *(Organization of Curriculum)*

If these questions are on your list, this may be the right book for you. There is a chapter on each question, and each question is clearly important. They are about areas with which all teachers deal, regardless of the age, subject, or grade taught. In a way, they define teaching; they *are* teaching. They are important things with which teachers inescapably come to grips, consciously or unconsciously. They summarize virtually all the decisions, actions, and situations a teacher has to handle with students in classrooms.

There are a lot of other important areas in which teachers need to function, too…like working effectively with colleagues, with parents, and in political and union forums; but they are not the subject of this book. *The Skillful Teacher* focuses on the classroom instructional skills of interactive teaching.

How will we go about answering the questions above? We will do so by drawing on the existing knowledge base about teaching, the stunning and rich knowledge base that has lain scattered on the barren littoral of cynicism, confusion and obscurity like a 1,000-piece jigsaw puzzle, complete, but waiting to be assembled.

The knowledge base tells us that there are many ways to handle the job implicit in each question (e.g., gaining attention to task—40+ ways; choosing a model of teaching—20+ models; choosing and writing objectives—five kinds). But it also tells us *what they are*. The knowledge base about teaching is not a set of prescriptions, a list of behaviors known to produce effective learning (though there are a few of these). Nor could it or will it ever be! The knowledge base tells us what our options are for dealing with each area, each major job of teaching, each question above. It further tells us that effective teaching lies in choosing appropriately from among our options to match given students, situations, or curricula. *In effective teaching, matching is the name of the game.*

To illustrate this, let's take a simple management situation—dealing with intrusions. Consider this situation: A teacher instructing a small group has an interruption from a student (Jimmy) who's stuck on an item on a worksheet; Jimmy has come to the teacher for help. There are several options for how the teacher can handle this, bearing in mind the need to keep the momentum of the group going but also to not leave Jimmy idle or frustrated: 1) wave Jimmy off; 2) wave Jimmy in but signal him to be silent until there is an appropriate pause to give help; 3) redirect Jimmy to another student for help; 4) teach students not to interrupt to begin with during instructional groups.

No one of these options is inherently "better" teaching. You can surely imagine various conditions under which each one would be the most appropriate response. For instance, if Jimmy doesn't have the confidence or social skills to approach another student for help, then waving-in may be better than redirecting. On the other hand, if Jimmy is overly dependent on the teacher, waving him off may be best, especially if there is confidence that he *can* do it himself if he tries again. The teacher's success in handling Jimmy will depend upon whether the teacher knows the options available for dealing with the situation, and can choose the best response by matching the options to that specific situation.

If, in a similar manner, there are many ways of dealing with each of the major areas of teaching identified in our list of questions, then skillful teaching involves continually broadening one's repertoire in each area and picking from it appropriately to match given students, groups, situations, or curricula. *The knowledge base about teaching to which we are referring is the available repertoire of moves and patterns of action in each of the above areas, available for anyone to learn, to refine, and to do skillfully.* In this book we will present the specific options we have discovered for each area, illustrate them with examples, and offer what is known about how to do the matching.

Parameters of Teaching

We're going to call these areas of teaching "parameters." Parameter is a technical word. In science it means "a constant whose value varies with the circumstances of its application." Applied to teaching, what's constant is the job—e.g., maintaining attention or communicating expectations—and what varies is the way to do that job in different circumstances.

Each question in our earlier list represents one parameter of teaching; the label we will use for that parameter is the italicized word in parenthesis following the question. Each parameter encompasses the many teaching responses and performance options that comprise the available repertoire within that particular area. In addition, since these parameters *together* make up teaching, it is important to recognize how the parameters are related to each other.

Some of the parameters have skills associated with them that are very specific. We will call such skills "moves," because they represent an action or a remark that takes but a second of time to perform. Moves are quick, discrete, and observable behaviors. They can be counted if you so desire. Many teaching skills can be explained in terms of moves, and many of them turn out to be related to classroom management: *Attention, Momentum, Expectations, Personal Relationship Building*. These are examples of what we will call Management Parameters.

Other parameters involve teaching skills that *can't* be performed or seen in a second. We consider being able to implement a model of teaching—for instance, Hilda Taba's 9-step Inductive Model—a skillful performance. A teacher skilled at that model orchestrates a series of events and follows certain specifiable principles for reacting to students. The whole performance unfolds over time according to a certain regular and recognizable "pattern." Being able to perform the pattern is the skill. It's a package: a cohesive, planful package that is greater than the sum of its discrete parts. To understand teaching (and to expand one's repertoire as a skillful teacher) one needs to be able to see "moves" as they stand alone and "patterns" of moves which make sense only when you look at them as purposeful packages. It's a different kind of analysis, and to understand teaching one must understand both. The parameters that are patterns we group together and call Instructional Parameters.

As if that weren't enough, some of the important things teachers do skillfully are hard to see at all! Some of these are covert decisions and can only be inferred if we're observing a class; others take place before school during planning or after school during the correcting of students' work. These skills generally involve choosing objectives, organizing curriculum, and evaluating student learning, and relate to what we will call Curriculum Parameters: *Objectives, Organization of Curriculum, Learning Experiences, Evaluation*.

So, we wind up with three kinds of parameters for skillful teaching: Management, Instructional and Curriculum. It is interesting to note that as an external observer of someone else's teaching you can only see these different types of teaching skills by looking in different ways. The Management Parameters are mostly moves. They are low-inference, meaning you can see and count them directly when they happen. For instance, you don't have to do much inferring to identify this Attention move: "Johnny, come on now. Get back to work." The Instructional Parameters are medium-inference skills. As an observer you'd have to watch for a while and put together the behaviors you see over time to identify the pattern. The Curriculum Parameters are high-inference skills, not to the teacher who is performing them, but to an external observer who has to put quite a few things together and make a mental leap to infer what the objective is in a given lesson. To understand skillful teaching, it is necessary to recognize these different types of, and different ways of looking at, teaching skills.

The three groups of parameters for skillful teaching have another relation, too—functional. The Management Parameters are the foundation of teaching—the *sine qua non*. If those jobs aren't being handled, no learning can take place. They contain the prerequisite skills for good teaching. The Instructional Parameters deliver the goods; their skills come to life during interactive learning time in classrooms. The Curriculum Parameters contain skills that provide the blueprints for instruction. They stand behind and above instruction and management. Management skills support and make possible instruction. Curriculum skills design instruction. And Instructional skills themselves deliver the goods. Altogether, these parameters delineate teaching: teaching is *all* of them. (See Figure 1-1.)

Plan of this Book

The Skillful Teacher moves from the here and now concerns of the Management Parameters, those most pressing and immediate needs for many of us, to parameters that address why we went into teaching to begin with—good instruction and caring about kids. We move then into Curriculum Parameters, the design skills for those most important decisions about what education is for, what shall be taught, and how we shall know if it's been learned. Thus, the chapters move from the specific and discrete to the complex, from those parts of teaching that are moves, to patterns of moves, to decisions about design.

Each chapter addresses a different parameter. We frequently start by describing why the parameter is important and how it relates to the bigger picture of teaching and learning. Then we define concepts and categories useful for understanding the parameter and go inside each category to lay out the repertoire of ways teachers handle pertinent situations. We do this with examples as often as possible. Next we usually examine what is known about matching teacher choices to students, situations, or curricula. At the end of each chapter is a "Checking. . ." page which lists all the key concepts of the parameter in a format designed to help teachers analyze their own repertoires and decisions.

It is not absolutely necessary to read the chapters in order, but there are certain cumulative benefits that make that desirable. Good discipline, for example, builds on a foundation of teachers' skills with the Attention, Momentum, Expectations, and Personal Relationship Building parameters. If you're struggling with a difficult class and turn to the Discipline chapter, you will find references back to the four

Figure 1-1

Understanding Teaching

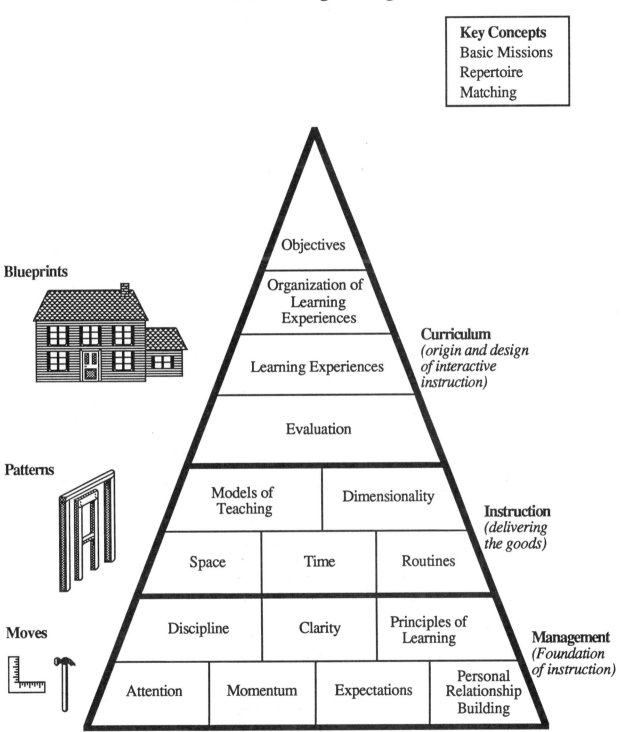

Management Parameters listed above; they're the first place to check oneself when working with difficult students.

Uses of this Book

Our audience is teachers and those who work with teachers around instruction—supervisors, evaluators, and staff developers. It is a professional book, a book we hope will be picked up by professional teachers and used to examine what they do. Even experienced teachers should check their skills against the repertoires available in each parameter to see if there are things that would add to their range, their effectiveness, and their ability to match the diverse needs we face these days.

We also desire through this book to build a common language and concept system for talking about teaching; not a dictionary of jargon, but at least a set of important and meaningful ideas about teaching that all educators can begin to use in common. If we can better understand each other, speaking and writing in clear and meaningful terms, then we can expect observation write-ups and evaluations of teaching to be more useful; supervision conferences to be more specific and productive; and staff development programs to be more focused.

We might also expect some of the barriers of isolation and loneliness between teachers to come down. We might expect teacher talk in teachers' rooms and other meeting places to be more open, more mutually helpful, and more about instruction. With a common professional knowledge base, discussing problems with each other might seem less an admission of personal inadequacy (a notion rooted in the "intuitive" teacher myth—if good teaching is intuitive and you're having problems, then there must be something wrong with you) and more a matter of a professional problem to tackle with knowledge and skills.

In undergraduate teacher education courses, in student teaching, and in graduate seminars this same focus on skills and on the development of common technical understandings should find a place. To recall an earlier theme, technical understanding of teaching casts no aspersions on the importance of humanism or child development or detailed knowledge of age and grade specific content, methods, and materials. Student teachers in the primary grades, for example, would do well to know about Cuisenaire rods and how to use them to teach place value. Likewise, student teachers in high school social studies would do well to know about the Amherst "Problems in American Civilization" Series and their uses. But teacher training (and in-service training) already deal with these things. In our development as a profession it is time to deal with teaching itself.

Source Materials

Joyce, B.R., Clark, C. and Peck, L. *Flexibility in Teaching*. New York: Longmans, 1981.

Polanyi, M. *The Tacit Dimension*. Garden City, NY: Doubleday and Co., 1966.

2

Attention

How do I get students to pay attention and stay on task?

Desisting
Alerting
Enlisting
Acknowledging
Winning

ATTENTION

The Attention parameter concerns teachers' skills in getting and keeping students *on-task* during classroom time; that is, engaging and involving students in legitimate curriculum activities. (In contrast to time spent on-task, off-task time includes behaviors such as setting up, getting ready, fooling around, waiting, daydreaming, socializing, and many others whose details need not concern us just yet.) In recent years many researchers have timed students in classrooms to see how much time they spend on-task, and then correlated on-task time with achievement (e.g., Bennett, 1978; Rosenshine, 1978). It is not surprising that they get fairly consistent positive correlations: the more time students spend seriously engaged in learning activities, the likelier they are to master the material. In this chapter we will examine the moves teachers make within the Attention parameter to maximize on-task time in the classroom.

In many ways, Attention is the bellwether parameter among the group of Management Parameters. Unless students are paying attention to the instruction, it does not matter how good the lesson may be otherwise. Engaging and involving students on-task in large group, small group, or individual learning experiences is what Attention is all about—indeed, what management is all about. It is the precondition for instruction, the *sine qua non* for curriculum implementation.

The Repertoire of Attention Moves

Skillful teachers make certain moves to engage students' attention: to capture it initially, to maintain it, and to recapture or refocus it when it wanders off course. This is the general class of moves referred to by the parameter label "Attention." Within this general class of Attention moves it is possible to distinguish five categories of teacher behaviors, which we call: Desisting, Alerting, Enlisting, Acknowledging, and Winning. The skillful teacher's repertoire for "getting and keeping students on-task" includes each of these categories of moves.

Desisting

Desisting moves carry the message "get with it." They are corrective and direct. They tell the students that they're doing something that they shouldn't be doing, and imply what the students *should* do (reengage the task). Among the various Desisting moves teachers make, individual moves vary in the degree to which they are corrective and direct: Some moves are more forceful or stronger means of conveying to students that they should "get with it" than others. The list below identifies the various types of Desisting moves we can observe teachers making—ordered from most forceful to least forceful—and gives an example of each.

1. <u>Punish</u>: "Well then, you'll have to miss recess if you can't get it done now."

2. <u>Exclude</u>: "Leave the group, Foster."

3. <u>Threaten</u>: "Stop it now, or leave the group."

4. <u>Sharp Sarcasm</u>: "Did you leave your head at home again, Grant?"

5. <u>Judgemental Reprimand</u>: "Can't you stop being such a pain?"; "Why don't you act like a fourth grader?"

6. <u>Order</u>: "Get back to work, now."; "Sit on your hands until you're absolutely sure you're not going to touch anyone."

7. <u>Specific Verbal Desist</u>: Teacher names the behavior to stop and gives the student the appropriate replacement behavior: "Stop the tapping, Jim, and get back to your handwriting."

8. <u>General Verbal Desist</u>: "Harry, cut it out."

9. <u>Mild Sarcasm</u>: Teacher says to a student who is whispering to his girlfriend, "Brendan, I'm glad you've found a new friend."

10. <u>Private Desist</u>: Either specific or general, but spoken softly so only the student addressed has his attention drawn to the teacher.

11. <u>Bring in Group Pressure</u>: "Fred, none of us can leave for gym until you're with us..." Classmates chime in, "Yeah, Fred, come on!"

12. <u>Peer Competition</u>: "John's ready. Are you, Beth?"

13. <u>Move Seat</u>: "Jimmy, move over to table four, please."

14. "I"-message: "It frustrates me when you talk to kids like that while I'm trying to teach, Clare. I feel like all the work I put into preparing this lesson is down the drain."

15. Urge: "C'mon Jill, will you please get in gear?"; "OK, let's sit down and be good listeners."

16. Remind: "What are you supposed to be doing, Shelly?"

17. Flattery: "You're too conscientious to waste your time this way."; "Back to work, handsome!"

18. Signals: Bell ring, raised hand, piano chord, etc.; or: without breaking the flow of talk with one student, the teacher holds up a hand in a "stop" gesture to a third student, signalling him to cease interrupting (or whatever he's doing) and perhaps implying by facial expression and body language, "Wait a minute, I'll be right with you."

19. Pause and Look: Teacher looks at the child...the 'long look'.

20. Name: Dropping a student's name into the flow of conversation (but *not* to call on the student) for purposes of attention: "Now the next problem—Jess—that we're going to tackle has some of the same elements—Jess—but the exponents are simpler."

21. Offer Help: "How can I help you with this, Charlie?"; "Do you need help, Charlie?"

22. Touch: Teacher places a hand gently on the student's shoulder or some other neutral place—may or may not be accompanied by the teacher stopping the activity and making eye contact.

23. Proximity: Being or moving physically near to the student with wandering attention (or whose attention is likely to wander).

Alerting

Alerting moves are often targeted at a group of students as opposed to individuals, and have the effect of keeping the students on their toes, minimizing distractions. There is no direct message conveyed in these moves; rather, they serve to generally keep the group alert and in anticipation. As with Desisting moves, the various Alerting moves teachers make differ in the degree of force expressed in the move. The continuum of Alerting moves, from most forceful to least forceful, includes:

1. Startle: Noticing that attention is wandering as a group listens to a cassette, the teacher abruptly hits the "stop" button and pops a question: "Why do you suppose Jefferson felt that way about Hamilton?"

2. Using Student's Name in an Instructional Example: "President John Lynn sits impeached and convicted. Who then would become president?...And we thought life was tough under Lynn! Now V.P. Christiane Baker becomes president. It's time to pack our bags and move to Canada!"

3. Redirecting Partial Answer: Teacher redirects a question to another student for completion of the answer.

4. Pre-Alert: "That's right. Now try this next one, Holly. Check her, Dwayne, and see if she gets it right."; "Now try this next one, Holly. Dwayne will help you if you run into trouble." (Both moves pre-alert Dwayne that he may have to answer. This is a way of focusing two students on one question.)

5. Unison: "6 x 6 is...Jane?...That's right. 8 x 8 is...everybody!"

6. Looking at One, Talking to Another: Teacher looks at one student but talks to another student. (Lasts but a moment.)

7. Incomplete Sentences: "...and so, as we all know, the thing that we put at the end of a sentence is a..."—teacher may or may not display open hands and raised eyebrows at the group, or use hand gestures, to encourage someone to respond.

8. Equal Opportunity: Teacher makes sure everyone gets called on or is checked, and students know from past experience that it will happen and could happen to them at any moment.

9. Random Order: Teacher calls on students out of sequence of their seating pattern so they can't predict when they'll be called on. [See the Note at the end of this list.]

10. Circulation: Teacher physically moves around the room.

11. Wait-time: Teacher pauses and allows a brief silence if a student

doesn't answer a question immediately. (This means having the patience to endure what may seem like an uncomfortable pause for five seconds, during which time the student may be able to generate a response if we don't jump in with cues or help. While the silence is going on, all other students are induced to focus on that question too, perhaps in anticipation that it will be referred to them.)

12. <u>Eye Contact</u>: Teacher makes eye-to-eye contact with the students in the group.

13. <u>Freedom from Visual and Auditory Distraction</u>: Teacher arranges the room so that small groups face into a corner or away from the main visual field in the room, or so that instructional or work areas are separated from noisy areas. Alternatively, the teacher directs the class to "Close your eyes and listen."

[Note: Brophy and Evertson (1978) found that random order questioning negatively correlated with achievement in low-socioeconomic-status schools, but not in high-socioeconomic-status schools. They reasoned that random order questioning generates higher anxiety and such anxiety is a mismatch for low-socioeconomic-status students, whom they feel may need more stability and support in their learning environment and less unpredictability.]

Enlisting

We call the third category of attention-getting moves Enlisting moves because their purpose is to enlist or "sign up" an individual student's or an entire group's voluntary involvement in curriculum activities. Enlisting moves serve to captivate students and sweep them away in the interest or excitement of the activity. They capture students' attention by emphasizing the appeal or attractiveness of the activity. Enlisting moves include:

1. <u>Voice Variety</u>: Teacher varies speaking tone, pitch, volume, or inflection to emphasize points and add interest.

2. <u>Gesture</u>: Teacher uses hand or body movements to emphasize points or add interest.

3. <u>Piquing Children's Curiosity</u>: "Now, I wonder what made that happen?"

4. <u>Suspense</u>: "Wait until you see what's in the box!"

5. <u>Challenge</u>: "This next one will fool all of you!"

6. <u>Making Student a Helper</u>: "Jim, will you hold up those letters for the group to see, please?" (Jim's attention has been wandering.)

7. <u>Props</u>: Teacher uses physical objects related to the content.

8. <u>Anthropomorphizing</u>: (mainly with young children) "Now boys and girls, let's see if we can fool the staircase on our way up and get to the top without it hearing us."; "Now, if Mr. W were to walk through the door right now and look for things that started with his sound, what would he find to make him feel at home?"

9. <u>Connecting with Students' Fantasies</u>: "If you had a million dollars, how many one-hundred-dollar bills could you have?"

Acknowledging

Sometimes students are inattentive for reasons that have nothing to do with what's going on in school or how skillful the teacher is. Some outside event is weighing on them (or exciting them). For example:

-   their best friend refused to sit next to them on the bus coming in this morning

-   their parents have just separated

-   the championship game is this afternoon, and they're playing in it.

At such times, merely acknowledging out loud to students your understanding of what's on their mind can enable them to pay more attention in class. It is very validating (and rare) to have one's feelings really heard, and simply acknowledging those feelings can, indeed, facilitate attention. For example: "I know you're excited about the hockey game tonight—especially with three stalwarts right here in our midst. But I'm asking you to put that on the shelf for a while, gang, because today's review is very important."

Another example: Seven-year-old Jennifer is distracted during reading group; her glance shifts repeatedly to the place she left to come to group (a display of dolls from foreign lands which she was arranging). In a flash, the teacher sizes this up and, knowing that Jennifer realizes that lunch will immediately follow reading, figures out that the child is feeling that she'll never be able to finish arranging the dolls. (After lunch can seem like forever to a seven-year-old.) So, the teacher makes an Acknowledging move: "Jennifer, I know it's important to you to get all the dolls neatly arranged. You can devote yourself to that entirely, right before we go to lunch, I promise. Only now you need to work with us on this reading because we won't be doing this later. I'll make sure you get back there." Getting the dolls arranged may not seem important from an adult point of view, but such seemingly trivial matters can be consuming to children and block their involvement unless teachers perceive and respond.

Here is one more example. Perceiving that Mary is concerned about something, the teacher makes this Acknowledging move: "You're afraid you'll miss your turn at the listening station, Mary?" Mary nods. "Look, take your time and do this paper well. I'll see to it that you get your turn as soon as you're done, even if we've passed you on the sign-up sheet."

Sometimes the teacher just asks, "Brenda, what's on your mind? You don't seem with us this morning." Further probing and active-listening may or may not release this block. However, sometimes just talking about what's on her mind, without any solution from the teacher, will be unburdening enough to permit the student to reenter "here-and-now" tasks.

Winning

Winning moves are similar to Enlisting moves in that they are positive and tend to attract rather than force students' attention to the learning experience. However, we have distinguished Winning from Enlisting moves because Winning moves focus students on the teacher, whereas Enlisting moves focus students' attention more on the activity. Winning moves rely upon the teacher's "winning" personality to mediate attention. The continuum of Winning moves that we can observe teachers making includes:

1. Encouragement: Teacher prompts students' on-going work, usually by means of voice qualities and facial expressions.

2. Enthusiasm: "That's a really interesting topic for a paper, Bob!"

3. Praise: "Oh, that's fine work, Angie."

4. Humor: (without sarcasm) Teacher jokes in a positive, supportive manner that is mutually enjoyable by students.

5. Dramatizing: Teacher acts out or performs material related to the lesson, or 'directs' students to dramatize experiences.

Analyzing Attention Behavior

One could order the types of moves from all five categories along a single continuum whose rule is: authority to non-authority; or alternately, force to attraction (see Figure 2-1). Moves and categories at the upper end of the continuum employ the most teacher authority, most directly and firmly applied. As one travels down the continuum, the authority component becomes less and less dominant.

Thus, the Attention parameter involves a more or less continuous scale of values along a functional attribute, the functional attribute being: moves whose end is to engage, continue, or reengage students' attention in the learning experience. It is this functional orientation that accounts for the merging of "praise", "enthusiasm," and "gesture"—variables previously studied by others for their own merit—into a larger parameter. We recognize that focusing students' attention is probably not the only thing "praise" or "enthusiasm" accomplishes (enhanced self-image? motivation?), and certainly not the only function with which these behaviors could be associated. We think, however, that from a functional point of view these moves at least logically do focus attention and, furthermore, that attention is a logical and necessary mediator to other outcomes with which the moves might be associated (e.g., achievement, motivation). Therefore, linking them within a coherent Attention parameter is productive for understanding teaching.

We suggest that teachers reproduce the continuum in Figure 2-1 and use it to profile their own teaching performance. Which Attention moves do you use? How many and which of the five categories do you use? What does your profile reveal about your Attention performance? Some teachers have had colleagues or supervisors use the continuum while observing them, checking off each move whenever they perform it. Then, the teacher or observer has drawn a simple graph representing the number of moves made in each of the five categories during the time observed. A sample graph might look like this:

Desisting	XXXXXXXXXXXXXXXXXXXXXXXXXXXXXXXXXX
Alerting	XXXXXXXXXXXXXXXXXX
Enlisting	XXXXX
Acknowledging	
Winning	XX

A teacher's self-profile or the pattern of moves shown in an observation graph can be used to examine the appropriateness of the teacher's performance of Attention behaviors, which leads to the issue of matching.

Figure 2-1
Continuum of Attention Moves

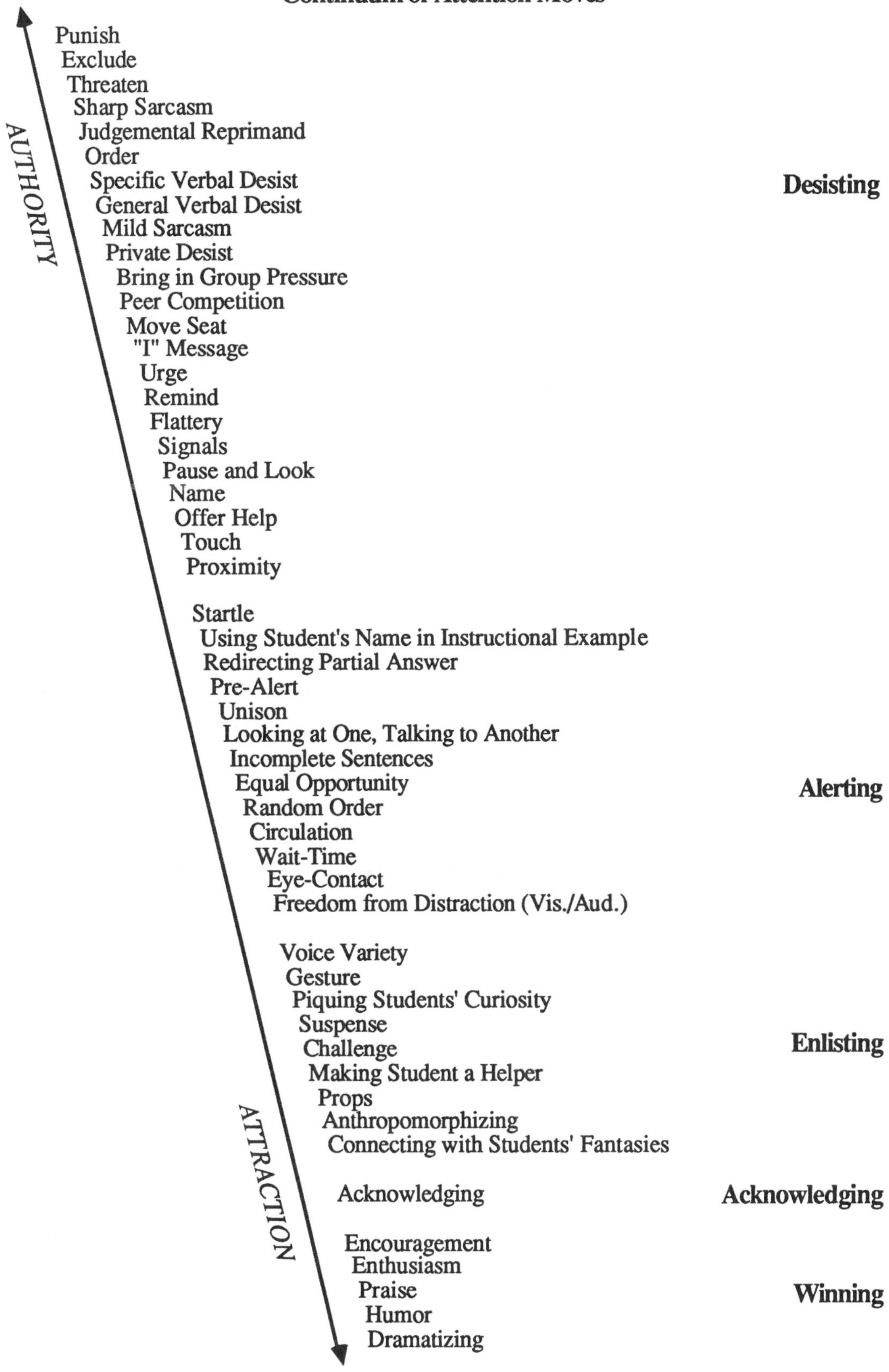

AUTHORITY

Punish
 Exclude
  Threaten
   Sharp Sarcasm
    Judgemental Reprimand
   Order
    Specific Verbal Desist
     General Verbal Desist
      Mild Sarcasm
     Private Desist
      Bring in Group Pressure
     Peer Competition
    Move Seat
     "I" Message
      Urge
       Remind
        Flattery
         Signals
          Pause and Look
         Name
          Offer Help
           Touch
            Proximity

         Startle
          Using Student's Name in Instructional Example
           Redirecting Partial Answer
            Pre-Alert
             Unison
              Looking at One, Talking to Another
               Incomplete Sentences
                Equal Opportunity
                 Random Order
                  Circulation
                   Wait-Time
                    Eye-Contact
                     Freedom from Distraction (Vis./Aud.)

              Voice Variety
               Gesture
                Piquing Students' Curiosity
                 Suspense
                  Challenge
                   Making Student a Helper
                    Props
                     Anthropomorphizing
                      Connecting with Students' Fantasies

ATTRACTION

                  Acknowledging

                  Encouragement
                   Enthusiasm
                    Praise
                     Humor
                      Dramatizing

Desisting

Alerting

Enlisting

Acknowledging

Winning

23

Matching with the Attention Parameter

Figure 2-1 is an objective list; that is, no judgements are implied about moves at the bottom being better moves than moves at the top, or vice versa. We are arguing, in fact, that *all* the moves have a place and each may be appropriate in a given context. (The one exception to this statement, in our personal opinions, is "sarcasm," which is always at least a small killer of relationships.)

Experienced teachers with good repertoires on this parameter may be observed to respond to different students in consistent but different ways. For example, the following descriptions illustrate how Mrs. T. skillfully matches her Attention moves to individual students.

Mrs. T. knows that Daryl looks for power conflicts; he invites tests of will with her or any other authority figure. When she uses most any of the Desisting moves with him he gets worse. For instance, he takes a "specific verbal desist" as a challenge to tap his pencil even louder and see what he can goad Mrs. T. into doing. So, she has learned to use Alerting and Enlisting moves with him. If he really gets out of hand, she will move firmly and remove him; but she often avoids the necessity for doing that, and does get Daryl to pay attention, by "challenging" him with a question, by "pre-alerting" him, or by using a "making student a helper" move. For instance, she uses the latter move when she sees him tapping the pencil and says, "...and so there really were four pyramids for the kings. Daryl, will you advance the filmstrip to the next frame so I can point to things from the front?"

Another student, Marsha, is a different sort of child. Though she also engages in frequent off-task behavior, Enlisting moves just seem to overstimulate her. Mrs. T. explains, "It's as if she interprets Enlisting and Winning moves as 'I-wanna-be-your-friend' or 'I-wanna-play' messages from me. She gets carried away with the interaction and focuses too much on me." While she looks for other ways and other opportunities to meet this need for closeness that Marsha seems to have, during work times Mrs. T. uses mid-range Desisting moves consistently with Marsha when she's off-task. And it works.

Different students...different needs...different moves deliberately matched to them by a skillful teacher.

Some experienced teachers are intuitive about the way they differentiate these moves across their students—and they are known as effective classroom managers. They may not be able to explain why, nor may their evaluators: It's just known that they've "got *it*"...whatever *it* is. Perhaps *it* is a subconscious acuteness at matching Attention moves to various students.

Whether or not we have this intuitive flair, all of us can benefit from reflecting about the patterns of inattention we see amongst our students and comparing them with the patterns of moves we seem to be making in response. We may discover that we are ignoring part of our repertoire because we get so irritated at Louise...or that our repertoire could be enlarged...or that we could do better matching if we looked for the reason behind the inattention. Talking about a student (or a group) with a colleague, with the Attention parameter's continuum of behaviors in front of us, can be a very productive activity.

Checking on Attention

1. Which kinds of Attention moves were displayed, and with what relative frequency?

   (Bar graphs constructed from raw notes can be used to indicate relative frequencies, or "moves" can be written directly onto the lines.)

   Desisting

   Alerting

   Enlisting

   Acknowledging

   Winning

2. Was there evidence of Attention moves being matched to groups or individuals?

   mismatch   no evidence   matched

Source Materials on This Parameter

Bennett, N. "Recent Research on Teaching: A Dream, A Belief, and a Model." *Journal of Education*, 160/3, August 1978.

Brophy, J.E. and Evertson, C.M. *Learning From Teaching*. Boston: Allyn & Bacon, 1978.

Hasentab, J. *Project T.E.A.C.H.*, Westwood, N.J.

Martin, D.L. "Your Praise Can Smother Learning." *Learning*, February 1977, 43-51.

McKenzie, R. and Schadler, A.M. "Effects of Three Practice Modes on Attention, Test Anxiety, & Achievement in a Classroom Association Learning Task." Paper presented at the American Educational Regional Association, Boston, 1980.

Redl, F. and Wineman, D. *Controls from Within*. Glencoe, IL: Free Press, 1952.

Rosenshine, B.V. "Academic Engaged Time, Content Covered, and Direct Instruction." *Journal of Education*, 160/3, August 1978.

Rowe, M.B. "Wait Time and Rewards as Instructional Variables: Their Influence on Language, Logic and Fate Control." Paper presented at the National Association for Research on Science Teaching, Chicago, April 1972.

Tanner, L. *Classroom Discipline*. New York: Holt, Rinehart, and Winston, 1978.

3
Momentum

How do I keep the flow of
events moving with smooth,
rapid transitions?

Provisioning
Overlapping
Fillers
Intrusions
Lesson Flexibility
Notice
Sub–Dividing
Anticipation

MOMENTUM

The concept of Momentum pertains to the smooth, ongoing flow of events in the classroom (Kounin, 1970). Teaching is full of pitfalls to momentum. When these pitfalls occur, students' concentration is broken. They are distracted from or prevented from becoming involved in learning activities. They experience "downtime"; i.e., time spent waiting for things to get ready, get started, or get organized. When momentum is not maintained, students get bored or look for things to do, potentially filling their time by daydreaming or engaging in disruptive behavior. On the other hand, when momentum is properly kept up, students experience smooth and rapid transitions from one event to another. Movement of students and equipment happens without bottlenecks, traffic jams, conflicts, arguments, or pushing and shoving. Observing such a room, one has the feeling that things are "moving along." In this chapter we will examine the behaviors teachers perform to maintain momentum and keep things "moving along" in the classroom.

In a general sense, many parameters relate to the concept of momentum. For instance: Attention does, insofar as students are kept interested or at least focused on learning experiences; Routines does, in that efficient design of routines for recurrent procedures expedites organizing and setting up, and speeds transitions; Expectations (for work) does in that teacher persistence and clarity about how things are to be done enables students to work more automatically, and makes students individually efficient at moving from one thing to another.

Other parameters of teaching also bear on momentum: Personal Relationship Building does, in that students' regard for the teacher makes them less likely to resist or disrupt the way "things-spozed-to-be"; Space does, in that effective arrangement of space facilitates students finding things and getting involved, and minimizes distractions; Time does, in that appropriate schedules provide for the ebb and flow of pupils' available energy and attention span, avoiding unreasonable demands.

Still further, one could look at the Curriculum Parameters of Objectives, Evaluation, and Learning Experiences for aspects that relate to momentum: mismatched material (too hard, too easy), inappropriately presented, can lead to bored or frustrated pupils who will certainly break the momentum of classroom flow!

In a broad sense, then, we can see that *any* mismatch of curriculum or instruction to students tends to break momentum. But to cast momentum so broadly is to subsume all of teaching under its umbrella. Indeed, any parameter of teaching, whatever the primary purpose of the behaviors it considers, does have a secondary effect on momentum. However, we believe that it is valuable to focus on aspects of teaching that relate *primarily* to maintaining momentum in the classroom. Therefore, we will narrow our definition of Momentum to eight key sub-parameters or kinds of teacher behavior *whose primary purpose is to keep things moving along*, and which, when improperly done or ignored, break the orderly flow of events.

Sub-Parameters of Momentum

The eight sub-parameters of Momentum are an eclectic group, comprising items that can be identified as being important in a management sense, pertaining to maintaining or at least enabling student involvement in learning experiences as all Management Parameters do. But unlike the behaviors in the other Management Parameters, which can be associated with other missions, these eight do not fit any other parameter and are primarily aimed at momentum. They are called: provisioning, overlapping, fillers, intrusions, lesson flexibility, notice, sub-dividing and anticipation.

Provisioning

Provisioning means having things ready to go—the space, the materials. With adequate Provisioning, one does not see the teacher call a group of students together and then leave them for a minute to fetch something needed for the lesson from the closet. One does not see students run out of needed materials during learning experiences so that they have to stop what they are doing and solicit new stocks from the teacher. (This does not preclude pupils restocking themselves from known and easily accessible storehouses or supply points. It's when the supply point is out of paper, for example, that momentum suffers.) One *does* see materials out and organized before the start of lessons and the space arranged as necessary before instruction begins; one does see the room equipped with those things the students will need or are likely to need for the activities that may predictably occur over the day.

Provisioning, like much of good management, becomes conspicuous by its absence. Nevertheless, there are many observable signs of good Provisioning. For example, for lessons: audio-visuals, charts, or demonstration equipment are set up in advance; the teacher writes information on the board behind a pulled-down map, so that the information is readily available when the map is raised; handouts are stacked near the site of a planned lesson. For the room itself: activities, kits, games, listening stations, books, manipulatives, and problem cards are laid out in an orderly and visible fashion for pupils to find and engage; supply points are adequately stocked; for primary grade children, a cassette is inserted on the proper side and wound to the proper point for the children to start listening; for even younger children, the volume controls on the headsets are in the proper positions. When skillfully done, a small amount of teacher time spent provisioning the environment during the school day results in a maximum amount of time available for focus on students.

Overlapping

We borrow this term from Kounin (1970) and expand on his definition: Overlapping—the ability to manage two or more parallel events simultaneously with evidence of attention to both. "Manage" here includes two aspects of teaching performance. First, *keeping in touch* with what is going on in several groups, areas, or activities at once (the teacher may be involved in one, more than one, or circulating among several sites); keeping in touch implies knowing the nature of the activity, the appropriate pupil behavior within the activity, and the current quality of the pupil's performance. Second, making moves to *help pupils over blockages*. Blockages may come from pupils not understanding directions, pupils not knowing what to do next, pupils' inability to resolve interpersonal disagreements (e.g., about sharing materials, or about how to proceed next as a group), pupils encountering material above their frustration level, pupils' attention wandering, or pupils finishing an activity and needing help making or planning transitions to the next activity.

"Withitness"—teachers having eyes in the back of their heads, seeing the whole room and letting pupils know that they know what's going on—is a prerequisite for Overlapping (Kounin, 1970). This "withitness" is necessary, of course, for noticing and responding to misbehavior in its early stages. But, in contrast to its disciplinary application, it is also the basis for Overlapping several simultaneous instructional events, as it enables teachers to keep in touch with the flow of all of the events.

Building on "withitness," teachers make moves to keep momentum going when they notice a blockage or potential blockage. For instance, below are a few examples of moves that maintain momentum by helping pupils avoid or work through blockages.

The teacher, seeing a student nearing the end of an art project, says, "Where are you going to put it to dry, Jimmy?" Jimmy replies, "Under the woodworking table." The teacher responds, "OK, fine. After that you can finish the book you started this morning." The teacher has provided a focus for the closure of the activity and the transition to next activity.

As a pupil across the room appears stuck on his lab experiment, the teacher says, "Mark, ask Jane for some help if you're stuck."

As the teacher sees a child using the last of the paint, he gestures for her to come over and reminds her to refill the paint jars when she's finished.

When the teacher sees a group arguing over the position of a senator on a bill, she says to them, "Where could you find out for sure?" This is a way of directing the students back into constructive involvement.

The point of Overlapping is that all of these moves to maintain the momentum of groups and individuals are made *while* the teacher may be instructing a punctuation skill group, tutoring a pupil in reading, inspecting a pupil's lab report, or engaging in some other primary focus. The teacher makes the management move without leaving, interrupting, or seeming to remove attention from the primary focus but for an instant. It is an accomplishment to perform Overlapping effectively at any time, and especially so when the teacher has a primary active role in a particular learning experience.

Fillers

It happens during the course of a day that teachers are caught with groups of students for short periods (from one to ten or fifteen minutes) where nothing is planned. Sometimes this happens in awkward places where standard classroom resources are not available: e.g., outside waiting for a late bus; in the hallway waiting for a late class to come out of a specialist's room (gym, music); in an instructional group just ended where students have had it with work, yet when there isn't enough time to assign them anything else or even to let them choose and start some other activity around the room before it will be time to line up for lunch. In such situations, what does the teacher do to prevent the disruption of momentum?

Some may be inclined to comment, why does the teacher have to do anything? The students will just have to sit and wait, that's all. Students should know how to wait: it's an occasional and unavoidable occurrence in life. It's not up to the teacher to entertain them at these times.... Yes, we would answer...a consummation devoutly to be wished. But it doesn't always work that way. For some groups not so in command of themselves, and for some situations, relying upon students to patiently sit and wait can be an unreasonable expectation—and may result in disruptions. In such instances, teachers may pull out a Filler to hold the class together for those few minutes. Below are some examples.

Since the clock in her room is wrong, Mrs. M. arrives with her first grade class five minutes early for gym. There's no use trekking all the way back to the room; they'd just have to turn right around and return. So she asks the children to sit against the wall and move close together so they can all see and hear her. "While we wait for the other class to finish up: raise your hand if you can think of a word that rhymes with...fish." (She calls on three students who give different rhyming words.) "You're clicking this morning...Now...one that rhymes with...lamp." (She calls on two more students.)

Another example: Surprisingly, tables 1 and 4 have finished their earth science experiments and write-ups early and put their equipment safely away, and ten minutes remain in the period. The teacher, Mr. L., knows the remaining tables will be asking questions and he'll need to be available for them. But to prevent down-time for tables 1 and 4 and fooling around (a distinct possibility with this freshman class), he quickly writes eight science vocabulary words on the board and calls up those two tables. He gets them seated and started on a 20-question review game in 45 seconds, and is then back circulating among the experimenters.

Sometimes Fillers are not as directly curriculum relevant as were the above examples. Primary teachers may just play "Simon Says". A fifth grade teacher may say, "OK, without anyone looking at their watches, raise your hand when you think 1 1/2 minutes is up. Go!" (This "feel of time" game is a good way to quiet a noisy bus for a few minutes.) Secondary teachers may begin chatting with a class about current events or school teams. None of these is necessarily a waste of time, but it is worth distinguishing between Fillers that pass the time and Fillers that bring in something of the current curriculum.

Intrusions

Sometimes a teacher's day can seem like a series of intrusions punctuated by moments of instruction. These intrusions take many forms: pupils wanting work corrected, wanting help, wanting directions clarified, or wanting disputes arbitrated; adult visitors; incoming messengers; public address announcements. Every intrusion has the potential to disrupt momentum; but teachers *can* handle intrusions in a way that minimizes their distracting influence on student's involvement with learning experiences. We find that there are four basic levels of performance that describe a teacher's ability to deal with intrusions:

- <u>allows intrusions to fracture momentum</u>

- <u>deals with intrusions in a uniform way</u>: For instance, *never* allows students from outside an instructional group to ask questions (that is, doesn't tolerate intrusions of any kind); or *always* refers intruders to peers for help; or *always* has intruders wait nearby until an appropriate moment to help them arises.

- <u>deals with intrusions in a variety of ways</u>: uses different ways at different times.

- <u>matches response to intrusion to the characteristics of the students involved, or to the particular situation</u>: For example, this may mean that the teacher knows that Jane (the child she's working with) has fragile concentration and that even a delayed response to an intruder will lose Jane for good. (Maybe it took 15 minutes to get Jane started!) At other times, it is the intruder's characteristics to which the teacher adjusts, sending off Charlie to get help from a peer because she knows that Charlie can handle that, but holding John in close while signaling him to be silent until she can briefly and quietly help him...because she knows John doesn't have the confidence to approach a peer. (Perhaps later in the month she'll call over a particular child to help John when he intrudes for help.) In summary, the matching may be to the student or students in the group (those intruded upon), or to the intruder.

Sometimes, the teacher matches the response to the situation rather than to the student(s). For example, the case of a fast-paced verbal game involving a large group may prompt the teacher to brook no intrusions at all, even from a student the teacher would normally accommodate, in order to preserve the momentum of the game.

As with all of the areas of teaching we will examine in this book, Intrusions remind us that the better we can match our responses to students or situations, the more effective we will be.

Lesson Flexibility
What do teachers do when lessons or planned activities are bombing? How do they control momentum? We can distinguish four levels of teacher performance:

- <u>presses on with the lesson anyway</u>

- <u>drops the lesson and switches to something else</u>

- <u>keeps the objective and tries to teach it another way</u>: varies the format of the lesson.

- matches a new format to the needs of the group and/or adjusts it for characteristics of individuals.

Here is an example of the latter. A group of students is full of energy, charged up after a fun gym period. They are having trouble settling down for paper and pencil exercises on contractions. The teacher, sensing this, draws a grid on the board, puts contractions in it, and calls the students up where they play a modified "concentration" game in which they can actively participate. The teacher has matched a new lesson format to the on-the-spot needs of the students. Momentum has been maintained by allowing the students to *productively* expend their energies.

Notice

Momentum can be broken if pupils are not prepared for transitions (Arlin, 1979): if they are abruptly directed to cease one activity and begin another without time to come to some satisfactory closure point in what they are doing. This is especially true when pupils are heavily invested in their activity, as is often the case with creative-expressive endeavors. They resent having to stop what they are immersed in much as a sound sleeper resents being rudely awakened.

Teachers anticipate and soften these transitions by giving pupils advance Notice of when a transition is coming, so they can get ready for it. Even with advance Notice some pupils have a hard time separating from their activities: "Just one more problem"..."Just let me finish painting this side"..."Just...." (School isn't the only place we meet this issue in life.) Teachers may simply hustle pupils along at this point: "Come on, I told you five minutes ago to get ready. Now let's go!" Or, they may discriminate how they handle this kind of resistance with different pupils. With regard to how teachers move pupils along when time has run out, we can distinguish these four levels of performance:

- no way: 'laissez-faire' (lets pupils deal with it themselves), or erratically urges children.

- one way: For instance, *always* pushes children along.

- presses with different degrees of fervor in different circumstances

- presses different students in different ways matched to perceived characteristics of the students: For example, the teacher says to Jenny, "By the count of three have your book away and be on your way to the door"...because the teacher knows Jenny is testing adult consistency in line with her dominant power issue. But for Noah, the teacher may allow a minute or two extra and quietly help him put things away since he has such a hard time investing, and he did a really nice job this morning, so the teacher wants to preserve its positive associations for him.

Sub-Dividing

When groups of students travel through the room during transitions between activities or between phases of an activity (to line up, to get their coats, to go to the library, to get microscopes, to hand in papers), they sometimes get clogged in physical bottlenecks. These jam-ups result in crowding and general unpleasantness, and at the very least cause downtime while students wait for the crowd to thin. Sub-Dividing (or Fragmentation, as Kounin calls it) means predicting these times and acting to prevent the jam-ups by dividing the groups into smaller units (individuals, pairs, tables, teams, children wearing sneakers) who move one at a time under the teacher's direction. Meanwhile, those students not in the unit currently moving are occupied with finishing tasks, putting away materials, or other aspects of the transition (perhaps a "Filler").

Some teachers use their Sub-Dividing moves to reinforce items of recent curriculum. For instance, they dismiss students for the bus by asking multiplication facts or spelling words, calling on individuals and allowing them to exit if they get the answer..."your ticket" some teachers call it.

The kinds of Sub-Dividing described above are most appropriate for primary age children. Older students who can manage themselves in situations involving potential jam-ups may simply be allowed to proceed. In this case, efficient teacher moves might include: detailing several students to pass out materials to the rest; storing materials at access points that accommodate several students "getting them" at once; sequencing and/or pacing activities so that small units of students naturally come up for materials (or pass the potential jam-up/downtime point) at different times—thus the sequential nature of the plan for the activities anticipates and precludes physical bottlenecks.

Anticipation

Consider this incident: The teacher has given the class advance notice to get ready to go down to the auditorium where a brass quintet will play for a middle school audience. "I hate concerts!" says Georgette. One minute passes—some children are putting things away. Two minutes—a few children are gathering by the door. Georgette is looking nobody in the eye and appears sullen. "Georgette, will you go down to the auditorium and see if the seats are set up for us?" says the teacher. Georgette goes. The class quickly line up at the door and the teacher sets off with them. They meet Georgette half-way there; she reports that the seats are set up and joins the class without protest as they proceed to the auditorium.

Skilled teachers perform this way every day. They anticipate trouble spots— incidents that will break momentum—and make moves to sidestep them. They move students out of the way of temptation, give resistant individuals face-saving ways to get out of self-made corners, anticipate situations or combinations of personalities that will break momentum and alter them—always before the trouble starts. Here are a few more examples of situations that benefit from a teacher's use of Anticipation.

When children are called to the rug or to a class meeting after cleanup, the teacher may anticipate that some will finish before others, that an ever larger group will slowly be assembling in the meeting area and waiting without focus (the meeting won't start until they're all there). The same may happen with a junior high class that filters into the room in dribs and drabs before the bell and at the bell is dispersed all over the room. In both cases, by anticipating what is likely to happen, the teacher can arrange to be present at the meeting area doing something of interest to absorb the children as they arrive (riddles, general chatter, a game, a brain teaser, writing something of interest on the board, holding a novel object). Some groups left without a focus at a time like this will provide one of their own...wrestling, arguing, or other momentum breakers. A teacher who can recognize the potential of the group will anticipate these times and be there to greet them with some engaging activity as they arrive.

Realizing that a small group will require much help and teacher time as they do follow-up work on a new geometry skill, the teacher will be sure the rest of the class are doing things they can handle comfortably, both in terms of procedures/ directions and content. Otherwise, the teacher may feel "nibbled to death by ducks" as Bob Hope would say, becoming overloaded with demands for attention and help. As a result, the students will experience downtime, conflict, and momentum will falter. So on the spot the teacher assigns a page of practice proofs from the *previous* section of the text (ones they can handle easily) to the bulk of the class, and calls up four individual students for a ten-minute review of the new concepts taught.

Anticipation is a difficult skill to observe, and for teachers to notice themselves applying, because those who excel at it typically perform Anticipation moves spontaneously and intuitively rather than pre-planning them. But teachers who experience difficulty in this area can often benefit from running advance "mental movies" of the day they have planned, expecially if they do so out loud in the company of a colleague who's helping them problem-solve momentum issues. In this way, potential stumbling blocks to momentum may surface and steps can be taken to avoid them.

At this point, readers may be getting foggy over the distinction between Fillers and Anticipation. They are, indeed, related. Anticipation is the quality of mind that warns a teacher that *without* a Filler at this moment, for this group, there may be trouble. But Fillers are only one particular response showing Anticipation. Anticipation is a bigger category than Fillers. It is a kind of thinking, usually spontaneous, and often tacit, that says, "If I don't do X, momentum will break down here." X may be many things besides a Filler. For example, Mrs. R., in ending a class meeting of first graders, picks children for the clay area first, then assigns other children to other areas. She does this because clay is the most popular activity and everyone wants to go there. She anticipates that if she doesn't deal with clay first and get it off everyone's mind, as well as reassure all children that they'll eventually get a chance there, it will be *on* everyone's mind while she tries to get kids to choose from among the other activity areas. Thus, the sequence in which she fills activity stations reflects her Anticipation of what would happen if she didn't deal with clay first.

At its most general level, Anticipation is a quality of mind inherent in all seven situations described in this chapter (Intrusions, Fillers, Notice, Lesson Flexibility, Overlapping, Provisioning, and Sub-Dividing). But teachers possessing that quality exercise it in many subtle movements outside the boundaries of those seven. So we need a general grab-bag category to hold and describe such situations, and this is it.

Reviewing Momentum

As you have seen, the Momentum parameter is clearly concerned with those teacher behaviors whose *primary* purpose is to keep things moving in the classroom. Within each of the eight sub-parameters, teachers perform a variety of moves specifically aimed at maintaining classroom momentum. The more skillfully teachers select from their Momentum repertoire to match their moves to the needs and characteristics of the students or situations involved, the more smoothly and efficiently transitions are made and the more successfully momentum is maintained.

On the following pages is a short Quiz which can help you review the eight sub-parameters of Momentum. You may choose to complete this Quiz as a self-test or as an exercise with a colleague to focus your understanding of this parameter.

Momentum Quiz

1. Summarize the Momentum parameter in your own words.

2. Match each sub-parameter to the item that most clearly relates to it.

A.	Provisioning	a.	"Try another way"
B.	Overlapping	b.	Distracting interruptions
C.	Fillers	c.	Physical bottlenecks
D.	Intrusions	d.	Managing two groups at once
E.	Lesson Flexibility	e.	"Simon says..."
F.	Notice	f.	Anticipating transitions
G.	Sub-Dividing	g.	Set up equipment in advance
H.	Anticipation	h.	Anticipate trouble spots

3. Describe some examples of:

Provisioning:

_____

_____

_____

Fillers:

_____

_____

_____

Dealing with Intrusions:

_____

_____

_____

4. Describe ways of Sub-Dividing when children are doing the following.

Lining up at the door:

_____

_____

_____

Handing in papers:

_____

_____

_____

5. What would you look for in small groups which are placed in different parts of the room to prevent loss of momentum?

_____

_____

_____

6. Complete the comment a teacher using Overlapping might say in each of these situations.

   A. A student across the room is obviously having difficulty with a worksheet.

   The teacher says: "_____

   _____"

   B. A student has completed her spelling workbook before the other students have finished theirs.

   The teacher says: "_____

   _____"

7. Which sub-parameter does each of these scenes illustrate?

   A. Students are returning from gym in ones and twos, a few at a time. The teacher is in the room holding several novel objects and asking the returning students what they are used for.

   This is an example of: _____

   B. A teacher says, "Boys and girls, we will be going to the lunch room in five minutes. Be sure your desks are clear and your books are ready to take to your locker."

   This is an example of: _____

   C. A group of students is obviously bored during a grammar lesson. The teacher who was lecturing stops and faces the group. She then asks the students to come to the front of the room, to act out several parts of speech, and to tell how these parts behave in sentences.

   This is an example of: _____

8. How is Momentum related to the Attention parameter?

   _____

   _____

   _____

   _____

   _____

Checking on Momentum

For items 1, 2, 3, 6, 7, and 8, circle whether each behavior: was displayed when appropriate (yes); was not displayed but could have been (no); or was not applicable (n/a).

For items 4 and 5, circle the level of performance demonstrated.

1. Provisioning: space and materials ready to go   n/a   no   yes

2. Overlapping: keeps track of several activities
   and helps students over blockages   n/a   no   yes

3. Fillers: makes constructive use of short
   unexpected waiting times with students   n/a   no   yes

4. Intrusions:

         fracture momentum
           uniform way of handling
             variety of ways
               matches responses

5. Lesson Flexibility:

         presses on
           drops & switches
             varies format
               matches new format

6. Notice: gives advance notice at transistions   n/a   no   yes

7. Sub-Dividing: breaks moving groups into
   smaller units   n/a   no   yes

8. Anticipation: anticipates and circumvents
   blocks to momentum   n/a   no   yes

Source Materials on This Parameter

Arlin, M. "Teacher Transitions Can Disrupt Time Flow in Classrooms." *American Educational Research Journal*, Winter 1979, 42-56.

Doyle, W. "Making Managerial Decisions in Classrooms." In *Classroom Management, 78th Yearbook of the National Society for the Study of Education*, Daniel L. Duke (*ed.*), Chicago: University of Chicago Press, 1979, 75-115.

Kounin, J. *Discipline and Classroom Management*. New York: Holt, Rinehart, and Winston, 1970.

Pierson, C. and Mansuggi, J. *Creating & Using Learning Games*. Palo Alto, CA: Learning Handbooks, 1975.

4

Expectations

How do I communicate to students what I expect of them, and are my expectations appropriate?

EXPECTATIONS

Nothing influences behavior so strongly as the clear expectations of a significant other.

—Jim Steffen
Management Consultant

Introduction

Classrooms are dynamic and complex societies that are rife with expectations: expectations that teachers have for students, and that students have for teachers and for each other. These expectations explain a good deal of what we see when we visit a classroom—both the good and the bad, the productive and the wasteful. But the expectations themselves can't be seen. They hang in the air almost like an atmosphere; they exist only between people and comprise a part of their relationship.

In this chapter we will discuss the Expectations parameter of teaching. However, you know enough about us from reading this far to know that we will not be satisfied to talk merely about "atmosphere." We are interested in behavior: controllable behavior, things teachers say and do to *produce* atmospheres. So, within this parameter we will explore what teachers say and do to create and communicate expectations to students clearly. We will also take up the issue of standards. The question about standards is: Are they high enough...demanding enough? (This is a question particularly of our times in education.) And finally, we will look at matching. With regard to standards: Are they reasonable? Are they appropriate as we look at a teacher dealing with different groups, different individuals? If they are, what does it take from a teacher to get these expectations met?

The quote under the chapter title above contains two key elements pertaining to Expectations. The first is the word "clear." Students have to know with certainty what a teacher expects. The second is the phrase "significant other." Teachers, like parents, are automatically significant others to students, if for no other reason than that they have power over them. If the relationship contains respect and regard too (and perhaps affection), the teacher becomes even more significant. *How* such relationships get built is the subject of another important parameter—Personal Relationship Building—and will be discussed in the next chapter. In this current chapter, we will look at the expectations themselves and the process for communicating them. The assumption of the introductory quote is that within limits, *what you expect is what you get*...and that we as teachers can raise (or lower) students' performance if we expect more (or less) of them. And that's quite a responsibility.

Three Key Messages

The bottom line of this parameter is sending the following three messages to students:

THIS IS IMPORTANT.
YOU CAN DO IT.
I WON'T GIVE UP ON YOU.

These are so important we wish to repeat them again: "This is important." "You can do it." and "I won't give up on you."

People of widely different personalities and various teaching styles can and do succeed in sending these messages to students. Success here is not a matter of style. From the lighthearted to the stern, from the free-flowing creative to the analytical, the best of teachers find ways to convince students that they, the teachers, are believers—believers in the students and in the subject. And such teachers do not do so by magic, do not communicate by osmosis. Words and actions, some quite subtle but, nonetheless, observable, send these messages. And we know it makes a huge difference in learning when they are sent, especially to low-performing students.

We can be just as behavioral in studying this parameter of teaching as we were with Attention and will be with Clarity. The approach will be the same: What is the repertoire of ways available to send the three messages? Around what kind of transactions are they sent? How do we match the ways we select to individual students?

Four Kinds of Expectations

As far as we have been able to determine, there are four basic kinds of student performance for which teachers have expectations:

- Quality and Quantity of Work
- Work Habits and Work Procedures
- Business and Housekeeping Routines
- Interpersonal Behavior.

In this chapter we will focus primarily upon the first kind of expectations. The others will be separately covered in other portions of this book (noted below). However, it will be helpful to briefly lay out all four areas of expectations here.

Expectations for the *Quality and Quantity of Students' Work* have to do with individual output and production rates for items of work. For example: How good is the work Jason is doing? When the teacher responds, "Well, he could be a lot more thorough."...or, "He's really sloughing off. I think he could do a lot better if he tried."...the teacher reveals a negative evaluation of the work Jason was *expected* to produce. The teacher has higher expectations for Jason than he's meeting.

Of course, depending on the teacher's expectation for Jason's work, there are other ways in which his evaluation may be expressed. Here are two other versions that reveal that the teacher's expectation *has* been met: "Just fine. That's really the quality I expect from Jason."; "Well, that's about all you can expect from Jason."

These expectations for students' *current* performance are different from expectations for students' performance growth over time. It's quite a different thing to ask from the teacher's point of view whether the increments of difficulty for new objectives or new lessons are appropriate for the students. ("Size of the bite" we call that. We will consider this in more detail later in the Objectives chapter under "matching.") Here, the subject is not so much the stretch which new work demands of the students with regard to what they have mastered recently; it is the current products and the teacher's expectations for how well the work, and how much work, will be produced.

The second kind of expectations—expectations for *Work Habits and Work Procedures*—pertains to *how* students shall go about their work, not the products of work themselves. Some of these expectations may focus on such things as getting assignments, following directions, getting help, handing in, and doing research. For example, a teacher may say, "Every time you do a paper, I expect you to make an appointment with me to go over your first draft at least one week before the final draft is due." Or, students may be expected to keep a log of books read with dates and comments, keep it accurately and up to date, and do so on their own without teacher reminders.

We are talking here about *on-going* habits and procedures, things students are routinely expected to do in their work, not directions on how to do individual assignments (that's "Structuring," see Chapter 13.) As an observer, one may hear a teacher reminding students of these on-going procedures from time to time; at the beginning of the year one may see repeated and direct attention to *teaching* them to students; but during most of the year (if they're working well) one won't hear them talked about at all. They just function—underlying (formatting, if you will) the academic work students are doing. These expectations may be for following routine managerial procedures in preparation for teacher-led groups (where to go, when, with what materials, what the order of events shall be); or may pertain to personal work habits such as writing posture, organization of math problems on a page, order of operations.

The third kind of expectations are for *Business and Housekeeping Routines*. These pertain to *non-academic* work-related procedures such as attendance, lunch count, cleanup and other operations that will be detailed later under the Procedural Routines parameter. For example, ninth grade students may be expected to organize and carry out their own lab cleanup at the end of each period. Third graders may be expected to move counters to register their attendance and use them further to indicate their choice of free-time activity when they first come to class in the morning.

Lastly, expectations for *Interpersonal Behavior* pertain to how students should treat each other and cooperate with the teacher. We will examine these later under the Discipline parameter.

In what follows we will be dealing with the first of the four kinds of expectations: *Quality and Quantity of Work*. Each of these four kinds of expectations has been considered separately because it is possible that a teacher with high expectations for quality and quantity of work may have few or unclear expectations for work habits and procedures; that is, there seems to be no necessary correlation between a teacher's behavior on one kind of expectation and the same teacher's handling of another. (Though one might not expect it logically, we have observed inconsistencies in numerous teachers on this parameter.) However, there is a strong correlation between the behaviors that serve to *communicate* all four kinds of expectations, whatever the standards behind them, and it is with these behaviors that we will begin.

Over the course of this chapter the following important aspects of the Expectations parameter will be considered:

- Do students know what the teacher's expectations are? How are these expectations communicated to students?

- What is the nature of the expectations themselves? What can be said about the standards embodied in them?

- How appropriate are those standards for groups and for individuals? How are they varied or adjusted (matched)?

Communication of Expectations

The first things to know about a teacher's expectations are whether, and how, they are communicated. Here are six important qualities to look for in the communication of expectations:

- <u>direct</u>
- <u>specific</u>
- <u>repeated</u>
- <u>communicated with positive expectancy</u>
- <u>modeled</u>
- <u>struggled for with tenacity</u>.

Let's consider what is meant by these six qualities.

Direct means that the expectation is explicitly brought to students' attention, usually verbally. *Specific* means that the details of the expectation for students' performance are clearly stated or otherwise specified in the communication (which may be written and not verbal). *Repeated* means that the expectation is repeated often to make sure students absorb it.

Positive expectancy means that the statement of expectation has a "you can do it" flavor: the communication of the expectation is not seen as an order to the student, but as an expression of confidence (sometimes challenge) on the part of the teacher that the student can and will meet it (Tanner, 1978). Another version of positive expectancy has a more imperative quality: "Of course you'll meet this expectation!" is the flavor..."It's what's done!" is the implication conveyed by tone and body language.

Modeled for expectations has two meanings. The first is model as in "show" or "demonstrate." One may make it clearer to students what is expected by performing the behavior oneself as a model of what to do. The purpose of this form of modeling is clear communication. The second meaning of modeling is to "practice what you preach" so that in one's regular practice and behavior one is a model of thoroughness, or of self-evaluation, or of courtesy, or of whatever else one is expecting of students. Whether it's expectations for procedures, inter-personal behaviors, work habits, or application of skills, students take powerful messages from observing how faithfully teachers follow their own dicta.[1]

Tenacity is a quality that surfaces in response to resistance. Tenacity subsumes repetition and consistency: one would not see tenacity without repetition, but repetition does not necessarily imply tenacity. When students resist teacher expectations and getting them met seems hopeless, teachers who struggle on nevertheless display, we can say, tenacity (presuming, of course, that the expectations are realistic, because if they aren't, "foolish" would replace "tenacious"). For example, we have observed teachers displaying tenacity in the following ways: teacher goes to study hall to get a student; teacher reminds a student she's expected at 1:15 to go

---

[1]Thanks to John Pierce of the Duxbury Public Schools for reminding us of the importance of modeling with Expectations.

over some work; teacher nabs students before and after class and makes appointments; teacher calls parents at home…. All of these are ways of reinforcing an expectation.

This quality or behavior we've called *tenacity* raises an issue for some teachers: "It isn't my job to chase them around if they don't do their work; it's their responsibility. And if they don't understand something, I expect them to come and ask me!" There is a certain "come-and-get-it…or else!" message in this attitude. That message can intimidate certain students and prevent them from learning what they might because it cuts them off from the person from whom they might learn—the teacher. On the other hand, the responsibility for assuring that learning takes place cannot rest solely with the teacher; students must do their part. As observers of ourselves and of others we have the duty to ask, "Are we doing enough, being tenacious enough without creating dependence, chasing students enough so that they get the message that we really *care* about their investment in their work?" Because that is the message that tenacity sends…we care.

These six qualities are important elements of the messages teachers send to students about what's expected. In addition, when it comes to students' work, the *feedback* they get about their products seems particularly important in communicating expectations. In our work, the following important attributes of this feedback show up again and again in our interviews with teachers and students:

- <u>Prompt and complete</u>: Products are returned to students within a very few days of submission…sometimes the same day; and there is evidence to the student that the teacher has looked at or corrected the whole work, i.e., given real and thorough attention to what the student has done.

- <u>Detailed</u>: Feedback contains detailed remarks, suggestions, or questions from the teacher to the student. Sometimes these are notes in the margin, sometimes responses in a student journal, sometimes they are delivered verbally.

- <u>Personal contact</u>: There are frequent occasions of face-to-face feedback to students—during class, especially before and after class, even in the hallway. Perhaps they'll be jocular: "Hey, Jimmy! Before you get locked up in your shoulder pads this afternoon you're going to see me with those corrections, right?"

- No excuses: · Teachers go after students. They do it personally and with tenacity. This behavior is an extension of both personal contact and tenacity. As an observer, what we see is teachers holding students accountable, putting them on the spot with "why" questions when work is not turned in, is late, or is inadequately done...and not letting them off the hook, not accepting inadequate explanations. Teachers give the work to students to correct or to do over again; set deadlines; frequently offer help when necessary or make provisions for students to get what they need to do the work (materials, peer tutoring, etc.). "No excuses" means giving consequences for poor performance too, but this can be done without rancor or anger; but often involves firmness of tone and body language (see below).

- Recognizes superior performance: When students do well, there is some special form of recognition that highlights their accomplishment: posting especially good papers on a bulletin board; displaying a product in a public place; complimenting in front of the class. (The issue this behavior raises is how a teacher provides for the student who might never produce a "superior" product and whether a teacher can adequately define "superior" for a student in terms of his *own* progress from past work.)

- Logical Consequences for Poor Performance: Equally important are consequences for non-performance or poor performance. If something happens as a result of not doing homework or classwork, or as a result of doing shoddy work (or as a result of tardiness or sloppy cleanup or the many other areas of performance for which teachers have expectations), then students become convinced the teacher "means it."

(In the Discipline chapter—Chapter 6—we will look more closely at consequences and what is known about how to make them effective. We will develop the details of the following attributes of effective consequences: (a) they are clear in advance to students; (b) there are a range of consequences rather than just one rigid one for each expectation; (c) they are logical rather than punitive; (d) they are delivered with appropriate affect; (e) teachers make clear to students that they— the students—have made a choice. At this point readers may wish to skip ahead to the section on consequences in the Discipline chapter.)

Standards

After examining the communication of expectations, the next aspect to look at is the relative standards embodied in the expectations. We find that a teacher's standards for expectations can be viewed along this scale:

- none

- few consistent

- low: Teachers demand less of the students than they might.

- too high: Standards are inappropriately demanding for most students.

- average: Standards reflect a mid-level of demand attainable by most students.

- inspirational-vague: This is an interesting one. These teachers often have excellent reputations. Students and parents like them; they are often charismatic, stimulating performers. Students *do*, in fact, work hard to please them. They may instill in students a feeling that the subject is important, worthy, dignified. And we may see significant investment on the part of the students as well as significant learning. All this is great. It's just that the standards of the teacher may never be clear, and each student's learning may richochet down the track in a somewhat uncontrolled manner, since they are never quite sure what the definition of good performance is. For a few students this lack of definition may actually antagonize them and neutralize the inspirational effect.

- high and demanding but reasonable: Standards are quite demanding; expectations are pushy on the part of the teacher, but are attainable for most students.

From an observer's point of view, figuring out where a teacher is on standards requires some knowledge of age appropriate norms for the students and some specialized knowledge of the population of the class in order to make valid judgements. But teachers can certainly analyze their own performance and strive to make the standards inherent in their expectations appropriate to their students.

A Note on Standards and Expectations

We make a distinction between what a teacher *thinks* students will do ("expectations") and what a teacher *wants* students to do ("standards"). Unfortunately, in everyday talk about schools one hears the word "expectation" used in both senses (and rarely hears the word "standards" at all). Yet, they are both important ideas. Unless these two ideas are separated and conceptualized clearly by practitioners, it is possible we may find teachers who have expectations in the sense that they have *forecasts* of what students will do, but who have no notion of standards at all—no goals or heights for which to reach (or have students reach)— in their behavior in the four areas of Expectations discussed here. Having expectations without standards may color much of teaching today.

Matching With Your Standards...Adjusting Them

Consider the following four statements and their implication for both the teacher's standards and how those standards are applied to students of different ability. Which one best describes you?

1. "I have the same expectations for everyone. There's a certain amount of work to be done in this course and I expect everybody to do it."

2. "I have different expectations for different kids. I know some of them can't be expected to perform as well as others; this is the way it is in any large group. There are certain demands I just don't make on the lower ability students."

3. "I have different expectations for different kids. I know some of them have better backgrounds for getting this material, and maybe they're just quicker. Anyway, I make special provisions for the slower students to try to bring them along as far and as fast as they can go."

4. "I understand that kids in here have different abilities and speeds of learning; but I also know what a quality performance is like from a student, and I know what it means to really know this subject. I press them all toward that standard of excellence. I provide extra boosts and help those who need it, and I know they'll still move along at different rates and with different degrees of success. But the standard is there and I push them all toward ever closer approximations of it. If they never get there, at least they learn about excellence and get rewarded mightily for their incremental steps toward it."

These statements represent real people and real attitudes in our profession. The beliefs and intentions behind the positions these people hold are worth spelling out in some detail because they translate into action that has a powerful and sometimes decisive effect on student achievement. So we would like to describe more fully what these four people mean. Though they are, we grant, stereotypes, they are nonetheless real—that is, there *are* people like this and understanding what they mean by their statements will help us examine our own expectations and how we communicate them.

Teacher 1 makes *no discriminations* between students. What's expected seems conceived more in terms of coverage or amount of work done rather than quality of performance. The same standards for productivity are rigidly applied to everyone. Due dates are enforced and students are expected to learn the material or take the consequences. These teachers can let low-performing students be invisible as long as they are passing. The students are invisible because they hunker down and the teacher teaches past them.

Teacher 2 is *differential and accepting*. The teacher forecasts that students have different abilities and will perform according to those abilities. Those performances are accepted as representing what the students are capable of, and no effort is detected to press them to new heights. They all get pretty much the same material and they do what they can do.

Teacher 3 is *differential and provisioning*. The teacher provides for students who look like they'll have difficulty with the material—maybe by tailoring their assignments down within their range, maybe by supplementing them through extra help, peer tutoring, or extra instructional materials.

Teacher 4 is clear about an *image of excellence* in the subject area. That standard is held out for all students as a challenge and as a purpose of the instruction. When students say the teacher "really makes me feel this stuff is important," it reflects this kind of teacher commitment. This teacher also knows students have different capacities for learning and different rates, and makes allowances (provisions) for these differences, not by tailoring assignments down, but by providing extra help, extra instruction for those who need it. The teacher rewards whatever incremental steps students make toward the standard of excellence, but never forgets that standard or lets students forget it.

Teacher 1 does no matching. Teacher 2 has different expectations for students that turn into self-fulfilling prophesies. Teachers 3 and 4 are both individualizing in the sense of adjusting instruction within the class to students performing at different levels; but there is more of a confidence about Teacher 4 that they *all can do it*, or at least get near it. 4's behave a lot like the Mastery Learning paradigm, whether or not they've ever heard of it: that is, for students who are struggling, they break tasks down into however many small steps each student needs to succeed. The tasks are sequenced toward the eventual mastery that's intended for all the students, and the *time* individuals spend on various tasks or subtasks is adjusted for what they need. But the same mastery is the target for them as for everybody, and the teacher won't give up on them. These teachers believe that all students can learn and show it. True 4's are uncomfortable with grades because grades interfere with the messages they're trying to convey to kids. They give much genuine praise for real progress that may still be far short of excellence and are always pressing students to outperform their stereotypes of themselves. 4's may bend C's to B's for students who are knocking themselves out, but not B's to A's. These teachers believe they can really make a difference, despite some students' difficult home environments (Dembo and Gibson, 1985).

A "4" *gone haywire* focuses on the standard of excellence without giving students adequate opportunity or help in meeting it. Thus, while these teachers may avoid the pitfalls of stereotyping students as "brights" and "slows," and while they may press everyone toward excellence, they don't provide the wherewithal to get there. Instruction is at fault. Such 4's who lose perspective may also lose sight of individuals in their passion for excellence. They may press Special Education students and low-performers too far and too fast and into failure. A "3" who loses perspective individualizes like crazy, has all kinds of different materials and techniques available; but these teachers don't demand enough of the students. They unconsciously form stereotypes of what the students can accomplish and stop pushing...or they borrow from a "2" and start accepting whatever students produce as representative of what they can do, without conscious classifying of kids. They continue to work very hard and match (or attempt to match) students' learning styles, but in their zeal to provide for all, such 3's are susceptible to overfocusing on affect and going soft on content. Thus, they may subtly sabotage their own rescue missions.

In sum, we wind up with four qualitatively different levels of teacher performance on the sub-parameter of matching expectations to different students, which we can label:

- no discrimination
- differential and accepting
- differential and provisioning
- working for high standards (excellence) with allowances.

Some might argue that "working for high standards with allowances" risks damaging the self-image of students who can never reach the teacher's standard of excellence, and that good teaching is being "differential and provisioning". Others would argue that "working for high with allowances" is more appropriate at higher grade levels and that "standards of excellence" does not apply so clearly in the primary grades, for example, where mastery of basic skills is the big agenda and we would do better to think in terms of segmental mastery learning rather that "excellence." Still others would argue that excellence is excellence, and everyone should be exposed to it, made to reach for it. The fact that students are not all equal is a fact of life—all *people* are not equal in ability. And the fact that not everybody does the same quality of work should not be concealed from students as long as they're not made to feel crummy about what they *do* do with effort.

Such cases could be made. It is not our intention to contradict them by delineating these four attitudes towards matching. It is our aim here to point out that *the distinctions between these four teacher attitudes exist, and that they show up in behavior*. As teachers we should examine which attitude *we* hold, and how that affects our teaching performance: How do *we* match our expectations and standards to different students?

Pygmalion Revisited

The preceding sections concerning Expectations are noticeably different from the literature that has unfolded since *Pygmalion in the Classroom* (Rosenthal and Jacobson, 1968). In our exposition, we have aimed to focus teachers' attention on their expectations for an individual student's performance at the item level—that is, for specific tasks—and have invited them to discriminate their expectations between students, and within an individual student, for different tasks and different kinds of tasks. Further, we have invited teachers to be explicit and up-front with themselves and with the students about what their expectations are, so that by virtue of being explicit, the expectations may assume the character of shared learning goals between teachers and students.

The literature has been on a different tack, shedding a different kind of light on the subject of Expectations. First, these other authors and researchers have not distinguished expectations at the task level within students and between students. They have not asked about a teacher's expectations for whether Jimmy could write better sentences, or Mary could do her math faster, and what it would take to get them there. Rather, by "expectations," they have meant a teacher's gestalt impression of a student's *general* competence or aptitude. In their work, these authors have demonstrated that teachers create classes of students—the "brights" and the "slows."

Second, these investigators have shown that teachers then communicate their gestalt impressions to students by subtle and indirect messages which are, nevertheless, read by students and which influence their academic performance (and probably self-image). Cooper (1979) has pulled together these subtle teacher communication behaviors into five categories, relabeled here: Climate, Demands,

Persistence, Frequency of Interaction, and Feedback. Cooper explains them as follows (emphasis added):

- Climate: "It was found that teachers who believed they were interacting with bright students *smiled* and *nodded* their heads more often than teachers interacting with slow students. Teachers also *leaned towards* bright students and *looked brights in the eyes* more frequently." (p. 393)

- Demands: "Students labeled as slow have been found to have *fewer opportunities to learn new material* than students labeled as bright." (p. 393)

- Persistence: "Teachers tend to stay with the highs longer after they have failed to answer a question. This persistence following failure takes the form of *more clue giving*, *more repetition*, and/or *more rephrasing*....Teachers have been found to *pay closer attention* to responses of students described as gifted...teachers allowed bright students *longer to respond* before redirecting unanswered questions." (p. 394)

- Frequency of Interaction: "...teachers more often engage in *academic contact* with the high than low-expectation students." (p. 394)

- Feedback: "Teachers tend to praise high-expectation students more and proportionately *more per correct response*, while lows are criticized more and proportionately *more per incorrect response*." (p. 395)

There are thirteen distinct behavioral items (items in emphasis) in the preceding categories; and they provide empirical evidence that many teachers do, indeed, classify students as "brights" and "slows" and act differently toward them accordingly.

An observer (or teacher monitoring himself) could adopt either of the two approaches described in this parameter for profiling a teacher's behavior: (1) examine the *explicit* nature of a teacher's communication of expectations in terms of its being direct, specific, repeated, positive, and tenacious for different tasks in different cases—and then look at the standards implicit in those expectations; or (2) examine the *implicit* nature of a teacher's communication of expectations in terms of the thirteen behaviors Cooper summarizes as indicators of class prejudice between the "brights" and the "slows." Certainly, it is well worth looking carefully at ourselves to be sure we're not falling into the bright-slow stereotype trap.

The important implication for us as teachers is that these two patterns of behavior on the Expectations parameter should be consistent with each other. What we say explicitly regarding "all students can learn" should be congruent with what we do. If we seek to overcome the constricting grip of bright-slow class prejudice, which researchers are telling us is an unfair restriction on the equality of educational opportunity offered to students, then we *will not* do the unholy thirteen Cooper has collected and we *will* be explicit with our expectations and attempt to press all students toward excellence. And we will give students a lot of opportunities to exceed our expectations.

Having completed three strife-torn decades of desegregation in schools with a high degree of success (at least according to the ratios), we are faced, nonetheless, with dramatic underachievement among Blacks, Hispanics, and other minorities in our society. Communicating positive expectations and dissolving our stereotypes—perhaps even *their* stereotypes of themselves (Howard and Hammond, 1985)—is especially important at this point in the history of American education. The roots of what a person will do are planted firmly in his beliefs about what he *can* do. What are we as teachers doing to help minority students become believers in themselves as achievers? Avoiding the Pygmalion behaviors is a good start, but what's next?

A steady stream of authors and researchers are telling us that new curricula and new tougher standards are not enough. "First, without a doubt, the indispensible characteristic of successful teachers in low-income-area schools is a positive attitude. It is not enough for a teacher to use the right words. The critical question is, what implicit and explicit messages are students getting from the teacher about their ability to learn?" (Frick, 1987).

Young children believe success comes from effort; in fact, effort and ability are synonymous to them (Nicholls, 1978). But as they get older, children start attributing academic success more and more to native ability rather than effort. This creates a bind, because if one is not doing well, the only possible conclusion is that one must be dumb. Thus, many low-performing students opt out of school and quit trying by junior high because it's better to be considered lazy than dumb. The more we can press for and attribute success to ability *and effort* as students go through school (rather than luck or easy work), the better our success will be with minority students; in fact, with all students. "If you have a 'C' average or below you should spend three hours studying for this test." Implication: That's what it will take to get an 'A', and you can do it.

Maybe every school needs a person in charge of "exceeding expectations," someone who shakes up teachers, who goes around periodically reminding us to re-examine what we're expecting and demanding of students in the way of performance.

Perhaps that will be one effect of this chapter on readers. For in the end, the hope and the promise of this parameter is that it will give us better performance from our students, and give them more fair and equal treatment from us.

A final thought: The Expectations parameter is an example of the way in which teaching is more a calling than a job. If we have to believe in students to make them believers in themselves (especially with low-performing kids), then we must be givers. And givers are not just technicians.

Checking on Expectations

1. Do I know clearly and with conviction what my expectations are?
   Have I communicated them clearly to the students in ways that manifest these characteristics?

   - direct
   - specific
   - repeated
   - positive expectancy
   - modeled
   - tenacious

   - prompt feedback on work
   - detailed feedback on work
   - personal contact for feedback
   - no excuses
   - recognition of superior performance
   - logical consequences for poor performance

2. Do I communicate these general messages to all students:

   THIS IS IMPORTANT.
   YOU CAN DO IT.
   I WON'T GIVE UP ON YOU.

   How?

3. Are my overall standards appropriate?

   None
      Few Consistent
         Too Low
            Too High
               Average
                  Inspirational-vague
                     High But Reasonable

4. How do I match my expectations to different students?

> No Discrimination
>> Differential & Accepting
>>> Differential & Provisioning
>>>> Working for Excellence with Allowances

5. <u>Pygmalion Effects</u>

Do I do any of the following:

smile and nod more toward "highs"	yes	no
lean more toward "brights"	yes	no
look "brights" more in the eyes	yes	no
give "slows" fewer opportunities to learn new material	yes	no
give "highs" more clues when they fail to get an answer	yes	no
more repetition	yes	no
more rephrasing	yes	no
pay closer attention to responses of "gifted"	yes	no
allow "brights" longer to respond	yes	no
have more frequent academic contact with "highs"	yes	no
give "highs" more praise per correct response	yes	no
give "lows" more criticism per incorrect response	yes	no
do I do any of the above more with girls than with boys, or vice versa	yes	no

Source Materials on This Parameter

Bennett, N. "Research on Teaching: A Dream, a Belief and a Model." *Journal of Education*, Boston University, Boston, MA, 160/3, August 1978, 5-37.

Brookover, W.B.; Schweitzy, J.; Schneider, J.; Beady, C.; Flood, P. and Wisenbaker, J. "Elementary School Social Climate and School Advancement." *AERA Journal*, 15/2, Spring 1978, 301-318.

Cooper, H.M. "Pygmalion Grows Up: A Model for Teacher Expectations, Communication and Performance Influence." *Review of Educational Research*, 49/3, Summer 1979, 389-410.

Covington, M.V. "The Self-Worth Theory of Achievement Motivation: Findings and Implications." *The Elementary School Journal*, 85/1, September 1984, 5-20.

Dembo, M.H. and Gibson, S. "Teachers' Sense of Efficacy: An Important Factor in School Improvement." *The Elementary School Journal*, 86/2, November 1985, 173-184.

Dweck, C.S. "The Role of Expectations and Attributions in the Alleviation of Learned Helplessness." *Journal of Personality and Social Psychology*, 31, 674-685.

Frick, R. "Academic Redshirting Two Years Later: The Lessons Learned." *Education Week*, January 28, 1987, 20.

Good, T. "Classroom Expectations in Pupil-Teacher Interactions." In *The Social Psychology of School Learning*. New York: James H. McMillan Academic Press, 1980.

Hentoff, N. "Teachers: Accomplices in Failure." *Learning Magazine*, July/August 1980, 68-74.

Howard, J. and Hammond, R. "Rumors of Inferiority." *The New Republic*, September 9, 1985, 17-21.

Means, V.; Moore, J.W.; Gagne, E. and Hauck, W.E. "The Interactive Effects of Consonant and Dissonant Teacher Expectancy and Feedback Communication on Student Performance in a Natural School Setting." *AERA Journal*, 16/4, Fall 1979, 367-374.

Nicholls, J.G. "The Development of the Concepts of Effort and Ability, Perception of Academic Attainment, and the Understanding that Difficult Tasks Require More Ability." *Child Development*, 49, 1978, 800-814.

Nicholls, J.G. and Burton, J.T. "Motivation and Equality." *The Elementary School Journal*, 82/4, March 1982, 367-378.

Rist, R.C. "Student Social Class and Teacher Expectations: A Self-Fulfilling Prophecy in Ghetto Education." *Harvard Educational Review*, 40/3, August 1970, 411-451.

Rosenholtz, S.J. and Simpson, C. "The Formation of Ability Conceptions: Developmental Trend of Social Construction." *Review of Educational Research*, Spring 1984, 54/1, 31-63.

Rosenthal, R. and Jacobson, L. *Pygmalion in the Classroom*. New York: Holt, Rinehart and Winston, 1968.

Van Houton, R. *Learning Through Feedback*. New York: Human Services Press, 1980.

5

Personal Relationship Building

How do I build good personal relationships with students?

Ways of Relating
Seven Key Traits

PERSONAL RELATIONSHIP BUILDING

The parameter of Personal Relationship Building concerns the relationships teachers forge between themselves and students, and the elements that go into making those relationships productive. Teachers have many good reasons for building relationships with students and one of them is good classroom management. Students who like and respect their teachers are less likely to buck the program, less likely to be discipline problems, more likely to accept instruction and focusing moves. Students who dislike or have affectively neutral relationships with their teachers are less inhibited from misbehavior, more likely to resist instructional focusing moves. But there are other reasons teachers build relationships, too, such as making students feel like worthwhile people, making the human environment of the classroom safe, pleasant and healthy, and making teaching fun! All teachers build relationships of one sort or another with their students, and those relationships are an important variable in understanding what goes on in the complex society of a classroom, and how students perform within it. This chapter is about those relationships and the important elements that go into making them.

There are two ways in which we can look qualitatively at the Personal Relationship Building that goes on between teachers and students: 1) the variety of ways teachers have of contacting students' personal worlds; and 2) the traits which, when manifested by a teacher, seem to engender affection and regard in a relationship. We will take up each of these topics in turn.

Ways of Relating

Let's get personal.

In order to relate to you as a person, I have to attend to you, focusing on you as an individual. If I am teaching math, I may be focusing on the math and not on you; but, on the other hand, if I am able *also* to focus on you, then I am alert to your responses and make moves to enable you, particularly you, to assimilate the concepts. I am then relating to you personally and in a particular way—as an information processor. If I relate to you as a feeling being with hopes, fears, dreams, and goals, then I am attending to those aspects of you, listening for cues to those states, thinking about you and your interior states—that is yet another way of relating to people at a personal, one-to-one level. If I play sports with you, I interact with you as a teammate or a competitor and relate to you around the game. Maybe I talk to you about current events, do craft projects with you, help you plan your work, talk over interesting personal experiences at home or outside school that are important to you. There are many possible ways in which I can relate to you.

Likewise, there are many possible ways in which teachers may relate to students: as information processors, as feeling beings, over current events, over shared interest in some activity or topic, and so on. Further, teachers may relate in different ways to different students, and in different ways at different times to any one student. It is useful to examine our own repertoires here, and look for opportunities to meaningfully match how we relate to the needs of students and the circumstances of our classrooms. In this area of the Personal Relationship Building parameter, we can distinguish four levels of performance teachers exhibit:

- does not relate to students as individuals at all

- relates to students as individuals primarily in one way: commonly relates to all students only as information processors; or perhaps only around sports; or just chats during breaks.

- relates to students in a variety of ways

- matches the way of relating to the student: This level describes teachers who seek points of contact with students as individuals beyond what may be obvious or easy. They may go out of their way to identify, or create, opportunities or events during or outside of the school day to contact particular students. Some teachers arrange one-to-one conferences with each student each month (say one a day). Others occasionally have lunch with individual students back in the classroom. Perhaps, for example, the first way to build a relationship with Chris will be around the piano where the teacher can play a duet with him, or just play a song he may want to learn.

Clearly, the better a teacher can match ways of relating to the individual students and to particular circumstances, the stronger and more productive relationships will be with all students.

Traits

Considering teacher characteristics or traits brings in a viewpoint generally foreign to our work, and obsolete in the field of studies on teaching. However, we feel that it is necessary here to highlight certain classes of teacher behavior that are repeatedly mentioned as important by students in interview studies when they are asked about their teachers (Johnson, 1976). The traits and behaviors that seem most important are: fairness, appearance, humor, courtesy, respect, realness, re-establishing contact, and active listening. It is reasonable to connect these traits with Personal Relationship Building in that, when present, they foster more personal regard for a teacher, which can be a basis of good personal relationships.

Fairness

This seems to be the *sine qua non* for personal regard. Unless students perceive teachers as being fair in making decisions that bear on them—e.g., making assignments, arbitrating disputes, giving help, choosing teams—they cannot begin to like them.

Appearance

Appearance is mentioned more than one might have expected when students describe teachers for whom they have regard. Perhaps students take good grooming and neat, clean clothes as signs of respect or regard from the teacher—that the adult considers them important enough to look good for them.

Humor

William Glasser says humor is a form of caring. Teachers need not be joke tellers, but those who respond openly to humorous moments or who can kid light-heartedly with students seem to strike particularly responsive chords.

Courtesy

A courteous move, even though it might be quite formal and almost ritualistic, is still a direct gesture in recognition of, and often in behalf of, an individual. As such, it is a personal gesture, however remote, and connected with this parameter of Personal Relationship Building. Students tend to respond to courtesy in kind. No case needs to be made for courtesy as a desirable teacher behavior. It is included here as a trait related to Personal Relationship Building because students mention it and because it seems reasonable as a basis for relationships in the same way fairness is...a *sine qua non* for personal regard. A lack of courtesy blocks relationships, creates resentment. It would seem that an acceptable minimum of courteous consideration would be discernible in a yes/no sense. Discriminations beyond that would be very difficult.

Respect

Teachers show respect to students, as people, in many ways (Moustakas, 1966). They may honor student interests by making a place in the day for students to pursue them, or attempt to integrate these interests into the meeting of standard curriculum objectives through learning activities. They may show respect for student ideas by allowing or encouraging students to express them without criticism (though not necessarily without correction). They show respect for students by correcting errors without using put-downs, or without making students feel dumb or as if they've walked into an ambush (Howe, 1966); by joining corrective feedback with recognition of strengths. They may show they value students' products by treating them with care, providing for their display, and giving feedback that shows the teacher has really examined the product, whether the feedback be positive or corrective. (For instance, saying "You really captured all the tiny parts of the spider in your drawing," rather than just saying, "Beautiful" or "Good work.")

Note: We don't argue that praise such as "good work" or "beautiful" is bad or meaningless, or even necessarily less good in certain circumstances than praise that specifies the attributes that are praiseworthy (Ginott, 1965; Martin, 1971). It's just that to tie feedback to respect rather than just praise, the statement must show some real attention to the product. Conceivably, the teacher could show this attention and respect for the student's product non-verbally by looking long and carefully at the piece, and then perhaps *sincerely* saying, "Good work, Julia."

Realness
Authority acts as a screen that obscures seeing the "boss" as a person; that is, as a thinking, feeling being with a life history of experience. Instead, we tend to see the boss as the boss, the teacher as the teacher—the authority role figure. Young children who address their teacher as "teacher" rather than by name are clearly in this mode. Children begin to see their teacher as real, as a person, only if the teacher lets them.

There are behaviors by which teachers reveal aspects of themselves that allow this image of authority figure to be tempered by images of teacher-as-real person. Teachers share anecdotes with students from their own lives, integrating personal experiences into explanations and presentations. "I" messages as described by Thomas Gordon (1970) are direct verbal behaviors by which teachers explicitly state their feelings and what behavior or circumstance made them feel that way. Effectiveness Training Associates reports numerous cases of children who, when confronted by "I" messages, change disruptive behavior: children who had no idea their behavior was affecting their teacher adversely. When these statements are used it is sometimes the first time students have been asked to see their teacher as a person with feelings.

Re-establishing Contact
When a teacher strongly reprimands a student (e.g., sends the student out of the room), or shows anger carrying out some high-voltage disciplinary move ("Stop that right now! You cannot destroy someone else's work...Then if you can't help him rebuild it, this area is closed to you for the day...Goodbye!"), their

relationship may be under a cloud of tension (as it should be). After such incidents, the teacher who keeps good relationships looks to interact in a positive, personal way with the student around some other context. This is re-establishing contact, conveying the message that the teacher is not carrying a grudge, that the relationship is still intact. It removes the tension between the teacher and student, and gives the student an emotional entry back into the flow of activities. There is no apology or "making up" in the teacher move, nor is there any implied backing down from the firmness of the previous move or from the anger. It's simply a way of saying, "OK, let's get in touch again"...a return to normalcy.

To observe this type of behavior, one would simply have to see a personal move with a student sometime close on the heels of a discipline or desist incident. We need not guess how far the teacher went out of his way to create the positive interaction; we just have to see the move in reasonable time proximity to the incident.

Active Listening

Reflective listening feeds back to speakers the content of their remarks and thus confirms to them that they have been heard. *Active* listening adds a feeling component to the feedback, and the listener restates or infers the feeling state of the speaker aloud. For example, an active listener might say, "You're stuck on these problems (content) and getting really frustrated (feeling)." Teachers who use active listening are communicating concern for students' personal feeling states directly. While it can be used manipulatively and insincerely, it is reasonable to argue that on-target and genuine active listening is a relationship building behavior. It is the verbal behavioral embodiment of empathy. When combined with accuracy and respect (Egan, 1975), active listening makes children feel understood and cared about (Aspy and Roebuck, 1977). "She really listens to me" is a common statement students make about teachers they like and respect.

The quality of relationships between teachers and students is a deep and constant backdrop to all that is transpiring in classrooms, and one well worth examining. In analyzing your own teaching behavior (or observing another's teaching) for these traits, it is important to bear in mind that the appropriateness of moves from any trait may vary with the form of instruction or learning environment in operation at any given moment. For instance, moves that show respect for students as individuals may not surface when students are in a period of programmed instruction and interacting with the system rather than with the teacher-as-person. So, it might take the course of a whole day, or even many days, for one to see a teacher display the full range of his repertoire for the seven traits described in this section. Thus, checking on these behaviors requires an extended observation, or perhaps even several repeated observations, in order to see the full range of behavior.

Checking on Personal Relationship Building

Examine your own teaching, or that of another, and see which of the following apply. For each behavior or trait that you credit, see if you can cite an event or an exchange to back it up. For those you wish to develop, see if you can note a time or an opportunity for trying them out. Be as specific as you can.

1. Ways of relating to students: Circle the level of performance.

    no way
       one way
          variety of ways
             matches the way to individuals

2. Traits: Check any that apply.

    ___ fairness
    ___ appearance
    ___ humor
    ___ courtesy
    ___ respect
    ___ re-establishing contact
    ___ active listening

Source Materials on This Parameter

Allender, J.S., Seitchik, M. and Goldstein, D. "Student Involvement and Patterns of Teaching." *Journal of Classroom Interaction*, 16/2, 11-20.

Aspy, D. and Roebuck, F.N. *Kids Don't Learn From People They Don't Like.* Amherst, MA: Human Resource Development Press, 1977.

Brophy, J. "Teacher Praise: A Functional Analysis." *Review of Educational Research*, 51/1, Spring 1981, 5-32.

Brown, L. and Goodall, R.C. "Enhancing Group Climate Through Systematic Utilization of Feedback." *Journal of Classroom Interaction*, 16/2, 1981, 21-25.

Egan, G. *The Skilled Helper.* Monterey, CA: Brooks/Cole Publishing Co., 1975.

Fraser, B.J. and O'Brien, P. "Student and Teacher Perceptions of the Environment of Elementary School Classrooms." *Elementary School Journal*, 85/5, May 1985, 567-580.

Ginott, H.G. *Between Parent and Child.* New York: MacMillan Co., 1965.

Gordon, T. *Teacher Effectiveness Training.* New York: Wyden Press, 1974.

Johnson, M.S. "I Think My Teacher is A..." *Learning*, February 1976, 36-38.

Joos, M. *The Five Clocks.* New York: Harcourt, Brace & World, 1967.

Mergendoller, J.R. and Packer, M.J. "Seventh Graders' Conceptions of Teachers: An Interpretive Analysis." *Elementary School Journal*, 85/5, May 1985, 581-600.

Moustakas, C. *The Authentic Teacher.* Cambridge, MA: Howard A. Doyle Publishing Co., 1966.

Rogers, V.R. "Laughing with Children." *Educational Leadership*, April 1984, 44-50.

6

Discipline

How do I deal with very resistant students?

DISCIPLINE

Section I
Introduction and Overview

"What do I have to do to get students to apply themselves to their work and stop fooling around and being disruptive?" That is the bottom line question of the Discipline parameter. Many teachers spend a disproportionate amount of energy dealing with it; some leave teaching because they find they rarely deal with anything else. There is no question that good discipline is a prerequisite for good education; we must bring all of our best knowledge to bear on it so we can stop the needless hemorrhaging of both teacher and student energy that it consumes. We have the knowledge and the capability to retire this issue and to move on to the question most teachers are more interested in, namely, "How do I build self-discipline and responsibility in students?"

In this chapter we will address both questions, but first things first. If students are inattentive and disruptive, there may be one or more of the following causes at work:

1. Poor general management (Attention, Momentum, Space, Time, Routines, Personal Relationship Building)

2. Inappropriate work that is too hard, too easy, or a glaring mismatch to students' learning styles (Objectives, Learning Experiences)

3. Boring instruction (Learning Experiences)

4. Confusing instruction (Clarity)

5. Unclear expectations and consequences (Expectations)

6. Student sense of powerlessness

7. Physical causes

8. Ignorance of how to do the expected behaviors

9. Value clashes

10. Heavy emotional baggage students bring with them (e.g., being convinced one is a failure)

Figure 6-1 represents these causes and some indicators. Let's take a quick look at the 10 causes and go into a few of the more important ones in depth.

The first four causes all have to do with other parameters, some of which we've treated earlier in this book. If these basic classroom management parameters (Attention, Momentum, Space, Time, Routines, Personal Relationship Building) are not in good shape, discipline problems will result. When there *are* discipline problems, these are the first places to look, especially if the problems are endemic to a whole class, because, for example, kids with time on their hands will find an outlet somewhere for their energy and creativity—and that outlet may well be disruptive. (With prolonged boredom, disruptions are probably a sign of mental health and physical vitality in normal kids.) Thus, competent handling of Space, Time, Momentum, and Personal Relationship Building forms a foundation for good behavior. Conversely, absence of their skillful handling creates distraction, fragmentation, down-time, and resentment.

Even if these parameters are well managed, we need to make sure the work is appropriate for the kids (Objectives). If it is too hard or too easy, then we risk frustration or boredom—either of which may induce disruptive behavior.

The environment of the class itself may be a mismatch for certain students, and a simple change of the environment can reduce or eliminate problems for them. The most obvious variable is the degree of structure in the class (Colarruso, 1972). High structure environments leave students less choice in what activities to do when, with whom, and where in the room. Low structure environments (which may, nevertheless, be highly planned and highly organized) have more student movement and more flexibility in who does what, when…since students are making more choices and are more in charge of their personal schedules. Similarly, teachers can manipulate the degree of auditory and visual stimulation. In *Teacher Effectiveness Training*, Thomas Gordon (1974) has some very useful checklists for other ways to modify the environment (under the categories of "enriching", "impoverishing", "restricting", "enlarging", "rearranging", "simplifying," and "systematizing.") When looking for ways to improve students' behavior, we should, therefore, look also at the appropriateness of the environments we have

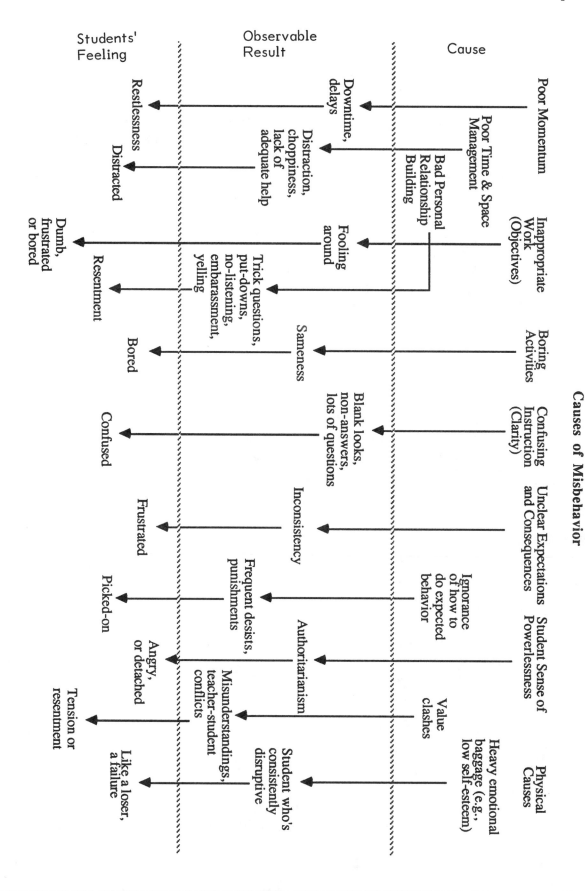

FIGURE 6-1
Causes of Misbehavior

created for them. We need to weigh how much these environments may be contributing to (rather than reducing) problems. The goal is obviously to arrange them so that we do not play to kids' weaknesses and trigger disruptive behaviors.

Finally, using the same format or activity structures day after day (too much lecturing, too many worksheets) may also induce boredom and acting out behavior in some classes. But, even if we are satisfied that basic management is handled well and instruction is of reasonable difficulty, there may still be problems.

A more serious, and more common, cause is unclear expectations and consequences; the intricate web of mutual understandings that go with them may not be clearly established between teacher and students. We have yet to find a teacher with widespread discipline problems (rather than just one resistant child) who didn't need help here. In Section II we will go into considerable detail to specify the essential "how to's" of building this web.

Schools as institutions resemble the army, prisons, and hospitals in the way they can systematically make students feel helpless. Schools can frustrate the basic human need for control of one's own fate by leaving little (in some cases *no*) room for initiative, decision making, and leadership. While this deprivation does not smart for the passive, for a large part of any population this environment makes children want to push back. And they do! If we use power skillfully, we can control these students—but we will probably also make them hate school and learn less. This is no pitch for free schools; learning is often hard work and requires doing assignments given by others, and that is okay. But without compromising high academic standards one iota, teachers can structure classes so that students feel some ownership and control of what goes on. When we take up "students' sense of powerlessness," we will see that every increment of progress in this direction takes pressure off behavior management because kids' energy starts to push *with* it instead off against it. In Section III of the chapter we will elaborate on how teachers can do this.

Sometimes seemingly inattentive students simply don't hear as well. They fail to carry out directions not because they're daydreaming or willful, they simply mishear key words. We have known "inattentive" students to be diagnosed with hearing loss after 2-1/2 years in primary school, and after much energy went into behavior modification and other focusing strategies for the children. So, the message here is simply to be sure to rule out physical causes when working with kids who appear resistant or spacey. These include vision, organic hyperactivity, thyroid irregularities, and a host of other possible physical problems.

Youngsters bring to school both the manners and the cognitive habits they have learned elsewhere. Failure to meet our expectations for lining up without running, for listening to directions, for lining up their work neatly on paper, or for putting materials away in an orderly way may simply come from the fact that they *don't know how to do so*! It is a fact that some kindergartners don't know how to walk rather than run in certain situations (which is to say they don't know how to predict consequences, control impulses, or plan physical movements). It is a fact that some older students simply don't know how to categorize objects to expedite a cleanup, much less plan their time and movements during it. In these cases, teaching the behaviors step by step is the antidote to the disruptive behavior, *not* clever consequences or contracts. There's no use trying to motivate youngsters to do something for which they lack the tools. It is our assumptions here that can cause us to overlook these possibilities. It may simply never occur to a teacher that the deepening cycle of threats and punishments has its origin in simple ignorance. We urge teachers facing disruptive behavior to examine the students carefully. More often than is realized, we assume capacities that are not there in students' behavioral repertoires. In these cases, putting the behaviors into their repertoires is what's needed. A question not to overlook when trying to figure out a resistant class or individual is, "Do they know *how* to do what I am asking them to do?"

Cultural clashes between teachers and students may underlie resistant behavior. This cause is rare, but real, and should be considered in classes where students' home life has strong ethnic roots in another culture.

Hardest of all—despite all the best efforts in responding to the issues above— there may be a few students who resist learning and, for one reason or another, do not function in school. They may be passive and withdrawn, or act out severely and consistently. The final section of this chapter will be about these students—the few, not the many; the troubled, not the norm. There are at least six major strategies for dealing with resistant students, each cohesive and each different, and they are all effective—*if* used with the right students. Our job shall be to learn what they are, how to use them, and how to match them appropriately to individual kids. Here, you will be challenged to broaden your range for responding to resistant students; you can acquire a repertoire from which to draw. You will be asked to look carefully at students and become practical diagnosticians so you can draw *appropriately* from your repertoire. There are no sure-fire formulas for matching students to strategies, but we are not reliant upon trial and error either. A good deal is known about what is likely to work with whom. You will have that knowledge to use here and apply in case studies of your students; but you will have to work hard to be able to use it. We will take up each of the six strategies and explore how-to-do-it and how-to-match.

The six strategies are named: Behavior Modification, Self-Awareness Training, Personal Influence, Logical Consequences, Reality Therapy, and Teacher Effectiveness Training. Each strategy has an intellectual parent, a central figure who has pulled it together and written extensively about it (except Behavior Modification which has so many parents, aunts, uncles and cousins it is hard to single one out.) Each strategy is distinctly different from the others. Each strategy has a particular series of steps to go through and a way for teachers to respond to disruptive students.

It will be our point of view that these six strategies are all good when used appropriately—that no one of the six is inherently better than any other. Furthermore, there are good grounds for believing that we can choose appropriately from the six...that we can match particularly resistant students with what we do, and that we do not have to rely upon—in fact, should not rely upon—just trial and error, eclectic sampling from available strategies. In Section IV we will first analyze the nature of each of the six strategies. Then, we will elaborate the components of each in detail and provide primary source references for further study. Finally, we will describe a rationale for choosing among them to match a particular student.

We now take some of the 10 causes of misbehavior for more in-depth treatment. Section II will deal with how to set up an effective system of expectations and consequences. Section III will deal with how to give students a feeling of control and influence in classroom life, thereby reducing discipline problems because kids have more of a stake in the school as a community. Section IV will describe the six Models of Discipline for severely resistant students and how to match them appropriately to which kids.

Section II
The Web of Expectations and Consequences

Are the rules and consequences clear and specific enough, both to me and to the students?

The prerequisite for strength in this whole area is that students have a clear and unambivalent picture of what the expectations for their behavior really are. Something must happen to get that information across. There are numerous ways this may be done: tell them directly, make up a chart, brainstorm or negotiate the class rules at a class meeting. Expectations are sometimes not codified as formal rules or laid out all at once, but they become known to students through what a teacher reacts to consistently. At any rate, the students must be clear about what they are, and thus expectations must be *specific* so there is no misunderstanding (or room for argument). It may not be enough to call for "silent reading time." The class may need clarification on what silence means. Does it mean absolute silence, or whispering, or quiet talking? Can the students discriminate the difference and modulate in a controlled way between those levels? If "silence" really means "quiet," then perhaps it really should not be called "silence"...and vice versa. If students are supposed to arrive on time for class, does that mean being no more than two minutes late, being in the room when the bell rings, being in their seats, or being in their seats with notebooks open and ready to go? *Where* these boundaries are drawn is less important than *that* they are established clearly. There must be no doubt as to when a rule has been broken.

Mendler and Curwin (1983) describe a comprehensive strategy for involving students in rule-making (called the "social contract") so that there is no doubt about what the rules are. After the teacher specifies certain non-negotiable rules and establishes consequences, students work in small groups to propose rules for the *teacher's* behavior, including consequences. (For example— "Rule: The teacher must call on students by their names. Consequences for violation: a) Remind teacher of rule, b) Teacher will apologize."; "Rule: Teacher should check our papers in private. Consequence for violation: Teacher will read to the class two chapters from the current book she is reading.") Mendler and Curwin explain:

> All of the rules and consequences are reviewed by the class to insure proper understanding of what they mean. Role play is often a useful strategy to illustrate the exact meaning of a rule or consequence. For example some students want the teacher not to yell. It is important for the teacher to speak louder and louder until agreement is reached as to what constitutes yelling. [Mendler and Curwin, p. 73]

Then, a careful process of decision making occurs in which the teacher and students decide which of the proposed rules and consequences will be incorporated into the contract. (For details see Mendler and Curwin, pp. 73-74). Finally, students take an exam that tests their knowledge of the contract. Classroom privileges can be earned by passing the test with a 100% score! This novel social contract procedure accomplishes several things: first, students developing rules for teachers gives them an added investment in making the process work; second, the test for comprehension and the link to classroom privileges sends the message that this contract is important and underlines the content of what the rules really are.

Do I convey positive expectancy?

Expectations need to be repeated, and often. One finds teachers, especially in the beginning of the year, restating and reminding students about expectations...eliciting expectations from students just prior to events that may strain the behavior. For instance: "We're going to the auditorium now kids. What might it be like there as we walk in? What will we need to do? What should we keep in mind for our behavior as a good audience?" Or: "Okay, we're ready to go to gym now. What do we think about when we are in the halls?...Why?"

An attitude of *positive expectancy* may be embedded in the utterances with which a teacher restates expectations. This positive expectancy has two aspects. The first has the flavor of "why of course you're going to do it"...this is not something the teacher says outright, but it is the assumption conveyed by body language and attitude. The other aspect of positive expectancy is encouragement, confidence, the "I know you can do it" attitude; it is often associated with positive statements of specific behaviors or questions ("Can you remember to raise your hand?") rather than direct desists ("Stop calling out!").

Another way to convey positive expectancy is to be assertive in the way we request appropriate behavior. Lee Canter calls for combining four attention moves— eye contact, hand gesture, the student's name, and touch—for an assertive effect:

> The teacher observed Steve roughly pushing and shoving the children standing beside him in line. The teacher walked up to Steve, looked him in the eyes, placed her hand on his shoulder, and stated, "Steve, keep your hands to yourself." (while gesturing with her free hand). [Canter, 1977, p. 75]

If students counter with excuses or other diverting moves, Canter recommends the "broken record" technique:

> Teacher: "Sue, I want you to raise your hand and wait to be called on before you speak." (Statement of want)
>
> Sue: "None of the other children do."
>
> Teacher: "That's not the point, I want you to raise your hand." (Broken record)
>
> Sue: "You never call on me."
>
> Teacher: "That's not the point, I want you to raise your hand." (Broken record)
>
> Sue: "Okay, I will."
>
> In this interchange, the teacher simply kept repeating (broken record) what she wanted from the child and would not become sidetracked by Sue's responses. The teacher maintained control of the interaction with the child.
>
> In utilizing a broken record, you first need to determine what you want from the interaction with the student (i.e., "I want Sue to raise her hand." This becomes your statement of want and the gist of your interactions. You can preface your statement of want with, "That's not the point, but...I want you to raise your hand", or "I understand, but...I want you to raise your hand.") No matter what manipulative response the student presents, if you respond with your statement of want—"that's not the point, I want you to...", or "I understand, but I want you to..."—your statement will be more effective. [Canter, pp. 79-80]

This technique can be surprisingly effective, especially with students who are verbal. Remember though, that when you use it you must know what consequences (or range of consequences) you are prepared to deliver if the behavior persists. Without that clear image, one's assertiveness will be hollow. Furthermore, after reasserting the expectation three times, a teacher had better be ready to implement the consequence.

Are the consequences logical rather than punitive?

Rudolph Dreikurs understood that punishment breeds resentment whereas logical consequences begin to teach students the reality of the social order. Punishment is any aversive stimulus (like being paddled...or writing "I will not throw paper on the floor" one hundred times) intended to discourage the recurrence of the behavior: you will be less likely to do the behavior next time because this unpleasant thing may happen to you again. Logical consequences, on the other hand, are connected to the behavior in such a way as to feel like fair retribution for the violation. If you have broken a rule against copying another's homework, it is a logical consequence to have to do it all over again under supervision (rather than stay after school as punishment). If you have littered the floor, it is a logical consequence to clean it up during recess (rather than write "I will not litter" one hundred times). If you have hurt someone's feelings with rude remarks, it is a logical consequence to do something nice for them (rather than sit detention). (More on logical consequences can be found later in this chapter in the section devoted to Dreikurs' model.)[1]

Do I have a range of consequences rather than one rigid response for every transgression?

If each rule has an automatic consequence tied to it, you can get boxed into a corner. One consequence only for each rule is a mistake. Mendler and Curwin cite the case of a teacher whose consequence for undone homework is staying after school to finish it. One day one of her best students says, "I'm sorry, Miss Martin, but my father was very sick last night. I had to babysit while he was taken to the hospital, and in the confusion, I didn't have time to get my homework done." The teacher is now in the dilemma of either being unfeeling and rigid ("I'm sorry, but you have to stay after school anyway") or letting the kid off and teaching the rest of the class that "good" excuses can pardon undone work. This could have been avoided if the teacher could pick from an appropriate *range* of consequences for each rule. For undone homework, the range might be:

Reminder
Warning
Hand in work before the close of school that day
Stay after school to finish it
Conference with the teacher, student, and parent to develop a plan.

---

[1] It is interesting to examine how "detention" is used in one's school in light of logical consequence theory. Sometimes detention can, indeed, be logical when a student has not done work and detention is used to get it done. But it is also quite possible for detention to be punitive and counterproductive when used as a consequence for, say, defacing a desk or talking back to a teacher.

With this range of alternatives, Miss Martin could gently remind Susan that homework is due on time, and then discuss how her father is doing, etc. In this way she is implementing one of the prescribed consequences, yet she is not being overly rigid with Susan. With another student who had been late six times that month, she might make him stay after and finish it. [Mendler and Curwin, *op. cit.*, p. 119]

Fair need not always be equal.

Do I deliver consequences in a way that is tenacious, consistent, prompt, matter-of-fact, and indicates student choice?

Every time an expectation is not met, the teacher must consistently react (not meaning react the same way, but meaning react every time). That is not to say punish. The reaction may be anything from a reminder to a consequence; but something has to happen. The teacher must *do* something, otherwise the students—especially resistant students—come to disregard the expectation (or else become confused over where it applies). The transgression usually cannot be ignored. (Sometimes the teacher may choose to ignore certain behaviors when they are minor and calling attention to them would just reinforce them...or the teacher may recognize them "economically" and briefly.) The general mission here is to communicate to students that one's expectations are really one's expectations...you *mean* them. They get this message when they find the teacher reliably calls them on certain behaviors—reliably and consistently *does something* about it. This "does something about it" is often cited as the most important of the attributes under communication of expectations (Rogers, 1972; Canter, 1977; Mendler and Curwin, 1983) and it will usually mean arranging some sort of consequence for the behavior. Mere admonishing and reprimanding without action that goes beyond words usually sends the message that expectations are weak.

Teachers must be *tenacious* about the business of restating expectations and consistently reacting. Individuals and sometimes whole classes will test teachers to the limits on this. The thing is not to give up, even though misbehavior continues in the face of specific expectations consistently upheld. Some very difficult students will push teachers this far to see if they really care (meaning care about *them*). If the reactions to the misbehavior are reasonable, appropriate, and fair, tenacity will carry the day.

Lee Canter (1977) tells the story of a very aggressive third grader, Carl, who consistently abuses other children, both verbally and physically. On several occasions he has also extorted money from his classmates! At a meeting with the child's parents, the principal, and the teacher, a contract is signed that Carl will be excluded from school if he does any of the following things: threatens children, cusses them, extorts money, or physically assaults them. The parents agree to follow through with the exclusion at home.

The next day, on the way into the classroom, Carl got into an argument with another student and roughly shoved him. Ms. S. immediately went up to Carl and simply told him, "You pushed Sol. You've chosen to go home for the rest of the day!" Ms. S. contacted the office: the principal called Carl's mother, who came to get him. Carl went home and spent the rest of the school day in his room doing the work he would have done had he stayed in school.

The following day, during a spelling assignment, another student refused to let Carl copy his work and Carl became angry. He threatened to beat the student up. Ms. S., hearing this, told Carl what he had done and that he would be going home again. His mother picked him up, and he spent the rest of the day at home in his room. Carl behaved appropriately for the next two days. On the third day, during free choice, Ms. S. observed him angrily cursing and screaming at a girl who would not give him the puzzle that she was playing with. Ms. S. repeated the same procedure of informing him of what he had done and that by behaving inappropriately he had chosen to go home. For the first time Carl became upset. He began to cry and say that he did not want to go home. Ms. S. simply told him that "he made a choice" and that he would be going home.

As was typical, the "third time was the charm." Ms. S.'s ability to deal assertively with Carl's behaviors let him know that his disruptions would not be tolerated. Carl thus chose to control his temper and behave in an appropriate manner with his fellow students.

Of all the sections in this chapter, this is probably the most important. It takes determination and tenacity to keep delivering consequences when the behavior persists. But without that tenacity students will not believe teachers are serious about their expectations. Follow through at the beginning of the year on plans such as the one Canter describes (assuming you have a student who needs such a strong plan) will be keenly observed by the rest of your class and let them know you mean what you say. Inconsistency and lack of follow through early in the school year is a common cause of school discipline problems.

Children may not care if you keep them after school once, suspend them every now and then, or send them to the corner infrequently. But there are few children who would not care if they knew that they would have to stay after school every day they chose to, even if it meant five days straight. There are few children who would not care if they knew they would be suspended every time they acted out, even if it meant three straight days of suspension. There are few children who would not care if they knew you would send them to a corner for their inappropriate behavior every time they chose to go, even if it meant five times a day.

What we are trying to say is this: if you really care, the children will really care. If you are prepared to use any means necessary and appropriate to influence the children to eliminate their inappropriate behavior they will sense your determination and quickly care about the consequences which they will have to face consistently if they choose to act inappropriately. [Canter, *op. cit.*, pp. 109-110]

Almost any behavior we really want to get, we can get if we have the determination…because we do have the power.

Does this mean that if one keeps delivering consequences persistently, the behavior is sure to change? First, it is possible to deliver a consequence over and over again consistently and have no effect. That can happen if the consequence is not strong enough, or if it somehow turns out to be a reward for the child. It can also happen if the behavior comes from a physical cause, ignorance, or a value clash. Second, the way in which the consequence was delivered in Canter's scenario had a lot to do with its success. The teacher did not blame, criticize or humiliate the student; she simply (but promptly) went up to him, noted the behavior ("You pushed Sol") and delivered the consequence ("You have chosen to go home for the rest of the day"). She pointed out that going home was the child's choice in this case since he knew that pushing Sol would lead to that. Thus, the teacher reacts with matter-of-fact emotion rather than anger. It is, in fact, easier to react that way when you know precisely what you are going to do. That knowledge (versus the helpless feeling of a child who seems outside your control) gives a teacher both confidence and calm which in turn allow for better judgments. So, being persistent with consequences can also fail if the consequence is not delivered in the right way.

The specific technique described in Canter's scenario is a strong one—systematic exclusion of a student to eliminate particularly disruptive and persistent behavior. But it can be very effective. Seymour Sarason describes another powerful exclusion technique that works without parents or contracts. It relies on the cooperation of another teacher into whose room the child is sent for exclusion. The host teacher has a special place the student goes that is not fun and where the student does work. For details see Sarason (1973), pp. 136-139.

Do I recognize and reward responsible behavior effectively?

No discussion of consequences would be complete without examining positive consequences—how we respond to students who are meeting expectations. There is a case to be made that good behavior should not be rewarded; it is expected; it should be the norm; no reward system should be necessary to maintain it. Nevertheless, with certain classes where discipline problems are an issue, explicit reward systems can play a useful role (and we're not just talking about elementary classes either).

Ingenious reward systems such as Canter's marbles-in-a-jar,[2] or numerous others such as those described in CLAIM (see Section IV), have been devised to acknowledge positive behavior in students. Curwin's (1983) approach relies more on social praise delivered in private. He likes to catch students being good, and goes out of his way to deliver both positive and negative consequences quietly so only the receiving student can hear. Thus, when he is bending over a student to say something privately, the rest of the class doesn't know whether it's something like, "You have continued talking to neighbors despite two warnings. The consequence is you'll have to stay after class with me and work out a plan to avoid this behavior..." or, "You've been focusing on your work and written two balanced sonnets this afternoon. That's what I call being productive!"

Do I take sufficient time and care at the beginning of the year to establish expectations?

One elementary teacher we know will not send her kids to specials for the first two weeks in September so she can insure solid learning of her expectations, establish routines, and begin to build class cohesion. Suspending specials may not be necessary, but the focus on expectations certainly is. It is useful to think of this period as one of teaching or training for the students. Training requires practice; thus, if students are noisy and disruptive in the hallway, one can say, "I can see we need more practice in hall walking from the way we just came back from gym." And you can, indeed, take the class out for some "practice" with you right then and there. This is not punitive, but logical as a consequence. (Mendler and Curwin (1983) cite a school that has an after school class in cafeteria behavior, including practice and an exam for those kids who have been disruptive at lunch. Students must get 100% on the exam to "graduate.")

Do I have high enough expectations for behavior no matter what the kids' backgrounds?

A teacher can control students, even if the expectations are inappropriate, by sheer power and fear. The presence of control, however, does not tell us anything about the appropriateness of the teacher's expectations. Making judgements about these standards for behavior takes us into a fuzzy but important area. If the demands we make on students are inappropriate, that will go a long way toward explaining discipline problems. We might create a scale for teacher standards going up the following ladder:

- no expectations evident: pretty much a laissez-faire treatment.

- few consistent expectations evident

- one uniform set of expectations that appears low: i.e., too easy, permissive, undemanding for what students seem capable of when judged by age and performance

- uniform set of expectations that are unreasonably high or age inappropriate (or in some other way inappropriate)

---

[2]Lee Canter (p. 140) advocates dropping marbles in a jar as a reward. The sound of the marble landing serves as an immediate audible signal to all that they are behaving appropriately. A full jar earns the class some predetermined reward such as a popcorn party or extra recess.

- uniform and average expectations

- uniform and high expectations: meaning demanding but still reasonable.

We could try to place ourselves on this ladder, but there would still be an important aspect of standards to examine. Once we have a general sense for our expectations-as-standards, we can look beyond and ask how we differentiate for groups or for individuals within these standards. Four separate and logical levels of performance have been identified which discriminate among teachers in how they apply their standards to different pupils. We can represent these levels in the following statements:

1. I have the same expectations for everyone.

2. I have different expectations for different kids, meaning I expect some to misbehave more than others, display self-control less. This may or may not mean I am more tolerant or understanding or accepting of this misbehavior from them; but anyway I don't demand that they meet the standards I do demand and expect of others.

3. I have different expectations for individual kids' ability to behave in different tempting or otherwise high-risk situations for them. I know their weaknesses and know the situations that can trigger them. I try to provide for them in advance of these situations.

4. I understand kids' differential abilities to behave in high-risk trigger-ing situations that are hard for them (as in the above entry), and I make some adjustments and allowances for them, *but my ultimate expectations for their behavior remain as high as they are for the other kids*, and I let them know that. I am striving with them toward ever closer approximations of those high standards. I am not surprised by their misbehavior when it occurs, so in a sense I 'expect' it from time to time; but I do not accept it. In fact, I work actively to change it.

When we look analytically at ourselves and try to get better control of behavior in our classes, it is useful to compare ourselves to these four statements. The third and fourth are distinctly different from the first two; they show up in teacher behav-ior that is also different and will have a marked effect of general discipline.

A distinction has been made between what teachers *think* a student will do (they may have "varying expectations") and what they *want* a student to do or measure up to (they may have different "standards").

Every year we work with at least one or two teachers, excellent teachers, talented and caring people whose effectiveness is reduced by their ambivalence about expectations. They are unsure how reasonable it is for them to expect...to push...kids toward more responsible and attentive behavior in class. They see the irresponsible "whacko" behavior of students who appear out of control, who have family and other problems, and feel they must make allowances. They thus under-sell the kids and undershoot with their goals for student behavior. Who says first graders can't sit still in a circle and listen to each other for a 15-minute meeting? Who says ninth graders can't learn to function in self-organized task groups to plan and organize a project?

Again and again, we have seen it demonstrated that you can get what behavior you want if you work hard enough at it, are tenacious and determined enough, are committed to the idea that it is right and attainable behavior for your students, and are willing to teach them the skills they may need to function at that level. (What you decide to "want," of course, can be unreasonable and age-inappropriate, in which case what you get is what you deserve!) This is true even for some disturbed students, though they tax you much more, your setting may need adjust-ment, and it will take considerably longer. Anything less is ultimately a disservice to our students.

If you have a clear notion of what you want and keep expecting, expecting, expecting *out loud* to students, with consequences when they don't measure up, with explanations of "why" over and over again, and with as much kindness and rationality as you can muster, you will get there; and that's no pipe dream. But first you must decide to do so.

Section III

Do I give kids a real and legitimate sense of control, influence, responsibility, and power in class life?

In the introduction to this chapter, we argued that teachers could structure classes so students felt some ownership and control of what goes on, and that doing so could reduce discipline problems. Bear in mind, however, that this is no substitute for clear expectations and consequences. They should come first. Inter-estingly, we know a first year teacher who never really did get expectations and consequences sorted out in her own head, but who nevertheless salvaged the year by starting an individualized contract learning system. The students invested in it and much energy that would have gone into fighting the teacher went into meeting their learning goals instead. But it was still a rocky year with less than optimal learning. If expectations had been established right from the beginning, her contract system would not just have salvaged this particular class, it would have put it into orbit.

Three excellent approaches for giving students ownership in classroom life are: negotiating Mendler and Curwin's "social contract," using the principal of learning called "Goal Setting" (see Principles of Learning, Chapter 8), and teaching through one of the five cooperative Models of Teaching (see Learning Experiences, Chapter 13).

While studying the Clarity parameter, an English teacher in one of our courses realized he often played guess-what's-on-the-teacher's-mind in his question asking. He confessed this to his class the next day and asked if they concurred. They did. He then asked them what they could do about it, specifically what action class members might take if he victimized them with such a question or if they observed him doing it to someone else. After collecting ideas in a general class discussion, they settled on the following procedure: when students feel that they have been asked such a question, they can call the teacher on it directly and ask him to restate the question. Alternately, students who cannot answer a question can redirect it to another student in the class by name. At other times the teacher will go around the class, in order, asking review questions about the text read for homework. If the student cannot answer a question or answers incorrectly, the next student gets the same question. If three students in a row fail to get the answer, the teacher acknowledges that it was somehow a poor question and rephrases it. The net result for these students, previously a low-performing class, was higher class participation and higher achievement. It is our belief, however, that there was a lot more going on here than simply eliminating guess-what's-on-the-teacher's-mind questions. First of all, the teacher was showing fairness and realness (Personal Relationship Building) in admitting that he could be the cause of a problem for students and looking in an open way for a solution. Second, what these techniques accomplished was giving the students some say in determining the rules of the classroom game and controlling the flow of events.

Another teacher we know tried to increase students' motivation for doing homework assignments well. It had been his practice to give students daily quizzes based on homework readings. One day he told them that if they got four 100's in a row, they could earn a free 100 points which they might then "spend" on future quizzes at any time and in any way they pleased. They could skip some future quiz and take 100 on it, they could take 30 points of it and elevate a 70 to 100 sometime in the future, or just save the points. He found that students' efforts on homework assignments and quizzes dramatically improved, even those students who had already been doing well. Our hypothesis is that what was powerful about this technique was the way in which it gave students something to control: namely, a bank account of earned points. Whether they earned them, and if earned how they would spend them, was entirely within their control. (For the students already scoring well, perhaps it was an insurance policy against future mishaps.)

Other teachers have replicated that technique, but have eliminated the require-
ment that the four 100's be in a row; simply attaining four 100's earns the 100 point
bonus. These ingenious experiments by the two teachers we have just cited suggest
to us that there are many places in classroom life where we can look for ways to
give students more legitimate control including, as these two people taught us, the
way we handle recitation lessons and the way we do grading.

**Do I explicitly build community in the class (knowledge about, appreciation of, and
cooperation with one another)?**

William Glasser's classroom meetings (Glasser, 1969), Gene Stanford's cycle
of activities for *Developing Effective Classroom Groups* (Stanford, 1975), relationship building activities (Wilt and Watson, 1978), cooperative learning (Dishon and
O'Leary, 1984): these are all specific (but not simple) strategies for building the
kind of affiliation and harmony in a class that prevents discipline problems.

Even without concerns about discipline, all four would be inherently worth
doing. But when relationships among class members are stressful or fractious (or
both), these strategies can lower the pressure and productively rechannel energy
that is going into fighting with one another.

Before describing the strategies, it is important to note that, as with a Model of
Teaching, one cannot read an article and then launch the strategy successfully.
These are not Attention moves or Clarity moves which are easily grasped and tried.
They are more complex patterns of moves and it is important to understand the
beliefs and the spirit behind them to make them work. Thus, people should: 1) take
their time in learning the strategies; 2) be willing to stick with them through the
rough ground of initial tries; and 3) perhaps most importantly, *not do them alone*.
You need someone else who's trying it also to check in with, to get feedback from,
and to troubleshoot with. Also invaluable would be a coach or an on-site person
knowledgeable in the strategy. Best of all would be both.

Over the past 15 years we have used classroom meetings with many of our
own classes, and as staff developers have helped others to make them a regular
feature of classroom life. We have rarely seen another practice so powerful for
building a general sense of community in a class or so directly useful for handling
problems such as scapegoating, bullying, and cliques.

Schools Without Failure is the book in which William Glasser describes in
detail how to conduct "Classroom Meetings." He reports, "I haven't met a child
incapable of thinking and participating to some degree in school if we let him know
we value what he can contribute" (p. 97). That belief is essential for a teacher who
wants to make classroom meetings work, because being non-judgmental and
accepting of student contributions is a key skill in leading meetings. The meetings

are the vehicle through which students experience both the participation, the sense of being valued, and a sense of being part of something real. Class meetings are held regularly (at least weekly and preferably several times a week), with students and teacher seated in a tight circle. Teachers lead the whole class in non-judgmental discussions about topics that are important and relevant to them. The three types are open-ended meetings, social problem-solving meetings, and educational-diagnostic meetings.

In open-ended meetings, either teacher or student introduce a topic for discussion. One of the teacher's roles is to build a focusing question for the students around the topic, which can be anything of current interest to the students. In citing a meeting where the students wanted to talk about Disneyland, the teacher asked, "Who would like to go to Disneyland?" Almost every child responded affirmatively. "Suppose someone gave me two tickets to Disneyland and said I should give these tickets to two children in my class. To whom should I give the tickets?" In addition to translating open topics into focused discussions, teachers use skills of active-listening and summarizing.

Open-ended meetings begin building a sense of involvement with each other, and lay the foundations for using the meetings for generating significant investment in academic work and the more difficult area of social problem solving. Chapters 10, 11, and 12 of Glasser's book are a good manual for learning and implementing these meetings, so we will not go into more detail here. We would, however, like to quote a literal description of a social problem solving meeting so as to create a more vivid image of how classroom meetings can be used to improve some of the more intractable (and usually untreated) sources of disruptive behavior in classes.

At another meeting, Mike was introduced as the topic. Physically overweight and not too clean-looking in appearance, with hair in his eyes and a very loud, offensive voice, and holes in all his tee shirts caused from biting and twisting and chewing on them, he was not pleasant to behold! Mike said he didn't like the class because they didn't like him. When asked why they didn't like him, he said it was because he was fat. The children eagerly disagreed. They said that had nothing to do with it. Mike wanted to know why, then. He was given the opportunity to call on those children he wanted to explain to him what they found offensive about him. Someone said it was because he wears funny hats to school, like the pilot's helmet he wore the day before. (Incidently, he never wore it again.) Some said he dressed sloppily. Martin said it was because he said things that hurt people. For example, when Martin came home from Europe and showed the class several treasures that he brought to share, Mike said he didn't believe they were from Paris and that he bought the same things here. Martin said that hurt his feelings. David said that when he shared things with the class, Mike blurted out similar derogatory remarks. (Mike still has not cured himself of this, by the way.) John, who had become much more introspective and perceptive, said it was because Mike always made funny faces and looked up at the ceiling with a disgusted look on his face when people tried to talk to him. While he was saying this, Mike was doing just that. John said, "See, Mike, you're doing it right now, and you don't even know it." Mike was asked if anyone, in his opinion, went out of his way to be nice to him. He said, only Alice, whom he liked. Everyone giggled. Alice said she didn't care if everyone did laugh at her, she liked Mike and was not ashamed to be his friend. She liked being nice to him. We talked as a group about the importance of having one friend at least. The others found that no one really tried to go out of his way to be his friend, but each person would try to make some gesture to show they would try in the next week. They really rose to the occasion, but soon forgot about it and were their usual apathetic selves. However, no one seemed to go out of his way to be nasty, which was a change. Alice continued being nice to Mike, and the children stopped teasing her about it. Harriet, who was one of the girls who was teasing Alice, apologized in a class meeting for doing so and she said she had once been teased for befriending someone without other friends, and that it took more courage to be his friend and yet she wanted to. She told Alice that even though it had hurt her feelings when the others teased her, she had forgotten and teased Alice and that she was sorry, and she could really understand how Alice felt. There has been a tremendous change in Mike this semester. He is not lacka-daisical about his work or appearance, speaks more quietly, uses more self-control, plays a fairer game in the yard, gets along much better with others, and has more (or some) friends. [Glasser, pp. 152-153]

We have had teachers read this account and get scared off by it. It seems to some like opening wounds or beginning a process that can get out of control. Yet two teachers with difficult classes with whom we worked last year, teachers who took six months to work up their courage to bring up comparable issues in their own classes, now view their own series of meetings as among the most significant accomplishments of their careers. We are glad they took time to work up their courage, because they were also working up their skills at leading meetings on safer topics. They also used many of Gene Stanford's strategies to build community in the class over that period (to be described shortly). But the point is that these kinds of issues fester and hurt and drain students' energy even if we don't address them; and bringing them out into the open with skillful leadership can make dramatic dif-ferences in class climate. Neither the teacher in Glasser's account or those with whom we have worked were specially trained in counselling techniques. They were regular classroom teachers who had the courage and the commitment to want to help students build strong community within their classes, and who knew that there were large dividends for the effort in academic learning as well.

A few notes on the Glasser excerpt above: phrases like "He was given the opportunity to call on those children who..." mask key decisions by the teacher-leader. What really happened was that at that point the teacher decided that Mike could benefit from specific examples of how his behavior put others off and called for them. Furthermore, the teacher decided that it would involve Mike more (and make it safer for him) if he (Mike) did the calling on kids. Later: "Mike was asked if anyone went out of his way to be nice to him." The *teacher* asked Mike that question, sensing an appropriate moment to turn the discussion around and focus on the positive. Then: "We talked as a group about the importance of having one friend at least." The teacher asked a few key questions to *guide* the discussion that way. It didn't just happen on its own. (The first two examples, especially, illustrate the misleading nature of the passive voice in effective communication.)

Learning to recognize such key junctures and opportunities is part of the skill learning we go through when we undertake social problem-solving classroom meetings. It is, indeed, not the sort of thing one rushes into on the first day. But these skills are within the grasp of most teachers. Overall, classroom meetings regularly practiced are one of the most significant climate builders for successful learning.

While teaching high school English, Gene Stanford came to the same conclusion and developed a carefully sequenced series of activities to build class cohesion over a year. In *Developing Effective Classroom Groups* (1975), he organizes the activities according to the stage of growth the class is in in its movement toward mature functioning. Students have to know something about one another before they can appreciate or become involved with one another, so Stage I is Orientation. In Stage II activities explicitly develop norms of Group Responsibility (through teaching awareness of others), Responsiveness to Other (meaning good listening skills), Cooperative Skills, Consensus Decision-Making Skills, and Social Problem Solving Skills. Stage III is Coping with Conflict; Stage IV is about Productivity; and Stage V is about Termination, that is, dealing with the end of the year, the end of the life of the group, and people's feelings about that. All this is integrated with an academic program and an emphasis on writing.

A number of specific Models of Cooperative Learning have been developed which structure academic tasks themselves in such a way that students build affiliation, mutual understanding, and class cohesion. (There is overwhelming evidence, by the way, that they are at least equally effective for academic learning as well. Many, such as Slavin, Johnson and Johnson, and Sharan, argue they are better.) Cooperative Models of Teaching usually have students work in groups. Contrary to most "group" work observed in schools, however, the activity is structured so that either task completion or reward (or both) depends on everyone's participation. Yet groups are not penalized for having slow students or rewarded for having the "best" students in them. For an excellent summary of how to implement these techniques see Dishon and O'Leary (1984). A further range of cooperative models is outlined in the Learning Experiences chapter of this book.

This section of the Discipline parameter has attempted to connect good discipline, meaning more narrowly an absence of disruptive and resistant behavior, with building a sense of community in the class. From our point of view, building community would be worthwhile in and of itself; but there is no denying it is also a powerful preventive force against discipline problems. Simultaneously, it is a wonderful source of strength for building environments that support the best kind of academic learning.

Now it is time to turn to the most resistant students, the group whom we have saved for last, the group who continue to resist and disrupt despite clear expectations and consequences, and despite our best efforts at creating ownership and building community in the class. These are the very needy kids who bring heavy emotional baggage through the door with them every morning and act out their needs in disruptive behavior that is resistant to standard measures. Fortunately, there are not too many of them. Most of the students who initially appear in this category just need more clarity, conviction, and tenacity from us about expectations and consequences. If you are pondering such a student now, be sure you have really gone the limit with standard measures before plunging onward. Yet these days it is not unusual to have at least one such student in a grade; and one is all it takes to create class-wide distractions and make us pine for June. The following section explores six comprehensive models for dealing with such students.

Section IV
Six Models of Discipline

In this section we will describe the how-to's of the six models in some detail. First, here is a brief description of the six strategies.

Behavior Modification is a very orderly approach based on the assumption that unproductive behaviors can be eliminated and productive ones can be substituted by analyzing and controlling one's environment and its rewards. Behavior Modification systematically: 1) clips (cuts off) rewards for unproductive behavior; 2) identifies substitute and more productive behaviors; 3) targets these new behaviors explicitly with the student; and 4) begins rewarding them on a schedule that starts out consistent and high in frequency, and gradually becomes variable and lower in frequency. Behavior Modification aims to work itself out of business as the new learned behaviors become inherently rewarding.

Self-Awareness Training teaches students to read their own signals so that they know when they're getting angry, afraid, frustrated, or whatever else leads to outbursts or other unproductive behaviors. Students can learn a set of coping strategies they can plug in when these things are starting to happen, coping mechanisms they eventually do on their own. At the beginning, the teacher plays a very active, verbal and supportive role to the student, that gradually diminishes as the student is helped toward greater autonomy with the system.

Personal Influence is based on strong mutual relations between the teacher and student. The teacher works hard to build this relationship in certain specific ways. Teachers bring in enough of their outside-school life and accomplishments so as to earn some respect as a figure in the world, a person of some interest and significance beyond the immediate classroom environment. Teachers then draw on this relationship like money in the bank and are quite firm with students when disruption occurs. They act quickly and decisively with consequences for disruptive behavior and let students know they are upset. They show their affect strongly without losing control.

Logical Consequences maintains a low level of teacher affect and draws upon creative thinking to have students experience not simple punishment, but consequences that are logically connected to what they did. Power struggles with teachers as authority figures are avoided. Teachers analyze student motivations and use these analyses to help students understand themselves. Students learn about the reality of the social order through logical consequences consistently applied and do not get moral lectures. They are also not let off the hook. There is a strong orientation toward democratic thought and the involvement of the group in establishing students' understanding of the social contract.

Reality Therapy gets students to face, to acknowledge, what they are actually doing. A non-judgmental but involved teacher gets students to evaluate what they have done in light of their basic needs. Students explore alternatives and are asked to make commitments to courses of action. This strategy is based on teacher involvement, follow-up, and tenacity. Students learn to face the reality of what they are doing and what that behavior in turn is doing to their relations with others. This is a strategy for developing responsibility and self-worth through the involvement of someone who won't give up on you.

In *Teacher Effectiveness Training* teachers and students clarify who really owns the problem, use appropriate skills, and if it's a mutual problem negotiate a no-lose solution using a set of sequenced moves. These solutions meet the needs of both the teacher and the student. It requires good "active listening" skills to find out a student's real need or real problem sometimes. And teachers need skill at sending "I messages" so students perceive the teacher's need. Good communication skills are required, and mutual respect grows from the problem solving process.

To be able to implement these strategies is not terribly hard, but each does take real study and practice and each is distinctly different from the others in the teacher moves it calls for. The behaviors and skills one needs are probably not outside the existing repertoire of most readers—you probably have made every move somewhere in your life. It is their order and application that takes time to learn; and believe us, they make a difference.

No one should think that by merely reading the balance of this chapter one is equipped to go out and do a strategy well. We issue this warning because we want the strategies to get a fair chance before someone who didn't really know how to do, say, Reality Therapy, comes back with no results after one try and says "Oh, that didn't work for me." It can work for anybody if you know how to do it and apply it *in the right cases*. And that brings us to that matter of knowing when and who is the right case. Matching is the crux of this chapter…the crux of teaching itself. But before we go into what's known about matching with the six strategies, we feel it necessary to develop each one in more depth so you have more of a context in which to read about matching. So, there follow now six sub-sections elaborating each of the strategies; then will come the final and most important section on matching, Section V, with brief profiles of students for whom a given strategy is appropriate.

Our objective in the following six sub-sections is to make the descriptions of the six strategies more vivid and more complete, to show how they differ and how they are designed to work. Upon completing these sub-sections interested readers can go to Wolfgang and Glickman's excellent *Solving Discipline Problems* (1980), where four of our six models are presented in full chapters including scripts of the strategy in operation. Beyond that, readers should move to the primary sources cited at the end of the chapter to start more rigorous skill building. (Some readers may wish to skip directly to the Section V on "matching" at this point, and then return to the sub-sections on the six separate strategies.)

Let us start by looking at the most structured of the six strategies, Behavior Modification. We will describe for you a particularly well constructed packaging of it for teachers called Classroom and Instructional Management—CLAIM. To analyze it and the other strategies, we will use a framework modifying and expanding categories Joyce and Weil (1972) use to analyze a model of teaching. The categories are: 1) definitions; 2) assumptions; 3) values; 4) goals; 5) rationale; 6) syntax (or steps); 7) principles of teacher response; 8) support system; 9) social system; 10) transcript; and 11) effects.

CLAIM
Discipline as Behavior Engineering

There are many who have applied the principles of Behavior Modification to classroom management. As an exemplar of this school of thought we have picked CLAIM, a recent and well-presented book from CEMREL, written specifically for teachers on how to practically apply these principles in classrooms. Some of CLAIM's values, assumptions, and goals may not be shared by all those who advocate Behavior Modification in the classroom. We point this out at the beginning so there will be no misunderstanding by adherents of this school. What follows is an analysis of one particular interpretation of Behavior Modification principles in a particular applied system. Other interpreters might differ in certain respects. What distinguishes CLAIM from many of the writings on Behavior Modification is that it is more fully a "model," than what is found elsewhere. (Or, as teachers have been heard to say, "It is more practical"...which is another way of saying, "It is good theory.")

Definitions

The following definitions are derived from the application of the terms within CLAIM, and are not necessarily consonant with definitions of the same terms elsewhere in the literature of Behavior Modification (see especially *modeling*.)

1. *Reinforcement*: anything which increases the frequency of a given behavior.

2. *Punishment*: anything which reduces the frequency of a given behavior.

3. *Schedule*: the relation of reinforcement to emitted behavior over time. Continuous reinforcement is reinforcement for every occurrence of the desired behavior. Intermittent reinforcement is reinforcement on an unpredictable basis for the occurrence of the desired behavior.

4. *Extinction*: elimination of a behavior, usually through elimination of the reinforcement, sometimes through pairing with punishment (negative reinforcement, aversive consequences).

5. *Response cost*: fines, usually in the form of removal of tokens or other forms of scrip redeemable for reinforcements.

6. *Baseline*: a record of the frequency of a given behavior over time

before beginning of selective reinforcement and/or extinction procedures.

7. *Reversal*: the restoration of a behavior to its baseline level, or near that level, when the selective reinforcement schedule is cut off.

8. *Shaping*: a gradual change in behavior accomplished through reinforcement of successively closer approximations of the desired behavior.

9. *Prompting*: giving necessary clues, hints, or prompts so that the subject can make the desired response in the presence of the appropriate stimulus.

10. *Target behavior*: the desired behavior to be achieved through application of Behavior Modification principles.

11. *Contingency*: the student response or behavior necessary to produce or earn the reinforcement; the job for which pay is given.

12. *Fading*: the gradual elimination of one reinforcer and its replacement by another reinforcer as the maintainer of the behavior.

13. *Modeling*: imitating the behaviors of others that are producing reinforcements for those others.

Many other terms from the universe of Behavior Modification are not defined here simply because they are not part of the CLAIM vocabulary (e.g., *operant conditioning, stimulus generalization, satiation...*).

Assumptions

1. All behavior is learned.

2. Teachers cannot deal with the source of a student's problems outside the classroom (e.g., home environment).

3. If unruly behavior exists and persists, the teacher has become responsible.

Values

Efficiency and Effectiveness.

Goals

1. Illegal behavior will decrease in frequency and be replaced by legal behavior.

2. Maximum academic progress possible for each student will be made.

Rationale

Systematic analysis of payoffs and systematic application of reinforcement theory to classroom behavior will yield an engineered environment most suited to maximum progress in learning. All behavior, even deviant behavior, is earning a payoff. If a teacher can identify the payoff and clip it, the behavior will be extinguished. If the payoff can be controlled and given for desirable (legal) behavior instead, the legal behavior will become established.

When misbehavior is reduced, the way is clear to efficient learning. Applying the same principles of reinforcement to learning tasks will effectively motivate individual students.

Steps

1. Pinpoint the target behavior...the behavior which you want to occur.

2. Observe deviancies from the target behavior.

3. Chart a baseline rate for the deviancies systematically over a period of time (often weeks).

4. Analyze what the reinforcement is for the deviancy; what payoff the child is getting.

5. Identify potential reinforcers the teacher can give for performance of the target behavior.

6. Choose a reinforcer likely to appeal to the child.

7. Design a progression and sequence of reinforcement for the child: his schedule of reinforcement, whether or not shaping will be used, specific increments of behavior change that will be reinforced if shaping is used.

8. Tell the student the target behavior.

9. Design a method for observing and recording behavior frequencies.

10. Apply reinforcement.

11. Record behaviors.

Principles of Teacher Response

1. Reinforcement should be immediate.

2. Beginning with schedules of continuous reinforcement, reinforcement should become intermittent to make target behaviors more firmly resistant to extinction.

3. Use ignoring, fines, time out from reinforcement, and simple aversive punishment to extinguish undesirable behaviors.

4. When your program seems to be failing, reevaluate your reinforcers to see if they are really reinforcing, and look back at your analysis of what payoff the student was (is) getting from the undesirable (deviant) behavior. Maybe the error lies there.

5. Associate social reinforcers with reinforcers in other categories (edible, activity, material).

6. Attempt to fade to social reinforcers.

CLAIM takes the view that inherent satisfaction in performing academic activities like reading cannot accrue to a child until reading becomes a part of his response repertoire. In other words, if a student can't read, he won't know reading can be fun. So Behavior Modification, therefore, should be viewed as a transitional technique, to bring a child to a certain level where inherent reinforcers can take over.

Likewise in the realm of social behavior, a student may not know how to gain attention in socially acceptable ways. Behavior Modification can bring him to a level of performance where he sees for the first time that other forms of interaction give him the attention he wants. If acceptable social behavior is simply not part of a student's learned repertoire of behaviors, he has no inkling that they can be reinforcing.

Thus the strategic goal embedded in CLAIM's syntax is to fade out the material, edible, and activity reinforcers they teach teachers to use, and wind up with the social and inherent reinforcers in effect.

Support System

1. Appropriate reinforcers must be available in the categories chosen (i.e., in either activity, material, edible, or social categories).

2. Time and personnel must be available to make the observations and record data for establishing baselines and compiling progress records once reinforcement is introduced.

Social System

1. The teacher is the identifier, author, and dispenser and withholder of reinforcement. The student is the receiver, the one operated upon, the one to whom "treatment" is given.

2. Authority: it rests clearly with the teacher.

3. Norms: established by the teacher, communicated to the students; conformance to norms is reinforced.

Effects

1. The direct effect of CLAIM's interpretation of behavior modification should be attainment of target behaviors by students as chosen by the teacher. Classroom deviancy becomes reduced; on-task, learning time becomes maximized. Learning carries on in an efficient and effective manner.

2. Implicit effects are to make for a passive student, accustomed to reacting in engineered ways to engineered reinforcements. An external orientation tends to develop a "payoff" mentality, though CLAIM tries to move against this tendency by fading to social and inherent reinforcers.

Others have raised questions about the effect of life in the environment of systematic behavior management upon creativity and upon initiative.

Self-Awareness
Discipline as Self-Control

The Self-Awareness model has several forms which we will present in this section. Therapists, teachers, and parents have used these strategies successfully with children of all ages, and in treating adult control problems. An understanding of the values of self-induced relaxation training and of self-control through inner-speech may finally make us realize that people who talk to themselves aren't so crazy after all!

Assumptions

1. Students may have no perception of the type, severity, or frequency of their behaviors.

2. Students may have no perception, or inaccurate perceptions, of their own feelings, their own interior states.

Values

This model values the mental health of students. What is important is that students become aware of their feelings and actions so that they can come to terms with them; thus they learn to anticipate and control impulsivity, outbursts, withdrawal, and other erratic behaviors that are symptomatic of their lack of awareness of themselves.

Goals

The goal of this model is to teach students to read their own signals and to engage coping strategies when the signals cue them that they are about to "blow" or follow some other dysfunctional pattern common to them.

Rationale

Students who are disconnected from their own inner selves need help in simply perceiving what their actions really are. An impulsive youngster may have no awareness that he jumped to his feet, knocked a book off the table, bumped two children while running to the door, and stepped on a painting as he went by the easel. All that he's aware of consciously is that "it's time to go." An older student may not be aware that he is getting increasingly frustrated at not being called on in an instructional group, that he is drumming his fingers and clenching his fists precedent to an outburst where he will lash out impatiently. Both of these students need to recognize these situations and read inner cues about how they're thinking and feeling. They need to be aware that these are triggering situations, and that something is happening inside them, before they can do anything about it. This model directly addresses with students what the triggering situations are for them, and then it teaches them to become aware of their reactions as these triggering situations develop. When they learn to read these reactions as cues to trouble, they need to know what to do. The Self-Awareness strategies offer a variety of techniques which students can learn, practice, and then use under stress to cool off, to control themselves, and to continue functioning effectively in school. The strategies include: 1) simple counting or graphing of behavior; 2) relaxation; 3) self-coaching through inner-speech (cognitive behavior modification).

Steps

Simple Counting

Anna-Marie is always calling out and interrupting in class. It is impulsive on her part, and the teacher decides to use simple counting to highlight the behavior, to call Anna-Marie's attention to it. After a group one day, the teacher says, "Anna-Marie, do you know that you call out an awful lot without raising your hand? It's really distracting to me and unfair to the rest of the kids who want to speak." "I'm sorry. I'll stop. I promise." (They have had these conversations before.) "Are you really willing to work on it? Well, I'd like to help you. How many times do you think you call out in a lesson?" "I don't know...maybe five?" (It's more like 25.) "Well, let's see tomorrow. I'll put a piece of masking tape on my wrist and every time you call out I'll put a mark on it without saying anything or stopping the lesson...but you'll be able to see me doing it and you'll know what it means. OK?" "OK."

This technique can be extremely effective in reducing habitual or impulsive annoyance behaviors when no more serious issues are involved than attention-getting and impulsivity. Simply seeing the teacher make a stroke on the tape reminds the student of the goal—to reduce calling out. "Oops," says Anna-Marie as she sees another stroke going down. Pretty soon she learns to anticipate a stroke *before* a call-out and starts inhibiting the call-outs herself. Afterwards, the teacher and Anna-Marie can add up the total call-outs and set a goal to reduce the total tomorrow. A week of this may be quite sufficient to teach the self-inhibition Anna-Marie needs to control calling out.

This technique and other forms of specific counting or record keeping about behaviors make students more aware of what they're doing, and make the reduction of unwanted behavior a mutual teacher-student goal. The counting is the feedback to students about their progress and needs to be prompt, complete, and frequent (Van Houton). Students have to be willing to try for the technique to work. Sometimes a teacher count of a behavior before discussing it with students produces data with which to confront them. They may be so surprised by how often they behave inappropriately that the shock value will motivate them. Teachers can use the technique on a whole class as well as on individuals. Here the goal becomes lowering the *class* total of call-outs or whatever is the inappropriate behavior being brought to awareness.

Relaxation

Bruno-Golden (1976) and Koeppen (1974) have produced scripts for teachers (or anyone) to use with students to achieve progressive muscle relaxation. These exercises involve students assuming a comfortable position and alternately tightening and relaxing various muscle groups in a systematic sequence. It's a good technique for any teacher to know. Which of us hasn't wished for some device to calm down a hyper class at one point or another?

For certain students, however, knowing how to relax can be a coping strategy against stress that might otherwise make them crack. In private or small group sessions, the teacher can instruct the student in the technique, and gradually fade out the coaching until the student can self-instruct through a set of exercises with minimal teacher guidance. A point can be reached where only a cue to start from the teacher is necessary and the student can carry out the exercise alone. "Robbie, you and I know you've been having a tough time controlling your temper these days, right? Well, I'd like to teach you something that will help. Are you game?"

Along with the training, teacher and student must discuss triggering situations, try to identify the settings and the conditions that set up the student for an outburst, and try to predict them. They need, further, to talk about the student's inner feelings, and the overt symptoms the student and teacher may observe, as pressure builds up on the student. For students who are out of touch with their inner selves and have a great deal of difficulty talking about their inner feelings, the two of them may do better by focusing on objective, observable qualities of events..."it's usually when you're in small groups...you start to clench your fists and your knuckles turn white." The point is, ultimately, for students to be able to read their own signals and turn on their coping mechanisms *before* they lose control. Along the way, they may need help from the teacher to recognize these cues. A code word can be set up between them. Or, the teacher may have to intervene beyond cue giving in any one of the following ways that Wolfgang presents (Wolfgang, 1977), getting more and more intrusive depending upon how much control the student has:

—proximity...looking on
  —"I see you starting to get out of control."
    —"You're getting out of control. I will help."
      —Physical interposing...verbalizing what the student is doing
        —holding student: "I won't let you hurt yourself or hurt others." (for young children)

For less disturbed children, coping strategies simpler than relaxation can be employed. Students can take a walk in the halls to cool off, or go to a private corner of the room. In both strategies, however, the teacher and students are confederates. They alone may be privy to the cuing system and the coping strategy. Students see the teacher as someone helping them to gain self-mastery. Teachers work to fade their active role to the minimum required to keep the student functional, delivering as much support as necessary but looking to reduce students' dependence on them.

Explosive youngsters badly out of touch with their feelings can be greatly helped by strategies such as this one, but may need therapy in addition.

Self-Instruction through Inner Speech
(Cognitive Behavior Modification)

In Self-Instructional Training, students are taught to use their own inner speech to talk themselves through difficult situations, difficult because they are struggling to contain impulses, to remain in control, and to employ alternate strategies. Teaching a student to alter his internal dialogue "will have directive effects on: (a) what the individual attends to in the environment; (b) how he appraises various stimulus events; (c) to what he attributes his behavior; and (d) his expectations about his own capacities to handle a stressful event" (Meichenbaum, p. 206).

One such approach is the Think Aloud technique. Meichenbaum describes a program conducted by Bash and Camp in which twelve aggressive second-grade boys were seen in small groups:

> The program began with a 'copy-cat' game, which introduced the child to asking himself the following four basic questions: What is my problem? What is my plan? Am I using my plan? How did I do? While the 'copy-cat' was being faded, cue cards similar to Palkes *et al.*'s were introduced to signal the child to self-verbalize. Over the course of training there was a shift from cognitively demanding tasks to interpersonal tasks ala Shure and Spivak. Initial results from this Camp *et al.* study were quite promising ...The results generalized to the classroom. The results of the Think Aloud training program take on particular significance when we consider Camp's findings that aggressive boys had verbal facilities that were comparable to normal boys on various performance tasks, but that the aggressive boys failed to use their abilities to think through and plan solutions to problems. Bash and Camp state:
>
>> 'Even when the rules of the game call for blocking the first stimulated response, aggressive children have more difficulty performing this inhibition (e.g., playing *Simon Says* game). Their natural inclination is to respond rapidly, but when specifically instructed to verbalize overtly before responding, they may achieve response inhibition more readily than normals.'
>
> The self-instructional training program, Think Aloud, successfully taught such self-verbalization skills. [Meichenbaum, p. 42]

In teaching these self-instructional strategies to students, teachers need to work with them alone or in small groups. Instruction starts with a situation that is often hard for the student to handle; e.g., a transition where the job is getting from a class meeting or an instructional group to the door, lined up and ready to go to lunch. At the outset of this chapter we described a child who jumped to his feet, knocked a book off a table, bumped two children running to the door, and stepped on a painting as he ran by the easel. The internal dialogue we eventually want the student to carry on with himself might go like this:

"Let's see, what's my job? To get to the line without bumping anyone."	Defining the Problem
"What do I have to do to get there? Start walking slowly...look where I'm going."	Focus attention on what to do
"That's it; not too fast now. Watch out for that easel rack." "How's it going...pretty well."	Self-evaluation, monitoring
"Hooray! I made it!"	Self-reinforcement

How does one teach a student to do that? Gradually. First the teacher has the student watch the teacher act out the motions and verbalize out loud the dialogue above. Then the teacher asks the student to walk through the motions of getting to the door while the teacher again verbalizes the dialogue out loud. The sequence then proceeds as follows through six phases:

TEACHER	STUDENT
1. out loud self-instructions performs motions	watches
2. out loud self-instructions	performs motions
3. whispers instructions	says self-instructions out loud, performs motions
4. moves lips only	whispers self-instructions performs motions

5. watches   moves lips only
performs motions

6. watches   inner speech for
self-instructions,
performs motions

Variations of this strategy, under different names (e.g., "stress innoculation"), are used with older students and with adults. But the principles remain the same. Students are taught to identify stressful situations for them, so that they can prepare coping strategies (relaxation, self-instruction) in advance. They are also taught to recognize their own signals of stress, so that when caught unprepared they can realize that they are on the edge of trouble and can spontaneously engage one of their coping strategies.

Social System

The teacher is a helping person in this model. Ultimate decision-making power on whether to use, and when to use, the coping strategies rests with the student, although the teacher is a trusted confederate and has the job of sending cues and prompts when the student is beginning to lose control.

Principles of Teacher Response

When the student loses control the teacher steps in as strongly as necessary to restore it, but no more strongly than necessary; after all, the object is to build the students' own capacity for self-control. Alertness, cue giving, and minimal response consistent with safety are the watchwords here.

Support System

Teachers need time and access to students outside normal class time—or the flexibility to get students alone in a private setting during class time. Teachers need to have identified in advance some triggering situations to work on with the student.

Effects

Successful practice of this model reduces outbursts and disruptive conflicts for students who are impulsive and out of control. It also builds their self-confidence and sense of accomplishment: this is, after all, a kind of mastery they are achieving. As a result, doors open for them to more productive relationships with other students who are less likely to regard them as "crazy" or be resentful and hostile toward them.

A related model is called "Interpersonal Cognitive Problem Solving." This model teaches youngsters "alternative-consequences" thinking. It is aimed primarily at young children and teaches them problem solving strategies they can use to replace fighting, bickering, and resolution of conflicts by power alone. The following script from Shure and Spivak (1978) is illustrative. The teacher leads children to review their actions and the consequences of those actions, then to generate alternate actions that might get the child's need met.

Teacher: Dorothy, were you working with these puzzles?

Child: Brian did, too.

Teacher: Did you and Brian work together?
(Teacher gathering facts of situation.)

Child: Yes.

Teacher: Is it fair for Brian to pick them up by himself and for you not to pick them up?

Child: No.

Teacher: Is it fair for you to pick them up and not Brian?

Child: No.

Teacher: What is fair?
(Teacher guides child to see problem from point of view of both children.)

Child: Brian won't help me.

Teacher: Can you think of a way to get Brian to help you pick up the puzzles?
(Child guided to think of solution to problem.)

Child: I could ask him.

Teacher: That's one idea. What might happen if you did that?
(Teacher guides consequential thinking.)

Child: He won't help.

Teacher: That might happen. What else could you think of to do if he says no?

Child: Hit him.

Teacher: You could hit him. What might happen then?

Child: We'll fight.

Teacher: Maybe you'd fight. Can you think of a third, different idea?

Child: You tell him.

Teacher: I could tell him. How will that help you when I'm not here?
            (Teacher continues to guide child to think of solutions to problem.)

Child: I could say I won't play with him anymore.

Teacher: Is that a good idea?

Child: Yeah.

Teacher: Why?

Child: 'Cause then he'll help me.

Teacher: Maybe. See what you can do to get him to help.

[Shure and Spivak, 1978, pp. 146-147]

The syntax that is embedded in the above dialogue is summarized by the authors in the following way:

1.   Elicit from the child his or her view of the problem in a non-accusatory way; for example: "What happened?" "What did the other child do or say?" "Why did he do that?" "What is it you want him to do?" "How do you know he won't do that?"

2.   Ask the child, in a matter-of-fact fashion, why he acted as he did. "Why did you call him a dummy?" "Why did you feel like hitting him first?"

3.   Guide the child to think about how he felt (feels) and how he thinks others felt (or might feel). You might ask, for instance, "How do you think he felt when you did that?" "How did you feel when he did that?"

4.   Raise the question of how one can find out how another child thinks or feels. "How can you find out if he likes your idea?" "How can you tell if he is happy or sad?"

5.   Ask the child to give his idea about how to solve the problem. "What can you do if you want him to let you do that (have that, let you play with him, stop hitting you)?"

6. Ask the child to think about what might happen next. "If you do that, what might your sister do or say?" "If you keep bothering him, what might happen next?"

7. Guide the child to evaluate whether he thinks his idea—regardless of its content—is or is not a good one, on the basis of his idea about what might happen next. "Is hitting back a good idea?" "Is trading a good idea?"

8. Encourage the child to think of different solutions to a problem, when relevant. "Can you think of a second different way to get him to give you a turn (let you play with them)?" "If they do not want to play now, can you think of something different to do that will make you happy?"

The responses of children indicate that they are more likely to take action when an idea is their own than when it is suggested or demanded by an adult. Although children do at times need to take adult advice, experience indicates that when the child comes up with a solution he likes, he tends to move to action with a spontaneous motivation that stems from the natural connection between his thinking and his action. If his idea fails, he thinks again and may try another solution before reacting with impulsiveness, frustration, or withdrawal. He has learned a problem-solving style of thinking.

Personal Influence
Discipline Through Personal Regard

In the Personal Influence model, teachers build strong relations with students and use these relationships to motivate students toward more responsible behavior. Teachers make deliberate moves to enhance their personal significance to students, and use their position of respect and regard and closeness to induce behavior change. Teachers show high affect and high commitment; students find their relationship with the significant teacher is a two-way street. While this may sound obvious and connect with what many of you believe you do already, a careful reading of this model may produce some surprises.

Assumptions

Students are more motivated to behave and to do good work if they respect and like the teacher.

Values

The things that are important in this model are student self-image and class order. The syntax reflects a conscious value that students build confidence in themselves as worthwhile people through a close relationship with a significant adult. It also has a clear commitment to class order and taking steps to stop disruption firmly when it occurs.

Goals

The first goal of the model is to build relationships between the teacher and resistant students in order to increase the personal influence of the teacher on students. The second goal is to establish clear expectations for behavior, with swift and consistent consequences for misbehavior.

Rationale

The relationship between teacher and student is like a bank account: it makes a student feel more comfortable, safe, and secure to have it. It enables a student to invest and grow, operating from a safe base to reach out tentatively to try new experiences. And it is something for both teacher and student to draw upon in times of need. A good relationship with a liked and respected teacher will motivate students to try harder both in their work and in their efforts toward better behavior. It will also make a reproof from that teacher more telling—and reproofs there should be! In this model teachers *show* students when they are upset with them: not losing control and ranting and raving, but showing anger, frustration, disappointment. And that means something to a student because of who the teacher is by that time to the student—a significant person. Students are less inclined to risk this relationship with a teacher through irresponsible behavior when the relationship is important to them. The teacher never uses the relationship as a threat, or the denial of closeness as a punishment. In fact, after reprimands or episodes where students must be removed from the room, the teacher looks for the earliest possible opportunity to relate to the student positively in another context, to reassure and rebuild the relationship. Nevertheless, though the teacher does not use loss of love threateningly as a club, the very presence of the relationship acts as a healthy inhibitor of disruptive behavior from the student. It is healthy because wanting to please those who are important to us by acting responsibly is a healthy thing. It is not the most advanced form of moral reasoning in the world, but for lonely and confused students it can be a definite step up.

Through this relationship students can gain confidence, try harder, and succeed more in their work. From the stable base with the teacher they can reach out and be brought into contact with other students in controlled settings, sometimes cooperative projects, so that they begin to extend their circle of successful relationships and begin to feel more worthwhile. As they can be accepted by more and more students, as they can see themselves as successful with others, so their capacity and desire to act in ways that will preserve these relationships grows.

Steps

1. Build a friendly relationship with individual student aimed at closeness and open communication by looking for, and capitalizing on, moments for positive, friendly, one-to-one interaction:

   a. few minutes before class
   b. few minutes after class
   c. inviting student to have lunch together in the room once in a while
   d. after school projects

2. Practice "Active Listening" and other behaviors detailed under the Personal Relationship Building parameter.

3. Share with the class things about yourself that are interesting …travels, experiences, especially any accomplishment or proficiencies you have (like playing an instrument or some craft ability) that make you real and significant in their eyes without appearing boastful. In general, this means showing them these abilities rather than telling about them. Bringing them in to show and share is more likely to be interpreted as "interesting" than boastful if not overdone.

4. Connect the student with other students in safe and structured ways. For example, teach a young student a game and then set him up for the first ten minutes of the day—typically a hard time for these children—to teach it to two other designated students. With older students, have them pass out materials, or play designated roles in group projects.

5. In one-to-one interactions with the resistant students, let them know exactly what your expectations are *explicitly* (see Expectations parameter). If appropriate, make behavior contracts and record keeping charts to help focus on what needs to improve and to keep track of progress.

6. When the student acts disruptively, react swiftly with consequences (which will frequently involve removal or isolation of some kind).

7. Always talk to the student afterward, calmly, but expressing some emotion. Get the student to analyze what went wrong and what needs to be done.

8. Look for an early opportunity after a disciplinary episode with a resistant student to have a positive exchange about something. "Gee, that's a nice piece of work, Jim"—especially if you've been very tough about the discipline. The purpose is to reopen communication and establish that your relationship is still alive. The caution is not to overdo it so the student learns a reward (e.g., after school project) will follow most serious disruptions. Keep the relationship rebuilding low-key, just enough to reopen and reassure.

9. Maintain frequent and direct contact with parents to involve them in the plan as much as possible.

Principles of Teacher Reaction

1. Active Listening during relationship building.

2. Go out of your way to find or make opportunities to build relationships.

3. Show affect when disciplining.

4. Be calmer and more analytical in post-mortems with students.

5. Rebuild relationships in low-key fashion after toughest episodes.

Support System

To carry out this model, a teacher needs sufficient access and frequency of contact with students to build relationships. Teachers need to be consistent with consequences and follow-up. Where this is limited by modular scheduling, the school should consider a more self-contained class setting, or at least fewer teacher changes for this student. The teacher needs to have a set of consequences figured out in advance for the student (and perhaps rewards, too, if this Personal Influence strategy is paired with behavioral contracting). These arrangements may require cooperation and agreement with other teachers or administrators (see Seymour Sarason's form of consequences in the following section). But the message is, "Have your ducks lined up." Know what you're going to *do* when the student's behavior crosses acceptable boundaries and gets too disruptive to continue instruction. Usually this will mean some form of removal to a mutual cooling off room or other site. You have to know *where*.

Social System

The teacher is the authority figure and the norms for behavior come primarily from the teacher. The class may be intimately involved in the setting of rules in general. But even when democracy *is* part of the class' life, and when it may be the way behavior norms are determined, Personal Influence does not intend to be a democratic model. If a student needs this model, democracy is not the cure to his ills.

Effects

Direct: Deviant behavior is reduced.

Nurturant:

1. The teacher provides a role model of caring and of responsibility, to which the student begins to attach.

2. The student begins to build positive relationships with other students.

Before leaving this model we wished to include one more specific strategy that fits in with it: an unusual, well thought out, and highly effective form of exclusion for disruptive students developed by Seymour Sarason and his associates. It appears in a book far removed from discipline: *The Culture of the School and the Problem of Change* (Sarason, 1971). It is a form of response to disruption that you may well find occasion to use, and that is also consistent with the Logical Consequences model coming up.

Sarason's strategy is a carefully sequenced set of steps to produce dramatic suppression of hostile defiance. The essence of it is pairing two teachers and removing the defiant student from one teacher's room to the other's. The success of the exclusion depends upon the preparation of the personnel, their pairing, and the support of the principal.

When a student is excluded from the sending teacher's room, that student must stay in the receiving teacher's room for one-half hour, be given a seat at the back, and excluded from any form of participation in that class' activities or interaction with the students there. If the student refuses to leave the sending teacher's room, the pair of teachers carry the child out (for children up to second grade). Older students who refuse to leave are informed that their parents will be phoned immediately if they do not go. Sarason reports that he has never witnessed a child refusing to respond to that pressure and that the excluded child under these conditions is never the slightest problem in the receiving classroom.

Sarason attributes the effectiveness of the strategy to its ability to immediately terminate defiant outbursts, and to its ability to underline with dramatic action the limits beyond which the student may no longer go.

The procedure must be introduced to the whole class at once, not as a punishment procedure but as a way of helping children remember to follow rules that allow them to enjoy learning. "It should be explained to the children repeatedly that a child will not be excluded because he is unwanted or disliked but because he needs the brief opportunity in another classroom to reflect on the rules he has been disobeying" (Sarason, p. 137).

Teachers are to give disruptive students one private warning that specifies what behavior must cease (and what replaces it) if exclusion is to be avoided. At the same time, the teacher must attempt to explain to the student how the class is being disrupted. If the child has to be excluded, the teacher explains to the entire class in the presence of the child being excluded why the step is necessary.

On returning to the classroom, the teacher should review the situation with the class covering reasons behind the relevant rules, alternative ways the excluded child might have behaved, and whenever possible having a brief discussion of how the class can help the excluded child in future.

After school, the teacher should have a short interview with the excluded child, explaining how the exclusion was to help the child remember class rules, not to cause embarrassment. Sarason places emphasis on the importance of this after school interview and its power to point out "how it is the child himself and not the teacher who decided whether he is to be excluded from the room" (Sarason, p. 138).

Sarason has used this strategy with students through fourth grade. We see no reason why it cannot be applied successfully in higher grades as well.

The following will summarize the major steps in this strategy:

1. Introduction

    a. Introduce exclusion move to whole class with its causes and consequences

    b. as a way of helping students remember and follow rules that allow them to enjoy learning

2. Implementation

    a. give one private warning with specification of behavior

    b. give public explanation of why child is being removed

    c. remove child, voluntarily or physically if necessary, or call parent

    d. maintain for one-half hour

    e. child is excluded from participation or interaction with second class

    f. review situation with class including:

        —alternative ways the excluded child might have acted
        —reasons for the rule
        —how to help him/her follow the rules

3. After School Interview

    a. to help, not to embarrass, is the motive

    b. teacher hopes warning will be sufficient in future

    c. teacher explains how it's the child who decided, by behavior, when to be excluded

    d. show affection and respect.

Rudolf Dreikers' Logical Consequences
Discipline as Social Contract

Rudolf Dreikurs seeks to eliminate the authoritarian use of power by parents and teachers, which he sees as inappropriate in a democratic age, and harmful to relationships between youngsters and adults. He blends Adlerian psychology with a new technique for responding to misbehavior called Logical Consequences. Reacting with logical consequences will take the acrimory—the child-adult power struggle—out of discipline and enable mutual respect to grow.

Definitions

1. *Natural consequence*: an aversive result to a child's behavior that occurs by itself, naturally, without any human engineering or intervention (e.g., tipping back in chair, child finally falls over).

2. *Logical consequence*: an engineered aversive result to a child's behavior that is logically connected to the behavior.

Assumptions

1. Equality is the only basis on which we'll ever be able to solve discipline problems.

2. The fundamental human need is to belong...and it develops into a striving to function in and with a group in order to feel worthwhile.

3. All behavior is purposive. The goal of self-determined direction motivates children's behavior.

Goals

Apply these values in dealings with children so as to:

1. Eliminate the "outright warfare" Dreikers sees between delinquents and society, between rebellious youngsters and parents and teachers.

2. Apply Adler's first social law—the law of equality, the logic of social living which "demands recognition of every human being as an equal" (Dreikurs and Grey, 1968, p. 8).

3. Provide the means by which the student can function properly in an atmosphere of freedom (properly here meaning with responsibility rather than license).

4. Eliminate autocratic methods of discipline.

5. To eliminate the obnoxious behavior of the average American child who "fights with his brothers and sisters, refuses to put things away or to do homework or help around the house" (Dreikurs and Grey, 1968, p. 10).

6. Cultivate relations based on mutual respect between children and adults.

Rationale

The goals can be accomplished if we understand the causes of students' behaviors, and stop trying to deal with them by autocratic methods. Our responses to behavior must manifest the reality of the social order by allowing students to take responsibility (and logical consequences) for their actions. When teachers/parents start generating responses to misbehavior from this framework of social reality, students will no longer resent, rebel, or feel oppressed because adult responses will no longer appear to be emanating from personal authority.

Furthermore, when the causes of misbehavior in individual students are understood, positive paths of action can be followed that relate to meeting the needs of the child. Thus, new responses to misbehavior based on democratic theory and positive programs of action to meet the needs of children who regularly misbehave will be the two prongs of the Dreikurs attack.

Students develop concepts, through learning, of what behavior will help them develop a place in the group. They may have the concept that cooperation will do so, or that being the center of attention will do so. We can find immediate goals behind every misbehavior. All misbehavior is the result of a discouraged student's mistaken assumption about the way he can find a place and gain status (see Glasser's view of deviant behavior as bad choices).

Logical Consequences has the student be impressed with the needs of reality and not the power of an adult. The principle of dealing with each other as equals yields a relationship based on mutual respect. Students are our equals now, not in power or size, but in their right and ability to decide for themselves instead of yielding to a superior force. Whereas punishment represents the power of personal authority, logical consequences, as the expression of the reality of the social order, operate at the impersonal level. Punishment says "You are bad"; logical consequences say "Your behavior yields this result." No judgement is made about "you" as a person.

Syntax

1. Observe the student's behavior in detail.

2. Be sensitive to your own reaction to the student's behavior.

If your reaction is:	The student's goal may be:
annoyance	attention
threatened	power
hurt	revenge
helpless	display of inadequacy

3. Give the student "corrective feedback". You stop the student, reprimand him, and see how he reacts. If he simply stops, the behavior may be simply a bid for attention. If the misbehavior increases, its goal may have been to express power. If the student seems hurt, the goal may be revenge.

4. Confront the student with the four goals asking one or more of these four questions, in order—but after a cooling-off period from the moment of conflict.

   a. "Could it be you want me to notice you?"

   b. "Could it be that you want to show me that you can do what you want to do and no one can stop you?"

   c. "Could it be you want to hurt me and the pupils in the class...to get even?"

   d. "Could it be that you want to be left alone?"

5. Note the recognition reflex; i.e., which one of the four questions the student seems to respond to verbally or with body language.

6. Apply appropriate corrective procedures depending on the student's goal as summarized in the chart below.

When using a logical consequence, pick an appropriate type. There are a variety of types of logical consequence from which to choose, as the following chart reveals:

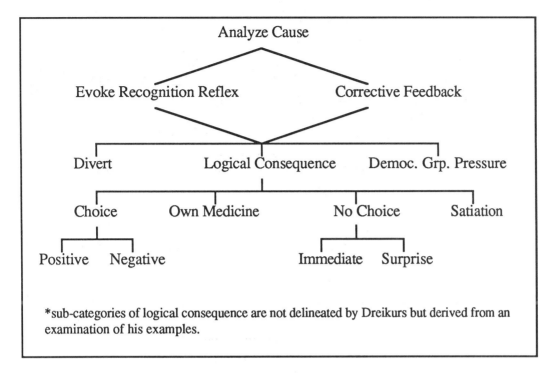

Analyze Cause

Evoke Recognition Reflex   Corrective Feedback

Divert   Logical Consequence   Democ. Grp. Pressure

Choice   Own Medicine   No Choice   Satiation

Positive   Negative   Immediate   Surprise

*sub-categories of logical consequence are not delineated by Dreikurs but derived from an examination of his examples.

In the CHOICE type of logical consequence, the student can avoid the logical consequence right away by choosing to alter his behavior. The positive choice is akin to Thomas Gordon's "owning the problem." (See the following sub-section on T.E.T.) If dallying with dressing and eating breakfast is making the student late for school, you simply let him handle the problem, own the problem. You may point out his choice to the student, but let him have positive control over handling the outcome. The adult's action is nil.

In a NEGATIVE CHOICE, the teacher/parent points out what logical consequence will accrue to the student *through the instrumentality of the teacher* if he doesn't perform in a certain way. Not doing assigned work in school will result in his having to stay afterwards to finish it. Having to finish it later is a logical consequence of not finishing it now. That's the way it is; staying after school is not viewed or presented as a punishment, it's just the way things are for people who don't finish their work. The teacher has to stay after too to finish up her work and can't go until it's done. This is the "social reality." This kind of logical consequence is considered NEGATIVE CHOICE here because the child is confronted with, "If you do X, then Y will happen." And Y is an aversive consequence for the child.

OWN MEDICINE type of logical consequence means giving it back to the student. Interrupt the interrupter; make an unliveable supermess around the sloppy student. In effect, hold a mirror of his behavior up to the student. There ought to be a certain amount of humor and appreciation of rational limits when employing this technique, certainly not vindictiveness.

In NO CHOICE logical consequences, the teacher levies the consequence upon the student right after the misbehavior occurs. What separates this from punishment is the logical connection the teacher must establish, at least in the student's mind says Dreikurs, between the behavior and the consequence. (The statement makes it sound like, for Dreikurs, the distinction between punishment and NO CHOICE logical consequences is not really so great, but that the trick is to convince the student there is a logical connection, whether there really is or not...and thus that the adult is not really dispensing punishment.) NO CHOICE logical consequences can be simply IMMEDIATE (removing two fighting children from a recess baseball game to sit out the recess) or SURPRISE, containing some element of novelty and originality (e.g., the teacher has rock throwers on the playground start rounding up all the rocks they can find, and then has them throw the rocks into a vacant lot to make the playground more safe). Other examples given of original reactions sometimes smack of embarrassment. One morning the seventh grader who continually taps his pencil in an annoying way is given a crayon instead of a pencil; the teacher states, "If you cannot use a pencil correctly, you will have to write with this."

SATIATION means the same to Dreikurs as it does to Behavior Modification people. Make the student do the illegal behavior over and over again until he is sick of it. Have the spit-ball thrower chuck spit-balls into a box all morning; have the wanderer walk around the room all afternoon.

In Dreikurs' last work, we hear that logical consequences are most useful in a goal one situation...attention getting. With power or revenge, logical consequences may backfire and should not be used. Natural consequences are alright anytime, however, except against goal four.

Principles of Teacher Response

1. Make sure the consequence is logically related to the misbehavior.

2. Present the consequence matter of factly, as an expression of the reality of the social order, not personal authority.

3. Make no moral judgements about the behavior or the student.

4. Be kind, use a friendly voice; never act in anger.

5. Be firm. In a NO CHOICE logical consequence, there really is *no choice*. This is what's going to happen to the student, and it must be carried through. Don't change your mind; don't give in; don't deviate from your announced procedure.

6. Act, don't talk. Too much talk (threats, warnings, explanations, exhortations) is the downfall of good discipline.

7. Be concerned with the "now", not with the past. There must be no element of "sin" in the teacher's view of the misbehavior, nor any element of retribution for past offenses in the consequence used.

8. Never get involved in a power struggle with a student. You will always lose. No contests of wills. ("I won't." "Yes you will, Jimmy Preston, and RIGHT NOW!") Simply refuse to be engaged in this kind of conflict. Sidestep it.

The *positive program*:

While refusing combat, be aware of the cause of the conflict. If the teacher diagnoses "need to show and assert power" as the cause, look for opportunities for the child to show pride in accomplishment. Try to channel that need to show power into positive paths. If the cause is need for attention, look for opportunities to praise accomplishments, ignoring deviant behavior that is attention seeking. If the misbehavior stems from assumed disability, treat it with encouragement; ensure success in the classroom; give responsibility, carefully chosen, but publicly visible. If the cause is revenge, then haul out your stamina and dig in for the long pull. Make the student feel liked. Dreikurs talks about group discussion and acceptance in this context, but leaves us with a direction rather than a syntax.

Use sociograms to gather data on popular and unpopular students, extroverts and introverts, he urges. Use this data in seating arrangements and class groupings to have isolates experience new skills of socialization, to put compatible students together.

Have regular class discussions once weekly to consider class problems. Stimulate students to learn to listen, to understand each other, and to help each other.

The positive program has four thrusts, each responding to one of the four causes of misbehavior that Dreikurs cites. But unlike the syntax of direct response to misbehavior, the positive program consists of general principles of teacher response to be applied in a prescriptive manner rather than specific actions. Another way Dreikurs has of talking about the causes of misbehavior is to consider the four causes as goals of the student. The positive program, then, seeks ways to meet these goals for the student without his having to misbehave.

Encouragement is the utility-infielder of this positive program, being applied to three of the four causes. Elsewhere, Dreikurs has written a whole book on the subject.

Support System

The Dreikurs model is claimed as most successful with children of elementary age. Beyond that age, more complicated and far-reaching motives add to the basic four with the onset of adolescence.

Effecting a logical consequence requires decisiveness on the part of the teacher, and, in some instances, an ability for novel or original thinking (the SURPRISE type of logical consequence). To levy a NO CHOICE, IMMEDIATE type of logical consequence, the teacher needs the self-confidence and quick response seen in experienced teachers who have developed a large repertoire of responses over the years. Failing the experience and the repertoire, the beginning teacher presumably must be able to think quickly on her feet and apply principles of teacher response to the situation, and develop a logical consequence for the misbehavior.

The teacher must keep her ego off the line, maintain a detachment, a separateness that enables her to avoid power conflicts with children...another difficult challenge, especially for the beginning teacher who is inevitably invovled to some degree with proving herself. It is this same kind of ego-detachment on the part of the teacher which will permit the student to own his own problem in the CHOICE, POSITIVE category. Furthermore, to try and convince a vicious-acting student that he is liked means liking an unlikeable child—this demands a most secure and giving, empathetic teacher.

Dreikurs' method demands firm, calm, non-judgemental ways of talking to students when handling misbehavior...also the techniques of sounding out and structuring the expression of the group's feeling about the misbehavior.

The space and time required for specific consequences that may be considered. (Will there be someone around after school to supervise finishing work, will shooting paperclips into a box in the corner of the room be too visibly distracting to the rest of the class in the set-up of this room, or too noisy?)

Social System

The teacher's role as autocrat is the target of the model. Get the teacher off the power pedestal, says Dreikurs; don't take the position of rule maker and enforcer as a personal role. Yet the teacher *is* the rule enforcer in his system; it's just that the rules are seen as not stemming from the teacher, but rather from the nature of things, from the social reality. It is the teacher who devises the logical consequence for a misbehavior, and it is the teacher who makes sure that the logical consequence is applied. If the consequence would apply all by itself, it would be a "natural" consequence. Logical consequences require human intervention to be affected.

Rule making is more democratic. Students are included in the constitutional process.

But when all is said and done, the teacher holds and openly uses power in the Logical Consequences system. This use of power is masked and blunted; resentment it might otherwise generate is reduced by having teachers avoid direct power struggles with children, and by clothing the consequence in an attitude of detachment on the part of the teacher, and logic in its relation to the misbehavior. It is not that power is used in a deceptive way, but rather that it is deceptive to think of the system as one that avoids the use of power. Logical Consequences cultivates an attitude about power in teachers and children that seeks to associate it with social reality rather than personal confrontation; but it does not reduce or eliminate its use.

In Dreikurs' last work (with Pearl Cassel, *Discipline Without Tears*, 1974), there is a qualification to the use of Logical Consequences that meliorate the above conclusions. Logical consequences are sanctioned in this book against goal one, attention getting, and *only* there, whereas in previous books there was no such limitation. One does not use logical consequences when the student's goal is power or revenge, or display of inadequacy. This, it seems to us, represents a shift of position from earlier Dreikurs' views. Taken at face value, this new position makes the Dreikurs model less reliant upon power and more reliant upon encouragement, and such things as use of sociometric data. The new book has a chapter on the evils of competition in school situations, a new theme for Dreikurs, and a chapter on how to conduct democratic class discussions, not a new theme for him. Several quotes from William Glasser suggest that these new emphases may come from a reading of Glasser's *Schools Without Failure* (1968), where the competition theme is found with similar arguments to those used by Dreikurs, and where the syntax of a class meeting is discussed in considerable detail.

Effects

Direct: Deviant behavior is reduced.

Nurturant: Teachers and students can relate to each other without the barrier of power struggles. Mutual respect is cultivated and democratic practices are supposed to become more a part of classroom life. Students become more realistic in their view of the world, more appreciative of the social value of cooperation.

Now let us examine a model of classroom discipline where exercise of sanctions by teachers is eschewed. We will start with the man who seems to have influenced Dreikurs at the end of his life—William Glasser.

William Glasser's Reality Therapy and Schools Without Failure
Discipline as Involvement

William Glasser translates the principles of Reality Therapy into a series of steps (syntax) for teachers to use in responding to misbehavior. By using these steps teachers can get students to take responsibility for their own behavior, and for altering their behavior if it is not meeting their own needs for self-worth, or respecting the rights of others to meet their needs. The result is a school climate of mutual respect, caring, and cooperative problem solving.

Definitions

Glasser establishes his basic definitions in *Reality Therapy* (1965). Some are translated into different vocabulary for *Schools Without Failure* (1968), but the meanings remain the same. RT will designate a definition from *Reality Therapy*; SWF will designate a definition from *Schools Without Failure*.

1. *Respect*: self-respect, a feeling of self-worth. (SWF)

2. *Self-worth*: a feeling of value to oneself and to others; feeling that one is a worthwhile person. (RT and SWF)

3. *Relatedness*: being connected or involved with other people in a relation of caring. (RT)

4. *Involvement*: relationship with a person or persons you care for and whom you know care for you in return. (RT and SWF)

5. *Love*: involvement. (SWF)

6. *Responsibility*: the ability to fulfill one's needs in a way that does not deprive others of the ability to fulfill their needs. A responsible person does what gives him a feeling of self-worth and a feeling he is worthwhile to others. (RT)

7. *Realistic*: action can be called realistic only when its remote as well as immediate consequences are taken into consideration, weighed, and compared. (RT)

8. *Identity*: state that results, is achieved, when one feels love and self-worth. In SWF, Glasser sees self-worth as necessitating confidence in one's knowledge and abilities in school. Love, in a school context, means social responsibility, caring for each other, helping each other.

Love is seen as the opposite of and the eliminator of feelings of loneliness and failure.

9. *Success*: an established identity; a state of having one's basic needs of relatedness and respect (or of involvement and self-worth) met.

10. *Failure*: a state where one's basic needs are not met. To understand Glasser's model it is important to keep in mind the full and special meaning of his definitions of involvement, responsibility, realistic, success, and failure.

Assumptions

1. The basic human needs of all people are:

   a. relatedness (involvement)
   b. respect (self-worth)

2. All people are responsible for their actions.

3. All people are capable of acting responsibly, regardless of their background, past experience, or current environment.

4. A change in behavior will lead to a change in attitude.

5. The first five years of school are critical to the development of responsibility and to the development of the ability to succeed.

Values

1. Caring for one another, affection.

2. Courage to attempt solution of one's problems in life.

3. Thinking versus rote learning in education.

4. Relevance to the issues children face in their lives built into curriculum content.

Goals

1. Achievement of personal success by individuals (defined as meeting the two basic needs of involvement and self-worth).

2. Achieving a social climate that manifests mutual respect, caring, and rational, honest, cooperative problem solving.

3. Structuring the expression of affection in schools; creating a form for it, and institutionalizing the expression of it. Making it a recognized part of the purpose, and building it into the activities, of school life.

Rationale

Success, as previously defined, comes through being realistic (as previously defined), responsible (as previously defined), and right (which means acting in accordance with accepted moral standards).

This can be restated as: Meeting one's basic needs of involvement and self-worth can be accomplished by considering the long range consequences of one's acts, by acting to meet the needs of others, and by acting in accord with moral standards.

To achieve this kind of success, one needs involvement as a starting point; one needs a "significant other" in one's life about whom one cares, and from whom affection is returned. When we have that, we can then begin to relinquish action based on the pleasure principle, that is, immediate gratification. But involvement alone isn't enough. After involvement exists, something must be done to raise the feeling of self-worth. We can only feel worthwhile if we maintain a satisfactory standard of behavior.

To maintain satisfactory behavior, we must become capable of, and practice, self-evaluation; we must look at our behavior and judge whether it is responsible (whether it meets our two needs) without depriving others of the ability to fulfill their needs.

Deviant behavior is unrealistic and irresponsible. Deviant behavior shows children have made bad choices about how to meet their needs. They can't make better choices unless they are involved with those who can.

Discipline, which is what those who love give us, points out unrealistic and irresponsible behavior and helps the child become realistic and responsible.

Steps

1. "Make Friends", says Glasser to teachers. "Become involved," he says to the therapist. "Establish a relationship," he says to both, "with mutual confidence in and expression of affection."

2.   Ask, "What are you doing?" when a student misbehaves. This is
     identifying, verbalizing, facing the reality of the behavior. This is a
     real step for some students, and not something they realize, much less
     ask on their own.

3.   Ask, "Is it helping you?" Evaluate. Judge the behavior. Behind the
     question is the thought that the behavior is not helping the child meet
     his two basic needs. But one does not talk explicitly about the two
     needs with students. One simply asks for an evaluation of the behav-
     ior: "Is it helping you?"

     Questions 2 and 3 may not be addressed by the students if the
     involvement is not previously established...and if they do not know
     that there will be no punishment.

4.   No punishment.

5.   Make a plan. The teacher asks the student to make a plan to avoid the
     behavior, or how to cope with the situation in an acceptable way next
     time it crops up. It is okay for the teacher to give suggestions, advice
     here (see versus Thomas Gordon's view). But the plan must be
     enough for the student so he can make a commitment to it.

6.   Get a commitment from the student to carry out the plan. This can be
     verbal or written.

7.   No excuses: "When will you do it?" And the teacher holds the
     student to the answer. No excuses are acceptable for not meeting the
     commitment. Though there is no punishment, the teacher holds the
     student to his commitment, and if the student does not meet it, asks
     the student to re-evaluate his plan, make a new one, or renew his
     commitment. The process may need repeating over and over again.
     The teacher who is involved is willing to start all over again repeated-
     ly. But always there is the expectation and the trust that the student
     will finally meet it. One expects and one expects and one expects.
     One never, however, excuses or condones or makes allowances, or
     fails to hold students to commitments.

8.   Class Meetings. These form a regular part of the response system of
     the teacher to misbehavior (as well as a format for establishing the
     requisite involvement). For a complete discussion of class meetings
     see Principles of Teacher Response to follow.

Principles of Teacher Response

1. Point out the reality of the situation...of the behavior.

2. Never condone irresponsibility.

3. Focus on the present, not the past.

4. No punishment, no sarcasm, no ridicule. Sarcasm and ridicule are destroyers of affection, of closeness, of relationships, of involvement.

5. Don't avoid speaking in the first person. "I want you to..." not "we should," or "you should."

6. The environment should never be manipulated so the child does not suffer reasonable consequences of his behavior.

7. Handle class problems in Class Meetings.

    There are three kinds of Class Meetings: Social Problem Solving Meetings, Open Ended Meetings, and Educational Diagnostic Meetings. Social Problem Solving Meetings are used to work out solutions to problems pertinent to the group or to any individual in the group. They are the kind of meetings that fit into the syntax of response to misbehavior. Open Ended Meetings discuss question of interest and relevance to the children's lives. In addition to making at least part of the day focus on issues of relevance to the students, however, these meetings perform a vital function in establishing involvement between the teacher and students, and among the students themselves. Educational Diagnostic Meetings are used to assess how well children are grasping aspects of curriculum and to plan future steps.

    The leadership of Social Problem Solving Meetings by teachers is handled in accordance with certain principles also:

    a. Solution to the problem is the focus of the discussion, never fault-finding or punishment.

    b. The teacher remains non-judgemental in his or her comments, though the students are not expected to do so. (Experiencing the feedback of his peers is one of the "reasonable consequences" a child suffers for an irresponsible behavior.)

    c.   Conduct the meetings in a tight circle.

    d.   Keep them short.

    e.   Don't overdwell on a single problem student (three times in a row on a class bully would be overdwelling).

    f.   Make the majority of class meetings in the other two categories (Open Ended and Educational Diagnostic).

    g.   Use Class Meetings as a vehicle for as much teaching of regular curriculum as possible.

Support System

1. Heterogeneous, home-room based classes. The class must spend most of the day together as a social unit for the feelings of involvement with each other and with their teacher to develop.

2. No "ABCDF" type of grading. (No labeling as "failure.")

3. Curriculum must have a "thinking" emphasis, so that...

4. Curriculum is relevant to issues in the students' lives.

5. Success in reading. Glasser sees this achievement as so much a part of social expectation about school and, in fact, so necessary for achieving feelings of success in school, that special attention must be paid to its accomplishment in design of school curriculum. To achieve it, he is even willing to dissolve the home-room class unit for a portion of the day.

6. Probably most important, the teacher must be the kind of person willing to make the personal commitment and investment of self to become "involved" with her students.

Social System

1. Non-punitive.

2. Students participate in rule-making.

3. Trusts and tryouts. The constant willingness of the teacher to start again with a student who has not met a commitment expresses a

confidence, a trust, in the student to eventually succeed. (It also expresses a depth of involvement on the teacher's part.)

4. The teacher's role is as a model of responsibility.

5. The teacher also has a role as a benevolent despot, not through punishment, but through rule enforcement and the holding of children to commitments they have made.

6. Reasonable rules. Participation of students in the constitutional process tends toward making the rules more reasonable. But Glasser realizes and approves of the fact that adults serve as major source for principles from which rules come. This is the practical reality. The statement that rules "should be reasonable" is something Glasser says to teachers and administrators knowing they will have and should have major say in what they will be. (Glasser is not a Summerhillian.)

7. The students are responsible for their own behavior and free to choose at all times what their behavior will be like. Their responsibility extends not only to themselves, or even to the teacher, but also to all the other members of the class.

Effects

Direct: Social problems are worked on openly with an orientation toward solution, not blame.

Relevance is stressed in curriculum.

Nurturant: Warmth and affection grows among students and between teacher and students.

Respect for each other's needs and rights is cultivated.

Empathy develops as students' needs are met and their responsibility grows.

The next model, Thomas Gordon's Teacher Effectiveness Training (T.E.T.) builds on the principles of the similar Parent Effectiveness Training and has been translated into an in-service course offered nationwide to schools and school districts.

Thomas Gordon's Teacher Effectiveness Training
Discipline as Communication

In the T.E.T. model, Gordon seeks to eliminate the conflicts and misunder-standings that cause poor relations between teachers and students by teaching them communication skills. The T.E.T. communication skills give students and teachers an alternative to power in resolving conflicts of needs. No longer does the teacher have to win at the expense of the student's needs (Method I), or the student win at the expense of the teacher (Method II). The "no-lose" Method III, taught in T.E.T., enables both students and teachers to meet their needs.

Definitions

1. *Active Listening*: listening for the feeling content (the encoded message) in a speaker's remark, and feeding this back to the speaker.

2. *"I" message*: a non-judgemental description of another's behavior, a statement of the behavior's tangible effects upon you, and a statement of the feelings generated in you by this behavior. These three elements in any order comprise an "I" message.

3. *Gear Shifting*: switching into active listening after sending an "I" message.

Assumptions

1. Acceptance enables change and growth. When a person feels he is "OK" as a person, accepted for what he is in the eyes of another, he will be receptive to changing his behavior. In addition to enabling change, acceptance is a near *sine qua non* for it. When one feels non-acceptance from a change agent, one resists the change. Gordon's base in Maslow and Rogers is evident here.

2. The Gordon system presumes relatively mentally healthy children; it is not designed for dealing with emotionally disturbed children.

3. A valued relationship exists between teacher and the student. The system applies only when the teacher has "bought into the relation-ship"; i.e., cares about the relationship, values it. (No wonder Gordon and Glasser are now giving training sessions together.) One won't be motivated to go through the steps of active listening and the others in the syntax if one doesn't care about the other party.

4. Students can take responsibility for, and solve, their own problems.

Values

Gordon values honesty and openness in communication. He values forthrightness in the recognition of, and respect, of one's own needs and those of others. He values non-judgemental communication as an expression of that acceptance. He values the mutual respect of meaningful relationships where people, in caring about each other, try to meet each other's needs. He lastly values behavior which facilitates the personal growth of others. These values translate directly into Gordon's goals.

Goals

1. Build a relationship between student and teacher whose result will be to make all teaching more effective.

2. Get students to take responsibility for their own behavior.

3. Increase the no-problem area (see Rationale below), and thus make more time available for teaching-learning.

Rationale

All classroom pupil behavior is either acceptable or unacceptable to the teacher. "The Rectangle" below illustrates this universe of behavior. Everything above the line is acceptable; everything below the line is unacceptable. The placement of the line (and thus the size of the areas) varies with personality, and within persons varies with time, mood, conditions, environment. Whispering to a classmate may be acceptable one day and unacceptable another, depending on other factors in the teacher's life (if the principal has just given her a tough grilling, for example).

```
+------------------+
|                  |
|                  |
|   Acceptable     |
|                  |
+------------------+
|                  |
|   Unacceptable   |
|                  |
+------------------+
```

Another way of looking at the universe of classroom pupil behavior is "Problem Ownership." Either a pupil behavior is giving the teacher a problem, giving the student a problem, (sometimes both), or is no problem for anyone (like working on math problems, or going to sharpen a pencil in an acceptable way). This no-problem area is called the teaching-learning area.

```
┌─────────────────────┐
│    Student Owns      │
│     Problem          │
├─────────────────────┤
│                      │
│  Teacher-Learning    │
│      Area            │
│                      │
├─────────────────────┤
│    Teacher Owns      │
│     Problem          │
└─────────────────────┘
```

The causes of misbehavior (behavior in the problem area) are unmet needs of children and teachers. Instead of trying to identify and deal with these needs, teachers often use power, which results in poor relations with students; poor relations aggravate poor communication, and the circle goes round and round. Using communication skills to identify and meet teacher and student needs without the use of power is Gordon's strategy for reducing misbehavior.

Steps

1. Determine if a problem exists.

2. Own the problem. This one is harder than it sounds. You, the teacher, only really own the problem if it is having a tangible effect on you. We (adults, parents, teachers) often "own," take responsibility for problems that are not really ours. For example, Margie is dilly-dallying in the morning, is slow getting down to breakfast. Mother, who always has to harass her to get her to school on time, is a nervous wreck by the time the school bus finally leaves. Whose problem is this? Mother has *made* it hers. But who really owns the

problem? Margie does. Right now Mother always solves it for her. If Mother lets Margie own her own problem, then Margie will have to deal with the consequences (walking to school, being late...waiting until Dad leaves for work and hitching a ride, also being late...). If we choose to take responsibility for a problem that is not really ours, it may begin to have some tangible effects on us (Mother is a tangible nervous wreck). But if we let the problem rest with its real owner, then only the owner feels the effects.

If the second grade teacher is recapping open paint jars every night and mumbling about the irresponsibility of her class, whose problem is the paint jars? If the teacher lets the children own their problem of leaving paint jars uncapped and having only dried cake to paint with the next day, whose problem is it?

If the students are working productively but noisily, and the class is next to the principal's office and the teacher is afraid the principal will get the wrong idea and give her a bad evaluation, whose problem is it?

3. Active Listening. Active listening, as defined before, is listening for the feeling content (encoded message) in the speaker's remarks and feeding that feeling back to the speaker. ("What do you like in a girl, Dad?"—really meaning, "You're wondering what to do to get boys to like you.") Active listening tends to get at the real root of the problem, which may be buried under several layers of feeling, only the topmost of which is showing at first. Good active listening extracts facts, meaning, and feeling content from heard remarks. While we are accustomed to listening for facts and meaning, we are not accustomed to listening for the important feeling content going on behind the remarks. If we are in the problem area, it may be this encoded feeling that is the cause of the problem, reflecting some unmet need. If we are dealing with a problem the student owns, "active listening" may help the student work his way through to a solution.

3a. The teacher owns the problem. "I" messages are brought to bear. For example:

Say the room is too noisy for her tolerance and her conception of a level conducive to learning...but the students are happy with it, aren't finding the noise offensive anyway. The teacher sends an "I" message with the elements previously described (non-judgemental, description of the behavior, tangible effects on her, feelings generated in her). "The noise level in this room is giving me a headache!" (Description...effect.) "I ache for some peace and quiet." (Feeling.)

4. Gear shifting. The "I" message may take care of the problem by itself. If the students have regard for the teacher and an okay relationship with her, they may be motivated to change their behavior. But if they have a need of their own which is not being met, we have a conflict of needs situation. In this case the teacher, after sending an "I" message, must gear shift into active listening to identify the needs of the students. After a period of this, she may restate her "I" message. If both teacher and students own the problem, a Method III solution may be called for.

5. Method III. Method I is teacher power: teacher wins, students lose. Method II is children use power: students win, teacher loses. Method III is the no-lose solution consisting of the following steps:

   a. define the problem in terms of needs
   b. students and teacher mutually brainstorm solutions
   c. they mutually evaluate solutions
   d. they mutually pick one acceptable to both
   e. determine how and when to implement
   f. appoint a later date for reassessment of the solution.
      Meet on the date.

   Method III is used only when it has been previously explained and "bought," at least for a trial, by the students.

6. Modifying the environment. Here the teacher takes the initiative to enrich, impoverish, restrict, enlarge, rearrange, simplify, systematize; or plan the environment, but not at the expense of the students (not making them "lose").

Social System

Students and teachers are both conceived as individuals with needs to be respected and met. Whoever has the problem takes the initiative to send "I" messages to the person or persons whose behavior is having a tangible effect on them. If the students are not skilled enough in sending "I" messages, the teacher is sensitive to their needs and uses active listening to bring them out. Conflict of needs is handled through the modified negotiation techniques of Method III or by having the teacher take initiative to modify the environment so that the behavior goes into the no-problem area. *Decisions are negotiated only when there is a con-*

flict of needs. When acting in the no-problem area, there is nothing to prevent the teacher from taking initiative and making instructional decisions based on other models of teaching.

Principles of Teacher Response

In the no-problem area the teacher can respond out of whatever framework she or he likes. Even the dirty dozen[3] can be okay! But when there is a problem, the syntax provides clear steps to take, starting with defining and owning the problem. At the basis of all the steps are mutual respect and a desire to meet the other's needs.

Principles of teacher response are empathy, separateness, facilitation, self-respect, and negotiation.

Empathy is manifested in active listening.

Separateness means allowing others to own their problems, not identifying with or assuming unto oneself the problems of others; letting people take responsibility for themselves.

Facilitation means that, though separate, one helps others find their own way to reach solutions to problems, one facilitates their progress.

Self-respect here means standing up for yourself too, not repressing your own needs, but recognizing, articulating, and seeking to meet them openly, at the same time as one is a helping person to others.

Negotiation is the principle at the root of Method III solutions, the method called into play when there is a conflict of needs.

Support System

1. Active listening requires of the listener:

   a. a trust in the ability of the student to solve his own problem.

   b. a genuine acceptance of the other's feelings.

   c. an understanding that feelings are transitory. ("I hate you!" Maybe he really does, at this moment, but not deeply, and probably not in five minutes.)

---

3 advising, ordering, sympathizing, threatening, moralizing, lecturing, judging, ridiculing, analyzing, interrogating, distracting, praising

d.   a real desire to want to help the student.

e.   separateness...an ability to psychologically separate yourself from another's problem, from identifying and assuming responsibility for the other...but not preventing you from helping.

f.   an understanding that students seldom start by sharing the real problem...that the real problem may be buried beneath several layers of feeling.

g.   a respect for the privacy of others, who may not want to reveal certain feelings to you, or intend them only for your ears when they do.

h.   time...enough time to go through the process (which you don't have in a crowded hallway with 30 kids on the way to lunch).

2.   "I" messages require of the sender:

a.   honesty in expressing feelings.

b.   risk: You are, after all, revealing a feeling to another person.

3.   Gear shifting from "I" messages back to active listening requires significant ego control. With a strong need of your own, just expressed in the "I" message, you have suddenly to tune in to the other person's need and actively listen to it. (This I view as the most underrated and demanding aspect of Gordon's system.)

4.   Method III requires that:

a.   students understand what it's all about and "buy" it.

b.   students believe you will do your part and not resort to power in the end.

c.   you have time to go through all the steps.

As you can see, the elements of the support system pertain to attitudes and beliefs on the part of the teacher, rather than physical supports. One must be a certain type of person, with certain understandings and beliefs, and have the time to carry out the system in a given situation, in order to make Teacher Effectiveness Training work. Thus, we may classify these support elements as belonging almost entirely to the "presage" category.

Effects

Direct: The direct effects of the system, according to Gordon, are that "teachers like kids and kids like teachers"; i.e., improved relationships. These improved relationships result from improved communication skills. Thus, the no-problem area expands in the "Rectangle" (see Rationale) and more time is available for teaching-learning. More teaching-learning takes place; teaching becomes more effective.

It is interesting to see that the result of this humanistic approach is related to more effective teaching. But, Gordon has a special understanding of "effectiveness."

Nurturant: Remembering his base in Maslow and Rogers, and carefully reading his comments on the benefits of such things as active listening, reveals that "effectiveness" to Gordon means facilitating personal growth; that is what one becomes "effective" at doing. The new T.E.T. communication skills create better teacher-child relations, which relations manifest themselves in a changed learning environment of warmth, responsibility, mutual respect, and acceptance. The new learning environment facilitates personal growth and, therefore, simultaneously enhances academic learning.

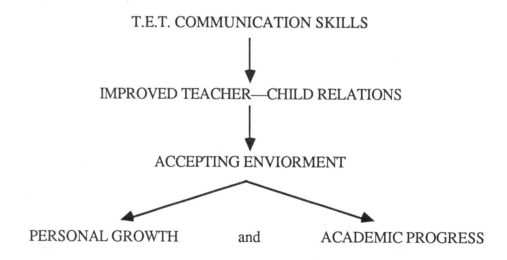

Other nurturant effects are student modeling of active listening, "I" messages, and Method III techniques.

A Final Comment on Models of Discipline

In contrast to the cohesive models analyzed above, the bulk of the writings on Discipline are not conceptually complete. Most writings do not consider or integrate many, or most, of the 11 categories we have used to analyze a model. The 11 categories of analysis may be said to comprise a functional definition of a "model" of Discipline. Unless a scheme has all 11, it cannot be said to be a fully developed model. A model without a syntax and/or a rationale, for example, would be no model at all.

Section V
Matching

One statement of Dreikurs' has always struck us as significant: "All behavior is purposive." While his four "purposes" (attention, power, helplessness, revenge) don't seem nearly to cover the waterfront of motives behind misbehavior, the basic notion is a powerful one—people do what they do for a reason...always. They may not know the reason consciously, but it's always there. From this idea, we can recognize that behind all previous patterns of student misbehavior are needs, felt psychological needs that the student is trying to meet through the behavior. This doesn't make us sappy, too "understanding," or permissive; it simply tells us: "figure out what the student is really trying to *get* through this behavior, and that will tell us a lot about how to respond." What the student may be trying to get, the unmet need that might be working actively inside him, may be:

Safety/Security.................... "I have enough trust. Things are at least minimally safe for me. I know what's going to happen next."

Self-Control........................ "I can control myself. I'm not afraid I'll hurt myself or others."

Affection........................... "Somebody significant cares about me."

Inclusion........................... "I'm accepted in this group."

Control as Power................. "I have some control over my fate, over what happens to me."

Self-Esteem........................ "I'm a worthwhile person."

Recognition........................ "Other people have esteem for what I've done, for who I am."

Self-Actualization................. "I'm realizing my potential."

Remember, now, that *most* misbehavior need not be traced to unmet psychological needs. Students who test a teacher by calling out, passing notes, or doing a thousand other things may be doing nothing more complicated, in fact, than simply *testing the teacher*. They're trying to see how much they can get away with. We're not talking about that here. We're talking about the one or two very resistant students who persistently misbehave despite appropriate treatment through Expectations and the other Management Parameters.

The psychological needs listed above are arranged in sequence starting with the most fundamental. We will develop the hypothesis that there is a relation between the psychological needs driving a student's behavior and the most appropriate response strategy, along the lines shown in this chart:

Psychological Needs That May Be Driving Resistant Students	Response Strategies
Self-Actualization	
	Teacher Effectiveness Training
Recognition	
Self-Esteem	Reality Therapy
Control	Logical Consequences
Inclusion	
	Personal Influence
Affection	
	Self-Awareness Training
Safety/Security/Trust	
	Behavior Modification

The six strategies are arranged, bottom to top, from least mature to most mature; from those that demand the least maturity and competence of the student to those that demand the most. Students with unresolved needs in the early (lower) part of the sequence seem to be less mature emotionally and require strategies from the less mature part of the continuum (Behavior Modification, Self-Awareness Training). Students driven by later needs (e.g., control) seem better able to respond to more mature strategies (Logical Consequences, Reality Therapy).

Over a long period of time with a particular student, we should try to move up the chart. That is, we should start with strategies appropriate to the student's current needs, but help the student grow by moving into more mature strategies. In this way, we are moving students toward more self-discipline, even if we have to start off doing all the discipline for them (Behavior Modification). Their growth toward improved mental health and emotional maturity is not just paralleled but fostered by our ability to modulate our strategies upwards over time. If this seems like a big demand to be making on teachers—to master and practice appropriately six different strategies of discipline—we agree. Teachers aren't trained to do that in college. But one doesn't have to be an expert to start using this framework for understanding behaviors and trying to tailor responses. The fact is, we already *have* these students in our classes and we have to start somewhere. Getting to know and try the different strategies takes time and practice, and proceeds much better if at least two teachers work on it together. But learning them *is* eminently doable, and an immense service to students who have no other stable anchors in their lives than their school and their teacher. But let's backtrack. Where did we get that list of psychological needs to begin with?

Many authors have brought to their work the notion of certain universal psychological needs shared by all humans. Some authors arrange them hierarchically, such as Maslow (1962):

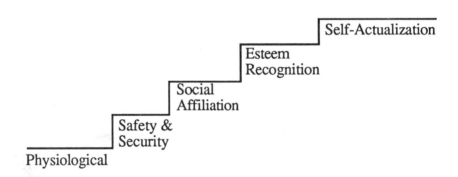

"Hierarchically" to Maslow means that lower needs have the greatest strength (e.g., physiological) until satisfied. For instance, if you're hungry you don't worry much about social acceptance. If physiological and safety needs are met, social affiliation needs come to the fore. One tries to meet that need and it could account for much behavior we see. This same person, however, would not be driven strongly by needs for esteem and recognition; at least, that would not be the dominant force behind behavior until social affiliation needs were satisfied.

Maslow and others do *not* view these needs as developmental steps which, once traversed, do not need to be reworked. People move up and down the ladder according to current circumstances: If I lose my job, I am suddenly thrown two or three steps down the stairs and begin operating out of my need for safety and security. If a student's parents get divorced, the same thing may happen.

In Figure 6-2 on the following page, we have spread out the basic psychological needs as described by a number of authors. While each author uses different terms and highlights a different number of needs, there is considerable overlap amongst them, boiling down to eight basic needs that seem to be included by all the writers.

Figure 6-2

Maslow	Dreikurs	Shutz	Glasser	Erikson	SUMMARY
Self-Actualization				Integrity vs. Despair Generativity vs. Sterility Intimacy vs. Isolation Identity vs. Identity Confusion	SELF-ACTUALIZATION
Esteem Recognition	(Helplessness)/ Competence		Respect	Industry vs. Inferiority	RECOGNITION SELF-ESTEEM
	Power	Control		Initiative vs. Guilt	CONTROL
Social Affiliation	Attention	Inclusion Affection	Relatedness		INCLUSION AFFECTION
				Autonomy vs. Shame	SELF-CONTROL
Safety/ Security/Trust				Trust vs. Mistrust	SAFETY/ SECURITY/TRUST

Note that we have included Erikson's eight psychological stages, or psychological crises, on our list, too. Erikson *is* a developmentalist; in other words, he does see these crises as stages which must be traversed before addressing later issues up the scale. And the crises usually do not reoccur once resolved, yet people (and children) can get stalled with unresolved crises at a lower level, which prevents their moving to healthy later stages of emotional development. What is relevant here is the connection between any one of Erikson's stages successfully navigated and the psychological need that gets met by that successful passage. There seem to be parallels between what Erikson sees happening—for example, during the crises of "initiative vs. guilt"—and what Shutz sees as meeting the basic need for control.

Taken together these writers seem to be sending some clear messages: 1) all humans have certain psychological needs in common; 2) the needs are related in regular ways (maybe hierarchical); 3) needs drive behavior. When a basic need isn't met, it motivates observable behavior and enables us to account in some way for what we see.

How can we use those ideas to match resistant students with the six strategies? What is the relationship between a strategy a teacher may choose and the need that may appear to be driving the student's behavior?

In this section we are about to offer some guidelines in answer to those questions, but the following caveat is necessary. We are not psychologists, and we are not trying to make teachers into psychologists. The last thing we want to do is to get teachers to label a student with a psychological need and begin "treatment." The whole business is much too 'iffy' for that. Even mental health professionals, we feel, diagnose too often and too early. We can't really know what's going on inside another person's head and why they're acting as they do; but we *can* have conviction that *there is a reason*, even if it remains obscure to us (and to them). And there is no other way to pick appropriate response strategies except to try to make some logical match-up between what *might* be the student's need and a strategy that's in line with that need. Don't diagnose; be very, very tentative—but try to use behavior to get clues to needs and make connections to strategies. That will be better than using one strategy with everyone as if it were **the** method of Discipline, and it will be better than random, eclectic bouncing around with different strategies.

Six Typical Profiles
Behavior Modification is the most controlling of the strategies; and one thing we know about it is that it really works. If you do it well enough, you can get a student to do most anything, even high school students. Why would a teacher want to be so controlling? One reason might be desperation: the class (or the student) is

so disruptive you can't think of anything else to do! Or, students may simply not have in their repertoires the behaviors they need to function properly: *not know how to* pick up and put away, *not know how to* do assignments in order; *not know how to* meet deadlines; *not know how to* resolve a dispute without fists. Behavior Modification can allow students to experience behaviors they would never try on their own and thus discover that there are other ways of doing things. Students in extreme inner states of insecurity or anxiety can be helped to function, to get through the demands of the day, by leaning on the strong structures of a Behavior Modification program. It actually supports them, helps them function as opposed to flop around, during times when they are weak and confused. Rather than controlling in these circumstances, Behavior Modification is supportive, even protective. It stops the negative cycle of behavior that is destroying a student's relations with others and confirming a self-image that is probably already poor. It gives students a lifeline to hang onto until they can gain some control over themselves. And that is what we want to work for ultimately—self-control, self-discipline.

We are always trying to move students up the list toward the more mature strategies because a person who can respond to the Reality Therapy approach, for example, is more emotionally mature than a person who needs Behavior Modification all the time. In any given year, you may find yourself starting off with Personal Influence for Jimmy, but able to move to Reality Therapy by the end of the year. Many connections and transitions between the strategies are possible, but one always tries to move up the list with a student. Over a period of several years in a public school, we have seen skilled teachers move a student along from Behavior Modification in grades K and 1, to T.E.T. by grade five. Other things outside the teacher's control must support a student's personal growth to enable dramatic progressions like that, but we are also quite certain it could not have happened without a team of teachers who shared this point of view and planned with each other to help the student grow.

The *Self-Awareness* strategies are also suitable for students in tenuous emotional states. These students may intellectually know the difference between productive and unproductive behavior but be unable to control themselves. Their tempers often flare out of control; they don't trust themselves and have difficulty forming friendships. They may withdraw, spend a lot of time drawing, reading, or wrapped up in some objective activity. If they have a bent for science or art, they may produce fabulous projects, and in fact only through these projects do they build the superficial relationships they do have with others. They hate to talk about their feelings, in fact, are unable to, afraid to, and may refuse to if pressed. When they do speak about themselves, it is in connection with events and objects, not people or feelings. For young children in this plight, the strategies of Wolfgang and of Lederman are right on target. For older students, the self-instructional strategies of Meichenbaum are more appropriate, though forms of these are also useful with young children (e.g., the "Turtle Technique").

Students who are suited to the *Personal Influence* model often generate love-hate feelings in you. They have likable, charming, even lovable qualities. One moment you feel like hugging them, and the next you want to throw them through the wall. One-on-one they tend to be great; in a group they can be poison, inciters, show-offs. Curiously, they are often quiet in large groups where there is more anonymity, but incorrigible in small groups where the social tensions of establishing themselves with the others are too much for them. When they come in in the morning they may drift around the room, checking out what everyone is doing, moving from thing to thing, settling in nowhere. They have a real need for affection and inclusion and those are often missing in their lives. In those morning meanderings they are looking for their place, wondering where they can plug in, and they don't quite know how to connect. Their reputations, their relations with the other students, don't make entry easy for them in unstructured situations. They long for friends, for closeness with other students and with the teacher, but they repeatedly behave in ways guaranteed to antagonize. The structure, the demands, the warmth, and the relationship building of the Personal Influence model help them bridge a difficult period in their lives.

With younger children, one may borrow from Behavior Modification to help these students gain more awareness and control over their most disruptive behaviors. With older students, contingency contracting can help supplement the "tough" half of the Personal Influence model.

Sometimes we meet students who say "no," who defy and are openly challenging of authority at every turn. These students may be candidates for the *Logical Consequences* model. They refuse to do their work or do it only when they "feel like it." They *look* for power conflicts with authority figures, actually invite them. Of course, there are some students who get into frequent arguments with peers and with teachers but who do not appear to deliberately set them up; the students we're taking about here, however, *do* set up challenges to authority, and the argument is usually about "doing it my way." Such students can be tyrants in games with others, and may do a considerable amount of bullying and outrageous pushing around of other students and of teachers, too, up to the limit they can get away with. Their psychological need for control is driving the behavior—only the need has gone haywire, gone out of perspective, and is damaging these students and those with whom they come in contact. They have come to believe, as Dreikurs would say, that the only way they count in the world is by showing their power, by controlling others. That is how they think they must act in order to be significant and worthwhile people. This mistaken belief must be changed if their behavior is to change in any way other than a temporary one.

Dreikurs' method avoids the power conflicts the student seeks and tries to teach the reality of the social order through logical consequences. These consequences do not represent the imposed power of the teacher, but rather the way things really work in the world. Thus, students can't get mad at the teacher and back into their old unproductive power game. They begin to see their behavior as having consequences for themselves because the behavior is incompatible with how the social order works, not because the adults "won't let me." They begin to learn something about the social contract. They are put in a position of seeing their behaviors in relation to what a society, a group, needs to function, and the group itself is used in classroom meetings to reinforce that message...which brings us to Glasser's Reality Therapy and Classroom Meeting model, where the use of the group is more developed.

Candidates for *Reality Therapy* are students who are acting irresponsibly—students who are always forgetting books, showing up late, not doing work, missing appointments and obligations, blaming others and not perceiving or at least acknowledging their own role in conflicts. These students may act quite disruptively, knocking over others' books, punching students they pass in the hallway, slamming lockers. But they are not premeditated or deliberate about these acts in the same way as an attention-seeker would be. They just seem to fall into these behaviors. They're like emotional drifters who are easily led into bad practices and bad company. When asked why they bumped into a student they'll likely say, "I don't know," and shrug. Given punishment and reprimands, they won't argue, won't comply, and won't change.

In Reality Therapy, students are brought up against the consequences of their behavior for their relations with *other people*. It is a more personal focus than the Dreikurs' model, where the intended learning is: "This behavior doesn't work in the world." Glasser's learning is more like: "It isn't working for *me*. Now what am I going to do about it?" This is toward the top of the scale of maturity among the six models because the responsibility for seeing, evaluating, and changing the behavior lies with the student, even though an involved teacher is necessary to get them into each step. Glasser, who doesn't focus much on the causes of misbehavior, likes to deal with the here and now. Many people, he believes, who act crazy, can decide *not* to act crazy. They have the inner control to do that if they can go through the Reality Therapy steps and decide that it is worth their while to do so—if they have someone who's involved enough to walk the road with them and not give up on them. So Glasser might be inclined to use Reality Therapy with students operating at quite a low level.

Classroom Meetings broaden the sense of "involvement" from between teacher and student to include students with each other. Eventually through these meetings, students gain a place to talk to each other about what's really on their minds. Resistant students get to hear how others are perceiving them, and the others are enabled to share those perceptions in a problem-solving environment.

A good candidate for *Teacher Effectiveness Training* (T.E.T.) is a student who appears resentful, maybe sitting out his school time like a prison term, occasionally rebellious or wise, but usually functional. Work may be satisfactory or inferior. These students may feel the teacher never listens to them, and the teacher may feel they have no respect for or understanding of what school is all about. There is poor communication between teacher and student and both feel their needs are unmet. Both are unsatisfied with their relationship in class even though overt conflict may not be frequent between them.

Such a student usually has a cumulative history of increasing hostility and seems ready to manifest it toward *all* teachers, unless they prove themselves otherwise. With other students relationships are often fine. It is to adults that the student has begun to generalize the notion that "all they ever do is give orders, tell me what to do. They never listen." And the student has given up sending messages about his beefs.

T.E.T. can also be right on target for a student with a problem where, through active-listening, a skillful teacher can help the student reach his own solution.

T.E.T. isn't a model that lines up with a particular psychological need like some of the others. It is the most mature of the models, because it calls on the student to have sufficient empathy or at least understanding to read a teacher's "I" message and be willing to respond through "no-lose" (or "win-win") negotiation. Method III solutions themselves require listening and sending skills on the part of both parties that are difficult for very troubled students. Gordon himself says that T.E.T. is not designed for disturbed students. However, it is our experience that Active-Listening and "I" messages are skills that are immensely valuable on their own, even when one is not using the whole T.E.T. model. Active-Listening is very helpful, almost necessary, in the Self-Awareness model, and "I" messages complement the Personal Influence model nicely. And, of course, Active-Listening is the key skill for unlocking the longer term resentment of the student profiled above.

To summarize, then, each of these six strategies seems most appropriate for a particular kind of student. We have offered a typical profile for each of the six as general guidelines for matching, and referred to psychological needs that may be behind the profile. To pick a strategy, a teacher must start with the student's behaviors themselves. They should be written down—the what, when, with whom, how often, and where of these behaviors. Simply listing behaviors and circumstances, however, will not be enough. *How* a behavior is done (as reported by an observer) is important, too, for from that "how" we will try to infer the motive behind it: Did Charlie knock over the books casually as he passed them, a kind of afterthought in his meanderings (Reality Therapy candidate)? Did he swagger down the aisle and knock them over with a cocky flick and insolent glare back (Logical Consequences candidate)? Did he let out some pent up resentment simmering all morning and knock them over in exasperation (T.E.T. candidate)? Did he knock them over in an impulsive pell-mell rush to get to his seat (Self-Awareness candidate)? What are the other behaviors that make up Charlie's profile? As we develop that profile, we may get closer to where Charlie is in life and see more clearly what strategy is most likely to help *him* function successfully and grow emotionally.

Figure 6-3

Behavioral Characteristics	Model	Teacher's Role
resentment	T.E.T.	an equal person
irresponsibility	Reality Therapy	therapist
defiance & attention seeking	Logical Consequences	representative of society
loneliness & attention seeking	Personal Influence	significant other
impulsiveness	Self-Awareness	coach & confederate
ignorance or lack of control	Behavior Modification	operating the system

It is interesting to reflect on how the teacher's role changes in different models (see Figure 6-3). In T.E.T. the teacher is conceived as an equal to the student: both have their needs and their rights, and both participate in looking for "no-lose" solutions that will consider both their points of view. In Reality Therapy the teacher functions as therapist; though involved with and supportive of the student, they are no longer equals: the teacher is now a helping person who regularly and directly brings the student back to earth and makes them face facts. In Logical Consequences there is more detachment yet, with the teacher now representing society. Teachers who use Personal Influence become admired authority figures to students. Self-Awareness Training turns teachers into coaches and systems designers, and is not far removed from Behavior Modification, within which teachers are not only systems designers, but operators of the machine.

As one goes down the list, the student's role diminishes and the teacher swells in authority, responsibility, control, and status. Conversely, as one goes up the list, the teacher diminishes in importance and the student grows as a fully functioning, socially aware person who can deal with life successfully. Through understanding teacher and student roles in the various models we can broaden our perspective on the relations of the models to each other, and underline the value of seeing them in a developmental progression. That perspective says to us simply: take students where they are, and help them grow in maturity.

The arrows in Figure 6-3 indicate some of the common progressions one can observe when students are able to respond to increasingly mature strategies. Behavior Modification can help a student get in control enough (calmed down enough) to enter Self-Awareness Training, or to respond directly to a teacher using Personal Influence. Both Personal Influence and Logical Consequences can be a springboard to Reality Therapy and Classroom Meetings. It is neither necessary nor appropriate to move through all six strategies with any one student. For a certain student, for example, the most natural step after Personal Influence may be Reality Therapy. At a certain point, the student may not need a teacher to act as his conscience, but may be able to move directly to evaluating his own behavior.

Section VI
Response to Illegitimate Behavior

To respond to a behavior one must see it (or hear it, or "feel it") or in some other way perceive it. Kounin has given us the term "withitness" for teachers who are particularly good at this: They seem to have eyes in the back of their heads, and not only know when illegitimate behavior occurs, but make some move so the students *know* they know. "Boy, you can't get away with anything on Miss Dooley!"

Once the behavior is perceived the question becomes: How does the teacher respond? We distinguish four levels of response:

- no withitness (no response)

- one general pattern of response

- more than one general pattern of response (variety); different patterns (strategies) at different times

- patterns of response chosen in light of the individual students' characteristics (matched).

Figure 6-4

Six Families of Response to Resistant Children's Behavior

CONSEQUENCES (Sarason) teacher pairings limits warnings removal enlisting the class	**(Dreikurs)** creative & relevant logical consequences no "battles" reality of the social order, not punishment opportunity »r leadership or demonstration of constructive potency	**REPLACING & TEACHING NEW BEHAVIORS** Behavior Modification I.D. target behavior tell child / goal set clip reinforcers keep count reinforce approximations note progress to child (Buckholt et al.) (Madsen & Madsen, etc.)
PERSONAL INFLUENCE Personal Relationship Building Clear expectations of a significant other Direct Specific Repeated Positive Expectancy "You can do it" Tenacity Consistent Reactions High teacher affect noticing (Hymes) (Wallen & Wallen)	**PROBLEM SOLVING** (T.E.T) Teaching Children to see their messages clearly, listen to others' messages accurately, and negotiate solutions. Active listening "I" messages Gear shifting Method III (Gordon)	Shure & Spivak teaching to think of alternatives, consequences of behavior, impulse control
	TAKING RESPONSIBILITY (Reality Therapy) What are you doing? Is it helping? (What do you want?) What are you going to do about it? Involvement Humor, no excuses, tenacity; seeing oneself as worthwhile and connected to others. (Glasser)	**SELF-AWARENESS** (Cognitive Behavior. Mod.) Looking on "I see you're starting to get out of control." "You're getting out of control, I will help." Intervening…describing what you are doing Hold Teaching children to read their own signals, be aware of their actions and feelings. (Meichenbaum) (Wolfgang, Perls, & relaxation)

Between variety and matching to individuals, we may be able to discriminate patterns matched to situations and to groups.

We know a teacher who displays basically one pattern of Discipline in her class: direct desists and logical consequences. However, she uses another pattern on the playground when children get into fights with each other (and are not challenging her or her classroom expectations directly). Out there, she uses the Glasser model. In other settings not directly confronting her clear classroom expectations, she will usually use methods not based on her own power (e.g., cafeteria disputes between children and lunch room aids when she is called in).

If we were to focus only on the classroom, we would judge her as using only one pattern. Broadening our consideration to the whole school environment, we would judge her as using "variety." If we focus on the playground only, we might see power moves against certain illegitimate behavior (e.g., dawdling in lining up to come in) and Glasser type moves when she intervenes in fights. What we are facing is the subdivision of "illegitimate behavior" into sub-classes: a) those that could be interpreted as challenging the teacher, those which children might consider as something to "get away with"; and b) those that do not challenge the teacher (fights, misbehavior in the lunchroom, in another teacher's class...).

If a teacher has only one way of operating in each setting, but acts differently in each setting, that is a kind of variety sure enough, but not the same kind as for a teacher who demonstrates variety in both settings. We may thus revise and finalize the judging for "response to illegitimate behavior" in the following way:

- no withitness

- withitness and one pattern of response

- at least one pattern each
  in two different settings   OR   • more than one pattern
                                           in each setting

- patterns matched to children.

The Positive Program

Omitted from this discussion has been any detailed consideration of the positive side of Discipline; that is, notions such as: self-discipline as the "purpose of it all"; building community and regard among students through deliberate activities; teaching students to work together cooperatively and effectively as group members; teaching students to listen to one another; making curriculum involving, interesting and relevant; making classroom life democratic so that students have a stake and a say in the order and civility of how they behave toward one another and toward the teacher.

All of these issues have been treated elsewhere and have often been related to reducing discipline problems (Stanford, 1977; Glasser, 1968; Dreikurs and Grey, 1968; Gordon, 1974; Aronson, 1978). These aspects of Discipline are not discussed here nor directly addressed as sub-parameters for two reasons. First, in a pure management sense, we have considered what teachers may control and the moves they may make to create the conditions for instruction. Illegitimate behavior blocks instruction and so its treatment as a Management Parameter under Discipline has been in a preventive sense: How does one prevent or respond to illegitimate behavior when it occurs? This is the minimum and universal maintenance level necessary in all classrooms for the continuance of instruction, regardless of the teacher's orientation toward a positive program. Second, the notions listed above can all be considered as curriculum goals for positive action, as guidelines for learning experiences or objectives for which learning experiences may be designed. Thus, these notions, when operative in a teacher's teaching, reflect curriculum decisions and would be noted when we look at instruction itself under the Dimensionality parameter.

Following, in the form of a Quiz, are some profiles of real students we have known. We invite you to read them and see which of the six models of Discipline you think would be most appropriate. What is your rationale for your choice? (This exercise is particularly beneficial when done with colleagues as a group.)

Discipline Quiz

For each of these student profiles, which of the six models of Discipline would be most appropriate? Write the model in the margin next to each profile.

Jimmy

Jimmy seems on the edge of life. He's quite unpredictable. Sometimes he behaves like a lamb, looking at you with those beautiful brown doe eyes. He likes to cuddle, responds to warmth and physical affection. He will try his work for a while, some days (not often) get quite involved in it. More often he does a little (or none) and is off around the room.

He'll grab things from other kids, push and shove, yell, be combative. In class meetings or instructional groups he may yell; when singing with a group he'll be the first to degenerate into shouting or meaningless yells. Occasional periods of passive immobility, anger and striking out, and out of control craziness (throwing things, messing things) speak of deep inner sadness.

Jimmy is six and from a single parent home. His mother is often, however, not there when he returns in the afternoon, but he's not always sure which afternoons these will be. He has a key. He walks home with his sister who is five. His mother is loving, but unstable and troubled herself.

In large and small groups, whether for a class meeting or for instruction, he often bursts out of control—yelling, shouting, tugging or pinching kids near him. He often smiles as he does this, as if it's a form of showing off, but he also responds quickly to teacher reprimands...for a few seconds. The expression that flashes across his face when reprimanded shows acknowledgement that he's done something wrong, but then there he goes again. He is often removed from groups to a corner of the room or the hallway.

He doesn't get much work done, has a short attention span, but is a bright child. He responds to warmth and cuddling, seeks out adult laps. He does considerable running in room, lots of grabbing, fighting, bumping. When removed from the group he may sob deeply and genuinely for considerable periods of time. These periods of wrenching sadness and crying are not uncommon. Often he will burst into tears for no apparent reason.

You never know how he'll come in through the door. But what you see the first few minutes usually sets the tone for the day. A frequent scene is Jimmy standing at the door, not coming all the way in, peering anxiously around looking at what is going on, being defensive about his space, probably getting bumped by a child behind him going in, and responding with a punch and angry face.

He will space out for short periods, looking sad and immobile; at other times he may get quite involved with a story or with a science activity. He can work cooperatively with other children, but these times will often degenerate into fights over sharing or over real or imagined slights. He is easily set out of control, especially at transition times.

If you call for cleanup and line-up for lunch, he'll throw things in the general direction of where they're supposed to go (or just leave them where they lie) and run to the door. Frequent bumpings and fights result at these times. Running seems the only response he knows for a call to go from one place to another.

At times, of course, he won't come at all, seeming not even to hear, being totally absorbed in blocks or clay. These periods of total absorbtion are less frequent than abuse of materials like sitting at the clay table making small balls and throwing them at nearby students...or pretending a large block is a bulldozer and crashing another child's building.

The only thing that seems to settle him down is physical restraint and cuddling. Sometimes you have to go through 5-10 minutes of restraint.

Ken

Ken is a ninth grader, though he looks a little young. He's always in hot water, rarely in class. Last week he got into a wrestling match—basically playful—with a buddy and destroyed bed of spring flowers under the principal's office window by rolling all over them.

In private, teachers call him a "wild-ass kid." He seems to live from moment to moment, and to have no roots anywhere, home or school. Others can get him involved into almost any kind of mischief...and often do...stealing, vandalism (painting dome of the new gym with silver spray-painted obscenities); it's getting so he occasionally thinks up a few things like that to do on his own.

He seems to act with no internal guidance system...an unguided missile; has no goals, nothing to shoot for, nothing to get out of school. Beneath the rollicking prankster seems a fearful young man who, when caught and confronted with his deeds, shrinks visibly. When being addressed by the vice-principal for discipline he will not talk much, shrug his shoulders, look very depressed and alone. He accepts punishment and it does absolutely no good. He makes promises and disregards them entirely.

Freddie

Freddie seems out of contact with his body, ungainly and awkward, almost disconnected from his limbs. He looks like he might bump into something at any moment without knowing it, and sometimes he does.

Freddie is 11, tall for his age, and has a high pitched voice.

He will come into the cafeteria, usually toward the end of the line. He walks with a lurching, shuffling gait, head bobbing. He will look around, head almost swiveling. By the time he's gotten through the line and to a table he will be talking very loudly, a little wildly. Squeezing into a seat at a table he may be abusive to adjacent children: "Hey, you slobbo, let me in!" Minutes later there may be wild laughter, grabbing or throwing of food, and very hyper, out-of-control behavior. The cafeteria over-stimulates him, as do other large group settings.

Freddie is not hyperactive though. In fact, in class he is most often completely absorbed in his work—his own work that is, not the teacher's. He likes to draw fantastic machines, to read about anything scientific, and will immerse himself in these activities at every opportunity, withdrawing from class participation.

In total class instruction and small group work he calls out, does a lot of things seemingly to be center stage, and is often silly. If he can withdraw, however, he will just as soon pass these times covertly drawing or studying something that interests him.

He can get very angry at other students and has hurt a few with hard punches or by pushing them into desks this year. He will lose his temper, have outbursts, and really get out of control.

He won't talk about his feelings, *can't* seem to respond to anything that asks him to talk from inside. He talks about things.

He knows a great deal about a number of scientific and technical topics and loves to repeat this knowledge to adults. As a younger child he was one of those fanatical and knowledgeable dinosaur experts. In general, his mind is very absorbent of facts and general information, but his lack of concentration seems to block him from making connections, from developing concepts you might expect from so verbally advanced a boy.

In skill work, like determining if a given word would be on a given dictionary page or learning the algorithm for long division, he has very little patience, tends to rip up papers if he doesn't get it right away. He won't ask questions, and when it's reexplained for him he'll leap into applying what he's absorbed before the explanation is even complete…almost with panic. Once he's got it, though, he can do it competently and generalize to new situations. He will race through work, however, and make many mistakes.

He doesn't have any real friends, but does play with other children in such activities as fort building outside. He will not enter organized games readily if at all. His play will be something that allows him to do his own thing, play his own part, focus his eyes and body on, say, the fort. His talk at these times will be about the fort or about some dramatic fantasy the children develop as they build the fort: "Hey, look at this cool slide here (that he's just made). They'll be able to go ZOOM over the wall there." He will seldom look at another child as he speaks.

Figuring Out Discipline Problems: 21 Questions

1. Is the work too hard or too easy?

2. Do I build good personal relationships with students?

3. Do I maintain good momentum in lessons?

4. Do I manage time and space well?

5. Do I make appropriate attention moves and make them promptly enough?

6. Is my instruction confusing to some students?

7. Do I vary instructional format and materials enough to avoid students being bored?

8. Are the rules and consequences clear and specific enough both to me and to the students?

9. Do I communicate expectations in a way that is...?

    - direct
    - specific
    - repeated
    - shows positive expectancy (both "you can" and "you will")

10. Are the consequences logical rather than punitive?

11. Do I have a range of consequences rather than one rigid response for every transgression?

12. Do I deliver consequences in a way that is...?

    - consistent and tenacious
    - prompt
    - matter-of-fact
    - indicates student choice

13. Do I take sufficient time and care at the beginning of the year to establish all of the above?

14. Do I have high enough expectations for behavior no matter what the students' backgrounds?

15. Do I refuse to accept excuses?

16. Do I give students a real and legitimate sense of control, influence, responsibility, power in class life?

17. Do I recognize and reward responsible behavior effectively?

18. Do I explicitly build community in the class (knowledge about, appreciation of, cooperation with one another)?

19. Are there physical reasons (hearing/vision loss, organic hyperactivity) for this behavior?

20. Is there a value or culture clash between teacher and students (or among students) that is behind the behavior?

21. Do the students know how to do what I'm expecting of them?

Planning for Very Resistant Students

1. Have I gathered enough objective data on the student's behavior?

2. Have I presented it to a team to get additional input and questions?

3. Have we come up with the best guesses as to the "psychological need?"

4. Have we picked a matched response model?

5. Have we worked out a coordinated plan for all teachers who contact this youngster?

6. Have we included the youngster's family in the plan?

7. Have we provided for periodic review and modification of the plan?

Source Materials on This Parameter

Adler, A. *The Problem Child*. New York: G.B. Putnam & Sons, 1963.

Aronson, E. *The Jigsaw Classroom*. Beverly Hills, CA: Sage Publications, 1978.

Buckholt, D.R.; Berritor, D.E.; Sloane, H.; Della-Piana, G.M.; Rogers, K.S. and Coor, I.F. *Claim—Classroom and Instructional Management Program*. New York: Walker Publishing Co., 1975.

Canter, L. (with Canter, M). *Assertive Discipline*. Santa Monica, CA: Canter and Associates, 1977.

Colarusso, C. *Diagnostic Educational Grouping: Strategies for Teaching*. Bucks County (Pennsylvania) Public Schools, 1972.

Dishon, D. and O'Leary, P.W. *A Guidebook for Cooperative Learning*. Holmes Beach, FL: Learning Publications, Inc., 1984.

Dreikurs, R. *Psychology in the Classroom*. New York: Harper and Row, 1957.

Dreikurs, R. and Cassel, P. *Discipline Without Tears*. New York: Hawthorne Books, 1974.

Dreikurs, R. and Grey, L.A. *A New Approach to Classroom Discipline, Logical Consequences*. New York: Harper and Row, 1968.

Ginott, Dr. G. *Between Parent and Child*. New York: MacMillan, 1965.

Glasser, W. *Reality Therapy*. New York: Harper and Row, 1965.

Glasser, W. *Schools Without Failure*. New York: Harper and Row, 1968.

Gordon, T. *Parent Effectiveness Training*. New York: Peter Wyden, 1970.

Gordon, T. *Teacher Effectiveness Training*. New York: Peter Wyden, 1974.

Hersey, P. and Blanchard, H. *The Family Game*. Reading, MA: Addision-Wesley, 1978.

House, E.R. and Lapan, S.D. *Survival in the Classroom*. Boston: Allyn and Bacon, 1978, Chapter 1.

Hymes, L. Jr. *Behavior and Misbehavior*. Englewood Cliffs, NJ: Prentice-Hall, 1955.

Lederman, J. *Anger in the Rocking Chair*. New York: McGraw-Hill, 1969.

Martin, G. and Pear, J. *Behavior Modification*. Englewood Cliffs, NJ: Prentice-Hall, 1978.

Maslow, A. *Toward a Psychology of Being*. Princeton, NJ: Van Nostrand, 1962.

Meichenbaum, D. *Cognitive Behavior Modification*. New York: Plenum Press, 1977.

Mendler, A.N. and Curwin, R.L. *Taking Charge in the Classroom*. Reston, VA: Reston Publishing Co., 1983.

Pierson, C. *Resolving Classroom Conflict*. Palo Alto, CA: Learning Handbooks, 1974.

Rogers, D.M. *Classroom Discipline: An Idea Handbook for Elementary School Teachers*. New York: Center for Applied Research in Education, 1972.

Sarason, S. *The Culture of Schools and the Problem of Change*. Boston: Allyn and Bacon, 1971.

Shure, M.B. and Spivack, G. *Problem Solving Techniques in Childrearing*. Washington: Josey-Bass, 1978.

Swap, S. "Disturbing Classroom Behaviors: A Developmental and Ecological View." Exceptional Children, November 1974, 163-172.

Van Houton, R. Learning Through Feedback. New York: Human Sciences Press, 1980.

Wallen, C.J. and Wallen L. *Effective Classroom Management*. Boston: Allyn and Bacon, 1978.

Wilt, J. and Watson, B. *Relationship Building Activities*. Waco, TX: Educational Products Division, WORD, 1978.

Wolfgang, C. *Helping Aggressive and Passive Pre-Schoolers Through Play*. Columbus, OH: Charles E. Merrill, 1977.

Wolfgang, C. and Glickman, W. *Dealing with Discipline.* Columbus, OH: Charles E. Merrill, 1980.

Wood; Bishop; Rogers; Cohen and Danna. *Parenting: Four Patterns in Child Rearing.* New York: Hart Publishing Co., 1978.

Additional Readings on Relaxation Training
compiled by Dr. Barbara Bruno-Golden

Bernstein, D. and Borkovec, T. *Progressive Relaxation Training: A Manual for the Helping Professions.* Champaign, IL: Research Press, 1973.

Bruno, Barbara. "Progressive Relaxation Training for Children: A Guide for Parents and Children." *Special Children,* AASE/Box 168, Fryeburg, Maine, Fall 1974 (Part I) and Summer/Fall, 1975 (Part II).

Jacobson, J.E. *Teaching and Learning New Methods for Old Arts.* Chicago, IL: National Foundation for Progressive Relaxation, 55 East Wahington St., 1973.

Koeppen, A. *"Relaxation Training for Children." Elementary School Guidance and Counseling,* October 1974, 14-20.

Northfield, W. *How to Relax.* The Psychologist Magazine Ltd., Denington Estate, Wellingborough, Northamptonshire, England, 1973.

[Also, commercially prepared cassettes for home training programs in adult relaxation skill development are available through Bio Monitoring Applications, Inc., Suite 1506, 270 Madison Ave., N.Y., N.Y. 10016.]

7
Clarity

What does it take to explain things clearly?

Cognitive Empathy
The Big Picture

CLARITY

Clarity is a variable that is long on research and short on meaning. It has been included in studies many times...even making Rosenshine's "Big Nine" (as we like to call them), the nine variables most related in correlation studies to student growth on standardized tests (see Rosenshine and Furst, 1973). But the problem has always been that we have not known what "clarity" meant to those researching it...nor have they (see Hiller, *et al.*, 1969; Belgard, *et al.*, 1971; Martin, 1979, for attempts at definition). High-inference judgement ratings of teachers' clarity don't inform us what the low-inference components of the concept are. Why is it that some people are better at explaining things than others? What do they *do* to be more clear?

Consider this episode: $2^2 \cdot 2^3 = ?$ is the problem and many in the class have gotten it wrong. "What many of you did," says the teacher, "was to multiply the 2's so you got $2^2 \cdot 2^3 = 4^5$. That's wrong. It's $\underline{2}^5$." He erases '4^5' and writes '2^5' in its place, "The 2 doesn't change." Then he moves on to the next problem.

The teacher has "covered" the problem, but he certainly hasn't explained it. The episode is notable for its omissions—for what *didn't* happen—more than for what did. The teacher didn't check to see if there was any understanding of the rule at work for doing this sort of problem ($N^a \cdot N^b = N^{a+b}$). He didn't check to see if there was any conceptual understanding of *why* the rule works. He didn't do any explaining of the process for doing the problem: he just indicated wrong and right answers. Importantly, he didn't elicit any student participation to see how many and who might still be confused. For instance, he didn't check to see if any students could now do a similar problem. There is little about this episode that is clear—to either the teacher or his students.

The behaviors we're concerned with in the Clarity parameter underlie the process of delivering clear instruction. The situations we will be concerned with here include: presenting new material; explaining concepts; giving directions when they are needed or explaining directions when they need to be elaborated; re-explaining old material; and dealing with student confusions. Over the course of this chapter, we will examine the repertoires that exist for dealing with these events.

Cognitive Empathy

Perhaps central to this parameter and to good teaching in general is something the Teacher of the Year, Mary Clark, said in a 1981 interview. In describing how to teach, she said, "Know what is inside your students' heads, including the information, feelings and goals they bring to the classroom."[1] This implies that Clarity involves a kind of *cognitive empathy* (as well as emotional)[2] that enables teachers to know *when* students don't understand, and then to zero in on *what* or what part of the material they don't understand.

Knowing when students don't understand and then determining what they don't understand are two different skills. Knowing *when* students don't understand suggests that teachers have means of *checking for understanding* during instruction. Determining *what* students don't understand implies that teachers have ways of *unscrambling confusions* that identify the specific point(s) of misunderstanding and deal with them. Since both skill areas are important to Clarity, we need to separately consider how teachers perform each.

Checking for Understanding

We'd like to use the word "checking" to describe when teachers are trying to determine whether or not students are confused. When teachers are checking they are reacting to the class, reaching out to students, getting outside of themselves to make a "yes...no...who?" judgement about whether confusion exists. How *do* teachers detect confusion? We've been able to identify six levels of performance, which we characterize with these headings:

- presses on
- reads cues
- "dipsticks"
- uses recall questions
- uses comprehension questions
- anticipates confusions.

Although each will be discussed independently, it is important to realize that these six levels of performance are not mutually exclusive; a teacher might display several of them at different points during the same lesson.

---

[1] Parsons, C. "Grading Teachers for Quality." *The Christian Science Monitor*, October 28, 1981, p. B6.
[2] Knowing what's going on with students' feelings and goals is also very important and is taken up again in Chapters 5, 8, and 13.

At the first level, teachers may simply not be responsive to students' lack of understanding. Remaining oblivious to students' confusion during instruction, teachers just *press on* with their explanations. Or, not being aware of the potential for confusion, they fail to give any directions for tasks that require explanation. Not checking and "pressing on" can occasionally be appropriate in fast-paced reviews of material previously taught if there has been thorough checking in the past and today the teacher's purpose is to highlight key terms or concepts. Even here, however, since checking takes so little time, it would be wise to do it.

At a second level, teachers may check for understanding by *reading cues* in students' behavior (e.g., body language, facial expressions) that signify confusion. Only when they notice such cues do they pause in their instruction. Relying on whether students appear to understand, however, can be risky. Students may not provide cues even though they are not following the instruction. For example, in a study of student thought processes during instruction, Peterson and Swing (1982) describe how students fooled observers who judged them to be attending to the lesson:

> Melissa's responses to the stimulated-recall interview suggested that she was not attend-ing [although observers judged from her behavior that she was] and instead seemed to be spending much of the time worrying about her performance and the possibility of fail-ure. For example, when asked what she was thinking after viewing the first videotape segment, Melissa replied: "...since I was just beginning, I was nervous, and I thought maybe I wouldn't know how to do things." After viewing the second segment, Melissa said the following: "I was thinking that Chris would probably have the easiest time because she was in the top math group." After viewing the third segment Melissa responded: "Well, I was mostly thinking about what we talked about before—I was making a fool of myself." Finally, after the fourth segment, Melissa stated: "Well, this might be off the subject. I was thinking about my crocheting meeting 'cause I wanted to have it done." [Peterson and Swing, p. 485]

Teachers, at a third level, may check more directly for general student under-standing with periodic questions. They probe to see if students are still with them, successfully comprehending the instruction. This checking may concern general understanding of content, procedures, or directions. Madeline Hunter talks about *dipsticking* to continuously monitor whether students are understanding. She and her colleagues teach students to use signals—thumbs up, thumbs down, thumbs to one side—to send periodic messages to teachers about how well they're under-standing something. There are any number of other forms of dipsticking teachers use to accomplish the same thing. For example, asking students to "Nod your head if you're with me so far," or calling for unison responses from the class, both of which can give a general reading according to how many students respond and how emphatic the response is. Some teachers pause in the middle of classes and give one-question quizzes...then circulate and look over shoulders as students are writ-ing to see how everyone is doing. This takes only a minute or two and gives an accurate dipstick reading of how well the students are understanding the material.

Good performance on dipsticking is indicated when there is evidence that a teacher is taking constant readings across all (or at least most) of the students in the class to see if they're still "with it." What is looked for is quantity, frequency. Effective use of dipsticking is characterized by frequent general readings of how well students are tuned in. Teachers may get these readings by simply asking a high volume of questions for a large number of students. Within this form of "dipsticking" it is important to distinguish checking *using recall questions* from checking *using comprehension questions*. Recall questions call for factual answers which come directly from the material presented. For example, "What is the formula for finding the area of a right triangle?" The answer is the direct recall of the formula: 1/2 the base times the height. On the other hand, comprehension questions can only be answered if students truly understand a lesson's concepts or operations. For example, "What is the area of this right triangle (one that has measurements marked, but no terms labelled)?" The answer requires both the recall of the formula and the understanding how to apply the formula to a specific triangle.

Comprehension questions are those that can only be answered if students understand the concept being checked. For example, "Why couldn't 'gobble' be on the page?"—where the guide words on the dictionary page are "hunt" and "mound." Students can only answer that question if they understand how guide words bound the range of entries on a dictionary page.

We are *not* introducing Bloom's taxonomy here and beginning a discussion of the levels of thinking stimulated by teachers' levels of questions. (That, however, is an important topic in itself and will be considered in the Learning Experiences chapter.) We are trying to point out that during "checking," we sometimes think we are getting a reading on students' comprehension, but in reality we are only checking their recall of key words. An example of this appears in the Quiz at the end of this chapter.

At a final level, teachers may check for understanding in advance of instruction by using what they know about their students to *anticipate confusions*, probable points of misunderstanding: e.g., items of information that might be difficult to assimilate; or that are likely to confuse; or that are embedded in material which assumes students have prior knowledge of, say, a term. By anticipating confusions, teachers become aware of when students are likely to have difficulty understanding and can spend time clarifying the material *before* students become confused. Anticipating confusions is often one of the most subtle and difficult checking performances to observe because students do not, in fact, become confused: teachers "head them off at the pass," taking care of the potential lack of understanding before it develops. But for this very reason it also represents the height of sophistication in checking.

One aspect of teachers' performance in anticipating confusions deserves special mention—dealing with students' pre-existing misconceptions as they affect instruction. A series of investigations by science educators (e.g., Eaton, et al, 1984) have revealed the many misconceptions students have about how the world works: for example, "air is empty space" and "my eyes see by direct perception" (rather than receiving reflected light). They bring these misconceptions to instruction and unless teachers discover them, surface them, and explicitly *contradict them*, students hold onto them and reconcile them with the instructional information. The resulting "maps" they create in their heads may seem logically consistent, but they're wrong and present serious obstacles to learning. This can happen even when the instruction is, ostensibly, clear as a bell—because of the failure to account for the misconceptions students bring with them to the instruction. And, though the research is most well developed for science concepts, there is no reason to believe the same thing does not happen with concepts from any discipline. The implication for us as teachers is simply to be aware that students do not come to class as blank slates. What's already in their heads has great bearing on how our instruction gets interpreted.

Question: How would a teacher be able to do all of this checking for understanding? Answer: because they are able to get inside of students' heads. The disposition to and the ability to *get inside students' heads* is the foundation of this entire parameter. Teachers skillful at Clarity want to know how it's going for their students, and have a repertoire of ways for finding out. They have a degree of "cognitive empathy" for the workings of the learners' minds—an ability to put themselves in the learners' shoes—and that guides everything they do.

Unscrambling Confusions
When teachers do detect *that* students are confused, the next Clarity move involves finding out *what* the students are confused about and tailoring re-explanations accordingly. We call this "unscrambling confusions."

When students have signaled (or teachers have discovered) that they don't understand something, and teachers are attempting to re-explain or clarify the point of information, we can observe five different levels of teaching performance:

- none
- re-explains
- isolates point of confusion with pinpoint questions
- perseveres and returns
- has student explain own current thinking

At the first level, teachers make *no response* to the perceived confusion. At a second level, teachers simply launch into a *re-explanation* of the item. It may be slower and/or more detailed than the first explanation, but it is basically the same thing over again without any venture into the students' thinking.

At the next level, teachers question the students with *pinpoint questions* to discover precisely where in the sequence of learning the students went off-track and became confused. When that point is finally pinpointed, these teachers swing in, economically omitting re-explanation of things the students have already assimilated, and move on with the re-explanation.

At another level, clear teachers *persevere* when they find a student confused over an idea. They will stick with students, perhaps have several exchanges with them if time allows, and then, most importantly, come back to them later in the period to see if they "really got it." This return visit may be via review questions, or by asking the student to apply the idea in some other context to make sure he really understood. Sometimes there isn't time in the period for a teacher to unscramble all the confusions of all the students...a reality we all live with in teaching. In that case, what one may see from a perseverant teacher is some way of noting or recording who, specifically, is still foggy on the new concept. Perhaps the teacher will make some provision for a return engagement with those students (arranging for a short small group session right then and there, or asking Bill and Mary to stop by after classes for a few minutes)...or some other move aimed at noting who still needs more explanation and creating a setting where they'll get it.

At a final level, teachers ask students to describe their thinking for more than sequence: they probe for *how a student thinks* about the concept or operation. They try to understand the student's frame of reference, his way of conceptualizing the item. They ask such questions as: "How did you get that answer?"; "How do you approach this kind of problem? Can you tell me what you did or thought about it?"; "What did you try first? Why?"; "What do you think this might mean?"; "What does 'city government' mean to you?" In this way, sometimes we discover that apparently "wrong" answers aren't really wrong at all if we understand the student's assumptions and logic. Using the student's frame of reference with *its* meaning orientation enables the teacher to re-explain the concept (or ask a series of questions that will bring the student closer to self-discovering the concept.) If the concept turns out to be outside the boundaries of the student's thinking system, then it's an inappropriate objective altogether. And that is a terribly important thing to find out.

Three authors stand out for their work in raising our consciousness about the importance of understanding students' thinking. Throughout the 1970's, Bill Hull conducted a series of "Children's Thinking Seminars" where teachers met regularly to discuss cases of children's processing. Through logs, writing and discussion, teachers were (and are, for these groups continue at many sites) stimulated to reflect on the children's thinking to try to see how and why they were interpreting phenomena and doing problem solving as they were. Hugh Mehan (1974) analyzed classroom discourse between teachers and children and showed that children's "errors" in following directions were really eminently logical interpretations of the adult talk when understood from the standpoint of *students*. Eleanor Duckworth (1981) conducted a series of investigations with teachers into youngsters' thinking, in which the starting point was teachers studying their *own* thinking and learning processes. The outcome was that:

> ...to 'give a child reason' became the motto, the aim, of much of the teachers' subsequent work. This was the challenge they put to themselves every time a child did or said something whose meaning was not immediately obvious. That is, the teachers sought to understand the way in which what a child says or does could be construed to make sense—they sought to 'give him reason'. [Duckworth, 1981, p. 6]

One of Duckworth's important messages is to point out that the main contribution of Piaget to teachers is not his stages of development; it influences teaching little to be able to identify a child's stage in the Piagetian hierarchy once we accept the value of using concrete materials (especially when we realize the value of teaching concretely even for adults). What matters, and what improves our teaching, is understanding Piaget's clinical interview technique "in which the adult role is to find out as much as possible about what the child himself believes about an issue" (Duckworth, *op. cit.*, p. 14). In addition:

> To the extent that one carries on a conversation with a child, as a way of trying to understand a child's understanding, the child's understanding increases "in the very process." The questions which the interlocutor asks, in an attempt to clarify for him/herself what the child is thinking, oblige the child to think a little further, also...What do you mean? How did you do that? How does that fit with what she just said? I don't really get that; could you explain it another way? Could you give me an example? How do you figure that? In every case, those questions are primarily a way for the interlocutor to try to understand what the other is understanding. Yet, in every case, also, they engage the other's thoughts and take them a step further. [Duckworth, *op. cit.*, p. 21]

(For further discussion of the way in which students' understanding can be deepened by having them reflect on their own thinking, see the "Summarizing" section at end of this chapter.)

Explanatory Devices

Checking and Unscrambling Confusions are essential to good Clarity behavior...probably the heart of it. But there are other things that bear on it too...like a teacher's repertoire of explanatory devices to assist in explaining. Such devices include: analogies; highlighting important items; mental imagery; physical models;

audio-visuals; use of charts or blackboard; translation into simpler language; modeling thinking aloud; use of simple cues; and use of progressive minimal cues. Most of these terms speak for themselves, but a few deserve additional comment.

Mental Imagery

Mental imagery means making pictures in your head. This can be done by asking students to draw, or asking them to close their eyes and create, images of what is happening in the text (or images of persons, events, or information presented in other ways). Clearly, this technique requires that teachers select content that lends itself to imagery: it is hard to imagine how one would use imagery to solve quadratic equations. But it could be very effective for understanding the scene in Lincoln's cabinet room when he put an end to Secretary Chase's White House ambitions, or when he fired General McClellan, or for understanding what happens inside a plant cell during photosynthesis.

Descriptions of successful imagery programs (Pressley, 1976; Escondido School District, 1979) usually include having students speak about and/or share their pictures: "What do you see?"; "Tell me about your picture."; "What else can you see?" Researchers (see McNeill, 1984 for additional references) have demonstrated increased student comprehension, retention, and ability to make inferences from material treated in this way.

Modeling Thinking Aloud

For teachers who like to role-play, this technique is right up their alley. When teachers model thinking aloud for students, they go through the thinking step by step as a student would, role-playing, as it were, just what one would do. This includes being puzzled, making mistakes, self-correcting, and checking themselves along the way. Modeling thinking aloud is appropriate for any kind of multi-step operation where problem solving is involved. By doing the thinking aloud, teachers get a chance to show students where the pitfalls are and how to get through common hang-up points, as well as model the appropriate steps. An example of modeling thinking aloud (partially) for the problem 7,301 divided by 45 might sound like:

"Let's see, I have to divide 45 into 7,301. So 45 will go into 7?...no, into 73, how many times? 2. No, 2 times 45 is 90; it must be 1. 1 times 45 is 45. 73 minus 45...borrow 1 from 7, 13 - 5 = 8. 4 from 6 is 2...26. Now I bring down...the zero. Try to put 45 into 260. So that's what?...."

Modeling thinking aloud is done by the teacher in front of the class. It is a dialogue with oneself. Beth Davey (1983) shows how the technique can be used to teach students a variety of comprehension strategies. For example, you come upon a word you don't know in the text: "Hmmm, what does that mean?...better reread the sentence...still don't get it. Maybe I'll read ahead to see if it gets clearer...Nope, still doesn't make sense. Let's see. Do I recognize any of its parts?...." In this way, the teacher can take a set of guidelines—reread; read ahead and back to see if the context gives a clue; look for parts you know, particularly stems, prefixes and suffixes—and show what they look like in operation.

Modeling thinking aloud is one of the least seen and most powerful of the explanatory devices. It is especially useful in teaching any kind of problem-solving or step-wise procedure.

Progressive Minimal Cues

In small group or one-to-one tutoring, one can often see a teacher using silent finger-pointing skillfully as a minimal cue to call a student's attention to an attribute of a word or a part of a problem he needs to look at again. The *minimal* part of the cue giving is important here, meaning just enough to get students looking at what they need to, but not so much as to deny them an opportunity for thinking out the error. For example, if a student reads "cot" as "cat"...the teacher silently points to the "o" in "cot"...a minimal cue. If necessary, the teacher progresses up the scale of cues, making successive cues less and less minimal until the student gets it. (The next step would be to spell the word aloud, stressing the "o"..."c-o̲-t", but not telling the word.)

To analyze their own (or observe another's) use of explanatory devices, teachers can make a simple count of how many and which are used to aid in explaining and clarifying information. There is no evidence we know of that any one of these devices is better than another; but there is considerable support for "variety" in teacher presentation as correlating with effectiveness. Using a number of devices in lessons is one form of "variety" certainly. And common sense argues that by using a repertoire of these devices, a teacher can increase the likelihood of retaining students' attention and engaging their learning style.

Speech

Another sub-parameter obviously involved in clear communication is the Speech of the teacher. It must meet certain minimum criteria for diction, pronunciation, enunciation, grammar, syntax, and then choice of words (appropriate vocabulary) in order for students to understand what is said. Smith and Land (1981) have analyzed speech patterns of effective and ineffective teachers. Their studies and those of others consistently show negative effects on students' achievement when teachers use "vagueness terms" and "mazes" in their speech. On the next page are some examples they cite.

Vagueness terms (underlined):

This mathematics lesson <u>might</u> enable you to understand a <u>little</u> more <u>about</u> <u>some</u> <u>things</u> we <u>usually</u> call number patterns. <u>Maybe</u> before we get to <u>probably</u> the main idea of the lesson, you should review <u>a</u> <u>few</u> prerequisite concepts. <u>Actually</u>, the first concept you need to review is positive integers. <u>As</u> <u>you</u> <u>know</u>, a positive integer is any number greater than zero. [p. 38]

Mazes (underlined):

This mathematics lesson <u>will</u> <u>enab</u>…will get you to understand <u>number</u>, <u>uh</u>, number patterns. Before we get to <u>the</u> <u>main</u> <u>idea</u> of the lesson, you need to review <u>four</u> <u>conc</u>…four prerequisite concepts. The first <u>idea</u>, <u>I</u> <u>mean</u>, <u>uh</u>, concept you need to review is positive integers. A positive <u>number</u>…integer is any whole integer, <u>uh</u>, number greater than zero. [p. 38]

As evident from the above, mazes are false starts or halts in speech, redundant words, and tangles of words. Vagueness terms take many forms (see Figure 7-1, following from Smith and Land, 1981). Hiller, et al. (1968) "presented evidence that vagueness occurs as a speaker commits himself or herself to deliver information that he or she can't remember or never really knew" (Smith and Land, 1981). It can also occur, it seems to us, when a teacher does not wish to appear authoritative about information and allows a confused sense of Personal Relationship Building to obscure Clarity. Such confusion can occur when a teacher goes overboard on a desire to be seen as open to student ideas and as a facilitator rather than an information giver. What results is a "tentative teacher" who uses many vagueness terms.

Beyond acceptable speech, there are some things that are not so obvious. We can discriminate teachers who speak in different ways to different students, perhaps varying their way of speaking by type of occasion too. They have, in short, a variety of ways of speaking. The difference may be in the range of vocabulary used; in the accent; in the use of slang; in the cadence, speed, or rhythm of the speech; in the formality or informality of the language (Joos, 1967). We are led to wonder if the teacher can speak to the students in their own language in language forms that are likely to be effective for explaining, clarifying, elucidating…in language forms that may be better suited to the kind of interaction occurring?

In analyzing teacher behavior, for teachers who speak in different ways at different times to different students, an observer can note "variety" with some objectivity on the Speech sub-parameter. If, in addition, there is some evidence that a

```
┌──────────────────────────────────────────────────────────────────┐
│                          Figure 7-1                                │
│                 CATEGORIES OF VAGUENESS TERMS                       │
│                                                                    │
│  Category                        Examples                          │
│  1.  Ambiguous designation       Conditions, other, somehow,       │
│                                  somewhere, someplace, thing.       │
│                                                                    │
│  2.  Approximation               About, almost, approximately,     │
│                                  fairly, just about, kind of,       │
│                                  most, mostly, almost, nearly,      │
│                                  pretty (much), somewhat, sort of.  │
│                                                                    │
│  3.  "Bluffing" and recovery     Actually, and so forth, and so    │
│                                  on, anyway, as anyone can see,     │
│                                  as you know, basically, clearly,   │
│                                  in a nutshell, in essence, in      │
│                                  fact, in other words, obviously,   │
│                                  of course, so to speak, to make    │
│                                  a long story short, to tell the    │
│                                  truth, you know, you see.          │
│                                                                    │
│  4.  Error admission             Excuse me, I'm sorry, I guess,     │
│                                  I'm not sure.                      │
│                                                                    │
│  5.  Indeterminate quantification  A bunch, a couple, a few, a     │
│                                  little, a lot, several, some,      │
│                                  various.                           │
│                                                                    │
│  6.  Multiplicity                Aspect(s), kind(s) of, sort(s)     │
│                                  of, type(s) of.                    │
│                                                                    │
│  7.  Negated intensifiers        Not all, not many, not very.      │
│                                                                    │
│  8.  Possibility                 Chances are, could be, maybe,      │
│                                  might, perhaps, possibly,          │
│                                  seem(s).                           │
│                                                                    │
│  9.  Probability                 Frequently, generally, in         │
│                                  general, normally, often,          │
│                                  ordinarily, probably, sometimes,   │
│                                  usually.                           │
│                                                                    │
│  Smith and Land (1981) as per Hiller, et al., 9 categories (1969)  │
└──────────────────────────────────────────────────────────────────┘
```

particular way of speaking at a given moment is chosen to match some characteristic of a group or an individual, then "matching" may be noted.

Explicitness

Explicitness means expressly communicating and not leaving to implication the:

- intention of cues
- focus of questions
- necessary steps in directions
- meaning of references
- reasons for activities.

These five events are the main places we can observe Explicitness in action. Having said that, let us recall that instructors don't always teach by explaining, nor do they intend to. They may teach inductively or Socratically or in many other ways. But when it comes to direct explaining behavior, especially where a student confusion has been detected, then we look for Explicitness.

Intentions of Cues

Effective explainers cue students explicitly to make the connections and use the kinds of thinking that will lead to learning the material. They leave no logical gaps. Teachers who are *not* explicit make assumptions (unfortunately, often faulty) about students' ability to read their cues or read their intentions. These teachers are often guilty of playing "guess what's on the teacher's mind" (or "guess why we're doing this"), a game that serves no purpose in learning and intimidates and confuses students. Here is an example of *in*explicit cuing behavior:

> "Before defining 'concave'," Orr asked, "Where do bears sleep?" He thought students would create an image of a cave that would help them remember the definition. Both students noticed this odd question and understood that it was supposed to provide a device for learning the definition. However, neither perceived that this device was an image. [Winne and Marx, 1982, p. 510]

Focus of Questions

Sometimes the focus of our questions isn't explicit, and we wind up in another version of "guess-what's-on-the-teacher's-mind." Here is an example: A Latin teacher has a student read a question from an exercise in a text. "What type of question is that?" the teacher asks. The student does not respond. No other students volunteer or appear to know either. What the teacher really means is: Which of the six types of question on yesterday's handout—questions with 'quid', 'cur', 'ne', 'quis or quem', 'ubi', or 'quo'—is this? He assumes the student realizes this—*but the student doesn't*. The teacher doesn't realize that "what type" is not a cue to the student to scan the six "types" on yesterday's worksheet and pick one. The universe of possible answers the student is scanning is not six choices, it is infinite, and so he is at a loss.

The episode continues: The teacher directs the student to turn to the handout and read the first item. The student obliges. In a tired voice the teacher says, "OK, read the next item." The student obliges. This second item is an example of the type of question from the text. The student finishes reading it. There is a pause. The teacher gives the student a wide-eyed look, "Well?" "Oh," says the student, and goes on to identify the text line as a 'quid' question.

This confusion would have been avoided if the teacher could have been explicit about the mental operation he wanted the student to do: "...and by 'what type', Jimmy, I mean which of the six types we discussed yesterday. Check your handout compared to the text line you just read. Everybody else check, too, to see if you'll agree." (This is an active participation move.)

The above episode is a good example of "guess what's on the teacher's mind." By contrast, teachers who are explicit show students directly how what they're doing now...or next...will help them get to the learning goal.

By looking for Explicitness in instruction, we look for clear steps that enable learners to know *why* questions are asked and *how* directions or examples relate to learning tasks. "He always asks us questions we can't answer," is a common report that students make on unclear teachers. They can't answer questions because the teacher fails to define or at least reference the domain the question is tapping. Consider this episode: "What is good writing?" asks Miss Jones, and she has a specified list of attributes in mind which she proposes to get up on the board. But the question is a 'sucker' question, because students are going to volunteer all sorts of plausible answers that don't fit in with her lesson plan. That would be okay if she were to collect them all, discuss them, and then perhaps compare them to the text list she has in mind. But, instead, she's going to say "no," and "that's not quite what I'm looking for," and invalidate much good student thinking as she 'develops' (that's how her lesson plan puts it) her list. She doesn't really mean, "What do *you* think good writing is?" She means, "What do *I* think good writing is?" In other words, "Read my mind."

Another easy trap for teachers to fall into regarding Explicitness is asking questions in series. Good and Brophy (1978), citing Grossier, describe a teacher who in discussing the War of 1812 asks in one continuous statement, "Why did we go to war? As a merchant how would you feel? How was our trade hurt by the Napoleonic War?" The teacher is trying to clarify his first question and to focus thinking upon an economic cause of the war. In his attempt, he actually confuses.

Questions in series are a temptation whenever we ask a question and get silence back from the whole class. We want to give a clue, so we ask another question that is intended to lead the students toward our focus. What we may accidently do, as above, is jerk students' train of thought around and leave them confused as to what we are really after.

Necessary Steps in Directions

Teachers may direct students to commence tasks but inadvertently leave out necessary steps in the directions. This can happen when we make unwarranted assumptions that students understand the conventions for how certain tasks are done. "Get together in groups of 4 or 5 and brainstorm as many endings as you can for this short story." This teacher has omitted to instruct groups to choose a recorder, and they have all started brainstorming without one.

Another example: "Fix these sentences and then move on to the next assignment." Some students have interpreted "fix" as cross out and write over the words that are wrong (which the teacher, in fact, intends). Others are recopying the entire sentences with the corrections, which is taking four times as long. As a result, they won't have time to finish the second assignment.

The injunction of this sub-parameter is simply to spell out completely what we mean in directions and not assume steps are inherently obvious to students.

Meaning of References

Sometimes teachers make references to famous people, ideas, events, or works which are intended to elucidate current instruction; only the students may not know the references and therefore they confuse rather than clarify. They may, in fact, subtract from instructional effectiveness in this way: while students are being puzzled about the reference and asking themselves what it means, they may miss the next one or two points that are made.

"Reading James Mitchner's *Hawaii* can make one feel like Sisyphus, which becomes apparent by about chapter 25." That sentence won't mean anything to students who don't already know that Sisyphus was a cruel Greek king who was condemned to be forever rolling a huge stone up a hill in Hades, only to have it roll down again every time he neared the top. Therefore to feel like Sisyphus means to feel hopeless about ever finishing.

Being explicit at times like these would not foreclose our using arcane references, but would cue us to explain them on the spot so students could benefit from them.

Reasons for Activities

This form of Explicitness simply means telling students why they are asked to do a particular activity. More particularly, it means explaining why the activity will help them learn something or contribute to a larger learning or task performance. "The reason we're doing this experiment is to show how hard it is to take data and record information simultaneously. You just can't do it. So, like all scientists, we're going to have to 'extrapolate' our readings. Remember that term from the graphs we worked on in the chapter?"

Another example: "The reason we're doing these sentence combining worksheets is so you can use these same techniques to make your own writing more interesting in the adventure stories we're writing."

Explicitness moves of the kind illustrated above build a series of bridges back to objectives from individual activities and between activities themselves.

The Objective

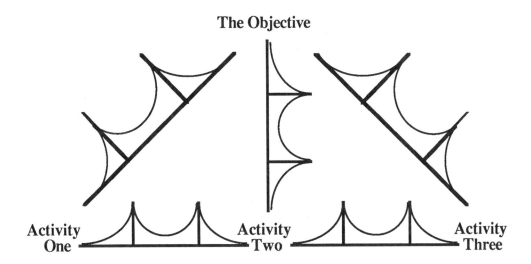

Activity One   Activity Two   Activity Three

Sometimes the move shows students how the current activity fits into patterns of other experiences they've been having or are about to have. "The reason I'm asking you to locate these references in the card catalogue is to build up your speed and check your accuracy. You'll have to use this card catalogue a lot next month when you start your research papers and I won't be around to help much of the time. So you've got to be able to use it independently to find books you want."

Without these explanations, many students do assignments mechanically, with minimal care and investment. They do them because they're "work" and you're supposed to do your work. But the work isn't leading in a meaningful way toward anything they understand. Those of our readers who have worked with learning styles and studied the intriguing work of Bernice McCarthy (1981) and Anthony Gregorc (1979) know that "quadrant one" learners especially need to understand these connections.[3]

We have been discussing moves teachers make to show students how current activities or assignments relate to intended learnings (objectives). That, indeed, is a form of Explicitness. For it to occur, however, students have to know what the objectives are in the first place; otherwise, there's nothing to relate the activity to. Before considering how well and how often we are giving students reasons for activities, we need to ask whether or not we're communicating the learning objectives themselves. This question will be early on our agenda in the following section, The Big Picture.

---

[3] McCarthy has synthesized several significant theorists on learning style into a model that categorizes learners into four main types. These are represented on a visual pie-diagram as four quadrants. One of the learning styles, quadrant one (also called "Innovative Learners"), has a particular need to know why a given learning is taking place. To serve those students well, teachers need to explain *why*.

The Big Picture

The last group of Clarity sub-parameters cluster together around a common mission we have christened "The Big Picture"; it is composed of behaviors which are thought to help students place current information or operations in a larger framework of meaning. These teaching behaviors can be considered in a simple presence/absence, yes/no way. They are:

- communicating what the students will know or be able to do at the end of the upcoming instruction (the objective)

- giving students the itinerary, the list of activities they'll be doing.

- activating current student knowledge about a new concept or curriculum item

- showing resemblance of the old and the new and integrating information into the context of previous work or previous knowledge "demonstrating to students how the things you are talking about resemble what they already know" (Friedrich, p. 78).

- providing transitions between items of information or ideas

- foreshadowing things to come or how present information will fit or relate to future work.

- summarizing.

These behaviors have been included because we or others think they might play a part in a future science of teaching, a future set of laws explaining teaching outcomes. Current research does show a correlation between them and improved student learning; but we cannot definitively claim cause and effect for them yet. One thing we do know, however, is that there are a variety of ways to accomplish each of them; and we know further that the repertoire for doing so has been developed by practitioners. That is where we have gone to discover the repertoires developed below, and indeed, in this whole book. Thus, this effort to assemble the professional knowledge base of our craft, teaching, is clearly dependent on continued partnership between two communities which should be one—teachers and researchers.

Giving Students an Itinerary

An itinerary is a listing or delineation of the steps that will occur over the course of an activity or period. An itinerary is like an agenda or roadmap. It tells where things are going and in what order. For example, it is common to hear a teacher say, "This morning we'll be going over your homework answers and then looking at the material in the new chapter. Then, we'll do some group work on your projects." This is useful for students to know. It gives them a mental sequence to follow and lets them know what to expect.

Communicating What Students Will Know or Be Able to Do (Objective)

Giving students an itinerary for the activities they'll do today is *not* the same as stating the objective of that work. There is nothing wrong with giving kids itineraries; its just that an itinerary is not an objective. Likewise, giving clear directions and outlining what procedures students are going to follow also is *not* the same as stating an objective (giving clear directions and outlining procedures are covered in the "Structuring Learning Experiences" section of Chapter 13). Below is a clear statement of an objective in which the teacher lets students know what they'll be able to do when the instruction is over:

"Today we're going to learn how to write on paper what you've been telling me out loud in math groups—that you have one-half or one-fourth or three-fourths of a whole something. Well, there is a special way of writing numbers that stand for those things and when we're done today you'll be able to use it."

Most teachers have been taught how to say and write behavioral objectives. That language serves a purpose, but it need not be used all the time. The objective may not *be* a detailed behavioral one at all. The example above happens, in fact, to *be* a behavioral objective stated in language to match seven-year-olds (give this teacher a checkmark for "matching" on the speech sub-parameter!). But other language patterns can serve as well. For instance: "We're going to look at this filmstrip and see what we can learn about the personality characteristics of Hemingway the man." Once again, students are oriented toward what they're supposed to know at the end of the lesson. Such statements frame the "big picture," give an overall orientation to what is to follow, a frame that helps the students make sense of subsequent activities. To note "yes" on this sub-parameter, an observer wants to see a teacher appropriately introduce lesson activities with something that casts them within a bigger frame, purpose, or objective, so that the students know what they're going to learn.

Before leaving this discussion of communicating objectives, there is a related but separate area we should consider: communicating to students *why the objective is worthwhile*. This is the "Who cares?" question. As a result of our skill at communicating objectives, students may know exactly what it is about the Viet-Nam War that we want them to understand at the conclusion of the lesson; they just may not think it matters. For some students, understanding the usefulness or relevance to them of a learning objective makes a big difference in their investment. Writing about "quadrant one learners," McCarthy (1981) says:

> Students need reasons to proceed with learning. All students do. But for the Innovative Learners "Why?" is an absolute necessity. It seems simplistic to mention that students need reasons, but they are rarely given. Teachers assume students know that what is taught to them is necessary. Teachers assume *their* reasons are sufficient, that students will value what experts say they should learn. Not so. Students need reasons of their own...Every teaching or training enterprise should begin by creating a desire. Even in adult education, where highly motivated students come for their own personal needs, teachers must give reasons why the program is important. The teacher *must* take the time to discuss what s/he hopes to do and *why*. Giving them a reason, a need of their own for proceeding, is so simple and fundamental that one can only marvel that it is not done. [McCarthy, 1981, pp. 92, 94]

Thus it would be particularly important for some learners (and useful to all) to know our reasons for wanting them to know the principal causes of the Viet-Nam War and our involvement. "The reason this is important to us is that the Viet-Nam War has causes in common with many other wars in history. If this country enters another war, it's very likely that many of you will be drafted into the Armed Services and have to fight. Therefore it will be important to you as citizens to be able to follow current events and the decisions of your leaders in government to see where we're headed. As citizens, you can make informed choices in voting for leaders who stand for policies you want. Our study here will help you decide in the future what you think we should fight for as a country—and at some point that choice is sure to be yours."

While not so dramatic as topics, we might be equally clear about why it is worthwhile learning geometric proofs; studying myth as a literary genre; or learning to identify by their attributes igneous, sedimentary, and metamorphic rocks.

Giving reasons for learning something isn't an event that should happen with every lesson. Most lessons are taking students one increment further or developing skill one degree higher on a particular objective. At the beginning of new units or topics, however, giving reasons for our objectives can be very appropriate.

Preparing to deliver these reasons to students can be a useful exercise for us as teachers, too. If we can't give a good reason for learning something, maybe we shouldn't be teaching it.

Activating Students' Current Knowledge About a Concept
Techniques that activitate students' current knowledge about a concept or topic not only tune them in to what's coming, but prevent the dreaded "Charlie Brown Syndrome!":

Recall what Charley Brown does when he gets a new book. Before he even looks at the book, he counts pages—625 pages—"I'll never learn all that!" He is defeated before he starts, before he has had a chance to realize that he does not have to learn *all* that. It is not all new. He already knows something about it. He has not given himself the chance to learn what he already knows about what he is supposed to know. [McNeill, 1984, p. 34]

What we want to do, in one way or another, is ask kids this question: "What do you already know about X?"...and record (or get them indivi-dually to record) what they come up with. As the concept or topic is developed, the teachers can go back to these initial lists or charts to compare what students learned with their original ideas. Sometimes, students find themselves fitting new learning into old charts, sometimes they find parts of their old conceptions contradicted. But in any event, having created an image of what they already know about a topic places before them a map against which they bounce (and into which they put) our new information. It is in this way that we are serving the "big picture."

Numerous techniques have been developed to accomplish activation of current knowledge. One is *semantic mapping*. McNeill (1984) provides the following description:

Begin by asking pupils what they think of when they hear the word X (X is the topic they are about to read about). Free association is desirable. As pupils offer their associations, list the responses on the chalkboard. Try to put the associations into categories.

For example, responses to *money* might be categorized into uses of money, kinds of money, denominations, consequences of having money, ways of earning, and other associations. Help the pupils label the categories and then ask them to read the selection to learn more about X. It is fine to encourage pupils to pose their own questions about what they want to learn about X from the text. Next, after reading the selection, the class gives attention to the set of categories and prereading questions related to X. Pupils at this time add new ideas acquired from their reading, correcting and augmenting the original map. [McNeill, 1984, p. 10]

Note that McNeill's description is of a semantic mapping exercise prior to reading a selection of text. But it could be used equally well before doing an experiment, viewing a film, or interviewing a guest. The point is that the teachers are getting students ready for new information by calling up their own maps (or "schemata" as the researchers would say) of what they already know about the topic. The effect is to make students more active listeners, watchers, and readers.

Other techniques like semantic mapping have been developed by practitioners and researchers in the reading and language fields and are well worth study by teachers from all disciplines. They have in common the effect of getting students cognitively active in relation to new in-coming information.

Showing Resemblance to Something Students Already Know

It is useful when teachers show how new learnings resemble previous work or students' previous knowledge, "demonstrating to students how things you are talking about resemble what they already know" (Freidrich, 1976). (Later we will see that this move is a labelled step in the Advance Organizer Model of Teaching. But it is appropriate to make this move within many styles of teaching or simple explaining as a good clarifier.) Below are some examples of this move.

[Comments in parentheses are student responses.] The teacher says, "When we first worked on multiplying you learned that it was related to addition...how?" (Repeated addition.) "Right! Meaning what?" (Multiplying is like adding the same number over and over again...as many times as you're multiplying it by.) "Okay, very good. Now this division operation we've been working on today is really a lot like multiplication, except what it's doing in short-cut fashion isn't *adding* a number over and over again, it's...what?" (Subtracting it.) "Right! Everybody see that? Jimmy?" [Score *yes* on 'Checking' for this teacher!] "Can you explain in your own words how division is like multiplication?" [Score *yes* on 'Comprehension Questions'!] (It's the backwards of multiplying.) "An interesting way to put it; I think you understand. Margie, what do you think Jimmy means by backwards? [Score *yes* on 'Comprehension Questions'!]

Here's another example from a beginning chemistry course. The teacher says, "So we've proven this welding torch burns hotter than the straight propane burner. Do you remember what we did at the beginning of the year, heating sodium chlorate in the test tube? What happened when we held a glowing ember over the tube?" (It burst into flame.) "How did we explain that?" (Heating the sodium chlorate drove off oxygen and the oxygen made the ember burn faster and hotter.) "Right! And a welding torch is like that. We've got these two tanks..." [teacher goes on to show how a welding rig mixes two gases, acetylene and oxygen, and that the presence of the extra oxygen vastly increases combustion temperatures].

The integrating of the old with the new that takes place on this sub-parameter builds intellectual links between items of information in such a way as to deliberately keep the picture of the whole emerging chain visible too. As students learn the new item, the new link, they simultaneously see the whole chain that is now one link longer. The link and chain analogy may break down for bodies of information that relate in other ways—like a web, for example—but the Clarity move serves the same purpose...linking the new item with the larger picture of established knowns (Ausubel, 1968; Gagne, 1974).

The difference between this principle and "Activating Students' Current Knowledge" is this: "Activating..." looks forward. It gets up on screen, as it were, students' present conceptions. Thus, their minds are warmed up and they have something to compare and contrast with the new learning when it comes along. What they already have "on-line" may or may not be accurate, may be complete or incomplete. The purpose of bringing it up is to get them in gear and give them a reference point to test against the new learning. They may ask themselves: Is what we learn about chemistry, indeed, what we thought chemistry to be?

The purpose of "Showing Resemblance to Something Students Already Know," on the other hand, is to look backward. The teacher wants students to see that the new learning coming up isn't really so new or different (or so hard); and he wants them to see that the new learning fits in with something they already know—that there already exists a structure or a continuum in their heads to accomodate it.

Providing Cognitive Transitions

These are brief, within-lesson transitions we're talking about here, and mostly applicable to direct instruction situations. (The teacher doesn't have the opportunity to guide transitions between items of information unless the teacher is leading the instructional activity.) In terms of Clarity, these moves are verbal markers that help the student follow the road map as the teacher makes a left turn here, a right turn there, or circles back to the point of origin. For instance: "Okay, that word problem required us to multiply. Now let's move on to the next one and see if it is the same."

Notice the difference between that remark and a teacher who simply says, "Okay, let's move on to the next problem." Telling the students to move on gets them from one place to the next sure enough, but does not provide a transition. A Clarity "transition" move takes something about what's just been done and relates it to what's coming up immediately. It provides intellectual links like "integrating" moves do, but instead of linking to the learner's past experience, or to learning from other disciplines or other times, "cognitive transitions" link is to what's come immediately before in the lesson.

Here's a good example: "So that's how the commercial banking system multiplies money deposited in checking accounts and creates new money. Now another way new money gets created is through consumer credit. Let's look at how all those plastic credit cards add to the banking system to create even more money."

Foreshadowing

Consider these two teacher statements:

"Well, you couldn't *have* two hydrochloric acid molecules on that side of the equation because it wouldn't balance. You don't have to worry about that now, but soon we will get to this notion that chemical equations must balance. When we talk about balancing equations, we'll be experimenting with the proportions of different chemicals that get used up in chemical reaction."

"...And if you think Laura worked hard helping Ma around the house, wait till you see what she did with Pa Ingalls around haymaking time. ('What's that mean?' a student asks.) Well, that's harvesting the hay, and that was a very important part of farm life then...now too. Anyway, haymaking is coming up in a couple of chapters. I think you'll enjoy that section."

These examples of foreshadowing take a term or an idea that crops up and create a brief image of what it will be like or what it will be about. This is done so that when the students get to that point, it's not totally strange territory. "Oh, I remember we talked about that last week," a student may say to himself, and start assimilating the ideas into his cognitive framework. Foreshadowing moves may crop up as moments of opportunity during instruction, and are often unplanned. For instance, in the case of our second example above, the students had commented on how hard Laura works around the house, and their remarks made the teacher think of the days of hard labor she spent with her father making hay, so she brought it up for comparative purposes, knowing it's coming up in a few chapters.

When teachers end a lesson with an introduction of a forecast of what the students will be doing next, that is foreshadowing of a kind, but we tend to see that kind of a move as a "cognitive transition." The difference is that a "cognitive transition" makes direct links between what's just been completed and what's immediately to come in the flow of instruction—even if 'immediately' is interrupted by overnight. "Foreshadowing" puts intellectual markers or hooks in place for items that are down the road and will not be dealt with the very next time the students work on this subject.

Summarizing

Teachers don't always summarize themselves; sometimes they ask a student to do it. It doesn't matter how it gets done; if somehow someone explicitly pulls everything together at the end of a lesson for all to see or hear, then summarizing has taken place and "yes" can be noted for the teacher on this twelfth sub-parameter of clarity.[4]

When students do the summarizing themselves, and when all of the students are involved in doing so simultaneously, two other powerful factors are added. First, the principle of learning called Active Participation is engaged (see Chapter 8). Second, students must get cognitively active with the material; they have to personally *reorganize* the information and concepts they have received so that they can state them in their own words. Asking students to do the summarizing inherently means asking them to say what they have learned in their own words. (It also means having to check their summarizing to see that it is accurate and complete.) It is that "in your own words" feature that is critical because it forces the learners to

---

[4] Asking students to make up a quiz on the important points covered in the class gets them *all* involved in summarizing nicely.

sift, reorder, and organize the information themselves. They can't just let the new learning lie on the library shelf of their minds as a memory trace. They have to pick up the pieces and put them together; and the very act of doing so strengthens the learning.

There are many ways to accomplish this summarizing so that all of the students get involved. Keeping a learning log (Pradl and Mayher, 1985) is one way.

> Typically, students make entries during the last five minutes of each period, responding to the following types of questions:
>> What did I learn today? What puzzled me?
>> What did I enjoy, hate, accomplish in class today?
>> How did I learn from the discussion or lesson?
>> How was my performance in class? [Sanders, 1985]

Teachers can also ask students to do this orally, in pairs at the end of class, or at appropriate stopping points within class. Mary Budd Rowe has demonstrated that students' retention increases when 2 minutes is provided for students to summarize and clarify for each other in small groups after every 10 minutes of teacher-led instruction. This "10-2" rule provides students the same kind of opportunity to get active with the material *in their own words*. Tobin (1985) comments, "The results [of this technique] are consistent with our interpretation that students need time to process lesson content in information-dense subjects such as science."

Summarizing questions can be made specific and tailored to any content: "Based on our discussion so far, tell your partner the principal causes of the Civil War. Then have your partner tell them back to you." If the class has reached consensus on the causes, this is a summarizing of the information. (If the class has not resolved the question, having pairs dialogue like this is more than summarizing—especially if they are asked to back up their respective arguments.) Additionally, a teacher may ask students to summarize in writing (perhaps in notebooks) the main idea of each section in textbook chapters. Having to stop and summarize periodically as one reads forces the kind of active cognitive processing we talked about above; you have to put it in your own words to write a summary—*Voila*, better learning! Studies have shown improved comprehension of text (not just stories) with convincing consistency (e.g., D'Angelo, 1983). And a number of writers have even offered useful models for *teaching* students how to do this summarizing-in-writing as they read (Hahn and Gardner, 1985).

In this chapter we described two behaviors that had to do with a teacher's cognitive empathy for students; we called them "Checking" (for finding out *when* students lose the thread of meaning) and "Unscrambling Confusions" (for finding out *where*, and fixing it). We were able to discriminate several different qualitative kinds of performance on both those sub-parameters. Then, we added an index of how many and which Explanatory Devices a teacher uses, and analyses of teacher Speech patterns and Explicitness behaviors. Finally, we described six teacher moves that help to clarify The Big Picture for students: Giving Itineraries; Communicating Objectives; Activating Students' Current Knowledge; Showing How New Knowledge is Like Something Students Already Know; Providing Cognitive Transitions Between Ideas; and Foreshadowing. Each of these is a functional aspect of the Clarity parameter.

We've just summarized the chapter. And that's the twelfth Clarity move—Summarizing. Can you now summarize what has been new learning for you in this chapter?

On the next pages we have provided a Quiz as a means for you to review, by yourself or with a colleague, the moves of the Clarity parameter.

Clarity Quiz

Read the following excerpts from classroom lessons. In the margin, label the Clarity move represented by each episode or quote.

1. A student has gotten several double-digit multiplication problems wrong on his homework assignment. The teacher goes to his seat: "It looks like you might be having difficulty with this type of math problem. Talk me through this one so I can see how you did it."

2. Physical education teacher to volleyball class (15 minutes into class): "To get better at receiving serves and not being afraid of the ball, we've been working this morning on tosses and bumps. Now we're going to concentrate on bumps and make it more realistic. We're going to set up a back row and play a game where you put that skill with bumps to work."

3. Teacher to class: "This period you are going to have a chance to work on your reading logs; then we are going to work with more problems that require careful reading. At the end of the period you'll have a chance to write your own careful reading problem."

4. A student is working on a chemistry lab experiment. The teacher comes by and asks, "Is this partially or totally dissolved?" (Student responds.) "Yes. Now what does that mean?"

5. Teacher to class: "Before we begin our study of the United States during the Great Depression, let's brainstorm all the things we already know about the Depression, plus the things we *think* we know, and the things we need to know. When you contribute a piece of information, just let us know which category it fits into."

6. Teacher to class: "Raise your hands when you get the answer to this problem on the board." (Teacher circulates while students are working.)

   OR

   Teacher to class: "Raise your hands if you have encountered a bug in your writing project." (Teacher takes down the names of the students she should get to during the period.)

7. A student's brow is furrowed while pausing over his work. The teacher walks over to him and asks, "Is something puzzling you?"

8. Teacher to class: "Before you begin translating today's date into a Roman date, be sure you remember how the Romans counted backwards. "OK, let's start with yours, Tim."

9. Teacher to class at end of defining 'Transcendence': "So that, in brief, is what it means. We haven't seen it a lot in the literature so far, but we're going to be talking about it when we get to poets. So be on the lookout for that term; we'll be returning to it.

10. Teacher, standing by seedling box, to class: "We've been measuring our seedlings and will have to come up with a class average eventually. So this morning our math worksheet will help us get ready for that. This morning in math we're going to spend some time on averaging to give you some practice in doing it."

11. Teacher to class: "So there *was* a real turning point in the American Revolution. What's the date we're looking for?" (Teacher waves in general direction of the blackboard on which the date is written.) (No student response.) "David just said it." (No response.) "Look at the board." (Students reply.)

12. A student has been a bit overwhelmed by what seems like so many steps in math word problems. The teacher sits down with her to go over some problems: "Here's how I solved this problem; follow along and see if you did the same thing: Let's see...it says, 'Ten full boxes of detergent weigh 100 lbs. The detergent alone weighs 90 lbs. How much does each box weigh alone?'...okay. That's without the detergent...what can I figure out here...hmm...if the total weight is 100 lbs. and the detergent alone is 90 lbs.,...hmm...I can subtract 90 from 100 and get the total box weight. Okay, that would be 10. Now...what does the problem want? Oh, the weight of *each* box. Well, if 10 is the total box weight and there are 10 boxes...I can divide 10 by 10. I get one. So that's it...one pound per box."

13. Teacher to class: "We've worked on a large number of problems during this unit and learned a number of different tips for solving them. Let's come up with a class list of all the problem-solving strategies that we've found to be effective during this unit."

14. A student has gotten a math problem wrong on a homework paper. The teacher, working with him, asks, "Let's see where you went wrong here. How many cubes did you count?" ("Six.") "That's okay. How many sides does each cube have?" ("Six...Oh!") "What number did you use for the number of sides?" ("Three.") "So that's where you broke down. Remember each cube

has six sides, so six cubes would have six times six sides or 36 sides altogether. Do you see where you went wrong?"

15. Teacher to class: "Remember when we developed criteria for judging presidents and then you each chose a president to evaluate using those criteria? Well, today we're going to do something similar. We're going to be developing criteria for judging legislation and then you'll evaluate a specific bill based on those criteria."

16. A student had consistently cross-divided instead of cross-multiplied on his algebra homework assignment the night before. Before the period began, the teacher went over the work with the student who appeared to understand what he had done wrong. Even though the class was focusing on another algebra concept that day, the teacher called on this student twice during the period when the process involved cross-multiplying.

17. Teacher to class: "I'm going to be giving you a fable for you to read and do some work on. Something will be missing from the fable; what do you suppose is missing?" ("Dialogue?") "No. Some element in a fable that's always in a fable and is missing." ("Setting?") "No." ("Plot?") "No." ("Moral?") "Right. You are going to have to figure out the moral."

18. Teacher to class: "I want to see if you really understand how photosynthesis works. What's the name of the substance in plants that makes them green?" ("Chlorophyll.") "Good. What does the prefix 'photo' mean?" ("Light.") "Great. In order to grow, plants need to be exposed to what?" ("Carbon dioxide.") "Super! You *do* understand. Let's move on to...."

Checking on Clarity

Examine your own teaching, or that of another, and see which of the following apply. For each behavior or level of performance that you credit, see if you can cite an example to back it up.

COGNITIVE EMPATHY: Circle the behavior(s) or the level of performance observed.

1. Explanatory Devices:

    charts or chalkboard   translation into simpler language   mental imagery
    analogies   physical models   simple cues
    A-V materials   progressive minimal cues   diagrams
    modeling thinking aloud   highlights important information

2. Checking:

    presses on   uses recall questions
      read cues   uses comprehension questions
        "dipsticks"   anticipates confusions

3. Unscrambling Confusions of Students:

    none   perseveres and returns
      re-explains   has student explain own current thinking
        isolates point of confusion
        with pinpoint questions

4. Speech:

    unacceptable   matched to group
      acceptable   matched to individual
        variety

5. Explicitness. Expressly communicating and not leaving to implication:

    intention of cues   meaning of references
    focus of questions   reasons for activities
    necessary steps in directions

THE BIG PICTURE: Check any of these that are observed.
6. ___ Gives Itinerary
7. ___ Communicates What Students Will Know or Be Able to Do
8. ___ Activates Students' Current Knowledge About Concept
9. ___ Shows Resemblance to Something Students Already Know
10. ___ Makes Transitions Between Ideas
11. ___ Foreshadows
12. ___ Summarizes

Source Materials on This Parameter

Anderson, L.M., Evertson, C.M. and Brophy, J.E. "An Examination of Classroom Context: Effects of Lesson Format and Teacher Training on Patterns of Teacher Student Contacts during Small-group Instruction." *Journal of Classroom Interaction*, 15/2, Summer 1980, 21-26.

Ausubel, D.P. *Educational Psychology: A Cognitive View.* New York: Holt, Rinehart & Winston, 1968.

Belgard, M., Rosenshine, B. and Gage, N.L. "The Teacher's Effectiveness in Explaining: Evidence on its Generality and Correlation with Pupils Ratings and Attention Score." In Westbury, I. and Bellack, A. *(eds.), Research into Classroom Processes.* New York: Teachers College Press, 1971, 182-191.

Brophy, J. "Teacher Praise: A Functional Analysis." *Review of Educational Research*, Spring 1981, 51/1, 5-32.

Bush, A.J., Kennedy, J.J. and Cruickshank, D.R. "An Empirical Investigation of Teacher Clarity." *Journal of Teacher Education*, 1977, 28/2, 53-58.

Cooper, C. "Different Ways of Being a Teacher: An Ethnographic Study of College Instructors Academic and Social Roles in the Classroom." *Journal of Classroom Interaction*, 1980, 16/2, 27-36.

Costa, A. *Teaching for Intelligent Behavior.* Orangevale, CA: Search Models Unlimited, 1985.

D'Angelo, K. "Precis Writing: Promoting Vocabulary Development and Comprehension." *Journal of Reading*, March 1983, 534-539.

Davey, B. "Think Aloud—Modeling the Cognitive Processes of Reading Comprehension." *Journal of Reading*, October 1983, 44-47.

Duckworth, E. "Understanding Children's Understanding." Paper based on talk given at the Ontario Institute for Studies in Education, February 1981.

Dunkin, M.J and Biddle, B.J. *The Study of Teaching.* New York: Holt, Rinehart & Winston, 1974.

Eaton, J.F., Anderson, C.W. and Smith, E.L. "Students' Misconceptions Interfere with Science Learning: Case Studies of Fifth-Grade Students." *Elementary School Journal*, 1984, 84/4, 365-379.

Escondido School District. *Minds Eye*. Escondido, CA: Board of Education, 1979.

Fortune, J.C., Gage, N.L. and Shute, R.E. "The Generality of the Ability to Explain." Paper presented at the A.E.R.A. Convention, Chicago, 1966.

Friedrich, G.W., Galvin, K.M. and Book, C.L. *Growing Together: Classroom Communication*. Columbus, OH: Charles Merrill, 1976.

Gage, N.L. "Exploration of Teachers' Effectiveness in Explaining." Tech Report No. 4. Stanford, CA: Stanford University Center for Research and Development in Teaching, 1961. EDO28 147.

Gagne, R.M. *The Essentials of Learning for Instruction*. Hinsdale, IL: Dryden Press, 1974.

Gregorc, A. "Learning/Teaching Styles: Potent Faces Behind Them." *Educational Leadership,* January 1979.

Good, T.H. and Brophy, J.E. *Looking in Classrooms*. New York: Harper and Row, 1978.

Graham, S. "Teacher Feelings and Student Thoughts: An Attributional Approach to Affect in the Classroom." *Elementary School Journal*, 85/1, 91-104.

Hahn, A.L. and Gardner, R. "Synthesis of Research on Students' Ability to Summarize Text." *Educational Leadership*, February 1985, 52-55.

Hiller, J.H., Fisher, G.A. and Kaess, W.A. "A Computer Investigation of Verbal Characteristics of Effective Classroom Lecturing." *American Educational Research Journal*, 1969, 6, 661-675.

Joos, M. *The Five Clocks*. New York: Harcourt Brace, 1967.

Martin, J. *Explaining, Understanding, and Teaching*. New York: McGraw-Hill, 1970.

McCaleb, J.L. and White, J.A. "Critical Dimensions in Evaluating Teacher Clarity." *The Journal of Classroom Interaction*, 1980, 15/2, 27-30.

McCarthy, B. *The 4MAT System*. Barrington, IL: Excel, Inc., 1981.

Mehan, H. "Accomplishing Classroom Lessons." In Cicouril, S.V. *(ed.), Language Use and School Performance*. New York: Academic Press, 1974.

McNeill, J.D. *Reading Comprehension: New Directions for Classroom Practice.* Glenview, IL: Scott, Foresman and Company, 1984.

Peterson, P. and Swing, S. "Beyond Time on Task: Students' Reports of their Thought Processes during Classroom Instruction." *Elementary School Journal*, 1982, 82/5, 481-491.

Pradl, G.M. and Mayher, J.S. "Reinvigorating Learning Through Writing." *Educational Leadership*, February 1985, 4-8.

Pressley, G.M. "Mental Imagery Helps Eight-Year Olds Remember What They Read." *Journal of Educational Psychology*, 1976, 68, 355-59.

Pressley, G.M. "Imagery and Children's Learning: Putting the Picture in Developmental Perspective. *Review of Educational Research*, 1977, 47, 585-622.

Rosenshine, B. and Furst, N. "The Use of Direct Observation to Study Teaching." In Travers, R.M. (*ed.*), *Second Handbook of Research on Teaching*, Chicago: Rand McNally, 1973.

Rowe, M.B. "Getting Chemistry off the Killer Course List," *Journal of Chemical Education*, 1983, 60/11, 954-956.

Sanders, A. "Learning Logs: A Communication Strategy for All Subject Areas." *Educational Leadership*, February 1985, 7.

Smith, L.R. and Land, M.L. "Low-Inference Verbal Behaviors Related to Teacher Clarity." *Journal of Classroom Interaction*, 1981, 17/1, 37-42.

Tobin, K. "Wait-time in Science—Necessary But Insufficient." Paper presented at the annual meeting of the National Association for Research in Science Teaching, French Lick Springs, IN, April 1985.

Winne, P.H. and Marx, R.W. "Students' and Teachers' Views of Thinking Processes for Classroom Learning." *Elementary School Journal*, 1982, 82/5, 492-518.

Special Note

Thanks to Hal Manley of Concord-Carlisle Regional High School and to Richard Deppe of the Carlisle Public Schools for assistance in generating examples of Clarity behaviors.

Principles of Learning

How do I make lessons more efficient and effective?

24 Packages of Power

PRINCIPLES OF LEARNING

This chapter describes 24 little packages of power—each package self-contained and ready for use by itself, each a possible addition to your teaching repertoire, and each certain to increase the rate and permanence of students' learning. A strong claim? Perhaps, but for once in education, a certain one.

What do these names mean to you: Pavlov, Thorndike, Hull, Watson, Guthrie, Mowrer, Spence, Tolman, Skinner?

We don't hear much about them these days. These are men who approached learning as a phenomenon about which universal laws might be deduced, operating principles discovered. And they discovered quite a few of them. The tradition of their research goes back to 1880 (Ebbinghaus) and is the strongest, longest, and soundest base we have in education for "how-to" recommendations. Taken together, their principles do not add up to a cohesive theory or approach to how to teach like we get from some of the moderns (Bruner, Ausubel, Piaget). Instead, these principles *each* were shown in their own way to make a contribution to learning effectiveness, and they lie scattered about the literature like so many precious stones waiting to be picked up. Many of them were collected in the 1970s and put into accessible form for teachers by Madeline Hunter and her associates (*Teach More, Faster* is an exemplary title of one of her books for teachers). But somehow these principles have not become part of the currency either of in-service teacher training or of college teacher education.

As you read this chapter you will recognize some of these principles from your own teaching. We find that most teachers routinely use six or seven of them intuitively, without knowing the labels you will learn for them as you read here. Some teachers use more, some less. We have yet to find a teacher who uses them all, however, and so believe that there is something new in this chapter for everyone.

We have been able to identify 24 of these principles in the literature (see such sources as Hilgard and Bower, 1966; Bugelski, 1971; Hudgins, 1977 for useful summaries and extensions of the principles). By studying them and looking for opportunities to use one or two new ones, you—we—anybody can expand our repertoire and improve student learning.

Later in this book we will study different "models of teaching" and explore both how to do them and what their different aims and theoretical bases are. When we get to models, we will be looking at teaching like a playwright looks at a script—we'll look at the design and sequence of the whole lesson and what discrete teacher moves have to do with the overall design of a particular kind of learning. We won't refer to any of these principles of learning then, but we won't be invalidating them either. They're always there, and always relevant.

Now, we will take up each of these principles in turn.

Meaning

The more meaningful and relevant the task or application of information is to the students' world, the easier it is to learn. Teachers using this principle may make explicit references to students' personal experiences as a tie or a hook for connecting content with students' lives; or they may actually simulate the experiences in the learning activity, or in some other way embed the new content in the students' meaning framework. One teacher using the principle gave us the following example:

> "The goal is to understand the difference between chronology and history.
> I do a two-part assignment. For one day, students are asked to keep a time line of their activities. The next day they are to write a narrative history of the one day for which they kept the time line, showing, where possible, cause and effect relationships."

This assignment makes a nice distinction between chronology and history around a context that has intimate personal meaning for the students...their own day's activities.

Similarity of Environment

Similarity of environment (actions, feelings, formats, routines) elicits the learner's "set to perform." This principle holds that certain features of the environment, when regularly associated with a particular type of learning or a period in which a particular type of attention or work is expected, trigger a mind-set in learners which "plugs them in," turns on their operators for that particular kind of lesson or activity.

Therefore, teachers can regularly use repetitive formats for certain kinds of learning—when the environment assumes certain space, time, and routine features—to create expectational mind-sets in their pupils for that kind of work. In addition, teachers may "warm up" students for a lesson by doing an activity that starts them thinking the way they'll be asked to in the lesson. For instance, suppose a teacher is going to do a lesson on outlining. Outlining requires students to categorize their ideas into topical groups. So, the teacher may warm up the class by playing Guess-My-Category: The teacher slowly develops the lists below on the board, writing the teams one at a time in the order indicated, under "yes" for positive examples of the category and "no" for negative examples. The students must guess the category to which the "yes" examples belong ("champions").

	YES	NO
	1. Lakers	2. Orioles
1986-87	3. N.Y. Mets	4. Bruins
Teams	5. N.Y. Giants	6. New Orleans Saints
	7. Dallas Cowboys	8. Seattle Mariners

When the game is over, the teacher says, "Now, the kind of thinking we were doing here is similar to what we have to do in this outlining activity for today. Take out your note cards and..."

Doug Russell (1980) points out that the above activity is also an excellent "sponge" for students arriving in class (see the Momentum parameter). It gets them involved with a meaningful activity right off the mark, yet does not penalize those who haven't arrived yet...eliminates down-time and waiting.

Contiguity

Events, objects, operations, and emotions close to each other in time and space tend to become associated in the mind of the learner. A first association, once learned, is hard to unlearn—whether it's calling Mary Ann, *Mary Lou* the first time you meet her, and finding yourself doing so every time thereafter; or adding the tens column first and then the ones, and finding that a hard habit to break.

Learners should not be allowed to practice errors and build an incorrect association. Students who practice footnotes in the wrong format the first time find that the wrong model interferes with the right one when they finally learn it. (Twenty years later one of the authors is still getting confused over the order of elements in a footnote, because he hasn't completely expunged the wrong model he was allowed to practice one night in homework with no corrective feedback!)

Thus, the implication for teachers is to anticipate errors where they are likely to occur; prevent these errors, even by giving the right answer where appropriate (e.g., a new sight word) *before* a student has a chance to guess wrongly (and thus learn a wrong association which must later be unlearned). Teachers should never allow a student to leave a learning situation with a wrong answer: let the last response that occurs be correct (for associative learning tasks at any rate).

Teachers should also be on the watch for potential negative *emotional* associations students may form. For example, students coming in to class after a recess full of fighting and negative emotions, who are then introduced to a new topic, may form negative associations with the topic that will interfere with future learning. This is not the time to introduce poetry for the first time. The teacher might preface the introduction to the topic with a brief activity that raises positive feelings in students.

Close Confusers

Insure an adequate degree of original learning before "close confusers" are introduced. Teachers following this principle are careful not to confuse or weaken recently learned items—say, the letter "d"—by introducing new items easily confused with it—the letter "b". In this example, the primary teacher will go on to "t", then maybe "f", then some other letters, all the while reviewing "d" in the expanding set of letters recognized, and then finally introduce "b" as a new letter when "d" has been thoroughly learned and practiced. To generalize the statement of this principle in other terms, teachers should not sequence new material so as to require fine discriminations between two contiguous terms when grosser discriminations can be used first. The making of fine discriminations can be demanded when at least one item of the content pair has had adequate opportunity to be thoroughly learned. (Note that textbooks unfortunately often introduce close confusers at the same time: e.g., rotation and revolution of the earth, or weathering and erosion.)

Likewise, exceptions to rules are not to be introduced until original rules are practiced and established sufficiently. Mindful of this principle, a secondary teacher writes:

> Constitutional law is a central part of any middle school social studies curricula. Instruction frequently involves explanations of the Bill of Rights, including illustrations of case law. For example, "freedom of speech" is usually tackled by considering yelling "fire" in a crowded theater. Before a teacher can realistically ask students to distinguish between acceptable and unacceptable forms of "free speech" he must be sure that they have a grounding in the basic concepts, including the important case law. Once they have this they can examine more complex situations.

Isolation of Critical Attributes

Teachers who practice this principle identify explicitly the critical unvarying attributes/elements of the item under study, and label them. Particularly with regard to definitions of new concepts, they isolate the qualities or *attributes essential to the concept*, attributes "without which, it is not" (without which the object is not the object but something else). In comparing two similar concepts (e.g., tattling and reporting), one may see the teacher develop two parallel lists of attributes and compare them. For tattling and reporting, they will be identical except for one item: intent. Intent (to get someone in trouble as opposed to giving needed information) is the critical attribute that discriminates tattling from reporting. What is the critical attribute that discriminates prejudice from discrimination? What are the critical attributes that define an estuary (clue: there are four)?[1]

When teachers highlight items as "important," that is *not* isolation of critical attributes. Highlighting is highlighting! Things can be important without being critical attributes. These four formulas may be the most important things to know in the chapter; these three events may be the most important things to know about the month preceeding the Civil War; but neither set of important things are the critical attributes of anything. Highlighting important items is something teachers do deliberately and usefully to focus students' attention on more important items. But that is quite different from identifying the definitional attributes of a concept.

In exploring the difference between a "developed" and an "underdeveloped country," the teacher may highlight certain critical attributes which define "developed"...e.g., mechanized planting and harvesting, efficient national market distribution system, infrastructure of highways and transportation networks. It is not enough, however, for this list of attributes to simply be presented (in the text...on the board). The teacher must see to it that the critical attributes are generated, call the students' attention to them (or elicit them from the students), and then have students *apply* the attributes in deciding which cases (here, what countries) do or do not contain those critical attributes.

When students can, on their own, apply their ability to discriminate developed from underdeveloped countries through analysis of critical attributes to *new settings*, to studies of countries where they're not specifically asked to look at them as developed versus underdeveloped, then we know this learning has transferred...and that brings us to our next principle.

Teach for Transfer (From Setting to Setting)

We know this principle is at work when we see teachers create a series of assignments or tasks in which the call for using a skill is progressively distanced from direct instructional settings.

---

[1] Answer: a) at outlet of a river; b) fan or delta shaped; c) silty deposits; d) brackish water (part salt-part fresh). All four of the above are necessary to have an estuary. Absence of any of them means you've got something else; therefore all four are critical or essential attributes.

Here is a good example of teaching for transfer. After defining fact ("that which is immediately verifiable by the senses, or that upon which most experts in the field would agree") versus opinion ("a belief; evidence exists to support differing beliefs"), the teacher has students label examples as fact or opinion: e.g., "Mary is wearing a sweater."; "Mary is the prettiest girl in the class." Examples get more and more difficult over time ("Some people believe in reincarnation.") until students are asked to generate the examples themselves. Then, they are asked to bring in newspaper articles (a new setting) which they are expected to analyze for fact and opinion. Finally, students are given cues to transfer their skill to settings where it isn't an assignment to distinguish fact from opinion—like text readings. (This example is based on Madeline Hunter's *Teach For Transfer*, 1971.)

Sometimes we don't need to do anything extra for transfer to occur...it happens by itself. If we have taught children to borrow in subtraction and they know how to do it, they will probably "transfer" that skill to the supermarket that very afternoon when buying supplies for a class party. But for many skills transfer will not happen spontaneously. We need to engineer a series of events that will induce it. And the final event in the chain, the actual "transfer" of the skill to a new context is one students take by themselves. That is what makes understanding this principle a bit tricky. We take students along a planned series of steps up to the edge of the water, but they have to jump in themselves for there to be evidence that transfer has actually occurred.

Mrs. Crane is teaching her junior high students about "characterization." They look at pieces of dialog and physical actions of characters in stories to see what these pieces of behavior reveal about the characters. The objective is to learn to recognize how authors develop readers' images and understandings of characters through dialog and physical actions. But in the long term, Mrs. Crane wants her students to be able to use "characterization" in everyday life, that is, to "read" people they encounter, to make inferences about what they are feeling and thinking from bits of dialog and physical actions the students observe. She wants them, in other words, to *transfer* their ability to recognize "characterization" as a literary device to their own ability to use it in understanding people they meet. So after analyzing the text in novels for "characterization," she assigns students to watch one of their favorite T.V. programs; they are to take down bits of dialog or describe physical actions they see that are in some way indicative of the character's personality. Later in the week her students are asked to bring in examples of "characterization" from their observations of people in their neighborhoods or their family. She is, thus, progressively distancing their use of "characterization" from the academic context of novels they are reading and pressing them to use the skill in ever closer approximations of real life.

If students have learned to read novels and plays for authors' biases, transfer has occurred if they then read nonfiction and magazine articles the same way. Teachers encourage this kind of transfer by proper sequencing of assignments and by pressing students to be aware of the multiple applications of their learnings. This principle is easily confusable with (but different from) Application in Setting, where a skill taught in an abstract setting is put to use right away in a realistic one. That principle goes as follows.

Application in Setting (From Skill to Setting)

Students should practice new behaviors or skills in the settings and in the way those learnings will be used in life. Thus, spelling will more likely transfer to composition if spelling tests embed new words in sentences (perhaps from dictation). The ability to listen to others will transfer to real discussions and to conflict resolutions if practiced in class meetings and real or simulated disagreements. Notice that we used the word "transfer" in both of these examples. Application in Setting is a principle which, when applied, makes it more likely that transfer will occur. As *part* of Teaching for Transfer one is likely to see several instances of Application in Setting. Application in Setting is something we see and give as a label to single instance activities which are having students use a skill in some real-life context—like identifying and labeling logical fallacies (e.g., the "straw man" fallacy) in arguments of current political candidates. But to claim Teaching for Transfer itself, we would have to see a *series* of such activities deliberately orchestrated so as to progressively distance the skill from abstract academic contexts. And each one of them singly may, indeed, have been by itself an example of Application in Setting.

Vividness

The vividness, liveliness, energy, novelty, or striking imagery of a learning experience is thought to more deeply impress new learning on students...perhaps through mediation of the attentional mechanisms. One can claim this principle to be in operation by virtue of observed student reaction to learning experiences, the "ooh...aah" reactions, the high level of arousal or emotion (surprise, fascination) we attribute to observed student behaviors (wide eyes, open mouths, rapt gazes, unusual stillness). In trying to practice what he preaches, one of the authors once introduced a group of teachers to the Principles of Learning by flamboyantly pulling a series of small gift-wrapped packages out of a case labelled "Idea Bag," to highlight that each principle is discrete and valuable, self-contained and important.

Active Participation

In classes of teachers who use this principle, students are operating, responding, moving, and talking during the course of the learning experiences. Sitting passively and listening is not characteristic of learning experiences embodying this principle. Active participation of all students might not require small or large muscle movement or manipulation: it could conceivably involve written participation with each student responding to each question; or it could be all verbal participation, with the setting structured in such a way that many students can talk at once (divided into pairs or small groups to reach consensus on something or debate some issue).

There are many techniques for structuring this kind of participation from students. For example, after finishing a presentation of the structure of an atomic nucleus, and the meaning of atomic number versus atomic mass, the teacher says, "OK now, explain to your neighbor what the difference is between atomic number and atomic mass." Teachers aware of this principle look for opportunities to make that kind of move.

Feeling Tone
Feeling tone propels learning in proportion to degree. This principle posits that students learn more and faster in proportion to the level of feeling provoked during the learning, either positive or negative feeling. The rule is held to apply, however, only up to a point. On one side, the more pleasurable the learning experience, the more the learning...up to the point where the pleasure takes over and begins crowding out the learning. There is, in other words, a point of diminishing returns for efforts to make learning pleasurable. Likewise, when teachers raise the level of concern of students ("I'm going to check you all individually on this material this period.") learning is potentiated, but only up to a point. Too much concern turns into anxiety, quickly interferes with learning, and blocks it. Again, a point of diminishing returns is quickly reached.

Application of this principle sees teachers either making moves to make learning experiences enjoyable (without becoming hedonistic) and/or raising levels of concern ("We'll be having a quiz on this material sometime this week."), but neither to extreme. Judging the extreme, or the point of diminishing returns, is not a judgment for which rules can be cited. To credit this principle as operative, however, an observer would have to cite evidence of teacher moves to raise positive and/or negative feeling tone, and be subjectively convinced (by watching student reactions) that extremes had not been violated.

Mnemonics
Teachers using this principle help students use mediational devices for remembering new learning, devices such as imagery, anagrams, or jingles ("30 days hath September"). Here is a familiar one:

Desert—one "s", all alone in the desert.
Dessert—you get bigger in the middle if you eat too much of it.

There are many mnemonic devices, and a growing body of research comparing their effectiveness. For example, one particularly effective technique is called the "Keyword" technique and is used for learning new vocabulary words (in any language) and new terms. Students are asked to learn a keyword (word clue) for the new term that sounds acoustically similar to it (e.g., "purse" for "persuade"; "he's a date" for "hesitate"). Then students are asked to remember the content of a cartoon (plain line drawing) that contains the keyword interacting in some way with the definition of the new term. Levin, *et al.* (1982) show a cartoon for the new vocabulary word "persuade"; one lady points to a purse in a store and says, "Oh, Martha, you should buy that PURSE!" Martha replies, "I think you can PERSU-ADE me to buy it." At the bottom of the cartoon is written, "Persuade (Purse): When you talk someone into doing something."

In these cartoons, one character's utterance contains the keyword and the other contains the new term to be learned. Studies have been highly positive and uniform in demonstrating the effectiveness of this technique for learning new words.

Sequence

It turns out that: the first and last items in a series are the easiest to learn; the one just past the middle is the hardest; learning can be accelerated by chaining a sequence backward from the last item; sequences can be broken into small parts to avoid interference. This set of principles is applicable to rote learning and is easily observed when practiced in math fact and spelling drills, or any body of items in some sequence that students are expected to memorize (poems). Teachers can use this knowledge to improve the learning of items in the difficult positions. The sequence (or list) can be shortened, split in half so the difficult item becomes first on the shortened list. The order of items can be changed; the hard parts can be given extra practice; the hard items can be made more vivid (darker print, use of colors). A high school Latin teacher writes:

Students are expected to learn ten new Latin vocabulary words each week. 1) They quiz each other from the list at the beginning of each class period for five minutes. 2) Then they drill alone on the ones they missed in the partner quiz. 3) They write the list in their notebooks along with the meanings, putting the ones they missed first and last in the reordered list (and second and ninth if need be). Words they know best are put in the just-past-the-middle position. They cover the answers with their hand and go down the list several times quizzing themselves. This pro-cedure is repeated each day with missed words in first and last positions. The whole thing takes about ten minutes, which I use to circulate and talk to individual students.

It is interesting to note that this principle of sequence and the importance of the first and last positions is also applicable to use of *time*. What happens at the beginning and end of a class period (or day, or term) is most easily remembered; thus these spots should be milked to maximum advantage for learning. How to do this will be expanded in the chapter on the Time parameter.

Knowledge of Results

Knowledge of results should be specific and timely. Practitioners of this principle give explicit feedback to students on their work as rapidly as possible after completion. The rationale is that this feedback has optimum corrective impact when most proximal to the student's engaging the materials, and that it has maximum communicative effect when it is both full and specific. (Under the earlier Personal Relationship Building parameter, it is argued that full and complete feedback is a form of respect by which teachers show students they value students' work enough to look at it closely.)

Here's an example of knowledge of results: Upon completing a worksheet on social changes as a result of the Industrial Revolution, students see answers displayed on an overhead (or revealed from behind a rolled-up A-V screen). They correct their own papers and then ask clarifying questions of the teacher.

Another example: Students correct all their own workbook and worksheet pages from answer books, fixing all individual mistakes.

Students simply getting feedback from a teacher does not mean this principle is in operation. Finding out how they did on a test is not the principle. Students find out how they did at some point in every class, but there's nothing special about that. What is special (and what empowers learning) is feedback that is rapid, specific, and complete. Computer games give instantaneous knowledge of results, though not always with specific information about how to improve.

Teachers can claim they're using "knowledge of results" if they're giving students feedback about how they did very soon after they perform, along with an opportunity to self-correct or at least see what would have to be done to improve.

Reinforcement

Reinforcement is anything that strengthens a behavior and can range all the way from edibles and tokens to teacher statements of recognition like, "You stuck with that hard one until you got it and you didn't give up!" Verbal reinforcement is our main focus here because it is so overworked in the literature, so common a part of teachers' vocabulary, yet it is astonishing how little it is used skillfully. Many opportunities pass for applying this powerful stimulus to learning. The knowledge base tells us that verbal reinforcement should be: 1) precise; 2) appropriate; and 3) when appropriate, scheduled from regular to intermittent.

1. *Precise* means that the statement should specify what it is specifically that the learner has done that is good. "You didn't rush today, and you got them almost all right" is better than "Good work." The student is much more likely to reproduce the high accuracy rate, which is due to not rushing, if not rushing is explicitly reinforced.

"You finished those problems and then you put your stuff away without me giving you any reminders, and you started on your writing. That's great." The student knows what is great.

"In your story today you used adjectives beautifully to describe those street scenes...especially in the second paragraph."

2. *Appropriate*. If a student doesn't want it, it's not reinforcing. Being praised in front of someone else may be embarassing. Being told his handwriting is "so nice" may turn off a sixth grade athlete and get him kidded by his pals; more appropriate feedback for him might be "John, you're one of our best ball players and I see your fine motor coordination is just as good as your coordination on the ball field" (Hunter, 1979).

Thinking about this makes it easy to see why studies of praise and reinforcement that count frequency of the behavior and look for correlations to student achievement can never get anywhere. Only *appropriate* use of reinforcement works.

3. *Scheduled*. B.F. Skinner discovered that behaviors established through operant conditioning become more stable and more durable if reinforcement is delivered with every occurrence of the behavior *at first*. But then reinforcement should skip occasional occurrences at random, and the span of unreinforced occurrences between reinforcers should gradually be lengthened. Such a schedule could be charted as follows:

```
delivery of reinforcers      o o o   o o   o o   o     o   o
occurrences of the behavior  x x x x x x x x x x x x x x x x
```

Use of intermittent scheduling to establish behaviors is more in line with a systematic plan for behavior modification a teacher might use to develop, say, hand raising versus calling out, or promptness versus tardiness to class.

Degree of Guidance

How much guidance will the students need to get the most out of (or just to get *through*) the task? Guidance should be high with new tasks and withdrawn gradually with demonstrated student proficiency. Evidence for this principle cannot be simply to observe teachers delivering different degrees of guidance to different students. Evidence must cite different degrees of guidance offered to the same student or group of students over time as they progressively show increased proficiency with the new material. This is sometimes difficult to see in short observations. One may, however, see a teacher introduce a new skill to a class and immediately provide adequate guidance in practicing it. This may mean working with just one group after introducing Haiku to the whole class, giving the rest of the class something else they still need to practice but without so much teacher guidance...then rotating through the class with groups that focus on the new skill. Or, it may mean the teacher puts on track shoes and gets around to everybody, giving guidance and help where needed. The latter is more time efficient if the teacher can pull it off (but pulling it off is not so much a function of teacher skill as good judgement: i.e., what new material will or will not require more intensive individual guidance for students to be able to use it proficiently).

Breaking Complex Tasks Into Simpler Parts

One often sees evidence of this principle when teachers are attempting to explain or clarify operations students have failed to grasp. The task is broken down into smaller parts and one part, now isolated, is focused on for learning. For example, if students are having trouble with word problems, the teacher may just have the students identify the central question and the operation called for without doing any computing. Or students may be asked to draw a picture of what happens in the problem as a way of conceptualizing it, again without any computing. This principle manifests as task analysis and insures that sequential prerequisites for present learning tasks are established.

Practice

Practice should be *massed* at the beginning of learning a new skill or operation (meaning frequent practice sessions, close together in time), then *distributed* over increasing intervals of time. The *smallest unit* of new information that retains meaning should be practiced at any one session and should be worked on for the *shortest* unit of *time* to allow the students to feel they have accomplished something. After achieving proficiency, learned items should be practiced two or three more times anyway to make the learning more permanent (*overlearning*). Unlike athletics and motor skills, where practice makes perfect and the more-the-better (up to a point), long practice sessions with academic skills quickly reach a point of diminishing returns.

For areas like the times tables, each fact is a unit of meaning on its own, separate from the others, and only one or two of them should be introduced at a time, embedded in groups of already known facts for drill. (Certain tables and groups of facts, however—e.g., the 10-times table—group all at once as a single unit of meaning.) In teaching students to analyze a story, which is a complex task, only one part would be assigned at first, say identifying the setting; later would come describing the plot. In practicing a difficult piece of music, one would practice not a page, not a bar (which might be too small a unit to have meaning), but a measure.

Practice sessions should be *short* (2-5 minutes, not 20) *and frequent* (twice a day rather than twice a week). This is quite at odds with the schedules we often see when we look at students laboring over workbooks in classrooms.

If a teacher wants students to practice writing news stories in a journalism course, the "leader" (opening sentence/paragraph that contains all the critical information of who, when, where, what) is a meaningful unit. Students may be asked to practice writing just leaders for frequent short practice periods before being asked to write entire stories.

Goal Setting

The point here is goal setting *by students*. This principle tells us that when students get involved in goal setting for their own learning, they learn more. As well as being common sense, this conclusion is strongly supported by a line of research (see Schunk and Gaa, 1981). When students take ownership for goals (either self-set, teacher-set, or jointly negotiated), both their motivation to accomplish them and their ability to self-evaluate (and self-regulate) increase.

Student goal setting, of course, will not happen by itself except for very motivated students. Teachers have to do something to facilitate the process, like taking a few minutes of class time and asking all the students to write their goal for the period (or the unit) on a piece of paper...or like having periodic goal-setting conferences with individual students at timely intervals (like the beginning of new units or projects). These conferences can be quite short, but the goals chosen should be recorded somewhere, and later on students should be asked to evaluate how they did.

Student goal setting does not automatically lead to increased student performance. Certain properties of effective goals need to be present; they need to be *specific*, *challenging* but attainable, and able to be accomplished *soon*.

Specific goals contain items that can be measured, counted, or perceived directly as criteria for accomplishment. "Try my best" doesn't fit this mold; "master the 20 spelling demons" does.

The more difficult the goal the more effort the student will expend, providing the goal is viewed as attainable. So in guiding students to set goals, teachers have to help them walk the tightrope between what is "duck soup" and what is unrealistic.

Finally, goals that can be accomplished in the short term work better than long term goals. This does not mean long term goals should not be set. It just means that long term goals need to be broken down into short term goals, or sub-goals with their own plans of action, if one is to be maximally effective in reaching them. (Divide and conquer.) Learning or work accomplishment goals for students seem to work best around specified skills and products and for time spans of one period to several days rather than over several weeks or months.

A common misinterpretation of this principle is that it means students are picking what they will study, i.e., the content. Not so. Much more often (and usually more productively), they are setting goals about speed, quantity, or quality. Here are some examples:

"Glen, how many of these do you think you'll get done in the next half hour?"
"I think this whole page."
"Really? Do you really think that's a reasonable amount?"
"Yes, I'll do it."
"OK, show them to me when you're done."

This is a speed goal. Students makes a commitment to how fast they'll do some amount of work.

"How many references will you use in researching that, Brenda?"
"About six."
"OK, if you think that's enough, put it down in your outline sheet."

That is a quantity goal. There is no particular rate at which the researching must be done (except ultimately the deadline of the paper). It is a commitment from the student to do a specified amount. The same kind of goal applies to how many books students will read for free reading, how many extra credit or supplementary exercises they'll do.

Quality goals are particularly interesting to us. In these goals, the students make a commitment to how *well* they'll do something. This can take the form of targeting what aspect of their work they'll focus on improving. As teachers, we can give them the assignment to tell us what they're working to improve (and maybe even ask for it in writing):

"So Jamie, what's your quality goal going to be on this paper?"
"I'm going to work on improving spelling and punctuation."
"How about you, Tara?"
"My goal's going to be to use less tired words."

By getting students to set goals, teachers do not relinquish their ability to make assignments: they enlist the students in making personal commitments to speed, quantity, or improving a particular aspect of quality. It *is* possible to have students choose content in some cases—"I want to learn everything I can about frogs," says Freddy—there are places where it will fit in with curriculum requirements and time available to help him do so (especially if one of the teacher's goals is to stimulate and support an inquiring attitude). But it may be equally powerful to get students to set quality goals, thus involving them inevitably in self-evaluation to come up with a target for improvement.

In our experience, this principle of learning, so plain sounding and simple to understand, is one of the *least* practiced in education. If devoted just a little time and energy to it, we might see big payoffs in student performance and in students' learning something directly about self-regulation and self-evaluation.

Concrete, Semi-Abstract, Abstract Progression

Teachers using this principle can be seen to use tangible or manipulative materials at one stage of instruction, move to pictorial representation of the same material, and at still later stages of instruction deal with the same materials with the students in purely abstract ways. This progression is thought to be effective not only with young children who are at Piaget's stage of concrete operation, but also with adult learners. Dealing with concrete materials anchors images and experiences, which later connect with and are summoned by the abstractions that refer to them. One doesn't have to learn everything by experience (you don't have to be bitten by a rabid dog to learn they're dangerous); but experience anchors learning in a powerful way. Epstein's recent work (1980) on brain growth and stages of cognitive development particularly highlights the importance of avoiding abstraction in initial learning and using concrete experiences with early adolescents.

Modeling

Learning can be enhanced by modeling new skills or operations and preserving these models for student reference during early stages of learning. After explaining and demonstrating the algorithm for two-digit multiplication (or the format for writing a book report, or anything with procedures and steps), the teacher leaves a model showing the separate steps on the board as students go to work practicing examples:

```
          2       2       1       1
 48      48      48      48      48      48
x 23    x 23    x 23    x 23    x 23    x 23
         4      144     144     144     144
                         6      96      96
                                       1104
```

Saying and Doing

This principle is not the same as advice to use multi-sensory teaching. That advice, useful as it may be, refers to the fact that students have different perceptual strengths; through multi-sensory teaching you have a greater chance of hitting more students' strong perceptual channel, thus improving learning. "Saying and doing" is a package recommendation to be built into as many learning experiences as possible, especially the saying part. The principle comes from aggregate statistics (i.e., research on the mean effectiveness of treatments on groups) rather than matching perceptual modes to individuals.

The research compared various combinations of seeing, hearing, doing, doing and seeing, seeing and hearing, saying and hearing, etc., to arrive at saying and doing as the most effective. Apparently, students gain something measurable in the way of learning and retention when they themselves articulate a new learning out loud. Class discussion is not enough; in discussion only one student may articulate the new learning. Pairs or small groups are more efficient where students review new learnings out loud to each other. College students, for example, find speaking their notes into a tape recorder an effective form of review and rehearsal of information.

Cumulative Review

Old learnings should be included in practice and drills of new material so that these old learnings are periodically exercised. As one moves on in a skill sequence, the range and number of skills demanded in the practice exercises grow cumulatively to include all the old skills. To prevent practice tasks from becoming unwieldy when the range of skills is big, only a representative sample of them is included in exercises focusing on new material.

Certain skill sequences automatically cumulate old skills in new products without any design steps required by the teacher...for example, report writing. As students learn new punctuation and grammar skills, these are automatically practiced each time writing takes place and are expected to be done correctly. Likewise, as students use more elaborate language forms and learn to organize ideas better, these also are automatically expected to be continued in future writing. But other skill sequences require more deliberate design for cumulative review to take place effectively.

In drilling on flash cards to learn times tables, each new pack should contain a representative sample of all previously learned facts; and occasional packs should be only reviews to solidify old learnings.

In learning geographical features of a country in South America, the features should come up again and again in the context of the questions about the country's elections, political system, economy. A violation of this principle would see students studying the geographical features of *all* the South American countries in sequence, then going back and studying all their political systems, then all their cultural highlights, and so on.

End Without Closure

Consider the impact of this teacher statement: "Think about three ways you might get out of this dilemma and be ready to share them with us tomorrow when you come in" (Doug Russell, 1980).

Leaving students *without* an answer and *with* something percolating overnight may be more effective in some cases than coming to a neat ending of each class with all issues resolved.

Keeping Students Open and Thinking

Teacher Responses to Student Answers

Art Costa has pointed out that the way that teachers respond to student answers is probably more important than the questions themselves. This statement implies that looking at the way teachers ask questions is not enough. Influential as questions may be in getting students interested, in stretching their thinking, and in guiding discussion, the questions alone don't account for the quality of discourse.

In this section we examine the repertoire of ways teachers respond to student answers because there is an important principle of learning at work in that situa-tion—a situation in which teachers find themselves dozens of times a day. The principle says simply: respond in a way that keeps students *open and thinking* (rather than shut down and afraid or competitive). Doing so makes learning more continuous and more efficient.

Students get powerful messages from the teacher's responses to their answers, and it is these messages that influence the way they participate in lessons from that point on. Depending on how the teacher responds, a student may get one or more of the following messages:

"I'm dumb."

"Well, I muffed that one!"

"My job is to guess the answer in the teacher's head and say it in precisely the way he's thinking it."

"I muffed that one and I should get back in gear. I know this stuff."

"The teacher thinks I can think this one through and get it."

"What I said was worthwhile, but there's more."

"My teacher really listens to what I say."

"My teacher really wants to know what I mean. There must be something worthwhile in what I said."

"My idea wasn't as good as that one. Boy, I'm glad I didn't get called on."

"Wow, I guess I did pretty well on that one, eh?"
"It's not safe to risk an answer in here unless you're really sure."

"It is safe to risk an answer in here. If I don't get it, I won't be put down."

"I can say what I think and be respected and accepted for that."

"If I can't get it, I'll be helped to remember or figure it out."

Clearly the effect of these messages can be powerful. And we have all received them at one time or another in our own experience as students. The effects are either to open us up or close us down; to make us feel more confident, curious, and encouraged to participate, or to make us more afraid, timid, protective, quiet, and defensive. Simultaneously, the effect is either to stimulate us to search, scan, wonder about, reflect, and in general *think*, or instead to try to get it right and shine, impress, win (and/or protect ourselves from getting wounded).

We invite you to take a look at the following list of ways teachers respond to student answers. Read the definitions, ask yourself what message (from those above) you think you, as a student, would get from each response? For instance, let's say the teacher asks, "How do you find the area of a circle?"

Criticize: "That's not even close. Come on, wake up!"

Give correct answer: "No, it's *pi* r^2."

Redirect to another student after you answer: "Judy, can you tell us?"

Redirect to get more, build, extend: "OK. You're on the right track. Judy, would you add anything to that?"

"Wrong" with the reason why: "Not quite, because you left out the exponent."

Supply question for which answer is right, cue, hold accountable: "That would be right if I asked for the formula for the circumference...Now, do you remember anything about the use of exponents in that formula? [Now student gets it right.] Right! And I bet you'll remember that after lunch if I check you, too. I'll ask you then, and I bet you'll get it!"

Wait-time: [...silence...]

Follow-up question to double-check or extend: [student answers correctly with *pi* r^2] "OK. And what precisely does 'r^2' mean?"

Acknowledge: "Um hmmmm."

Restate in fuller language: "OK. So you get the area by multiplying *pi* times the radius of the circle squared."

Ask student to elaborate: "Can you tell me more about what you meant by that?"

Praise: "Way to go!"

These responses form a repertoire. Like the Attention continuum (see Chapter 2, page 23), no one of these moves is inherently best, and matching is the name of the game. One could create the context in which each of them, even criticizing (but not put-downs), could be appropriate. Several of them, however, are particularly

Figure 8-1
Teacher Responses to Student Answers

*Ways of
moving on
to another
student*

Criticizes "Come on. That answer shows no thought at all!"

"No," and redirect to another student

"No," then give correct answer

"No," with reason why (which may serve as a cue)

NO

"Try again."

Validate what is right or good about an answer,
then cue, sticking with student

Ignore answer and cue

Wait-time II

*Ways of sticking
with a student who
hasn't gotten it
yet, or hasn't gotten
part of it*

Follow-up question to double-check or extend

Follow-up with expression of confidence or
encouragement. "I think you know."

Redirect to another student to add more, build,
extend. "Would you add anything to that, Jim?"

Ask student to elaborate answer

Call for self-evaluation of answer

**M
A
Y
B
E**

Follow-up question to clarify. "You're saying that…"

Acknowledge "Uh hmmm."

Repeat student's answer

Restate student's answer in fuller or
more precise language

*Ways of affirming
or acknowledging
without judgement*

"Right."

"Right," with reason why

YES

Praise

effective for specific purposes, and should be considered for inclusion into any teacher's repertoire. Wait-time is one such behavior.

Mary Budd Rowe discovered almost 20 years ago that if teachers waited three seconds or more after asking a question (that is, were willing to endure at least three seconds of silence) some very desirable things happened. (She also discovered that hardly any teachers do so; the average wait-time after asking a question before the teacher jumps in with cuing, redirection, or telling the answer is .5 seconds!) When teachers were willing to wait the three seconds, students who ordinarily didn't answer did so; answers tended to be in full sentences rather than single words or phrases; answers were at a higher level of thinking; and students were more likely to start responding to each other and to comment on each other's answers.

Similar findings have been obtained when a student *has* answered, and the teacher waits 3 seconds again before commenting on the answer. Waiting *after* a student has responded is called "Wait-time II." (Waiting after asking the question but *before* the student has answered is called "Wait-time I.") This response behavior achieves similar desirable outcomes to Wait-time I: teachers tend to increase the cognitive level of their questions; students increase the cognitive level of their answers; students speak in more complete and more elaborated sentences; and students who would otherwise not elaborate do so.

Supplying the question for which the answer is right, cuing, and holding the student accountable accomplishes several things. First, it salvages a little student self-esteem. You don't see or hear as much if you're smarting with humiliation. As Hunter says, "When someone is humiliated or feeling unworthy, their perception narrows. Our job is to help learners be right, not catch them being wrong" (Hunter, 1979). This strategy also strengthens a connection between the answer and the question it *does* go with...by supplying that question.

Applying this principle doesn't mean the teacher is never allowed to say a simple "no" or "wrong" again, in fear of damaging student learning. Quite the contrary, it often doesn't do any harm at all to say "nope" pleasantly and move on to the next student. And to use this strategy with *every* wrong answer would take forever. It is an excellent strategy to use frequently, however, and especially when there's a question to link up the wrong answer with, often an item of recent learning.

A follow-up question to double check or extend (called a "probe" in research literature) is a way of checking to see if the student really understands the meaning of an answer or is just parroting. For example, in the case cited above, a student might be able to recite "*pi* r squared" without knowing that r stands for the radius of the circle.

Acknowledging a student's answer non-judgmentally leaves the door open for further comment from other students...or for adding to the original answer by the same student.

Restating in fuller language is a move a teacher would do for the benefit of the other students...to make sure they understood what the answer meant.

Asking students to elaborate on their responses helps *the teacher* know what they really meant: "Could you explain that a little further?" "I'm not sure what you meant by that, Jerry. Can you say a little more?" "You need to be more specific, Jane. How far exactly are you saying the fulcrum has to be from this end?"

Praise can be an effective response to a student answer, but only if used well. Jere Brophy's definitive review of the research on praise (Brophy, 1981) summarized how to praise well. To be effective, teacher praise must be *specific*, *contingent*, *genuine*, and *congruent*. We would add *appropriate* to the list.

Specific praise specifies exactly what is praiseworthy about the student's performance: "John, I'm impressed with the variety of verbs and sentence patterns you used in this composition. This is your best work so far."

Contingent means that the praise is dependent on successful student performance and not given randomly or for encouragement. Non-contingent praise (i.e., given randomly and sometimes for incorrect answers) is frequent and found "most often among teachers who have low expectations for student learning...and within any given class, it is most likely to be directed toward the lowest achievers....No doubt such praise is given in an attempt to encourage the student. However, it seems likely that, to the extent that the students recognize what the teacher is doing, the result will be embarassment, discouragement, and other undesirable outcomes" (Brophy, 1981, p. 13).

Genuine means simply that the teacher means it; that the praise is not manipulative, not given to "reinforce" (translation: engineer) a specific behavior, but reflects real appreciation on the teacher's part.

Congruent pertains to body language. Gesture, tone of voice, stance, and posture must send the same message as the words. If the teacher leans back, looks away, and says in a bored tone of voice, "I can see you really worked hard on these problems, Freddy," Freddy is not likely to be convinced.

Finally, *appropriate* refers to choice of words, setting, and style that is matched to the particular student involved. Public praise to individual junior high students can embarass them. Public praise for certain behaviors can make them want to crawl under the table: "Oh, John, your handwriting is so tidy and neat" (said to a macho 8th grader).

Brophy also points out that effective praise: uses students' own prior accomplishments as the context for describing present accomplishments; is given in recognition of noteworthy effort or success at difficult (for *this* student) tasks; attributes success to effort and ability, implying similar successes can be expected in the future; fosters endogenous attributions (students believe that they expend effort on the task because they enjoy the task and/or want to develop task-relevant skills).

Each of the behaviors just described (Wait-time, follow-up question, acknowledgement, restate in fuller language, asking students to elaborate, and praise) has research to support it as an effective teacher behavior (see Costa, 1985; Dunkin and Biddle, 1974 for summaries). In addition, one can find similar support for "redirecting" in the literature, and even a case for the appropriateness of criticism with certain students as long as the criticism is not a put-down (Graham, 1984)...which brings us to the issues of repertoire and matching in this business of teacher responses.

Since many of these response techniques are inherently effective in and of themselves for stimulating thinking and attaining clarity (or so the research would suggest), they are worth adding to our repertoire in this parameter. And it is a good bet that, among the list cited, there are several new ones for any teacher. (Least frequently seen, in our observations, are Wait-time, asking students to elaborate, and effective praise.) But beyond incorporating them into our repertoire, there is the issue of matching. Are we using our repertoire of response techniques appropriately, in the right situation, with the right students? Wait-time, for example, is inappropriate when we're asking low-level questions or doing drill. Giving students time to think and process is most effective when higher-level thinking is called for. Redirecting prematurely can deny a student the opportunity to think through an answer or refine one already given. Restating in fuller language can aid the understanding of the rest of the class, but if done unnecessarily or to excess can teach students not to listen to one another. So the bottom line here, as elsewhere in our quest to understand teaching, is to first work to expand our repertoires so we *can* respond more appropriately to more students in different situations; and second, to look carefully at what we are pulling from our repertoires for individual students so we can improve the effectiveness of our matching.

If Students Don't Answer

The previous section has made an assumption—that students are answering our questions. Students often do not, however, have the answer at their fingertips and there is that pregnant second or two in which we must decide what to do. Are we embarrassed for the student—do we want to get the spotlight off that child? Do we stick with the student, giving cues? Do we ask the question over again? Do we redirect the question to another student?

Let's reframe those questions. What are the options—what is the repertoire of moves for us to make when students don't answer questions? What is known about their effects? How do we pick which one to use with Jerry here, who's looking at the ceiling and grimacing hideously as he gropes for the answer?

As in the previous section, we can identify a repertoire of responses teachers may make to keep students open and thinking; in this case, moves to make when students don't answer:

—Wait-Time I
 —Repeat question
  —Cue
   —Ask simpler question
    —Ask fact-only question
     —Give choices for answer
      —Ask for yes or no response
       —Ask student to repeat or imitate answer
        —Ask for non-verbal response such as shaking
          head or pointing
          —Instruct student to say, "I don't know."

The benefits of Wait-time have been described above. Simply enduring a little silence (at least 3 seconds) while Jerry grimaces may give him the time he needs to come up with the answer. *Modeling* this behavior can have a powerful influence too.

One of the authors once attended a session where David Perkins was asked a question; David turned his head, looked sideways, then up at the ceiling, and continued in silence for a full 10 seconds. By this time the author was getting nervous for David as a presenter and looking for something to say, some way to jump in and rescue him from what seemed like a paralytic attack. But just at that moment, David looked the questioner calmly in the eye and delivered a brilliant reply. He didn't appear in the least ruffled; he had for the past 10 seconds simply been comfortably thinking out his answer. It was the author who had been uncomfortable with the pause, not Dr. Perkins!

Several other times in that session similar pauses for reflection followed complicated questions from the audience. After the first time, the author was not worried about David any more and spent the time thinking about the question too. In fact, David Perkins' modeling of wait-time for *himself* to think through an answer had an immediate effect on the class. The whole discussion became more reflective and thoughtful. And by having our instructor model his willingness to think before he spoke, we in turn became more comfortable doing so. The result was to elevate the level of the entire discussion.

Wait-time is a behavior where coaching, or some form of peer feedback, is particularly helpful. We are so used to filling silences with talk that unless we specifically commit ourselves to try wait-time and get someone in to *watch* us trying it, we will likely fail to learn this valuable behavior. The very presence of an observer will remind us of our commitment and increase the likelihood of successful practice.

Turning to the other behaviors on the continuum, we see a progression where less and less is required of the student, until finally only imitation or head-shaking is requested. This continuum was developed by Good and Brophy (1978) for non-responsive students. Their point is that students should not be allowed to "practice" non-responsiveness, but instead be expected to participate. Referring to Blank's work (1973) with inner-city children, they write:

> If they fail the initial question, the follow-up question should be a simpler one that they can handle. In general, questions that require them to explain something in detail will be the most difficult. Progessively simpler demands include factual questions requiring short answers, choice questions requiring them only to choose among presented alternatives, and questions that require only a yes or no response. If the students do not respond to any level of questioning, they can be asked to repeat things or to imitate actions. Once they begin to respond correctly, the teacher can move to more demanding levels as confidence grows....Inhibited students need careful treatment when they are not responding. As long as they appear to be trying to answer the question, the teacher should wait them out. If they begin to look anxious, as if worrying about being in the spotlight instead of thinking about the question, the teacher should intervene by repeating the question or giving a clue. He or she should not call on another student or allow others to call out the answer. [Good and Brophy, 1978, p. 226]

Reviewing Principles of Learning

Within this chapter, we have described 24 "little packages of power"; 24 techniques teachers can use to increase the rate and permanence of students' learning. Figure 8-2 on the next page summarizes these "double dozen" principles of learning.

Following Figure 8-2, we have provided a Quiz that will give you the chance to review and put into your own words the value of these principles of learning. As you complete the Quiz, take a moment to reflect on any of the principles that may be new to your repertoire, and consider how you can incorporate those into your teaching.

Figure 8-2
PRINCIPLES OF LEARNING—The Double Dozen

1. **Application in Setting**: students practice new behaviors in settings where they'll be used
2. **Meaning**: connecting to students' personal experience.
3. **Teach for Transfer**: engineering a planned sequence of activities that progressively distance the skill from abstract academic contexts.
4. **Isolate Critical Attributes**: highlighting and labeling them.
5. **Concrete—Semi-abstract—Abstract**: follow as a progression with the introduction of new material.
6. **Modeling**: step-wise products, procedures, and processes preserved for student reference.

7. **Similarity of Environment**: an activity which gets minds in gear for upcoming events.
8. **Active Participation**: any way you can (unison, check with a partner, signals...).
9. **Vividness**: and varying of practice formats.
10. **Feeling Tone**: fun, but not too much; worry, but not too much; raising level of concern.
11. **End Without Closure**: but with follow-up at a later time...to invite percolation.

12. **Breaking Complex Tasks**: down into simpler, smaller pieces; isolating trouble spots for focused work/practice; higher frequency practice/repetition of new items.
13. **Degree of Guidance**: high with new tasks; withdrawn gradually with familiarity.
14. **Close Confusers**: insure an adequate degree of original learning before close confusers are introduced.
15. **Say—Do**
16. **Mnemonics**: tricks to aid in memory (keywords, images in sequence, jingles...).
17. **Sequence and Backward Chaining**: first and last are easiest; just past the middle is hardest.
18. **Practice**: massed at beginning, then distributed; smallest meaningful units; short practices; overlearning.
19. **Contiguity**: don't allow practice of errors, especially with new learning.
20. **Cumulative Review**: in practice, periodically include representative sample of previously learned material.

21. **Knowledge of Results**: promptly through monitoring.
22. **Reinforcement**: precise; regular; intermittent.
23. **Goal Setting**: by students; ownership, specific, challenging; able to be accompished soon, then longer term.
24. **Keep Students Open and Thinking**: e.g., supply question for which answer is right, deliver prompt, hold accountable.

Quiz
Vignettes on Principles of Learning

For each vignette below, do two things:

1) determine what is important about what the teacher did; why is it likely to support effective learning?
2) in the margin, write the name of the principle of learning in operation.

Note that some vignettes may exemplify more than one principle, though there will be one that is dominant.

If you have a colleague with whom to work, share your answers.

1. Each spelling test covers this week's words, 3 words from last week, and the 2 most frequently missed words from previous weeks' lists.

2. The teacher is illustrating the permeability of membranes by pushing various-sized balls between the bars of a metal milk crate. "We'd call this semi-permeable because the marble will go through, but, as you can see (pushes...it finally goes) it goes through with difficulty, not just gliding through like the peas did." Later in the period he has them draw diagrams to illustrate the permeability of membranes they have been experimenting with. On their unit tests and in the review session before it, they will be asked to explain permeable, semi-permeable, and impermeable in sentences.

3. After reading orally part of a story in a basal reader called "Flat Stanley," the teacher asked the students some questions. One set of questions was: "Have you ever seen a grate in the road? Are you more likely to see them in the city or in the country? What are they for?" Later when they got to the part of the story where Stanley goes to California, the teacher asked: "Have you ever been to California? How did you get there? How long did it take you, Jeff, when you drove?" When one student mentioned the time change, the teacher looked at the clock and said, "What time do you think it is in California?" Having determined that it was 8 A.M., one student said, "They aren't even in school yet."

4. The teacher told his group of 11th graders that he wanted them to clearly understand the concepts of prejudice and discrimination and be able to under-

stand them. He defined prejudice, writing it on the board: "Social prejudice is a hostile feeling toward a person or persons because of their membership in a particular group." He underlined the words feeling , membership, and particular group. He then went on to define discrimination as "preferential treatment" of a person or persons because of their membership in a given group. After writing this on the board he underlined the words treatment, membership, particular group. He emphasized that the discriminating attribute in each concept was feelings versus treatment or actions. Probing students further on these concepts, he asked what the difference was between disliking someone and being prejudiced against him. A student suggested that the key was whether or not the dislike was based on the person's membership in a particular group. The teacher asked if someone could provide an example of prejudice. A student said, "If an adult doesn't like a kid because he's a teenager." The teacher asked the class, "Is this prejudice? Why?"

5. 3rd grade P.E. lesson on jump roping skills:
    The teacher took a few minutes at the beginning of class to let the children express what they had successfully accomplished by the end of the last class (e.g., jump 10 or more times), and to decide individually what they were going to work towards (e.g., jumping more times without missing; jumping into the rope while it was turning; two people jumping at the same time). He checked with individual children from time to time, talking with them about what they'd said they'd try for, and helping them make modifications when appropriate.

6. (…in that same P.E. class)
    The teacher had the kids in groups and made sure each was involved all the time; for example, 2 children were turning the rope, one (or two) were jumping, and one was counting. The children in a group would switch tasks after the jumper(s) had a few turns.

7. (…same P.E. class)
    The teacher said most children could only jump rope a few times and were not at all skilled when he started this series of lessons. Therefore, he wanted to focus on this activity for a few classes, organizing tasks so that they would have enough practice to really improve. They were now jumping 10 or more times and most were increasing the variety of conditions they were working under (e.g., jumping in; jumping with different children turning the rope; two children jumping at the same time).

8. (...P.E. class)
   I observed this teacher stay with a student who was having trouble for about 4 minutes at the beginning of class. During this time, the teacher isolated the variables that the student needed to attend to in order to jump rope successfully (keep your eye on the rope; start jumping when the rope goes over your head; stay in the middle of the rope; jump to the rhythm set by the rope and the "counter.") He also provided the student with specific feedback about his performance and asked the student to tell him what he was going to try to remember. When the student started to successfully jump ten times without missing, the teacher moved away to other children and other groups. However, he returned to this one student several times during the class, providing as much help as necessary (e.g., taking the rope from one of the turners who was having trouble keeping a regular rhythm and turning the rope himself; asking the student to look where he was standing).

9. The teacher began this section of the class by asking who could explain the story: "Now this is a difficult story. Could any of you explain to a younger student why the author wrote the story?" To the 5 or 6 students who raised their hands, the teacher said, "Write your reasons on the board." As the students were writing, the teacher told the class that the rest would have to vote in a minute for the answer they believed to be correct and therefore they should look at them carefully and choose.

10. Suddenly the teacher yelled at a student who had just dropped a book (the whole event was staged). Students looked shocked at the teacher's over-reaction. Then the teacher smiled and explained, "You all looked very worried. Why?" Students responded with obvious reasons, generally saying they had never seen the teacher behave that way before—lose her temper. She then went on to make a connection to the character in the story who begins to act in unexpected and unaccustomed ways...

11. The goal is to understand the difference between chronology and history. I do a 2-part assignment. For day one, students are asked to keep a time line of their activities. For day two, I ask them to write a narrative history of the day for which they kept the time line, showing, where possible, cause and effect relationships.

12. A child read "quit" for "quite." The teacher says, "That would be right if the word didn't have an 'e' at the end. What does the 'e' do to the vowel in the middle?...Right. So what is the word?"

13. When I have the students drill each other on the symbols in the periodic table (names and symbols for elements learned in chemistry courses), they introduce one or two new ones at a time to each other in flash card packs. I teach them to do it this way: "This is a new one. 'Fe' is iron. You say that." ["'Fe'...iron."] "Right. Now, what's 'Fe'?" They're not to let their partners guess or try to figure it out, if they get a hint the partner is going to guess and get it wrong. I don't want them to practice any wrong associations. As I flip through the pack I make sure the ones they're missing come up more often than the others, too. As they learn them, I get more willing to let them hesitate when they see one.

14. The teacher draws individual numerals or letters on large sheets of paper (kindergarten). As the children watch, she draws the first part of the numeral or letter with the side of a broken purple crayon and the second part with a green crayon. Baretta-Lorton claims that "this really helps eliminate reversals and gives the children a sequential pattern to follow when writing numerals or letters." The teacher-drawn letter or numeral sequence cards are then hung in the room so that they can be easily seen by the children throughout the school year.

15. Students have had instruction on reading and writing big numbers (tens of thousands, hundreds of thousands, milllions, tens of millions, etc.) but they are having trouble. They are getting confused with the place value and tend to start at the left with a guess about millions or hundreds of thousands, disregarding the commas. To get them to remember to count places from the right and observe the commas, the teacher gives a lesson where all the examples have blank places such as: _ _ _ , _ _ _ .

On the board is a model:

billions, hundreds of millions, tens of millions, millions, hundreds of thousands, tens of thousands, thousands, hundreds, tens, ones

—— , —— —— —— , —— —— —— , —— —— ——

There are also a number of problems on the board with no numbers, in these forms:

_ _ , _ _ _   _ _ , _ _ _ , _ _ _

_ , _ _ _ , _ _ _   _ , _ _ _

_ _ _ , _ _ _   _ , _ _ _ , _ _ _

When called on, students start from the right and count out to the last place. They are expected to respond in the form, "ones, tens, hundreds, thousands, tens of thousands, hundreds of thousands." After doing a number of examples like this in unison, then calling on various individuals, the teacher has the students do a practice sheet by themselves in the same form while she circulates giving help.

Later on they will move on to reading big numbers with the numerals back in, but no medial zeros. When they show competence there, the teacher will add medial zeros to the examples she expects them to read and write.

Source Materials on This Parameter

Barringer, C. and Gholson, B. "Effects of Type and Combination of Feedback upon Conceptual Learning by Children: Implications for Research in Academic Learning." *Review of Educational Research*, Summer 1979, 49/3, 459-478.

Beeson, G.W. "Influence of Knowledge Context on the Learning of Intellectual Skills." *American Educational Research Journal*, Fall 1981, 18/3, 363-379.

Bellezza, F.S. "Mnemonic Devices: Classification, Characteristics, and Criteria." *Review of Educational Research*, Summer 1981, 51/2, 247-275.

Blank, M. *Teaching Learning in the Preschool: A Dialogue Approach.* Columbus, OH: Merrill, 1973.

Brophy, J. "Praise: A Functional Analysis." *Review of Educational Research*, 51/1, Spring 1981, 5-32.

Bugelski, B.R. *The Psychology of Learning Applied to Teaching.* Indianapolis: Bobbs-Merrill Educational Publishing, 1971.

Costa, Arthur. *Teaching for Intelligent Behaviors.* Orangevale, CA: Search Models Unlimited, 1985

Dunkin, M.J. and Biddle, B.J. *The Study of Teaching.* New York: Holt, Rinehart and Winston, 1974.

Good, T.J. and Brophy, J.E. *Looking in Classrooms.* New York: Harper and Row, 1978.

Graham, S. "Teacher Feelings and Student Thoughts: An Attributional Approach to Affect in the Classroom." *Elementary School Journal*, 85/1, 1985, 91-104.

Haughton, E. "Aims—Growing and Sharing." In Jordan, J.B. and Robbins, L.S. (*eds.*), *Let's Try Doing Something Else Kind of Thing.* Arlington, VA: C.E.C., 1972.

Hess, R.D.; Dickson, W.P.; Price, G.G. and Leong, D.J. "Some Contrasts Between Mothers and Preschool Teachers in Interaction with 4-year-old Children." *American Educational Research Journal*, Summer 1979, 16/3, 307-316.

Higbee, K.L. "Recent Research on Visual Mnemonics: Historical Roots and Educational Fruits." *Review of Educational Research*, Fall 1979, 49/4, 611-629.

Hilgard, E.R. and Bower, G.H. *Theories of Learning*. New York: Appleton Century Crofts, 1966.

Hudgins, B.B. *Learning and Thinking: A Primer for Teachers*. Itasca, IL: F.E. Peacock Publishers, 1977.

Hunter, M. *Motivation*, 1967.
------------- *Reinforcement*, 1967.
------------- *Retention*, 1967.
------------- *Teach More—Faster*, 1969.
------------- *Teach For Transfer*, 1971. El Segundo, CA: T.I.P. Publications.

Hunter, M. "Improving the Quality of Instruction." A.S.C.D. Conference, Fifth General Session, Houston, March, 1977.

Levin, J.R.; McCormick, C.B.; Miller, G.E.; Berry, J.K. and Pressley, M. "Mnemonic versus Nonmnemonic Vocabulary-learning Strategies for Children." *American Educational Research Journal*, Spring 1982, 19/1, 121-136.

Pressley, M., Levin, J.R. and Delaney, H.D. "The Mnemonic Keyword Method." *Review of Educational Research*, Spring 1982, 52/1, 61-91.

Rosswork, S. "Goal Setting: The Effects on an Academic Task with Varying Magnitudes of Incentive." *Journal of Educational Psychology*, 1977, 69, 710-715.

Russell, Doug. "Teaching Decisions & Behaviors for Instructional Improvement." Talk given at the A.S.C.D. Convention, 1980.

Schunk, D.H. and Gaa, J.P. "Goal-Setting Influence on Learning and Self-Evaluation." *Journal of Classroom Interaction*, 16/2, 38-44.

Sefkow, S.B. and Myers, J.L. "Review Effects of Inserted Questions on Learning from Prose." *American Educational Research Journal*, Winter 1980, 17/4, 435-448.

Trabasso, T. "Pay Attention." In DeCecco, J.P. (ed.), *Readings in Educational Psychology Today*. Del Mar, CA: CRM Books, 1970.

Special Note

We are grateful to the following teachers for sharing examples of their applications of the principles of learning with us: Nadine Bishop, Carol Callahan, Nancy Dennison, E.G. Downes, Joan Grossman, Matt King, Dave Mayall, Ellen Epstein Maxwell, Heather Robinson, Alan Ticotsky, Sal Trento, Jim Treweiler, Joe Walsh, and Mary Wilinsky.

9

Space

How do I get the most out of my space and furniture?

Matching to Instruction
Ownership and Privacy
Nine Checkpoints

SPACE

Architects, interior decorators, and environmental engineers all believe that the way things are arranged in space (including the space itself) makes a difference in how people function. These professionals make their living helping people to be happier and to function more efficiently through better use of the physical environment. We need to apply their insights to education for similar payoffs—increased satisfaction and productivity.

In this chapter on the Space parameter of teaching, we will explore ways in which teachers can make the most advantageous use of classroom (and school) space. There are two equally important but different ways of looking at teachers' use of Space. One is to look at the way arrangements of furniture, materials, and space support the kind of instruction going on. What are the goals of the lesson? What kind of learning environment does it ask for? How does the use of Space support the lesson? Since lesson goals and lesson forms change, Space arrangements can be expected to change also. There are a variety of Space arrangements teachers may use, and those arrangements can be rationally matched to the active form of instruction.

The second way of looking at Space focuses not on its varying uses, but rather on how certain *constant* space-related issues of student life are handled: ownership and privacy. Different students have different needs in these areas, and there are things teachers can do to match to those individual needs.

We will look at Space in both of these ways.

Matching Space to Instruction

Teachers experience a wide variety of office arrangements when they confer with school principals. Some principals speak to teachers across a desk; some have the teacher's chair next to the desk so that the conversation takes place across the corner of the desk. Other principals have their desk in a corner facing a wall, and turn their chair around to confer. Still others leave their desk and confer with teachers around a coffee table where two or three chairs are set.

Each of those arrangements sends a different message about authority, and uses physical setting to set the climate for the kind of interaction the principal desires. Likewise, teachers' arrangements of classroom space send messages about their image of the learner and the kind of learning they intend. Jacob Getzels has associated four such images with four different patterns of classroom space:

1. He ties the "empty learner" image to the *rectangular* room arrangement: "In these classroom designs, which were the standard in the early 1900s and continue to be the most prevalent today, the teacher's function is to fill the learners with knowledge. Hence all desks face front in evenly spaced rows toward the front of the class and the source of knowledge, the teacher and his or her desk" (Getzels, in Lewis, 1979).

2. Getzels next connects the image of the "active learner" to the *square* room arrangement: "In these rooms furniture is movable, arrangements are changed, the teacher's desk joins those of the children and the learner becomes the center..." (*ibid*).

3. Getzels' third model is the "social learner" and the *circular* classroom: "Learning was perceived as occurring through interpersonal actions and reactions..." (*ibid*). It is in such a shape that many of today's affective education programs occur. One commercial affective education curriculum guide even calls its program "The Magic Circle." Children learn about their own feelings, the feelings of others, and study levels and consequences of interactions.

4. Getzels' final model is the "stimulus-seeking learner" and the *open* classroom: "where learning centers, communally owned furniture, private study spaces, and public areas replace classrooms, halls, and traditional school furniture. The learner is seen as a 'problem finding and stimulus seeking organism'" (*ibid*).

Learners are, of course, all of these things. It is appropriate that students in school should sometimes be good receivers of information, sometimes active learners within teacher-planned tasks, sometimes heavily involved with each other in discussion, and sometimes shapers of their own activities (the "stimulus seeking" learner). No one of these physical environments is the best; they are simply different and exist for different purposes. When we look for variety in the way teachers arrange their class space, it is not random change and variety for the sake of variety that we look for. Rather, it is patterns of space that support different forms of learning appropriate to a particular lesson's goal.

Teachers can change Space arrangements quite quickly for different purposes. One high school teacher we know sometimes has four different arrangements for four successive periods. The changes are made easily and quickly because the students know the basic formats and do all the moving of desks in one or two minutes, usually between classes. The teacher spends time at the beginning of the year explaining these formats to the students and doing a bit of practice arranging them, so the students can set up quickly from then on.

On one day we observed, the first class (seniors) started with desks in rows for a recitation and presentation lesson on Russian short stories. The second class (juniors) quickly rearranged the desks into clusters of six and began "committee work"; i.e., cooperative team work on planning and preparing analyses of various American playwrights' works. The teacher signaled the format as students were entering the room, asking the first few students to set up for "committees" as they came in. Others then joined in. The third class (sophomores), again on signal, quickly put the desks in a large circle around the perimeter of the room for a discussion of a class book writing project involving elementary school children in a neighboring school. As a class, they were going to make some decisions and lay out a schedule for the project. The next period a new class (also sophomores) had a drill and practice lesson analyzing themes for variety in sentence pattern. Their desks were arranged, as you may have guessed, facing the teacher.

Some basic arrangements lend themselves more easily to this kind of flexibility. For example, "Mr. Orr's grade five class sat at individual desks placed around the perimeter of the room [perhaps facing the wall]. The open area at the center of the room was used for more of the formal instruction and for small group activities" (Winne and Marx, 1982, p. 496). This type of arrangement gives students some privacy and insulation from visual distraction when they are doing individual work. For a class meeting, all they have to do is turn their chairs around and they're in a circle...the same for total group instruction. They can go to tables in the middle for small group work, either with a teacher or in cooperative groups.

As we look at our use of Space, we can note whether it is a rational use. That is, have we arranged things *deliberately* to best support the kind of instruction under way? If the answer is yes, we can go on to ask whether we vary the arrangement when our instruction changes. In this manner, our use of classroom space can be classified according to one of the following statements:

- <u>no teacher impact on space</u>: Teacher takes it the way it comes (from custodian, from previous period's teacher, from tradition).

- <u>space arranged by teacher according to a conventional design</u>, and used conventionally, consistently, but without variation.

- <u>space rearranged periodically but experimentally</u>, without clear rationale, mostly just for "change" itself.

- <u>space arrangement constant but is appropriate for instruction</u>

- <u>space used flexibly for different instructional purposes at different times, matched to curricular goals</u>.

Within a given arrangement of space, the placement of materials can further support instructional goals. We find primary grade teachers are often particularly thoughtful about the placement of various items in relation to each other. For example, art materials may be placed near a creative writing area to encourage painting as a follow-up to creative writing. This kind of attention to location and activity flow, though, applies equally well to senior high school. A display of 19th-century American art may be placed over the supply table where students periodically go for assignment sheets and to turn in papers in an English class. The display might serve as a stimulus for a unit on American authors of the period. References and connections to the pictures can be made when the instruction starts.

Ownership and Privacy

Lewis (1979) raises the issue of what spaces *belong* to the students in a classroom (or a school). She provides the following table:

Desk	Probably the most valued and protected space. In very traditional classrooms it may be the child's only source of personal space. In more open classes it may be shared with others, or no longer be a part of the school furniture.
Locker	Often shared with others. Considered a convenience space.
Special Class Seat	In music, art, library, if seats are assigned, a certain degree of ownership will be attached to the seat.
Chair	Often individuals and the group will recognize individual ownership of chairs. Robert Sommer (1969) notes: "People who remain in public areas for long periods—whether at a habitual chair at a weekly conference or on a commuter train—can establish a form of tenure. Their rights to this space will be supported by their neighbors even when they are not physically present."

Boys' or Girls' Bathroom	Definitely a child's space and not a teacher's. A private retreat for tears, anger, fights, secrets, mischief and daydreams. In some-schools it becomes the communal news center for the underground student communication network. In some secondary schools it may become the property of a group of students or it may be locked by the administration.
Playground	Child owned and shared with other children. Powerfully real and memorable considering the relatively limited time spent in recess.
Hall	A no-man's-land in most schools. A public avenue. Perhaps the sense of ownership would be similar to that felt for one's lane or street at home. In secondary school, the hub of socializing.
Classroom	A wide range of possible feeling here. In some rooms children feel a sense of ownership for the whole room or sections of it. In other rooms the desk may be the only owned space.
School Building	Feelings of ownership increase with the years spent in the build-ing. Variations in intensity also depend upon school philoso-phies, building dimensions, and the degree to which children participate in school activities. [Lewis, 1979, p. 130]

Having a place of your own—not just a cubby or a mailbox—but a workplace to *occupy* that is regularly yours is a strongly felt need by many students. One of the authors consulted on a weekly basis in a school system for several years with-out such a space, and it drove him crazy!

Left on their own, junior and senior high school students regularly take the same desk in any given class. It becomes "their" seat. College students and adults do the same. As teachers plan classroom space, they should consider whether they have adequately met students' needs for ownership of space. That need varies considerably with individuals, as does their need for privacy.

Private spaces restrict visual distraction and noise—places like carrels or, at the most private, individual practice rooms. There are students who benefit greatly from having such places created for them or put at their disposal. Skillful teachers look for these individuals and match them with spatial arrangements that suit their needs. As they look at their classrooms and other school facilities (libraries, media centers), they ask themselves if enough private spaces have been provided to accommodate such students, because there are always some of them.

The literature on use of school space is sparse and the research is even thinner. A survey showed support for the following nine recommendations, which we pass along. They are not what we could call a scientific knowledge base, but rather a useful conventional wisdom. They can serve as a checklist from which to survey one's classroom and make judgements. As with checklists in general, it reminds us to ask questions we might otherwise forget.

1. Materials students use should be visibly stored and accessible to facilitate efficient getting and putting away.

2. No dead space, meaning open purposeless space whose use lends itself to random or illegitimate student activity.

3. In some settings, for reasons of safety or control, it may be appropriate for space to be arranged so the teacher can see all of it with no blind spots. (In other settings this guideline may be inconsistent with goals relating to trust, privacy, and independence.)

4. Vertical space (walls, dividers, closets, and moveable cabinet doors) should be employed productively—e.g., for display, learning stations, or storage of materials—thus effectively increasing usable space in the classroom. Hanging artifacts or displays from the ceiling, or multilevel use of space in addition to the floor (lofts, for example, or other erected structures), can further increase effective usable space within a room.

5. Dividers placed on a diagonal with respect to the 90° orientation of the walls can channel student movement and visual fields in interesting and deliberate directions.

6. Have a display area where students' work, art, various kinds of products can easily be seen and examined.

7. Keep active areas distant from quiet areas in a room. The rationale for this recommendation is to minimize distraction and interference.

8. Likewise, adjacent activity areas should be far enough apart, or clearly bounded from their immediate neighbor, so as to prevent distraction and interference.

9. Have clear traffic paths connecting functional areas of the room that do not necessitate students walking through one area (and disturbing things there) to get to another.

Overall, the message we get from reviewing the literature on Space and class-rooms is to be deliberate about its use. We can make our instructional spaces more attractive, more efficient, and more flexible; in short, we can control and change these spaces to best support instruction even as we move from lesson to lesson.

Checking on Space

Mark the descriptions that apply to these aspects of the use of Space. ['n/a' means 'not applicable']

1. Classroom arrangement:

    no teacher impact
    conventional
    varies experimentally
    uniform but supports instruction
    flexible, varies to support instruction

2. Is 'ownership and privacy' provided for?   n/a   no   yes

3. Are private spaces made available for
   those individual students who need them?   n/a   no   yes

4. Are the following used?

    • visible, accessible storage   n/a   no   yes

    • no dead space   n/a   no   yes

    • no teacher blind spots   n/a   no   yes

    • use of vertical space   n/a   no   yes

    • diagonal dividers   n/a   no   yes

    • display area   n/a   no   yes

    • active separated from quiet   n/a   no   yes

    • boundaries between areas   n/a   no   yes

    • clear traffic patterns   n/a   no   yes

Source Materials on This Parameter

Abramson, P. *Schools for Early Childhood.* New York: Educational Facilities Laboratory, 1970.

Gross, R. and Murphy, J. *Educational Change and Architectural Consequences.* New York: Educational Facilities Laboratory, 1968.

Kohn, J. *The Early Learning Center.* New York: Educational Facilities Laboratory, 1970.

Kritchevsky, S., Prescott, E. and Walling, I. *Physical Space.* Washington, D.C.: NAEYC, 1969.

Lewis, B.V. "Time and Space in Schools." In Yamamento, K. (*ed.*), *Children in Time and Space.* New York: Teachers College Press, 1977, 128-169.

Marshall, K. *Opening Your Class with Learning Stations.* Palo Alto, CA: Learning Handbooks, 1975.

School Review. *Learning Environments.* Whole Issue, Vol. 82 No. 4., August 1974.

Winne, P.H. and Marx, R.W. "Students and Teachers View of Thinking Process For Classroom Learning." *Elementary School Journal*, May 1982, 496.

Zefferblatt, S.M. "Architecture and Human Behavior: Toward Increased Understanding of a Functional Relationship." *Educational Technology*, August 1972, 54-57.

10

Time

How do I time events and regulate schedules so that students get the most productive learning time?

Allocation
Time to Learn
Instructional Time
Beginning and Ending Minutes
Pacing and Rhythm

TIME

Time is the currency of life, and teachers run the bank for their students about six hours a day—an enormously powerful position. They run the bank even for "free choice" times where the options available are those offered or allowed by the teacher.

When students do what, in what order, and for how long is largely under teacher's control; and we know from recent research that controlling it well has a big impact on student learning. This includes time spent in places other than the classroom too, places like the cafeteria. How long students spend in each of the environments school offers and the quality of that time is something faculty members control. This chapter is about being as deliberate as possible in managing student time use for maximum learning. It draws on the growing knowledge base of the field to help us be better time managers for our students.

The issues of time management for students center around *allocation* and *efficiency*, and *pacing*.

Allocation

A superficial look at the research on student time use may prompt one to say, "So what else is new?" Obviously, if students spend more time on math and lose less time fooling around they will learn more math! But there is something new, and there are insights—perhaps surprises—for all of us when we start getting accurate data on how our students are really spending class time.

Through the 70's, time-on-task research worked its way through a series of more refined and powerful concepts represented in the following diagram:

Time in School

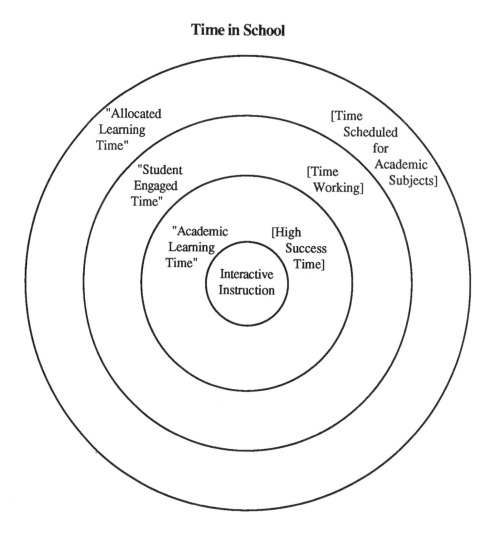

Starting with *Time in School*, each of the concepts of the chart includes and subsumes the one(s) below and inside its circle.

Time in School is self-explanatory.

Allocated Learning Time means time scheduled for academic work in a given area.

Student Engaged Time is the number of minutes students are actually working or attending during academic periods, and not daydreaming, fooling around, or getting organized.

Academic Learning Time is the time students spend engaged with a high rate of success. The high success rate distinguishes it from Student Engaged Time and makes it a subset of Engaged Time.

Interactive Instruction is time spent directly with a teacher getting instruction (one to one, small group, or large group), as opposed to time spent alone doing seatwork or projects or working with a group that's not interacting directly with an instructor.

Of the time spent in school, a portion is allocated for academics. Research has found little difference between Time in School across schools, but very big differences in Allocated Learning Time across schools and between classes. For example, as cited by Caldwell, *et al.*, (1982), Dishaw reports:

> ...time actually allocated for fifth-grade math ranged from 18 minutes to 80 minutes; allocated fifth-grade reading time ranged from 51 minutes to 195 minutes. Allocated time may also vary enormously within a class; for example, in one study (Dishaw 1977) one fifth-grade student spent 39 minutes each day on math while another student spent 75 minutes. These differences in actual allocated time suggest that some students may have two to four times as much opportunity to learn specific academic content as other students.

Time scheduled for different subjects should reflect some consensus across a school about what is important and what the priorities are within those things that are important, for there are surely many of them. Is it fair that because of a particular elementary teacher's talents and inclinations, her class gets a great reading and writing program but practically nothing else? One of the needs this Time parameter brings up is to look at student's school experience from a long range point of view. Over the years, what amount of time is spent learning what subjects as a student goes through school? Is there some consistency and rationale to this expenditure of time? If not, then we are not really in control of the education we are delivering. If not, we do not even *know* what we are delivering.

While such wide variances might not show up in a similar analysis of allocated time in high school, they probably would for the next category.

Of the time allocated for academics, students are only engaged or attending for a portion of that time—on average about 75 percent of it. But there, also, the range of student engaged time is very big—50 to 90 percent (Fisher, *et al.*, 1978). It is the *percentage* of student engaged time (as a percentage of allocated time) that seems important, not just the absolute number of minutes.

> "Several studies indicate that engagement rates are significantly related to student achievement (Anderson, 1975; Fisher, *et al.*, 1978). Thus variations in engagement rates are highly predictive of student achievement, accounting for as much as *three-fifths of the variations* in achievement (Bloom, 1974)...reanalysis of the Stallings and Kaskowitz data (Rim and Coller, 1978) showed that classrooms with more engaged time in reading or math generally showed higher achievement in that subject. However, gains

in student achievement did not always directly vary with engaged time. For some grade levels and subjects the relationship between student achievement and engaged time leveled off and then became negative when engaged time was larger than a certain value." [Caldwell, *op. cit.*]

The above makes sense, given that some students master new material very quickly. For them, part of the engaged time can be wasted practicing material they already know.

About 25 percent of time allocated for academics seems, inescapably, to go into management tasks (getting papers, setting up equipment...) and student inattention (daydreaming...). Even the best classroom managers seem able to reduce this only slightly by squeezing 5 percent back from inattention. Thus, a 75 percent engagement rate is considered good. When students start falling below this, teachers should reexamine their management strategies and work to get engagement back up.

We also need to examine the *teacher's* engaged rate. What percent of allocated time is the *teacher engaged with students* as opposed to preparing materials, correcting papers, or doing other management tasks. Research is clear that this percentage should be high (Stallings, 1980). A major study of secondary school teachers found the average engaged rate to be 73 percent. Teachers who had lower rates of interaction with students had classes with significantly smaller achievement gains (or no gain at all), especially for low-performing students. This is true even if *students* are on-task most of the time. As Stallings (1980) explains:

> The students are on-task, but the teacher is not teaching. In those classrooms where no gain was being made, the students were doing written assignments 28 percent of the time and reading silently 22 percent of the time, and teachers were doing classroom management tasks more than 27 percent of the time.

Finally, students experience a high rate of success for only a portion of the engaged time. That time is called "Academic Learning Time" in the literature (why not call it "high-success time"?) and as before, the amount of it students experience across classrooms varies hugely—in basic skill work, for example, anywhere from 16 min./day in a group of low-average classes to 111 min./day in a group of high-average classes. High- and low-average does *not* refer to the ability level of the students, by the way. It refers to the *teachers'* ability to get more Academic Learning Time for students. High average teachers provide "more than twice as much academic learning time as in the average case and more than six times as much as in the low-average case" (Caldwell, *et al.*, 1982). These startling figures prompt us to take a careful look at how our students are experiencing school time, because high-success time correlates strongly with achievement, and data show that teachers who do study their time use make significant changes (Stallings, 1980) and get better student learning.

One of the authors once studied the time usage of students in five classrooms of a K-5 school using a technique adapted from Engel (1977). He scanned the class every five minutes, making a notation for each student on a class roster. The notation captured what the student was doing, and with what level of attention or involvement. From these data, a color bar graph was constructed for each student with colors coded to study activities showing student time use over a whole morning. Coded cross marks in black were overlaid on the color bar to indicate degrees of inattention or non-involvement. Putting all the bars together on one graph for the class gave the teachers an enormous amount of data, both on individual students and on patterns across the class. One teacher was losing a great deal of time in classroom management: passing out papers, setting up in the morning, getting ready for transitions, etc. Another teacher had students with a low level of involvement due to social chatter at table groups—quiet, unobtrusive, but persistent and interfering with their work. Another teacher found her students were involved pretty consistently with individual tasks and projects, but sometimes received only five minutes of direct teacher instruction in the course of the day. All these teachers made changes to increase their effectiveness after they saw the data. The changes involved more attention to momentum, rearranging space, rescheduling their own instructional time, and clarifying their expectations for student behavior. The point we wish to make is that the obvious was not so obvious to them until they directly faced objective data about their own students and their own classes. When they had the data, they were able to improve their own effectiveness. Academic Engaged Time and student time spent in Interactive Instruction may sound obvious enough to you and me, but you may find some new priorities emerging when you get the numbers on your own classes.

Lienhardt, *et al*. (1981) comment that "teachers must be vigilant in their search for children who are losing out. While the average off-task rate was 15 percent, some students were off-task more than 30 percent of the time. While the average amount of teacher instruction (in reading) was 16 minutes a day, the range was from 1.4 minutes per day to 35 minutes per day (within the same class). While the average time spent in silent reading was 14 minutes per day, some students spent no time at all reading silently. Fortunately, teachers can dramatically change the experience and performance of those students who seem to be losing out without changing things for those who are not." But first the teacher must become aware of who they are, and how the time is being lost.

Time to Learn

Benjamin Bloom's work on Mastery Learning has added another important concept to our knowledge base about time—"time to learn." The idea is that most students can learn anything if they have the prerequisite pieces of knowledge and skill in place and are given adequate time to learn it. Giving them adequate time to learn doesn't mean giving them material and just waiting until they've gone over it long enough to absorb it; it means task analysis of new learnings, careful ongoing assessment, and reteaching loops for items and to students, who need it...and for only those who do.

The view of time from Mastery Learning puts teachers on the spot along with students. We can't just blame the students if learning isn't taking place. We must examine our own determination and be able to prove we are offering students appropriate-size bites of new learning; for instance, not leaving them in the dust with Chapter 2 if they haven't yet grasped the items in Chapter 1.

Mastery Learning is a form of individualizing instruction, but individualizing means more than self-paced here, more than marching through programmed material. It means clear and comprehensive sequences of instruction laid out in advance, broken down into pieces, and with options for how to deliver instruction of those pieces to students. Above all, it means monitoring what students know and not giving up until they have met mastery criteria.

Efficiency

Another area researchers have looked at is how much Interactive Instruction students experience, meaning time with a teacher actively working on material as opposed to seatwork, written assignments, or silent reading. For Interactive Instruction the findings have indicated: the more, the better (Stallings and Kaskowitz, 1974). The point is simply that when teachers are teaching, students are more likely to be learning—and that workbooks and other solo assignments that occupy students' class time don't teach...not a very surprising finding when one considers the importance of teacher feedback, knowledge of results, degree of guidance, and other Principles of Learning we have considered previously. This finding has led some (Rosenshine, 1981) to advocate the Direct Instruction pattern of teaching for whole class groups as the most efficient form of instruction. This recommendation really misses the point. Research is convincing that the proportion of Interactive Instruction time is important, but the Direct Instruction pattern is only one way to get it, and suitable only to one kind of teaching—skills. All the Models of Teaching in the next chapter can provide interactive teaching time. Peer tutoring can provide interactive teaching time. It is the *attributes* of Interactive Instruction that are important any way you get them, and those attributes are, it seems to us, clear explanation, prompt feedback, knowledge of results, and appropriate degree of guidance.

Furthermore, there are learnings for which the Direct Instruction pattern is clearly not the only or the best way—like teaching students to evidence positions (see Jurisprudential Model); like teaching the scientific method (see Discovery

Model). So, we urge our readers to put the current vogue for Direct Instruction in perspective. Direct Instruction is effective for teaching skills, and it works to the degree that it provides high proportions of Interactive Instruction time. But there are other learnings besides skills, and two dozen other models that can provide Interactive Instruction.

Now, having said that, it is time to return to the point and ask ourselves and the teachers with whom we work if there really is enough direct teacher contact with students, regardless of the Model of Teaching in use. Individualized programs are at high risk here. If poorly managed, students, though active and involved, may get only a few minutes a day with the teacher and that is not enough. If that is happening to you, then either you need to do more group work or manage individualization so students get more feedback and guidance.

But how much time-with-teacher is enough? Rosenshine (1981) concludes, "Currently, the need for students to spend 60 to 75 percent of their time working alone is a fact of classroom life. Whether this percentage can be reduced, or whether instruction can be organized so students are more engaged when working alone, are major areas for future research" (p. 22). Thus, we can infer that 25 to 40 percent of a student's academic time directly involved with a teacher would be pretty good. There are certainly many classrooms where the figures are nowhere near that.

We must also remember that what goes on during the Interactive Instruction may or may not capture the essential attributes of good Direct Instruction. Leinhardt, et al. (1981) found in a sample of classrooms that 14 of the 16 minutes of teacher instruction in reading went for "general instruction"—which sounds like presentation and direction-giving. Of the remaining two minutes, students spent one completing a task in the teacher's presence, and one getting explanations of modeling of correct elements of reading. Thus, even within Direct Instruction time it is possible for students to get very little in direct feedback and clarification.

All of this leads us to wonder what accounts for the large differences in engaged time, high-success time, and interactive instruction time we find in different classes? What do the "high-average" teachers do that the others don't?

Skill at the Management Parameters (Attention, Momentum, Expectations) is a large part of it. Research from Kounin to Evertson and Brophy correlate student achievement with these teacher skills. They work to get more student engaged time and less time lost in management and disciplining. Thus, with more time spent in actual learning, one would expect better test results. It is interesting to note, however, that no matter how good a manager one is, "nonengaged time seems inevitable. In average classrooms, students are not engaged about 16 minutes per hour of allocated time in reading and math; the three high teachers reduced this amount to 12 minutes per hour. In classrooms of both average and high teachers, students spend eight to nine minutes in interim and wait time. Thus, the difference between the teachers who had the highest academic engaged minutes and the average teacher was about four minutes of nonengaged minutes per hour, and most of this difference occurred because the high teachers reduced off-task time to about four minutes per hour" (Rosenshine, 1981). But the high teachers also allocated more time to the subject. So after Management skills we can add another to our list of reasons for the variation across classes in academic engaged time: clarity and deliberateness about priorities for time allocation.

Variance in high success time must be traced to the appropriateness of assignments, the diagnostic acuteness of the teacher, the adequacy of instruction and direction-giving before students are turned loose on individual tasks. In other words, the teacher's skill at Clarity, Structuring Learning Experiences, and Matching Objectives to individuals and groups. But this is not much help if we are looking at Time as a parameter and wondering what skills are particular to managing it well. So far, we seem to be saying that good time management comes from handling a number of *other* parameters well. And, indeed, to a great extent it does. If you see students who are on-task, productive, and experiencing success, you are seeing more than good time management; you are seeing successful education. Seen this broadly, good use of student time is a criterion for good teaching, an outcome of *all* the things that go into good education. But there are some skills that are distinctly part of efficient time mangement itself. Let's look at those aspects of the Time parameter that allow it to stand on its own as an area of teacher skill.

Beginning and Ending Minutes

In the Principle of Learning called "Sequence," we stated that what happens at the beginning and end of a class period or a lesson is best remembered. Teachers should therefore pay particular attention to what happens in these two slugs of time. We're talking about *short* slugs of time here...probably around five minutes. In what way should teachers take advantage of them?

The first lesson is simply not to waste them. Do not, if at all possible, let them be eaten up by organization and management—passing back papers, getting furniture arranged, getting kids seated, waiting for latecomers. Do not let the class end limply with students working on their own, starting homework, cleaning up, or socializing. Clean up the five minutes *before* the last five minutes and use the last five minutes to do something with the students: e.g., pull them together and have them highlight important points in today's lesson, lab, or whatever. Get them reviewing, summarizing, highlighting, or in some way engaging something important in those minutes.

Teachers with good Momentum skills are in the best position to take advantage of the opening minutes. Teachers who regularly "summarize" with students are likely to take advantage of closing minutes. But summarizing is not the only way to use closing minutes well. Giving assignments slowly and carefully, posing challenging dilemmas for students to ponder ("end without closure"), getting personal involvement or commitments from students on controversial issues or on contracts may be appropriate uses, too. The main point is to use it, not lose it. Give some sharp focus and purpose to the beginning and ending minutes.

Flexibility in Pacing and Scheduling

"Matching" has been an important theme with each parameter. We have advanced the notion that a parameter contains a repertoire and that skillfulness comes in matching choices from it to individuals, groups, and curricula. So it is with pacing and scheduling. The same pace will not work equally well for all classes. Carolyn Evertson (1982) found that the way teachers paced activities varied greatly and corresponded to their success with high- and low-ability classes, but made quite a difference in low-ability groups. Students in low-ability classes have a clear tendency to drop in and out of participation, especially during seatwork periods. Some students refuse to participate at all. Evertson provides the following descriptions and commentary (excerpted here) on two junior high teachers' classrooms to show how differences in pacing affect low-ability students.

[First example: Teacher B.]

> (The teacher has just put the seatwork assignment on the board.) Marie says, "I don't have a book." The teacher says, "Look on those shelves," pointing. Marie says, "Those aren't ours." The teacher says, "Some of them are." Marie gets herself a book. Chico raises his hand and says, "I need help." About five students start the assignment right away. (There are 12 students present.) The others are talking, have their hands raised, or are going to the teacher's desk. The teacher says, "Come on up, Randy," when she calls on him. When he gets there, "Larry, leave him alone." Larry stands and visits by the teacher's desk. Chico puts his hand up again. The teacher says, "Chico, what do you need?" He says, "Help." The teacher says, "Okay, wait a second." Larry sits down by the teacher's desk and looks on as she tells him something. Chico calls out, "Miss ___ , are you going to help me?" She says, "Yes, Chico, but come up here." He says, "Aw, Miss, it's too far." The teacher ignores him, and he goes to the teacher's desk. (At this point, five students...are at the teacher's desk.)

This classroom description shows rather dramatically the difficulty students in a lower-ability class can have in getting started and participating successfully in an activity. At one point, five students were at the teacher's desk and most of them were waiting for help. (The teacher eventually helped nine students at her desk during this seatwork activity.) Having so many students in such close proximity to each other frequently created problems and led to misbehavior to which the teacher was forced to respond.

The dialog also illustrates the poor task orientation which generally characterizes the lower-ability classroom. Chico's behavior here is typical of many slow students. He did not take academic activities seriously; he was not willing to begin work on learning tasks; and he was not interested in participating. Poor task orientation on the part of one student also can lead to disruptive behavior from others, as we find when we continue this activity.

> While the teacher is trying to work with Marie, Marie follows Chico's lead in teasing the teacher. She grabs the stapler. The teacher says loudly, "Uh uh, come on Marie." Later, Marie grabs her paper away from the teacher, wads it up, saying, "You wrote on my paper. You're not supposed to write on my paper." Marie sits down. Billy, meanwhile, has continued to play around and talk to Larry. The teacher says sharply, "Billy, you come up here!" Larry says loudly, "That's exactly what Miss ___ says, and it works for her, too." As Billy scoots his desk up, Larry sings, "Row, row, row your desk."

When the teacher had to give individual attention to so many students, she could not monitor the class efficiently, and it was more difficult for the students to get the teacher's attention according to the prescribed procedure.

> Chico, who has his hand up, calls out, "Miss, I can't wait forever." The teacher says, "Just a minute."...Mark yells loudly, "Miss!" The teacher ignores him and continues helping Marie. Then she goes to Pam, who has had her hand up for a long time. A girl calls out from the front of the room, "I need help." She has her hand up, but she calls out. The teacher looks at her and says, "Okay, I'll be there in a second."

It should be noted that two of these students here do not simply call out; they have their hands raised. However, they know that simply raising their hands is not as effective a signal as calling out. The teacher did not consistently enforce (in fact, hardly enforced at all) the rule against calling out under these circumstances.

> Chico calls out, "What time is it?" Billy tells him what time it is. The teacher ignores them both. Billy and Chico are trading epithets like, "Dumbhead." The teacher, helping the girls near the front, ignores them. Then, she looks up and says, "Chico, do you need something else to do?" Chico says, "No." The teacher says, "Then be quiet."

A basic conflict existed in lower-ability classes between two demands of the teacher: the need to help students and the need to control inappropriate, disruptive behavior. In this example, the teacher [teacher B] did not want to interrupt her interchange with the girls near the front, but she was finally forced to respond when their off-task behavior threatened to become disruptive.

[Second example: Teacher F.]

The comparatively high achievement gain of Teacher F's lower-ability class recommends it for closer examination. Teacher F allocated considerably more time for checking and discussion of work (13.7 minutes) and the presentation of material—lecture or introduction to seatwork (14.4 minutes)—and considerably less time for the final seatwork activity (22.5 minutes) than was characteristic of the lower-ability classes in general. In addition, the lecture or introductory phase of seatwork was structured differently, frequently punctuated by two or more very brief, highly focused seatwork activities. In this class, the lecture or introduction to the final seatwork activity usually exhibited the following pattern:

> Teacher F goes to the board, where there are 25 numbers written, and begins rounding off the first one. He has the students do this on paper. He says, "I want you to do the first five." They are in columns of five. He continues, "Then put your pencils down." They are writing these numbers down and he moves around the room. He stops the class (after about 6 minutes) and asks David what his answers were. David frowns and says that he didn't get anything. "Who can help him out?" asks the teacher. Robert says, "I got it." The teacher moves on to the rest of the column and then goes on to the A column which should be rounded to the nearest hundredth. The students then do this column. Kermit calls out, "Are we going to have homework, too?" The teacher says, "I'll assign that in a minute." Kermit says, "Well, we don't have time to work on it if we're going to do all of these." Teacher F says, "Oh, we are not going to do all of these." The teacher goes to the board and asks for the students' attention and begins to go through the second column. He asks Jackie to help him round off the first, and she says she didn't get it. He says, "I just asked you to help." She looks at it and begins to try it. He walks her through the problem. (At this point, when there are approximately 10 minutes left, the teacher gives the seatwork assignment.)

[The following is another instance of a lecture or discussion interrupted by brief seatwork periods.]

> (The teacher) says that they will be talking about addition of decimals. He says that this is not really much different than adding whole numbers. The teacher has Johnny write the first problem out for him. He says to him, "Tell me what to put down." Johnny adds three and two and says that it's five. Then he adds six and nine and says that it's 15; put down the five and carry the one. The teacher then asks him, "Where do I put the one? Down here?" Johnny says, "No, you put the one over the eight." Then he adds the eight and gets nine. He tells him to put the decimal between the nine and the five. When he's through, the teacher says, "Very good." The teacher then starts asking them review questions on decimals. As he asks questions, he reminds students to "Raise your hands and tell me what place the decimal is in." The teacher calls on Gracie to do the second example on the board. She declines, and then the teacher goes on to call on Edward. Edward works through the problem and then says, "Tell me what's wrong." The teacher says to him, "Well, let's find out. How can we tell?" The students call out

that they can subtract to check. At 9:28 the teacher puts up a third example. He tells the class that they'll be doing the assignment on their papers, and that they should go ahead and do number three to see if they can get it right. The teacher starts walking around checking to see if students are getting the problem right. There's some quiet talking in the room and the teacher is still walking around. At 9:41 the teacher says, "Let's look up here." (He works the problem on the board. After that, he assigns them another problem to do at their seats and walks around checking them.)

Teacher F copes with the problem of sustaining seatwork in his lower-ability classes by incorporating some of the seatwork into the lecture (or introduction to seatwork) in very brief segments, placing the responsibility for maintaining lesson continuity with the students for only a very brief period of time. The advantages of this format appear clear. First, a very brief seatwork activity is more likely to have a high task orientation than an extended activity. Surrounding seatwork periods with lecture allows the more easily maintained lesson continuity of the lecture to help support seatwork. Second, these brief seatwork activities incorporated into the lecture enable the teacher to provide more immediate feedback than extended seatwork activities. The teacher can thus modify his or her explanations during the lecture, if necessary, rather than interrupt a long seatwork activity, as frequently happens in the lower-ability classes....

In summary, the lower-ability class of Teacher F presents an important contrast with Teacher B's lower-ability class. Teacher B had a significantly longer seatwork period and shorter checking and lecture activities, possibly adding to her difficulties, inasmuch as seatwork is often a problematic activity in lower-ability classes. In contrast, Teacher F minimized this problem in his lower-ability class by reducing the length of independent seatwork activity, which contributed significantly to the higher task orientation of his class, as determined by observer ratings. The comparison suggests that long, extended seatwork activities are counterproductive, adding to management problems and minimizing good task orientation in low-ability classes.

Many teachers in junior and senior high school have both high *and* low ability classes in their schedule. Are they able to make adjustments, such as Teacher F above did, and pace classes differently for different groups? That is what we mean by "Flexibility in Pacing" in the heading to this section. One can look to see teachers structure time for certain individuals, as Teacher F did for a whole class. And the reasons for varying it certainly go beyond the global word "ability." In the Evertson study, "ability" really meant achievement on C.A.T. tests. So what we had was a distinction between high- and low-*performing* classes. There are many reasons for high and low performance besides native ability with its implication about intelligence. Very intelligent but impulsive or disturbed students may learn best when their pacing is regulated for short bursts of highly focused activities. Skillful teachers look to create such arrangements for those who need it, while the rest of the class may be paced quite differently.

We should be able to look at how a teacher handles pacing and decide which of the following applies:

- no pattern to pacing

- stable routine

- variations for teachable moments

- flexibility for changing curriculum priorities

- matching to individuals and groups.

Checking on Time

Does time allocation per subject match teacher
and school priorities?   Yes   No

Is student engaged time 75% (or above)
of the time allocated for academics?   Yes   No

Does the teacher interact with students
for 75% or more of allocated academic
time (as opposed to using his/her class
time for organization and management
tasks...correcting papers, preparing
materials)?   Yes   No

Do students get adequate time to learn
with reteaching when necessary?   Yes   No

Is high-success time adequate for
students' independent work?   Yes   No

Do individual students get enough interactive
instruction time with teachers?   Yes   No

Are beginning and ending minutes used
fruitfully?   Yes   No

Scheduling and pacing shows:

    no pattern to pacing
      stable routine
        variations for teachable moments
          flexibility for changing curriculum priorities
            matching to individuals and groups

Source Materials on This Parameter

Anderson, L.W. "Student Involvement in Learning and School Achievement." *California Journal of Educational Research*, 26, March 1975, 53-62.

Bloom, B.S. "Time and Learning." *American Psychologist*, 29, September 1974, 682-688.

Caldwell, J.H., Huitt, W.G. and Graeber, A.O. "Time Spent in Learning." *The Elementary School Journal*, 82/5, 1982, 371-480.

Dishaw, M. "Descriptions of Allocated Time to Content Areas for the A-B Period." Beginning Teacher Evaluation Study Technical Note Series, Technical Note IV-2a, San Francisco: Far West Laboratory for Educational Research and Development, 1977.

Engel, B.S. *Informal Evaluation*. Grand Forks, ND: University of North Dakota Press, 1977.

Evertson, C. "Differences in Instructional Activities in High and Low Achieving Junior High School Classes." Paper presented at the Annual Meeting of the American Educational Research Association, Boston, April 1980.

Evertson, C. "Differences in Instructional Activities in Higher- and Lower-Achieving Junior High English and Math Classes." *Elementary School Journal*, 82/4, 1982, 329-350.

Fisher, C.W.; Filby, N.N.; Marilave, R.S.; Cahen, L.S.; Dishaw, M.M.; Moore, J.E. and Berliner, D. "Teaching Behaviors, Academic Learning Time and Student Achievement: Final Report on Phase III-B, Beginning Teacher Evaluation Study." San Francisco: Far West Regional Laboratory, 1978.

Hillerich, R.L. "That's Teaching Spelling???" *Educational Leadership*, May 1982, 615-517.

Karweit, N. and Slain, R.E. "Measurement and Modelings Choices in Studies of Time and Learning." *Educational Research Journal*, 18/2, Summer 1981, 157-172.

Leinhardt, G.; Zigmond, N. and Corley, W.M. "Reading Instruction and Its Effects." *American Educational Research Journal*, 18/3, Fall 1981, 343-361.

Powell, M. and Dishaw, M. "A Realistic Picture of Reading Instructional Time." *Reading Research Quarterly*, 1981.

Rim, E. and Coller, A. "In Search of Nonlinear Process-Product Functions in Existing Schooling Effects Data: A Reanalysis of the First-Grade Reading and Mathematics Data from the Stallings and Kaskowitz Follow Through Study." Philadelphia: Research for Better Schools, Inc., 1982.

Rosenshine, B.V. "How Time is Spent in Elementary Classrooms." *Journal of Classroom Interaction*, 17/1, Winter 1981, 16-25.

Stallings, J.A. "Allocated Academic Learning Time Revisited, or Beyond Time on Task." *Educational Researcher*, 9/11, December 1980.

Stallings, J.A. and Kaskowitz, D.H. "Follow Through Classroom Observation Evaluation, 1972-1973." Menlo Park, CA: Stanford Research Institute, 1974.

11

Procedural Routines

What procedural routines are important, and how do I get maximum mileage out of them?

Clear Communication
Standards
Multiple Purposes

PROCEDURAL ROUTINES

Where would we be without routines in our daily lives: routines for getting up and ready for the day; routines for finding and storing important items at home and at work; routines for doing certain recurring tasks? By "routine," we mean any recurring event or situation for which there could conceivably be a regular procedure.

Clearly, routines are essential to our daily lives. We all have hundreds of routines that we practice unconsciously; they become layered one upon another, operate automatically, and free us for the more thoughtful and interesting projects we may wish to address. The same applies to the role of Routines in the organization of classroom life. Good routines are important, even vital to successful classrooms. When they are poorly thought out—or not thought out at all—the results are seen in disorganization, poor Momentum, and often discipline problems.

Classroom routines need to be *efficient*, and they need to be *clear*. The students need to know what the routines are and how to do them. We will highlight those two notions in this chapter, plus the idea that routines can teach. Routines themselves can be curriculum, by virtue of their particular purposes and the learnings embedded in them.

The Routines parameter encompasses a variety of kinds of classroom routines. Some routines pertain to *housekeeping* (e.g., attendance; lunch and milk counts; getting and/or maintaining supplies; organizing boots and coats; clean-up; snack distribution). Other routines pertain to operational features of *class business* (e.g., making announcements; noise-level control; leaving the room; turn-taking and population limits; what to do with the first ten minutes of the day or of the period; how to carry chairs, scissors, pencils, etc.). Still others pertain to *work habits and work procedures* (e.g., how to sit; how to study spelling words; use of lab equipment; procedures for using an easel; what form to use on book reports; a timetable and milestone chart of events to be checked by the teacher when students are preparing an oral report or a term paper.) When skillfully performed, all of these routines are valuable ways of organizing and managing a class.

Clear Communication and Standards

To get the most out of routines, teachers need to communicate them clearly. The first set of questions to ask about the use of routines comes from the earlier chapter on Expectations: Do the students know clearly what's expected of them in the way of procedures and routines? Do they know what they're supposed to do?

Teacher behaviors that account for *good communication* of Routines are similar to those for communicating expectations for work. Good communication of Routines is (see Expectations, Chapter 4, for expanded definitions):

- <u>direct</u>: routines are explicitly brought to students' attention.

- <u>specific</u>: all important details are explained.

- <u>repeated</u> to make sure students absorb them.

- <u>communicated with positive expectancy</u>: has a "you can do it" flavor.

- <u>modeled</u>

- <u>tenacious</u> in persistently (within reason) addressing routines until students master them.

- <u>consistent</u>: especially in that the teacher *reacts* whenever expectations for routines aren't met.

Similarly, the same kind of thinking applied within the Expectations parameter also goes into examining *the appropriateness of the standards* inherent in the routines, and how the standards are adjusted (matched) for individuals and groups. Therefore, as with standards for Expectations, standards for Routines can be viewed along the scale below (see the Expectations chapter for expanded definitions):

- <u>none</u> exist

- <u>few consistent</u> standards are used

- <u>low</u>: teacher demands less of students than he might.

- <u>too high</u>: teacher demands too much of students.

- <u>average</u>: standards are appropriate for most students.

- <u>inspirational-vague</u>: teacher motivates students, but the standards for their behavior are unclear.

- <u>high but reasonable</u>: standards are very demanding, but *are* attainable by students.

As with academic work, it is in our interest and that of our students to match our standards for Routines to the needs of individual students or groups. (See the Expectations chapter for a discussion of various levels of matching standards.)

Now, with those issues under our belt, we're ready to move into new ground: What about the routines themselves? Why *are* they as they are, and how much mileage is being gotten out of them?

Matching Routines to Purposes

The nature of a teacher's classroom routines is determined by the teacher by abdication, by negotiation, or directly. Seven levels of performance that describe teachers' use of routines can be distinguished:

- <u>no conventions or procedures</u> for relevant events: *ad hoc* teacher reactions.

- <u>a few conventions erratically followed</u>

- <u>stable routines</u> for most relevant events: usually established through training.

- <u>stable and highly efficient routines</u> for all relevant events.

- <u>varied routines</u>: the teacher modifies, experiments, uses alternative forms.

- <u>routines matched to the group</u>

- <u>routines matched to characteristics of individuals</u> and mapped to goals for them.

The above scale spans a range of answers to the question: Why are our routines the way they are? They may serve efficiency and, indeed, this is a valid and common orientation among teachers. They may serve a general goal—giving students security through the predictability of certain recurring events. They may map to more specific goals for groups or for the class as a whole, such as: having students routinely record books they have read in a register so that they take some responsibility for a form of record keeping and get to see and participate in building a cumulative index of their books read; clean-up by assigning teams to areas of the room so that the children have to come to grips with group responsibility, handling the division of labor, and dealing with individuals who won't carry their weight.

Routines may be created or adjusted by teachers in service of objectives for specific individuals. For example, in a primary-grade class, Tim may start each day by taking down a few chairs and then moving into woodworking or clay...something with a motor emphasis; whereas Josh's starting routine may be worked out to reflect academics and time in a private space. In an older class in which students are routinely expected to check the noteboard for morning assignments or for feedback from previous work, Clara may need a personal "greet" and escort over to the noteboard, or a folder of her own in which this information is placed. Tenth-grader Margaret may be asked to end each study hall with a log entry on what she's accomplished as a way of focusing her. Marvin may be asked to arrange the furniture for committee work at the beginning of each social studies period as a way of settling him down (and getting him to class on time).

Below are some examples of procedural routines that serve different purposes. Some serve efficiency and effectiveness—a worthy goal. These are related to *momentum*; that's the kind of efficiency meant here—an efficient flow of events without delays. For example, one such routine is:

> Finished work goes in my "in" tote tray; workbooks are left open to first page needing correction. This eliminates the problem of "What do I do with this paper?"

Other routines are aimed at increasing the effectiveness of cognitive learning. They are routines that are oriented toward *academics*. For example:

> Word Bank and Word File are on-going collections of words the children have found hard to spell. The student finds the correct spelling of a word, writes the word on a card, and then tapes the card to the "word bank," which is a set of 26 pockets—one for each letter of the alphabet—mounted on the wall. Cards are later filed in a permanent "word file" for future use in spelling.

A third group of routines shows how much additional mileage can be gotten out of routines if they are used thoughtfully and deliberately. These routines reveal what many would call the "hidden curriculum"; i.e., the indirect *personal and social learning* students receive just from being present in a particular classroom. "Personal learning" refers to students' learning something about themselves or some ability that might be described in terms of character development rather than skill. "Social learning" refers to students' learning something about others, about groups, about people together (cooperation, sharing). An example of such a routine is:

> After I call on the first student to read, he in turn calls on the next reader. This keeps a larger percentage of the students involved. It also raises questions of fairness (boys shouldn't *only* call on other boys) and consideration of differential reading abilities.

We believe that teachers should be as aware and explicit as possible about their hidden curriculum, and it is through this parameter that they can see much of it. If teachers want, they can make their routines serve multiple purposes.

To illustrate the array of purposeful routines that can comprise a teacher's repertoire in this parameter, we have provided a sampling of routines in the following Quiz. In the Quiz, you will label each routine by the general purpose you believe it serves: *momentum*; *academic*; or *personal and social learning*. This will help reinforce for you the intentions underlying teachers' performances in the Routines parameter.

After you label the routines, we invite you to think about your own classroom routines. What routines do you use that are momentum-related?; that have cognitive learnings built in?; that foster particular personal or social learnings? Is there any way you could milk your routines for more, develop them for bigger payoffs?

Procedural Routines Quiz

The following are actual routines as reported by the teachers who use them. (We, the authors, have commented within brackets upon some of them.) For each of the routines, label one or more of the following in the margin:

- Momentum
- Academics
- Personal and Social Learning (abbreviate this PS).

To help make your choice, ask yourself what the routine is for, what it seems to accomplish. Then decide which of the three categories that purpose seems to fit best. Some may overlap two categories. Review the examples provided earlier in the text if needed.

1. "Extra credit on enrichment papers: If a student finishes a math or reading assignment early, I have a set of follow-up 'fun' sheets which give extra practice in or extension of the concept we are studying. I give the set of papers to the first student finished, and I then direct other early finishers to get their extra credit papers from that first student. This gives the first student finished early some extra responsibility and it frees me from breaking up another group to get enrichment materials."

2. "When we go somewhere, I ask the first child in line to hold the door. He then goes to the end of the line. This has helped eliminate some of the rush to be first since he who is first shall be last. There is often no rush for second because usually we go through several doors."

3. "The children are given a new pencil at the beginning of each month. Except on rare occasions, they will not be given another one until the following month (they must borrow one or bring one from home...) This discourages misplacing pencils."

4. "Story folders...contain all second drafts of student's writings; give each child the ability to re-read a past story, to note improvement and to simply enjoy his/her own stories. Also nice to have during conferences."

5. "Children who come to work with me as a specialist each have a Duo-Tang folder in which they keep work papers completed and others still to be done or in process. These folders are kept in a plastic milk carton crate with oak tag dividers for each group. When the children come to their session they get their materials from the box. On the outside of the folders

lists can be kept which indicate books read, materials being used, schedule of sessions and other pertinent information."

6. "Each Friday morning, I sit down with a predesignated student [presumably different each week]. Together we mark out a dummy copy of the weekly [class] newspaper. I guide the story and write it correctly. Then the student copies it over on a master. This provides a positive writing experience for the student. There is little technical risk, and the feedback helps to encourage other types of writing."

[Authors' note: This also provides guaranteed *one-to-one* time with each student periodically for an extended period of time. Although around an academic/fun activity, it gives the opportunity for teacher-student relationship building, important to good teaching. As an activity it also affords opportunity for *community building* in the classroom; the articles may be directly about the class, its members, and things they did or things that happened to them together over the past week. Thus, the newspaper creates a kind of class history and can be compiled over the year. Everybody's interested in reading it when it comes out that afternoon. After all—it's about them!]

7. "Another technique I have learned aids in math boardwork. If we are working on unlined math papers, I guide the class in folding the paper before we begin. This creates boxes for the problems and helps organize the paper. It is also a lesson in the exponential powers of 2."

[Authors' note: Some teachers insist math be done on large-box graph paper only to aid in the organization and alignment of columns. They then reduce the size of the boxes and gradually "fade" out the use of graph paper, demanding that students keep work aligned and organized.]

8. "...I feel this method [posting long-term assignments on the board, with deadlines, and expecting students to work on them with free class time] helps the children take the responsibility of organizing their time to do the assignments and by checking the list frequently it helps them to learn to meet deadlines."

[Authors' note: This routine is concerned with students learning to manage their time; to plan projects that have parts and apportion tasks to time periods so that they meet a deadline. Children may not, however, be very good at this, and the procedures should accommodate some teaching or some strategies to help them learn time management. The first part of the strategy is to give the assignment with the deadline. This gives students the opportunity to succeed and also to fail, thus the questions can be asked: "How did you/what did you learn from this experience? How can you fix that next time?" Provisions have to be made for asking those questions to individuals. Some teachers provide check-in points along the way where students have to report how far they've gotten in a long-term assignment. They may reserve certain free periods or regular class periods for meeting briefly with every student to check progress. These brief check-ins, in addition to providing feedback on how work's going and motivating some laggards to get in gear, may be opportunities for a needed bit of tutoring or explaining or redirecting.

The question is, if you want kids to learn time management and organization, what aspect of your procedures *helps them learn that*, beyond just giving them responsibility for long-term assignments?]

9. "Three times a week the class has a period of silent reading, at which time the children may read books, magazines, articles, etc., of their choice. At the end of the period they add to a list, which is kept in their folder, the title of the reading material they read that day and also they indicate the date. I have the children keep this record and collect the sheets about once a month. This helps me keep tabs on what they are reading and to see if they are selecting books at their reading level. I feel it helps the children also to be conscious about how much they are reading. It seems to give some of them a really supportive boost!"

10. "Today's Work Chart—lists the work to be done each day [large piece of paper, two axes, students' names up the side, kinds of work across the top; thus, a matrix. Student can look across opposite his name and see which tasks have been marked for the student to do today]. Provides a means of individualizing daily assignments and holds children accountable for knowing what they should be doing each day. Children check off assignments as they are completed, giving sense of control."

[Authors' note: Often for a couple of children in the class it is very effective (needed) to make a personal "work chart"...or have the student make it. He keeps it right with him and checks off things as they are accomplished. He also builds in, through negotiation with the teacher, activities he especially likes to do. The chart can cover a period anywhere from one day to one week.]

11. "When students are singled out to do something special in class, such as coming up to play a rhythm instrument, I vary the routine of choosing who participates in these ways:

a) Number off down the row.

b) Begin at either the top or the bottom of the class list.

c) Have the children who have already played give their instrument to a 'quiet' person who hasn't played."

12. "Weekly clean-up. On Friday afternoon, I assign students to clean or straighten certain *areas* of the classroom. I alternate the jobs, and on some weeks kids may have no assignment. Then they can straighten their own desks or notebooks. Gets a clean neat classroom and cooperation on the job."

[Authors' note: It's not clear here, but perhaps *teams* of students are assigned to the areas of the room. Some teachers do that to encourage cooperation; the *group* is responsible for getting its job done. This raises questions such as "What if one member of the team doesn't carry his own weight"...fairness...or voluntary support, letting a fellow student in a jam finish his assignment and covering for him in the cleanup.]

13. "Give students options of any one of three ways for learning new vocabulary words...flash cards, write word three times with meaning, or make a 'flip-sheet' for studying and saying the word with its meaning. This helps students learn alternative ways of memorizing and, hopefully, discover the one which works best for them."

14. "I have often prepared visuals to organize the time during which students are arriving at and 'settling in' for class activities. At various times the transparencies may contain quizzes to review skills, directions for an activity that might involve special preparation of a paper (i.e., margins, numbering, etc.) for work that will follow, a list of words to be copied into notebooks, or instructions for specific group work. In the upper right-hand corner of the transparency I indicate the time at which the overhead will be turned off. Students understand that I expect work directed on the transparency to be completed by that time.

"I've found that this technique encourages prompt arrival at class, provides a focus for student attention from the time they arrive, and gives me a chance to take care of routine matters without having students slip into conversations orother involvements that must be cut off in order for class to begin."

15. "I have a decorative tin can sitting on my desk with a sign 'Notes from Home'. The children are to put notes that they bring in the morning in the can. This way I'm not interrupted each time a child comes in with a note and it enables the children to have a place to put them if I am busy at the time."

    [Authors' note: Some teachers use a similar device for receiving notes from the children in the class who are finding it hard to get the teacher's ear...or who have a private message they just would rather write than say directly. In both this and the above case, the teacher has to remember to periodically look in the note can/box. That proves to be no obstacle, however, if it is regularly used.]

16. "The art cart always carries half the boxes of crayons, pastels, marker sets which would be needed to give each child a set. Sharing and mutual responsibility are the goals."

    [Authors' note: Here we have planned scarcity to make children learn how to deal with it...also requires good mediating skills from the teacher. Active listening is appropriate here, also Glasser's "what are you going to do about it then" approach. (See Discipline chapter.)]

17. "As one or two children approach a finished product (this is a manipulative, project-oriented class) the new lesson is then introduced [to everybody; presumably the teacher calls for everybody's attention and introduces the new project]. The new materials are left on the table so the children can start their new projects by themselves (when they finish the old one)...finished products are put in the cabinet. Then I take children who are finished and show them a next logical step with the project they've just finished (enrichment). I give them the option of starting the new project or going one step further with the one they've just completed. Nine out of ten times they are motivated enough to continue the *old* project."

    [Authors' note: In project or lab-oriented courses the above procedure tends to keep the class together, even if students work at widely different rates, offers enrichment to those who will benefit from it, and minimizes confusing transitions.]

18. "Papers are passed in from two certain (specified positions) people moving in opposite directions. This I do to facilitate paper collection, avoiding wasting of time." [Two people are probably opposite the teacher in a circle and sitting next to each other. They start the passing in opposite directions.]

19. "Assignments…are designed to permit students to help each other at the same time that each is required to give individual answers. This supports students' learning from each other and legitimizes talk among peers in class by making it work-related. It makes copying obvious and unacceptable."

[Authors' note: This introduces the subject of cooperative learning and *how* to structure assignments and working environments so that it takes place productively…a topic of the "Learning Experiences" parameter coming up later.]

20. "Instruments in the musicmobile are distributed in an assembly (also could be done in a class) fire-brigade fashion, when each child is to have an instrument. The teacher can remain at the front of the group as the instruments move and not lose momentum."

[Authors' note: This also gives each student something to do, but probably requires practice with a group, especially younger students, so one child dropping an instrument doesn't cause a traffic jam.]

21. "Students will bring the correct books to class according to the 'book chart' in my classroom. The reason is to avoid 'I forgot my book', etc.…"

[Authors' note: It could be that this "book chart" is posted on the door or in some other highly visible spot so that students see as they go out or come in what books are required for the next class.]

22. "As a motivation to speed up and ensure student completion of revision activities for writing projects, use masking tape or colorful tapes to divide a large bulletin or chalk board into a series of 'frames', each large enough to display a student's final draft and each labelled with an individual student's name. As students complete work and have it checked, they are permitted to display it in their personal 'frames'. P.S. The idea works! Students are very anxious to 'fill in their frames'."

23. "Two girls (or boys) are responsible, on an alternating basis, for taking the morning attendance and delivering it to Mrs. Brooks. This develops responsibility and cooperation and allows me to talk with students informally in the morning when I can often catch an important fact about what has happened recently in the student's life."

[Authors' note: The important thing here is the teacher's goal—to have the first five to ten minutes of the day free of any management tasks so that the teacher can make personal contact with some students. The point of this contact may be relationship building, getting information, or filling full the cup of an attention-demanding child early on so he/she doesn't have quite the need to get attention later and fracture class momentum in doing so.]

24. "Every week or two I hold a lottery and parcel out jobs to my class....The whole process of choosing deals with arithmetic, chance, choice, reading, etc...."

25. "Re: Rules and Procedures

    When presenting a musical play to the school or to parents, these rules are followed:

    a) Participants arrive one hour early and meet in the music room for makeup and final touches on costumes.

    b) Only the stage manager, lighting people, and stage hands are allowed in the auditorium before the performance.

    c) When everyone is ready, songs from the play are sung for a warm-up and solo songs are begun but not finished.

    d) During the performance, everyone not on stage at the moment remains in the room—not behind stage or milling about in the halls.

    e) An attempt is made to keep everyone in a calm state, rather than allowing loud, boisterous behavior before the performance.

    f) All the leads are responsible for their own props.

    g) Each student is responsible for his/her own costume before and after the performance.

    Following these criteria guarantees the best possible performance."

26. "Bulletin board—Any articles from local papers which might interest the students or which include their name(s) are put up on the bulletin board. I also put up the weekly lunch menu, various cartoons that the kids would like, pictures or poems. The kids also can bring in clips to display. Kids take pride in seeing their names in print. I can also follow-up class topics."

[Authors' note: The last sentence, "...follow-up class topics," puts this procedure in the "cognitive" category. But there are other things going on here, too. The whole thing might be seen in terms of its role in community building in the classroom. The board happens to be located by the door, is often seen and the topic of conversation while kids are lining up or just coming into the room. It seems intended to be a conversation stimulator. This raises the question of displays in general and challenges us to get as much mileage out of them as we can, besides reinforcing skills and looking attractive.]

27. "When children are involved in a variety of activities, I take a moment to glance quickly about the room and note [on paper] where each child is and with whom. Gives me concrete information regarding children's choices of materials and friends. I can see activity patterns forming. Gives me insight to make constructive suggestions or introduce another concept to some activity and/or children."

[Authors' note: Anecdotal notebooks like the above can be used for note taking and record-keeping throughout the grade levels. When used in this way the teacher does *not* have to reserve time at the end of the day to sit down and record anecdotal notes for each child. Instead, a class roster in a looseleaf notebook is dated with the current date and left open on top of a cabinet, shelf, or desk. Teachers write words or phrases next to students' names as things come up, or when they happen to be passing the shelf where the notebook is kept. The notes might be about activities, as is the teacher's above, or about behavior, skill needs, or virtually any kind of performance. If the blank back of yesterday's roster is used to write or block out today's plans, the notebook may double as a plan book, too. The notes beside students' names may indicate things to get to with them today, reminders for the teacher; they also constitute an ongoing and cumulative record of student performance with dates...very useful at conference time...a rich data base difficult to get any other way.]

28. "When square dancing or any kind of dance that involves a partner of the opposite sex, I make it clear that:

a) As boys are chosen they are asked to fill in the first, second, third, or fourth place in each square.

b) Girls are then numbered off and asked to go to a certain square and stand by whatever boy has the corresponding number.

c) After each dance, the girls switch to another square but keep their same number positions.

d) No one is allowed to make derogatory comments about his/her own partner or anyone else's partner.

e) No one is forced to dance if he or she doesn't want to.

f) Those students not participating are assured they can come up next and either form a new square themselves or choose a partner by taking someone's place who has already danced.

These procedures encourage consideration of each other, especially in a situation which at first feels a little uncomfortable because of the closeness of the opposite sex."

Quiz Answers

 1: Momentum and Academics
 2: Momentum
 3: PS
 4: Academics
 5: Momentum
 6: PS and Academics
 7: Academics
 8: PS
 9: Academics
10: PS
11: Momentum
12: PS
13: Academics
14: Momentum
15: Momentum
16: PS
17: Momentum
18: Momentum
19: PS
20: Momentum
21: Momentum
22: Academics and PS
23: PS and Momentum
24: Academics
25: Momentum
26: Academics and PS
27: Momentum
28: PS and Momentum

Checking on Procedural Routines

1. Check any aspects of the communication of routines that apply, and see if you can cite an occasion to back up your claim with something that was said or done.

    ___ direct
    ___ specific
    ___ repeated
    ___ with positive expectancy
    ___ modeled
    ___ tenacious
    ___ consistent

2. Circle the one that applies. Are the standards embedded in the routines...

    none
        few consistent
            low
                too high
                    average
                        inspirational—vague
                            high but reasonable

3. Matching: Circle the performance level that applies.

    no routines
        few erratic routines
            stable routines
                stable and highly efficient routines
                    varied routines, alternatives
                        routines match group
                            routines match individuals

Source Materials on This Parameter

Randolph, N. and Howe, W. *Self-Enhancing Education.* Palo Alto, CA: Stanford Press, 1966.

Taylor, J. *Organizing the Open Classroom—A Teachers' Guide to the Integrated Day.* New York: Schocken Books, 1972.

Special Note

We appreciate the contributions of the following teachers, who were kind enough to share some of their routines with us:

Nadine Bishop, Steve Bober, Peggy Bowlby, Jeff Levin, Ann Lindsay, Barbara Lipstadt, Betty Murray, David Negrin, Loren Robbins, Sally Springer, Gene Stamell, Bill Tate, Alan Ticotsky, and Joe Walsh.

12

Models of Teaching

How can I vary my teaching style?

MODELS OF TEACHING

For the student of teaching, few efforts are as rewarding and as challenging as learning new Models of Teaching. This is an area where even the most mature and sophisticated of professionals can add to their repertoires and to their power to reach a broader range of students.

A Model of Teaching is a particular pattern of instruction that is recognizable and consistent; you can recognize it and label it when you see it, yet it is distinctly different from patterns in other Models of Teaching. A model has particular values, goals, a rationale, and an orientation to how learning shall take place (e.g., by induction...or by discovery...or through heightened personal awareness...or by wrestling with puzzling data...or by organizing information hierarchically...). And that orientation is developed into a specific set of phases teachers and students go through, in order, with specific kinds of events in each phase. The term "Models of Teaching" is capitalized because each one is a particular entity with very specific components, well worked out, and with markedly different appearances and effects.

Each "Model" is, in reality, a design for planning lessons so as to achieve two outcomes: 1) the teaching of content; 2) the teaching of a particular kind of thinking. There are dozens of Models, but each aims at those same two things— teaching content and teaching thinking. Almost any Model can be used to teach a given piece of content: however, although the information learned may be the same, the intellectual experience for students will be different. For example, if Mr. Jones uses Taba's Inductive Model for a lesson on Hemingway, he wants students to learn not only about Hemingway but also to think inductively. The model is carefully sequenced to get them into that kind of thinking. If he teaches through the Jurisprudential Model, he may want the same learnings about Hemingway, but he also wants his students to think like lawyers, to take positions and argue them with evidence. If he uses the Group Investigation Model, he may still want students to learn the same core information about Hemingway, but in addition he wants them to learn about group process, leadership, and coordinated plans of inquiry. If he uses the Advance Organizer Model, he wants them to learn about hierarchical thinking and subordination of ideas. Models of Teaching give us a way to be more articulate and more precise about implicit learnings students take from our instruction. They enable us to broaden the ways we instruct, and thus broaden the range of students' intellectual experience in school.

Research over several decades has shown no one model superior to the others for achieving learning as measured by test scores. But that only stands to reason, since that was not their intention. Models of Teaching were not created to be more efficient hypodermics to inject knowledge into students' heads. They were intended to teach students how to learn and think in different ways. One can use a variety of models in one's teaching to match students' preferred learning style; one can also use a variety of models to broaden students' capacity as thinkers and learners beyond their favored style.

Teachers who have multiple models in their repertoires may use several different ones in a day, or even switch models within a class period. Teachers who master additional models find themselves able to modulate across them like connoisseurs, thus giving professionalism a new dimension. But lest we wax poetic too early in the game, let us examine the models themselves, first with a more detailed description of what a model is, and then with a look at a number of specific models.

As an example, the Inductive Teaching Model has nine logical steps: 1) enumerating; 2) grouping; 3) labeling; 4) discriminating; 5) comparing; 6) inferring; 7) hypothesizing; 8) evidencing; and 9) generalizing. This script is very different from the Synectics Model: 1) introduce new material; 2) select an analogy; 3) describe direct analogy; 4) personal analogy; 5) point out similarities between new material and analogy; 6) point out the differences; and 7) review new material. By comparing the different Models of Teaching we can identify salient features and deal with important questions related to their application in curriculum, their use in specific situations or with different individuals, and their relation to content, subject matter, and the kind of thinking they prize.

Hilda Taba's Inductive Teaching Model, for example, prizes developing students' ability to make inferences from data. Like all models, Inductive Teaching has a series of phases that unfold over time, like acts and scenes in a play. Each phase looks and sounds different from the previous one; but like scenes in a play, each is carefully articulated with the previous and the succeeding phases to achieve a cumulative effect.

If we wished to use Inductive Teaching to present a lesson on Ernest Hemingway, the man, we might start by showing a filmstrip biography of Hemingway's life. This would be *phase one* of the Model, gathering data. After the filmstrip, we would ask students to tell us items of information they remembered. And we would record them on the board or on charts. The items might appear diconnected and random. "...Had a fishing boat named the Pilar." "He went to Spain three times during the Spanish Civil War." "He had a house in Key West." "He liked to write early in the morning while sitting on a balcony overlooking the streets of Paris." Perhaps we might collect two dozen such items which students would remember and contribute to the data base.

In *phase two* of the Model, we would ask students to group the items from the data base that belonged together. Students would look at the sentences on the board and put certain items together because they bore some relationship with one another.

In *phase three* of the Model, we would ask students to give a title or a label to the groupings they were creating. We might see students label a collection of items as "Hemingway's work habits as a writer." Another grouping might be "Hemingway the outdoorsman," in which information about hunting on the Serengeti and fishing in Michigan would appear. Students around the class might group items in similar clusters, but there would also be some differences in the categories students would create.

In *phase four* of the Model, we would see to it that the groupings of the items about Hemingway created by the students were displayed in some fashion for all to see (charts, overheads). In this phase, the Discrimination phase, the teacher asks students to explain the thinking behind their categories. What really makes this grouping hang together? The categories and the thinking behind them are compared and contrasted as the teacher guides the students through a discussion of the different ways the information could be grouped and why.

In *phase five* of the Model, the teacher asks the students if there are any ideas occurring to them about Hemingway as a result of what they have done so far. Are there any inferences they would be willing to make about Ernest Hemingway as a man? In a recent demonstration lesson we did with adults, one person said at this point, "I think Hemingway was really a very lonely man." At no point in the filmstrip does Hemingway's biographer ever make that point explicitly. No single item of information in the filmstrip would ever lead a viewer to that conclusion. Yet as a result of having been through these phases and manipulating the data in the way those phases require, inferences such as this and others become available to students. There are several other phases to this Model which we will not develop in any detail at this point; our objective is to show that the steps or phases in a Model of Teaching unfold in a planful way so as to lead students towards developing a particular way of thinking. We could summarize the first five phases of Taba's Model presented above by listing the key question of each phase.

Phase One—What is the data?
Phase Two—How would you group the data?
Phase Three—What name would you give to your categories or groups?
Phase Four—What makes your groups really hang together?
Phase Five—What inferences would you be willing to make about the topic?

Similar questions could be generated for succeeding phases. Remember, we are not arguing that Taba's model is superior to any of the others, we are simply trying to make concrete our earlier statements that a Model of Teaching is a particular pattern of instruction that is recognizable and consistent. Furthermore, we are trying to show how this pattern aims at developing a particular kind of thinking in students.

The notion of Models of Teaching was first introduced by Bruce R. Joyce in 1968 through the "Teacher Innovator: A Program to Prepare Teachers," an HEW-funded project. In 1972, Joyce and Weil published their text, *Models of Teaching,* which described a large number of models in detail. These descriptions have been updated in two subsequent editions, (1980, 1986) which have added Models and elaborated prior descriptions until we now have over two dozen Models of Teaching well described with anecdotes, examples, and outlines of steps. These books were an important contribution to the literature on teaching because for the first time the theoretical approaches to learning developed by such luminaries as Bruner, Ausubel, Skinner, Glasser, Suchman, Piaget and others were made operational—that is, Joyce and Weil spelled out what a teacher would do and what the lesson would look like if a person taught according to these theories.

Furthermore, to analyze each Model of Teaching they asked and answered each of the following questions for each theorist:

1. What is the orientation to knowing and learning to know in this Model? Does the teaching appear to be aimed at specific kinds of thinking and means for achieving it?

2. What sequence of events occurs during the process of instruction? What do teachers and students do first, second, third...?

3. How does the teacher regard the student and respond to what he or she does?

4. What teacher/student roles, relationships, and norms are encouraged?

5. What additional provisions, materials (materials and support systems) are needed to make the Model work?

6. What is the purpose of the teaching? What are the likely instructional and nurturant effects of this approach to teaching?

For the first time we were able to see the range of teaching alternatives, to compare them and to distinguish their unique features. Whereas the debates about methods of teaching always seemed in the past to be clouded by lack of clarity of terms—e.g., "lecture", "recitation," or "direct instruction"—the language of Models enabled us to visualize clear patterns of action in teaching. Thus, we could not only talk more precisely about what we might *do* if we taught a lesson through a different Model, we could talk more precisely about *why* we might do so and what the expected effects of using a particular Model might be.

We have provided a review of ten models of teaching; each is described in only the briefest details, and we need to remind ourselves that much study is required for the teacher to gain skill in them. What we hope to illustrate is the range of Models that have been developed and the wonderful menu for learning that lies before us as teachers. Most teachers already do one or two of these Models, but very few of us have been exposed to the full range available, much less trained in the subtleties of implementing them and matching them to different students and curricula.

Because we have the Joyce and Weil book available, there is no need for us to elaborate the steps or phases of each model in detail here. To do so would take an entire book anyway. Our intention is to lay out the different thinking objectives of a variety of models so that readers can focus further reading and learning on Models that best meet their current priorities.

At the end of the chapter, we provide a bibliography of original source works on the Models that will allow those readers interested in doing so to go beyond the chapter on a given Model provided by Joyce and Weil.

To make the models more vivid, we use a specific content in our survey, beginning geometry.

Advanced Organizer Model

Advanced organizers are concepts derived from well-defined bodies of knowledge; e.g., mathematics, grammar, sociology, etc. The following set of geometry concepts illustrates a well-defined, integrated, and progressively differentiated set of organizers:

GEOMETRY

Point

    Space   **Integrative Reconciliation...................**

P   Line Segment
r
o   Line
g
r   Ray
e
s   Angle
s
i   **D**   Vertex
v   **i**
e   **f**   Side of Angle
     f
     e   Congruent
     r
     e   Right Angle
     n
     t   Acute Angle
     i
     a   Obtuse Angle
     t
     i   Straight Angle
     o
     n   ....

In the Advanced Organizer Model these concepts are introduced by the teacher progressively, one by one, through lectures, films, demonstrations, or readings. Next, the student applies the organizer and demonstrates mastery of the geometry concept. For example, the teacher might define an acute angle as any angle that is less than a right angle (less than 90 degrees), and then she might further clarify specifics through examples. In phase two, the student might be asked "to make a drawing that represents an acute angle, and to label it ABC." From exercises such as this one, the teacher can determine student mastery, step by step, and then move on to subsequent organizers.

Why would a teacher use such a Model of Teaching? What value is there in this manner of instruction? Primarily, the teacher seeks to advance the conceptual organizers of this body of knowledge and to promote a meaningful assimilation of information. "Meaningful" means within the context of a hierarchical arrangement of knowledge. Students are expected to learn these organizers because they are basic and fundamental to academic knowledge. Some consider these conceptual organizers the bread and butter of school learning.

Concept Attainment

Closely related to the Advanced Organizer Model is Concept Attainment—learning by logic, analysis, comparison and contrast. The teacher knows the concept but instead of advancing the concept, she presents the data in the form of positive exemplars and the students search for attributes to identify the concept. The teacher also uses nonexemplars which do not contain attributes of the concept to assist students in determining relevant attributes. What is the concept illustrated below?

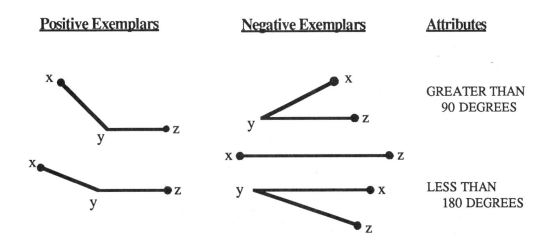

The student is expected to arrive at the concept "inductively," to learn by identifying the salient features and formulating an abstract statement: "any angle that is greater than a right angle and less than a straight angle." The mathematical label is less important than the student's awareness of these defining attributes.

Why use concept attainment as the strategy for the mastery of these concepts? The values of the Concept Attainment Model include not only the concepts themselves, but the awareness of how concepts are formed from attributes, sensitivity to logical reasoning, and a deepening regard for alternative points of view. These instructional and nurturant effects are learned through practice with concept attainment; the student in effect reconstructs knowledge through guided learning.

Inductive Thinking Model

Consider the following array of data:

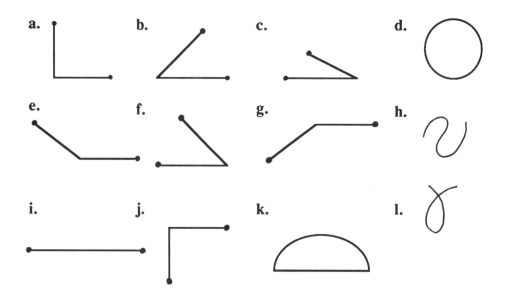

What do you see?
Which ones belong together? Why?
What would you call them? Why?
What do you notice about one of the groups?
What similarities and differences do you see?
What do these tell you about geometry?
What do you think would happen if...?
What evidence would you use to support your guess?
What can we say is generally true?

This series of questions leads students through a systematic sorting of the basic angles. The likely concepts from such a logical process might more or less approximate formal knowledge of geometry, but there is no guarantee, nor does it matter to the teacher that she doesn't know the concepts in advance. The teacher values student thinking; i.e., attention to logic, sensitivity to language, awareness of building knowledge, and concept formation. The students work cooperatively toward building ideas about these shapes. The Inductive Thinking Model enables students to generate knowledge as if they themselves were scholars responsible for producing insights into factual reality.

Inquiry Training

A problem: Make 2 squares and 4 equal triangles out of a rectangle measuring 5 inches by 1 inch.

In inquiry training the student is expected to put his or her knowledge to work to solve a problem. In the process there is more knowledge to be gained, both in substance (mathematical knowledge) and process (inquiry training). To solve the problem, the student needs to construct a solution consisting of geometry concepts: a process of verifying relevant facts about objects, properties, conditions, and events; and simultaneously hypothesizing possible configurations of space, shape, and size. For example, the student might think through the following solution:

Step One

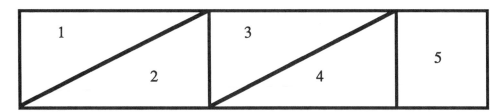

Step Two

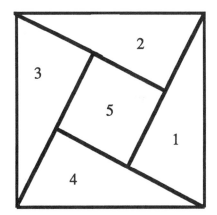

After being presented with the problem, students are encouraged to inquire together as a group while the teacher answers "yes/no" type questions; seeks clarification; encourages student verifying, hypothesizing, and explaining behavior; and guides the group dynamics.

Why should a teacher use the Inquiry Training Model over the other three academic Models of Teaching? Obviously, this model introduces a more tentative knowledge in which organized knowledge from the disciples is synthesized and employed in the formulation of a solution. Mastery of knowledge is not the goal of instruction, rather the student is expected to test out his or her knowledge. In addition, students learn strategies for inquiry by witnessing their own inquiry behavior. This happens when teachers and students go over their problem solving behavior following the cooperative exercise. There is an independence in inquiry learning, too. It provides the learner with experiences which prepare her or him for the uses of knowledge in more life-like situations.

Awareness Training Model

The preceding Models of Teaching were developed from information processing theory and represent traditional approaches to teaching. However, knowledge of space and points in space can be a personal experience as well. Awareness Training attempts to bridge the individual's experiences with other people's; for example, in this case, those of a mathematician. Imagine students with a rope who are able to experience geometric configurations equivalent to line segments and triangles.

a.   b.   c.

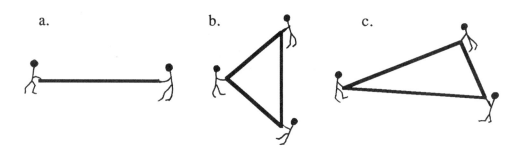

After experiencing "geometry" this way, students should be encouraged to discuss their feelings and thoughts; that is, to give form to them in language within the social context of the classroom. While these experiences may appear elementary in nature, they are, in fact, extremely rich in personal relevance and serve to integrate knowledge and self. The teacher values the students' world and their ability to express themselves. Awareness is often thought to be a first type of knowing which can undergird subsequent learning; however, it is a very special personal ability that marks the individual's maturity. We all like to be around a person who can express their personal realities as well as those more commonly held by communities of scholars.

Synectics Model

The Synectics Model has been derived from a set of assumptions about creativity and analogies. Creativity means seeing connections between the familiar and strange and exploring new solutions to old problems. It means experiencing psychological states such as: detachment, involvement, autonomy, speculation, and deferment. We attain these psychological states through analogies which, in turn, lead the attainment toward the mastery of new and difficult material and novel vantage points for reconsidering problems. Both the means and ends of teaching are influenced by these assumptions.

In "Making the Strange Familiar" the teacher introduces the new material or content through lecture, film, or demonstration. Without comment, the teacher then solicits a possible analogy and asks students to describe it. To personify the analogy, the students act it out. Describing and acting out the analogy provide the particulars for the fourth and fifth steps, listing the similarities and differences between the analogy and the new material. Finally, the students return to the original material to examine and review it, and to discuss details which might have been omitted from previous activity during the analogic thinking. Consider the following example:

Step one:	The teacher presents material on Geometry.
Step two:	The students select an analogy; e.g., a tree.
Step three:	The students describe the tree in detail.
Step four:	The students act out being parts of a tree.
Step five:	The students point out similarities between the tree and geometry; e.g., the "angle of the branches to the tree trunk" or "the points from where the branch begins to end."
Step six:	The students point out differences; e.g., "the crooked branches not being straight lines."
Step seven:	What aspects of geometry were not covered in the discussion of similarities and differences...?

The synectics process induces creative thinking and mastery learning of content. It is both a personal experience which integrates geometry and personal knowledge and an analogic one which capitalizes on the student's ability to make connections. In addition, it is a wonderful group experience. We diversify our efforts to learn through the synectics model; we achieve several goals: mastery of subject matter, analogic thinking, personal integration, fun, and group productivity.

Nondirective Teaching

"John, we're going to study geometry for the next three weeks, and I'm hoping each person will plan a personal project."

"What do you mean, Mr. Rogers?"

"Well, what would you like to learn about geometry?"

"I'll be honest, I never thought about geometry. To me it's just another school subject."

"I understand. We plan so much of your activity in school that it just doesn't seem right to have to think about it for yourself. However, it is important to me that you have this opportunity to set your own goals, to develop the project, and to share with me in assessing your progress."

"I wouldn't know where to begin."

"I'd like to help you. As a teacher I've learned a great many planning skills. I guess that's what makes this project so important to me."

"What do you mean?"

"Well, I want you to learn to organize your own learning, to feel a sense of responsibility for where you're going and how you get there. More importantly, that you feel progress. I know you can do it, and I want to help you."

From this transcript we can learn a great deal about Nondirective Teaching. "Learning" is a personal experience. The individual experiences planning, responsibility, and a teacher who values the student's perspective. Acquiring one's own responsibility for learning and the skill to plan and to develop those plans is no small matter, but if you want students to become independent learners, Nondirective Teaching establishes the interpersonal relationships which can facilitate personal productivity.

This type experience for the student is not casual or mindless teaching. In its own way it is a rigorous experience for both the teacher and the student. The teacher who normally plans and organizes instruction uses that knowledge and skill to facilitate the student's own efforts. It is necessary to share the student's anxiety and anger, yet remain firm in your efforts to support him. The student lacks the know-how to move along, but with courage, with experience, and with feeling progress, structuring learning becomes easier and more productive.

Why would a teacher want to function in nondirective ways? There are some very persuasive reasons. Students learn to take charge of their own school lives, not in the sense of excluding teachers and other students, but in the sense that some part of what goes on is from the individual: it belongs to the student. Personal development is a real goal. Students also become aware of their feelings and thoughts about themselves and others, and they are required to deal with them. Finally, students learn to plan and to organize, to carry out, and to evaluate learning.

Group Investigation

When a teacher thinks about teaching Geometry, he is less likely to consider social-oriented Models of Teaching. The traditions of mathematics education have been centered on the individual and mathematics content. However, there are many opportunities for group activities which would not only promote affiliation and interpersonal skills, but they would provide opportunities for collective inquiry and other problem solving experiences. The individual gains mutual support during the time spent learning problem solving behaviors. These are relevant to students not only during schooling, but after graduation when the application of mathematics is done in the workplace as members of teams.

Group Investigation is a problem solving model for groups of students which consists of the following events:

1. Experiencing a puzzling situation.
2. Students discuss their reactions.
3. Students identify the problem.
4. Students make a plan and discuss roles.
5. Carry out the plan.
6. Students reflect on their experiences.

In these events, the teacher guides the group dynamics and acts as a resource person. The social climate is cooperative.

An example of the application of group investigation to teaching Geometry would be the problem of measuring heights. Such things as flag poles, buildings, trees, etc., are difficult to measure with devices, and getting students to plan and carry out original strategies for problem solving has both the effect of practical problem solving plus enhancing the more mathematical solution to the problem. The students need to explore aspects of the problem in practical ways, and attempts to resolve these practical problems would provide varied experiences which would, in turn, help students appreciate a more generalizable solution.

In order to teach Geometry through Group Investigation, a teacher has to appreciate both the instructional and nurturant effects of instruction. The experience involves respect for different people's points of view and knowledge construction, learner independence from the teacher, effective group process, a commitment to group inquiry and social dynamics, and disciplined inquiry. Group Investigation synthesizes these value orientations; from an observer's vantage point, we need a polyfocal perspective to appreciate the richness of this model of teaching.

Patterns of Instruction

Besides the Models of Teaching, there are three other common patterns of instruction one sees in classrooms today: lecturing, recitation, and direct instruction (which probably between them account for the majority of what one might see).

A good *lecture* will be systematic and sequential, and convey information in an orderly and interesting way. The effective lecturer will draw skills from the Attention, Clarity, and Learning Experiences parameters, as well as from the Objectives and Curriculum Organization parameters. The pattern of teacher behavior in lecturing, however, draws nothing from any internal theory of good lecturing, or cohesive theory of learning. A lecture is a composite animal with no secondary goal about learning-how-to-learn. (When the lecture is a step in the Advance Organizer Model, then the story is different.) Nevertheless, a good lecture is a worthwhile educational experience and certainly has a place in schooling.

A poor lecture, when it is poor, will be so because of poor performance on one or more of the five parameters listed above, not poor performance of a model called "lecturing."

A poor lecture may qualify as no-teaching-at-all, if we want to label it. Even an interesting speaker who holds our attention and/or keeps us amused with clever anecdotes may be doing no teaching if the content is not organized around the course objectives and not designed with the principles of organization in mind. Students can look forward to class, be well entertained, and leave without having learned a thing.

A *recitation* is an oral test. The teacher asks questions, students respond, and the teacher makes value judgements on the responses. Its goal is to cover the material, to go over it, to ask questions, see who knows what. By the time it's over, all the important stuff should be out (or have been said by someone and heard by all). Reviews for tests are often recitations. A recitation doesn't have a series of steps, but we could construct a checklist of events and qualities that might discriminate a good recitation as follows:

- covered all the material
- highlighted important items
- identified student confusions

- got maximum student participation
- took opportunities to stimulate higher level thinking.

For the rest, if we wanted to judge the quality of a recitation lesson, we'd have to go back to Management Parameters again—like Attention, Momentum, and Clarity. Recitations have a place in school, but not, we think, as large a one as they seem to occupy. When one is over, students and teachers are aware of who knows what, who read the assignment, and who gets A's. As an educational experience used for more than occasional review, it is something that has no guiding principles or point of view behind it, and little chance that the students will get better at learning in some particular way.

Direct instruction is usually used for skill work and does have a syntax:

1. Teacher states aims of lesson.
2. Teacher presents concepts or operation.
3. Teacher gives examples or demonstrates.
4. Teacher asks questions to check student understanding.
5. Students practice with direct monitoring, feedback, help and hints from the teacher, usually right there in the group.
6. Students practice alone (seatwork or homework).
7. Teacher corrects and decides:
   a) reteach
   b) regroup
   c) move on.
8. Frequent tests.

Direct instruction lacks model status because it has no theoretical basis, teacher/ student response pattern, or social/technical environmental conditions tailored to optimize a specified learning behavior. But we know that good direct instruction in groups with high time-on-task produces mastery of skills. Direct instruction reflects the current trends toward training, task analysis, and bio-feedback. These preferences for instruction evolved from the business community. They reflect values of efficiency and effectiveness.

Lecturing, recitation, and direct instruction are all prominent patterns of classroom instruction. To most teachers they are the models of teaching. In theory and practice, they are not models at all...nor are they ever likely to be so. Models of Teaching have elaborate theoretical statements and descriptions of patterns of behavior which teachers can be trained to perform. There are discrete teacher/ student interactions which characterize one Model and distinguish it from another. Models are similar to theatrical plays, though not so closely scripted; if teachers know the Model, they can visualize the classroom activity before it occurs, and use that image to monitor and regulate the flow of activity. The content and goals of Models are equally distinctive. In one Model the content is derived from an academic discipline—e.g., mathematics—while in another it would draw from recent student experiences for the content. A Model will be chosen not only to convey content, but to stretch the way students think and learn about learning.

Models of Teaching allow us to say of good teaching, "Good for what?"...and to answer out of the things a particular Model is designed to be good for (e.g., logical thinking, inductive reasoning, personal self-organization, cooperation and group skill...or whatever we feel our students need).

How many Models of Teaching do you use? Which ones? How could you better match some of your students with different Models?

Checking on Models of Teaching

1. The teacher's repertoire of models includes:

   no patterns
     recitation
       direct instruction
         a partial model _____
           a complete model _____
             a complete model & segments of another _____
               several complete models

                 _____
                 _____
                 _____
                 _____

2. Models of Teaching used are:

   inappropriate for students and/or material
     appropriate to material
       matched to group
         matched to individuals

Source Materials on This Parameter

GENERAL:
Joyce, B.R. and Weil, M. *Models of Teaching.* Englewood Cliffs, NJ: Prentice-Hall, 1972, 1980, 1986.

I. Social Investigation Models

1. *Group Investigation Model*
   <u>Major Theorists</u>:
   Herbert Thelen
   John Dewey

   <u>Mission</u>:
   Development of skills for participation in democratic social processes through combined emphasis on interpersonal and social (group) skills and academic inquiry. Aspects of personal development are important outgrowths of this model.

   <u>References</u>:
   Dewey, J. *Democracy and Education.* New York: McMillan, 1916.
   Thelen, H. *Education and the Human Quest.* New York: Harper and Row, 1960.
   Thelen, H. *Dynamics of Groups at Work.* Chicago: University of Chicago Press, 1954.

2. *The Jurisprudential Model*
   <u>Major Theorists</u>:
   Donald Oliver
   James P. Shaver

   <u>Mission</u>:
   Designed primarily to teach the jurisprudential frame of reference as a way of processing information, but also a way of thinking about and resolving social issues.

   <u>Reference</u>:
   Oliver, D. and Shaver, J.P. *Teaching Public Issues in High School.* Boston: Houghton Mifflin, 1966.

3. *Social Inquiry Model*
   <u>Major Theorists</u>:
   Benjamin Cox
   Byron Massialas

   <u>Mission</u>:
   Social problem-solving, primarily through academic inquiry and logical reasoning.

Reference:
Massialas, B. and Cox, B. *Inquiry in Social Studies*. New York: McGraw-Hill, 1966.

4. *Laboratory Method Model (T-Group)*
Major Theorist:
National Training Laboratory, Bethel, Maine
Leland P. Bradford

Mission:
Development of interpersonal group skills and through this, personal awareness and flexibility.

References:
Bany, M. and Johnson, L.V. *Classroom Group Behavior: Group Dynamics in Education*. New York: MacMillan, 1964.
Bennis, W.G., Benne, K.D. and Chin, R. (*eds.*). *The Planning of Change: Readings in the Applied Behavioral Sciences*. New York: Holt, Rinehart and Winston, 1964.
Bradford, L.P. (*ed.*). *Human Forces in Teaching and Learning*. Washington, D.C.: National Training Laboratory, National Association, 1961.
Bradford, L.P., Gibb, J.R. and Benne, K. D. *T-Group Theory and Laboratory Method*. New York: John Wiley, 1964.
Human Relations Laboratory Training Student Notebook. Washington, D.C.: U.S. Office of Education, 1961.

II. Information Processing Models

1. *Concept Attainment Model*
Major Theorist:
Jerome Bruner

Mission:
Designed primarily to develop inductive reasoning.

Reference:
Bruner, J., Goodnow, J.J. and Austin, G.A. *A Study of Thinking*. New York: Science Editions, Inc., 1957.

2. *An Inductive Model*
Major Theorist:
Hilda Taba

Mission:
Primarily designed for development of inductive mental processes and academic reasoning or theory building, but these capacities are useful for personal and social goals as well. Model developed from a specific kind of thinking which underlies scientific inquiry.

References:
Taba, H. *Teaching Strategies and Cognitive Functioning in Elementary School Children.* San Francisco: San Francisco State College, Coop. Research Project No. 2404.

Taba, H. *Teacher's Handbook for Elementary Social Studies.* Reading, MA: Addison-Wesley, 1967.

3. *Inquiry Training Model*
Major Theorist:
Richard Suchman

Mission: Primarily designed for development of inductive mental processes and academic reasoning or theory building. Generalized model of inquiry was developed from a general analysis of the methods employed by creative research personnel.

References:
Suchman, J.R. *The Elementary School Training Program in Scientific Inquiry.* Urbana: The University of Illinois, Report of the U.S. Office of Education. Project Title VIII, Project 216, 1962.

Suchman, J.R. "A Model for the Analysis of Inquiry." In Klausmeier, H.J. and Harris, C.W. (*eds.*), *Analysis of Concept Learning.* New York: Academic Press, 1966.

Suchman, J.R. *Inquiry Box: Teacher's Handbook.* Chicago: Science Research Associates, 1967.

Suchman, J.R. *Inquiry Development Program: Developing Inquiry.* Chicago: Science Research Associates, 1966.

4. *Biological Science Inquiry Model*
Major Theorists:
Joseph J. Schwab
Jerome Bruner (curriculum reform movement)

Mission:
Designed to teach the research system of the discipline but also expected to have effects in other domains, as for example sociological methods may be taught in order to increase social understanding and social problem solving.

Reference:
Schwab, J.J. *Biological Sciences Curriculum Study, Supervisor. Biology Teachers' Handbook.* New York: John Wiley, 1965.

5. *Advanced Organizer Model*
Major Theorist:
David Ausubel

Mission:
Designed to increase the efficiency of information processing capacities to meaningfully absorb and relate bodies of knowledge.

References:
Ausubel, D.P. *The Psychology of Meaningful Verbal Learning.* New York: Grune and Stratton, 1963.
Ausubel, D.P. *Learning Theory and Classroom Practice.* Toronto: The Ontario Institute for Studies in Education, Bulletin No. 1, 1967.

6. *Developmental Model*
Major Theorists:
Jean Piaget
Irving Sigel
Edmund Sullivan

Mission:
Designed to increase general intellectual development, especially logical reasoning, but can be applied to social and moral development as well.

References:
Furth, H.G. *Piaget and Knowledge.* Englewood Cliffs, NJ: Prentice Hall, 1969.
Kohlberg, L. "Moral Education in the School." *School Review*, 74, 1966.
Piaget, J. *The Origins of Intelligence in Children.* New York: International University Press, 1952.
Sigel, I.E. "The Piagetian System and the World of Education." In Elkind, D. and Flavell, J. (*eds.*), *Studies in Cognitive Development*, New York: Oxford University Press, 1969.

III. Personal Models

1. *Non-Directive Teaching Model*
Major Theorist:
Carl Rogers

Mission:
Emphasis on building capacity for self-instruction and through this, personal development in terms of self-understanding, self-discovery, and self-concept.

References:
Rogers, C.R. *Client Centered Therapy.* Boston: Houghton Mifflin, 1951.
Rogers, C.R. *Freedom to Learn.* Columbus, Ohio: Charles E. Merrill, 1969.

2. *Classroom Meeting Model*
Major Theorist:
William Glasser

Mission:
Development of self-understanding and self-responsibility. This would have latent benefits to other kinds of functioning; i.e., social.

References:
Glasser, W. *Reality Therapy*. New York: Harper and Row, 1965.
Glasser, W. *Schools Without Failure*. New York: Harper and Row, 1969.

3. *Synectics Model*
Major Theorist:
William Gordon

Mission:
Personal development of creativity and creative problem-solving.

References:
Gordon, W.J. *Synectics*. New York: Harper and Row,1961.
Gordon, W.J. *The Metaphorical Way of Learning and Knowing*. Cambridge, MA: Synectics Educational Press, 1970.

4. *Awareness Training Model*
Major Theorists:
William Schutz
Fritz Perls

Mission:
Increasing personal capacity for self-exploration and self-awareness. Much emphasis is placed on the development of interpersonal awareness and understanding.

References:
Brown, G. *Human Teaching for Human Learning*. New York: Viking Press, 1971.
Schutz, W. *FIRO: A Three Dimensional Theory of Interpersonal Behavior*. New York: Holt, Rinehart, and Winston, 1958.
Schutz, W.J. *Expanding Human Awareness*. New York: Grove Press, 1967.

IV. Behavior Modification Models

1. *Operant Conditioning*
Major Theorist:
B.F. Skinner

Mission:
General applicability. A domain-free approach though probably applicable to information processing function.

References:
Schramm, W. *Programmed Instruction: Today and Tomorrow*. New York: The Fund for the Advancement of Education, 1962.
Skinner, B.F. *The Science of Human Behavior*. New York: MacMillan, 1956.

Skinner, B.F. *Verbal Behavior*. New York: Appleton-Century Crofts, 1957.

Taber, J., Glaser, R. and Halmuth, H.S. *Learning and Programmed Instruction*. Reading, MA: Addison-Wesley, 1965.

13

Learning Experiences

How can I adjust for students' learning styles?

The Variables

LEARNING EXPERIENCES

The term "learning experience" is not the same as the content with which a course deals nor the activities performed by the teacher. The term "learning experience" refers to the interaction between the learner and the external conditions of the environment to which he can react. Learning takes place through the active behavior of the student; it is what he does that he learns, not what the teacher does.

—Tyler, Basic Principles of Curriculum and Instruction, p. 63

What This Parameter Will Get You

The main point of this parameter is to enable you to survey the activities you offer students so that you can describe them in a new way. This new way may help you with several things: 1) it may give you a fuller picture than you have had before of what students are experiencing in your class; 2) it may give you a picture of what they are *not* experiencing, i.e., out of the possible range of options, what characteristics your learning experiences do not have. This latter information could enable you to make one of the following statements:

1. "That's fine...it's OK not to have these features. What I'm doing is really on-target for this curriculum and those wouldn't be.

2. "Well, there are some things there I'm not doing that would be good to do. I'd like to do them but there's just so much time to work with. Think I'll just put them on the back burner for now and look into adding that when things slow up a bit."

3. "Well, there's a few things I really hadn't thought about much before. They'd be really good and I'd like to try them now."

One may be able to make all three statements about different parts of one's teaching. The point is you should be able to look at your teaching or that of another and see more than you have before—and then make some decisions based on that. You may come away from this chapter newly aware, or perhaps reminded of some important things we can design into students' experiences.

This parameter is constructed from the student's point of view. We ask first, what are students experiencing in their environment? What are the attributes of the activity? What is it like from the student's angle to be in this, doing this? Second, we ask, "So what?" What difference does it make? Of what importance is what students are experiencing on this particular attribute? What does it mean about their overall school learning? This enables us to make choices, because the shape of the learning experience is, after all, something we control as teachers.

We analyze a student's learning experience almost as if it were a real, tangible thing like a rock. It *isn't* tangible, but it is *real*, and has just as describable features as does a rock. A rock has attributes (e.g., shape) and possible values on each attribute (e.g., spherical, egg, cylindrical, cube; for the attribute of color the values might be brown, grey, blue, reddish, silver). So does a learning experience. Take "supervision." That's an attribute with three possible values (or options): independent, facilitated, or directly supervised. Which are students experiencing right now? They may be closely and directly supervised right now, and independent later on in the day. Their learning experience, then, may change based on this attribute, and when it does, it's a different learning experience.

A learning experience takes place over a time span with a beginning, middle, and end. It can be quite short—a matter of minutes—or extend to hours. When it changes on significant attributes, we say it's a different learning experience.

What do we get out of being able to do this kind of analysis? First, we get a very full and accurate picture of what the student is really experiencing in some activity we've planned. Second, we can look at activities we plan (or allow to be set up for students) over a period of time and see what patterns, what range, we are building into these experiences. Third, we can decide if the range is O.K. Are we ever giving students a chance to work cooperatively, for example, or is it always competitive or individualistic? What are the sensory input channels we stimulate? Do we ever use kinesthetic? What is the balance between concrete and abstract in our teaching? This parameter provides a set of questions with which to survey our teaching periodically and see if we are offering what we want to offer. Finally, the parameter give us some sharp focus lenses for looking at matching and adjusting learning experiences for individual students or groups.

In the following sections, we will describe the attributes of Learning Experiences one by one, and lay out the possible forms each may take. You may choose to profile yourself as you go, noticing which of the options characterizes learning experiences *you* offer, and then deciding if those choices are broad enough and appropriate.

Source of Information

Definitions

We examine learning experiences to determine whether the information the students are working with is conventional or constructed. "Conventional" shall mean it came from conventional sources such as a text, a reference book, the teacher, or some other source that *gives* the information to them. "Constructed" shall mean the students constructed the knowledge through some process of their own such as observation, experiment, interview, deduction, induction, application of logic, discussion, debate, or questioning.

Looking something up will always be a conventional source of information. It may be the student's own initiative, his own objective, and his own choice of learning experience behind the act of "looking up," for instance, design features of airplanes, but the source of information is still conventional.

Significance

It is significant to know whether or not students are ever challenged or put in positions where they are able to use their own resources as active agents for the generation of new knowledge (new at any rate to them, even if others have discovered the same things for themselves each generation), as opposed to receiving information that has been assembled and/or organized and/or predigested for them. Neither source of information is "better" than the other, but they are clearly different in their effects on the learner. If we find teaching that uses either source at the exclusion of the other, we are led to ask whether this is consistent with the nature of the curriculum and the goals of the program.

Resources Used

Definitions

Students may use any one or more of the following resources in the course of their work:

a text
the teacher
peers
parents
interviews with outside people (not parents, not teachers or peers)
observation
audio-visual materials
reference books
their own imaginations
their own experiences

We use this sub-parameter as an index to the breadth of resources brought to bear on the student's learning experience, and can tally a simple count of how many we have evidence are used.

Significance

Over the course of a student's education, we would expect all of the above resources to play a part, to be used. In any one course, grade, or more precisely in examining the learning experiences offered by any one teacher, we would ask which resources and how broad a range were appropriate and desirable, and compare that with the reality. In examining an individual student's educational experience, we could usefully ask how many of these resources were brought to bear across different courses, and evaluate the fit of the operating range of resources to the intentions of the program.

Personal Relevance

Definitions

On this attribute, learning experiences are found to be: contrived, simulated, or real. The degree to which the learning experience relates to aspects of life that have personal meaning to the students is indexed here. Does it connect to their "real" world outside school?

Doing a workbook page which contains problems of adding money in the form $124.35 + 3.50 = ?$ would be judged as "contrived" since it—the doing of the problem on a workbook page—is not connected to the students' world of experience outside of school. But, if the class has set up a model store selling grocery items (or anything they might find in a "real" store), and the students are buying things using play money (or real money), then this activity "simulates" real experiences from the students' lives. Further, if the class takes a trip to a supermarket and spends money it has made through some project to buy supplies for a party, and they collect, purchase, pay for, and get change, then the activity is judged "real"; that is, integrated, connected, and related directly to the real world they have experienced outside of school.

"Contrived" here does not have negative connotations in its use. Much of learning and knowledge construction is "contrived" in that it does not simulate or reproduce the "reality" outside school...nor could it. It is impractical for almost all of us to learn about the history of India by visiting historic Indian sites (though that would be nice). And aspects of historical study necessarily involve the reading of books and other "contrived" (versus "real") experiences to proceed effectively with the learning. There is no general value implied in this attribute that "real" learning experiences are superior to "contrived" ones. One does not have to leave school on a field trip to enter the realm of "real" learning experiences either. The act of painting is "real" no matter where one does it. Painting is painting and not a simulation of painting whether or not one does it in school or in an art studio. The same applies to creative writing or aesthetic work of any kind. Having a debate is a real experience between the debaters and not simulated just because it is not taking place in a court of law or a legislative chamber. Many experiences in the school are inherently real for students. Settling a dispute with another student over how to share materials is a real experience in which they play a deliberate role and act as mediators according to certain designs.

Significance

To many educators it is important that as many learning experiences as possible connect to students' real world of meaning, connect to their world of experience outside of school. There is a school of learning theory that holds that such learning experiences are more effective, more powerful, and more lasting in effect (Dale, undated). The student in this way of thinking has a context in which to embed the new information and because of its relevance to his personal life is more impelled to attend to what's going on, to participate in what's going on. This then guarantees a level of involvement on the part of the student with the learning experience that will maximize learning. To people of this persuasion it would be important to know just how much realness was characteristic of learning experiences being offered. Early childhood educators and open classroom educators are especially interested in this attribute of learning experiences (Bussis and Chittenden, 1976).

Regardless of one's beliefs about the learning theory of personal relevance, it is a distinction we can make between learning experiences. It produces data we can bring to an analysis of teaching-in-action in comparison with teaching's intentions. We can look at curriculum designs to see where and how often opportunities for "realness" exist, and how appropriate such experiences would be to the content and to the learners involved. We can evaluate the efficiency of a curriculum in terms of the balance between contrived, sim-ulated, and real experiences that is best for accomplishing the objectives of the instruction in the time allowed.

Competition

Definitions

Johnson and Johnson (1975) have a three-point typology for learning experiences: cooperative, competitive, individualized. They don't use the term "learning experiences," they say "goal structures."

A goal structure specifies the type of interdependence existing among students. It specifies the way in which students will relate to each other and to the teacher.

One might say they have taken a specific aspect of the social climate, that aspect related to competition and its presence, absence, or opposite, and defined it in detail.

> When students are working together to find what factors make a difference in how long a candle burns in a quart jar, they are in a cooperative goal structure. A cooperative goal structure exists when students perceive that they can obtain their goal if and only if the other students with whom they are linked can obtain their goal (Deutsch, 1949). Since the goal of all the students is to make a list of factors that influence the time the candle burns, the goal of all the students has been reached when they generate a list. A cooperative goal structure requires the coordination of behavior necessary to achieve their mutual goal. If one student achieves the goal, all students with whom the student is linked achieve the goal. When students are working to see who can build the best list of factors influencing the time a candle will burn in a quart jar, they are in a competitive goal structure. A competitive goal structure exists when students perceive that they can obtain their goal if and only if the other students with whom they are linked fail to obtain their goal. If one student turns in a better list than anyone else, all the students have failed to achieve their goal. Competitive interaction is the striving to achieve one's goal in a way that blocks all others from achieving the goal. Finally, if all students are working independently to master an operation in mathematics, they are in an individualistic goal structure. An individualistic goal structure exists when the achievement of the goal by one student is unrelated to the achievement of the goal by other students; whether or not a student achieves her goal has no bearing upon whether or not other students achieve their goals. If one student masters the mathematics principle, it has no bearing upon whether other students successfully master the mathematics principle. Usually there is no student interaction in an individualistic situation since each student seeks the outcome that is best for himself regardless of whether or not other students achieve their goals. [Johnson and Johnson, 1975, p. 7]

Johnson and Johnson have an observation checklist with a series of yes/no questions for classroom organization, student-student interaction, and teacher-student interaction. The outcome scores of the checklist are three percentage figures for the three possible goal structures. There is the recognition here that a learning experience will rarely be exclusively cooperative; for example, without some elements for at least some of the time of competition and/or individualization, too. From the percentage figures of Johnson and Johnson's observation checklist, one could make a statement about the dominant quality of the learning experience along the sub-parameter "competition."

An important body of research literature is emerging on the effectiveness of cooperative learning for cognitive ends as well as affective. This is accompanied by an emerging technical literature on how to do cooperative learning. At least five different forms of cooperative learning are developed and available for teachers to try:

Group
Investigation

Johnson and
Johnson
Type Cooperation
Activity

Jig Saw

STAD
Student
Teams
Achievement
Divisions

TGT
Team Games
Tournament

They are arranged in ascending order of the demands they place on students for interaction and communication skills.

In rating oneself on this sub-parameter, one wants to be able to look at single learning experiences and characterize its dominant quality—cooperative, competitive, or individualistic. How can such a distinction be made when all three may be present?

In certain science lab courses we have observed, groups of students worked together sharing apparatus, ideas, and information as they performed a common experiment. This we considered significant cooperation. At the same time, these students were recording experimental results in individual lab notebooks which were separately graded by the teacher. Different groups of students were at different places in the sequential programmed curriculum. Some were working alone, either because no one else was at the same place as they or because they wanted to work alone (which was also allowed by the teacher). Students took tests individually and when they felt ready to ask for them from the teacher. Individual pre-test feedback was given by the teacher to students and tests were graded individually. This was significant evidence for calling the learning experience "individualistic." In this lab course there were no observed instances of students comparing test scores in a competitive way, though in interviews teachers cited cases where that happened. Indeed, even if we had observed students comparing scores it wouldn't necessarily merit a judging of "competition" as a value of the learning experience on this attribute. It could be argued that comparing test scores reflects competitive qualities inherent in children, in humans, in the culture, or in the process of testing itself ("Whadjaget?").

Figure 13-1

Five Formats for Cooperative Learning

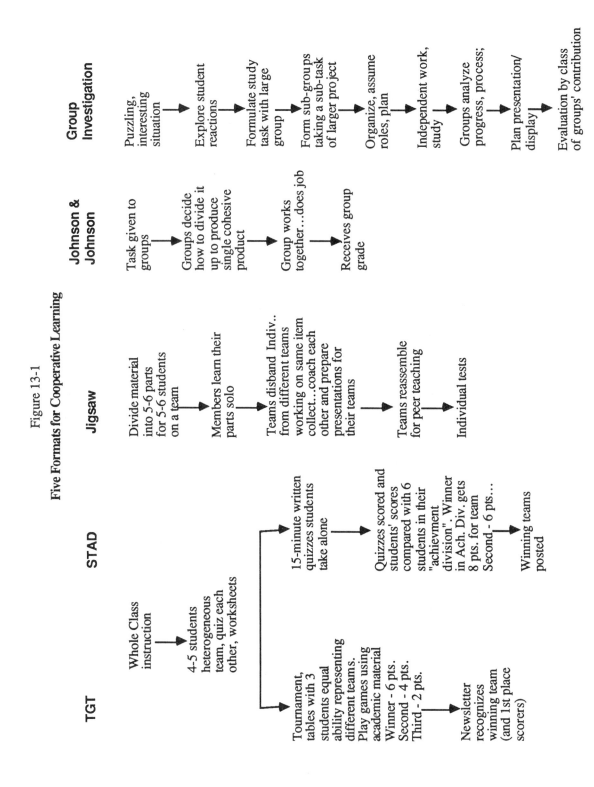

The kind of competition we looked for was one designed into the learning experience by the teacher and/or the curriculum...something like a team game, or a contest for speed or accuracy involving a group of students, or a recitation period where a student gives right answers in competition with peers. Many competitive forces emanating from students themselves, from peers, from parents, or from the culture and community may affect student behavior. These forces are not examined in this sub-parameter. It looks at aspects of the *design of the learning experience* that set up, by virtue of that design, intereactions that are competitive, cooperative, or individualistic in nature. Only students' behavior of these three types that is encouraged or arranged by the design of the learning experience will enable us to make a judgement on this sub-parameter. Competitive, cooperative, or individualistic bahavior of children that cannot be attributed to the design of the learning experience that comes from some (any) other source, is deemed irrelevant to the judging of this sub-parameter.

In the case of the science lab course previously discussed, competition would not be scored as a significant quality of the learning experience because whatever of it there was couldn't be traced to the teacher or the design of the learning experience.

Significance

It is not hard to get a discussion started among educators, or parents, or passers-by on the street for that matter, about the merits or evils of competition. It is a condition of life we have all experienced and about which we all have formed some values. This sub-parameter of teaching calls our attention to our ability to control in aware and deliberate ways *how* competitive, cooperative, or individualistic are the experiences of students in our schools. Educational decision-makers bring different values and different histories to their settings as has always been the case. But whatever their decisions about the shape of learning experiences, these decisions can be informed and deliberate if made by professionals who know the full implications of their acts. This sub-parameter gives you tools for surveying your own teaching to see just how much of cooperation or competition you are putting into students' experiences. It further offers you resources for getting the balance you want.

In this sub-parameter as in all the other sub-parameters of learning experiences we have touched, there is a seeable, analyzable nature, an emergent reality to the experience students have on each attribute. That experience is in the form it is because an educational decision-maker has made it that way—either deliberately or in ignorance. Each attribute is controllable, alterable, and subject to change by educators who seek to be knowledgeable and deliberate about the environments they create for learners.

Matching

"Yes" for matching will be supported by evidence that the teacher differentiated between groups or between individuals as to the competitive, cooperative, or individualistic quality of learning experiences.

Supervision

Definitions

Students may be directly supervised by a teacher who checks on what and how everybody is doing, may be independent and responsible for their own work, or the teacher may facilitate their work by which we mean being available as a resource person and occasionally intervening with suggestions, recommendations, or stimulating questions (Dunn and Dunn, 1978). During observations, the number of these three possible conditions present in a teacher's teaching can be counted.

Significance

A limited range on this attribute; for example, a teacher who always supervises all learning activities, excludes certain kinds of learning in a classroom. The breadth or narrowness of a teacher's range on this attribute is something we can look at for its nurturant effects on students; that is, the effects on them of living in an environment of that kind. We (or the teacher) can then ask if that is what is wanted. And we can, of course, compare this range of supervisory modes and the nurturant effects attached with the goals of the curriculum and of the teacher.

Matching

Teachers who discriminate among students on how much supervision they require or can tolerate so as to maximize their performance "match" the amount and kind of supervision they provide to the characteristics of students. Jane flourishes if left to work independently much of the time, checking in occasionally for conferences with the teacher. Working under direct supervision for the bulk of the day unnecessarily limits her learning experiences. But Martha can't seem to get herself organized; she'll have several false starts and then may socialize away her morning if not directly supervised in her work. Her teacher provides much direct supervision for her, much independence for Jane. The same kind of distinction can be made for sub-groups of the class and would enable us to conclude "yes" for the matching attribute of supervision.

Expressing the Self

Definitions

Students may or may not be given the opportunity to express something of themselves in a learning experience (Chalmers and Stuart, 1976). If they are given such an opportunity, the self-expression may be delivered through: 1) drawing, 2) creative writing, 3) performing, 4) speaking, 5) building or construction of some sort. Merely to respond or recite is not to express oneself as meant here. Expressing one's self means expressing something that is unique to the individual or expressing some standard information in a way that encourages students to bring in something of themselves to the expression. An assignment to diagram mitosis for biology (though different students will embellish the product to different degrees) is a prescribed product that has the student express mitosis, not himself. An assignment to represent the 1812 Overture in paint is also prescribed, but frees the student to express things unique to him that are stimulated by the music. A recitation question asking a student to summarize Turner's Thesis of the American Frontier does not allow for self-expression as would a question asking a student to say how he would have responded to the offer of free western land had he been alive 100 years ago.

Significance

The significance of this attribute relates to the value placed on self-expression by those responsible for the educational program. Data on the attribute tell us what we have and enable us, as before, to raise the attribute as an important and perhaps overlooked aspect of learning experiences over which program designers and teachers have control. And, as before, we can compare realities with intentions, where intentions about self-expression have been considered by program designers and made explicit.

Matching

We may look to see if teachers who allow for or encourage expression of the self allow for differences in ways students can best do that expressing. If matching were present, one would see not only range on this attribute but also negotiations or direct planning of students' activities where they were asked to or permitted to express themselves in ways different from other students.

Degree of Abstraction

Definitions

Learning experiences can be scored as concrete, representational (iconic), or abstract (Bruner, 1966). Concrete means manipulative: students are touching or seeing real objects that are integral to the learning experience. Iconic means representational: a picture, image, or other facsimile of real objects is embedded in the materials with which the learner is interacting. Abstract here means symbolic: words or thoughts are the stuff of which the learning experience is made without support from facsimiles or concrete objects.

Significance

We can compare the range of levels of abstraction offered to the nature of the content, and make judgements concerning appropriateness. Similar comparisons can be made in consideration of the age and learning style of the students. With young children, for example, we might expect to see more concrete experiences than at other grade levels.

Matching Levels of Abstraction

As students of the same age are often at different levels with regard to their ability to process abstract information, we might expect a teacher to discriminate among students and adjust the level of abstraction of the learning experiences offered to characteristics of individual students. We might also see matching at the grosser level of groups.

Recent research on stages of brain growth by Herman Epstein suggests that middle/junior high school students are still in a stage of concrete problem solving. There is a close correlation between Epstein's stages of brain growth and the boundary years of Piaget's stages of intellectual development. Conrad Toepfer (Toepfer, 1981) and others have applied these insights to middle school curricula and found that much of it demands formal operational thinking of students, a kind of thinking that only 12 percent of American youngsters are capable of at age 12. Toepfer makes a strong case that if we matched the level of thinking to the student's stage of brain growth, especially in the plateau period of 12-14 years of age, we could make a huge difference in school failure rates. He and his colleagues further recommend testing students for their level of thinking (onset of concrete operations, concrete operations, initial formal operations, established formal operations) and basing instruction on the stage. Intelligence, he points out, is different and un-correlated to stage of thinking. Super bright kids go through the same stages of growth and in about the same proportions per given age as normal and below normal IQ kids.

This sub-parameter of learning experiences bears a hard look. Coming research may help us use it to serve students much more effectively by tailoring instruction to accurate assessment of a student's stage of intellectual development.

Cognitive Level

Definitions

Bloom's taxonomy (1956) gives us six cognitive levels to consider: recall, comprehension, analysis, application, synthesis, and evaluation. We can examine learning experiences to see what cognitive level of performance they ask of students. We can further look across learning experiences offered by teachers to see what is the range of thinking embedded in them. We can count the number of levels for which evidence can be produced.

Significance

Researchers have long investigated such things as the number of higher-level questions teachers ask students in verbal interaction. This research implied that the more higher-level questions the better, and studies attempted to correlate proportion of higher-level questions with student achievement (Winne, 1979). However, large doses of high cognitive levels may be quite inappropriate for students who have not worked through lower levels with the same material. When we considered the Models of Teaching parameter we saw that for certain models (like Taba's) it was the *order* in which cognitive operations are demanded of students that is important and not the raw amount at any level.

Focusing on the cognitive level embedded in learning experiences offered by a teacher enables us to collect data on the range offered. Any predominance of one or two particular levels will prompt us to ask "Why?" If a teacher or a curriculum has some specific thinking objectives in mind, we can compare, as often before, intentions with reality.

Matching of Cognitive Level

If we see a teacher tailoring or adjusting learning experiences on the same or similar material so that the cognitive level demanded is different for different students, then we can attribute "matching" to this teacher. We may see this matching across sub-groups within the class or among individuals within the class. Either case properly evidenced will justify a "yes" on matching.

It is useful to look now with a higher resolution lens at how certain aspects of the learning experience get structured. The following sections on "structuring" take this up.

Structuring

We have all heard people refer to students who need a high degree of "structure." We have often wondered exactly what is meant by that word and discovered, not too surprisingly, that people mean different things. Sometimes they mean the student has to be watched—closely supervised. Sometimes they mean the task has to be broken down into small pieces and the student told exactly what to do, when, and how. Structuring there means leading students carefully, step by step, being explicit about all the details so that students don't get hung up not knowing what to do. We find out how structuring is being handled when teachers give directions. We would have called this section "giving directions" except that teacher giving directions is only one way activities get set up. Sometimes students are asked to set procedures, and sometimes teachers and students negotiate what to do and how. One way to analyze differences in teachers' teaching is to examing how much and where these different kinds of structuring are occurring—by teachers (high structure), by negotiation (moderate structure), or by students (low structure). Another thing to ask is if teachers differentiate between students along this sub-parameter of who structures activities. That, of course, would be matching.

When teachers give directions they will often structure (that is, make decisions and give instructions about) the content to be worked on, the procedures to follow, the behavior to do (e.g., "write", "discuss", "compare", "listen"...), the form of student products, and the point of closure (signaling when it's over). Content, behavior, procedures, products, and closure: those are the big five of structuring.

WHO DECIDES

No one decides	Student decides	Negotiation	Teacher decides

(low structure -------------- high structure)

1. Content
2. Behavior
3. Procedures
4. Products
5. Closure

A similar breakout appears in Berlak, *et al.*, 1975.

Let us look at each of the five and some examples of what each might look like with different degrees of structure.

Content

By content we mean information or objects dealt with at the item level. Who decided/introduced/is responsible for the presence of the particular items students are operating upon, working with? To make reliable assignments of responsibility here we must be clear on the unit of analysis. Just how big or small is an "item?" Some examples will help.

Activity	Item	Responsible Party
Recitation/review of Civil War battles with teacher leading questioning in chronological order seeking identification and sequence	Pieces of information elicited from students	Teacher
Teacher says, "Read this book and answer the questions at the back."	The book The questions	Teacher
Teacher says, "Pick a book you'd like to read and summarize it verbally for me."	The book	Student

(Note: Even though the use of time is structured by the teacher, and the behavior, writing, is also structured, the *content*, what is operated upon, written about, comes from the student.)

| Teacher suggests, "Use the blocks to make a model of the store we visited." | Model of store | Teacher |

(Note: Even though the student controls the shape of the product, what the store will look like, the item on which he is operating—blocks—and the model of a store was directed by the teacher. If the student was free to represent the store in any media he chose, e.g., paint, clay, then the *behavior* would have been attributable to the student as well as the shape of the product; but the *content* would still be the teacher's decision, the decision about *what* to represent.)

| Class discussion about the pros and cons of busing to integrate public schools. Teacher serving as facilitator and clarifier, not taking a stand, trying to get students to evidence their positions. | Arguments, positions, and evidence for positions | Students |
| Following a discussion of "movies," students form interest groups to study selected aspects of movie production: special effects, casting, scriptwriting, shooting schedules. Students nominate themselves into groups and teacher mediates which groups may form and the membership. | Special effects
Casting
Shooting schedules
Script writing | Negotiated |

At the most general level the teacher is almost always responsible for content. In the example above where students debate the pros and cons of busing, the teacher probably introduced the subject (though not necessarily). The teacher is responsible for the topic, the area being treated, but clearly that is above the item level. If teachers are responsible for the responses the students are producing in that they ask factual questions or leading questions, then we can also say they are responsible for the content. But if the students are bringing in information not directly tied to the teacher's questions, items or objects that could not be the only reply to the question or the lead-in of the teacher, then the students are responsible for the content at the item level (though perhaps not the general topic).

What can be said about a discussion where the teacher starts off being responsible for the content, say a recitation, and then switches to more open-ended exploration of the same material? And all within the same discussion? "And now what would you have done in General Lee's position? Do you think he did the right thing? Can you justify your position?"

In the above example, the responsibility for content has shifted from teacher to students, and an important attribute to the learning experience has changed. We will be interested in knowing what other attributes of the learning experience have changed.

For individual learning experiences we can note who is responsible for the content at the item level. Across learning experiences we can note which of these parties are responsible if we survey a number of lessons: teacher, student, or negotiation.

Behavior

To determine who has structured the student behavior within the learning experience one asks what verb describes what the student is doing? Who is responsible for that operation (verb) being the operation: the teacher, the student, or negotiation?

The student is reading, writing, summarizing, responding verbally, building, painting. Who chose that for him to do? These are questions we ask of individual learning experiences. Then, when we look across learning experiences and note a teacher's range on the structuring of behavior, we ask how many of the three possibilities were exercised: 1, 2, or 3? Or none? It may be that the teacher has a behavior in mind for the learning experience but fails to state it. This is of no consequence if the behavior is obvious or understood by the students. ("Doing" a page in a workbook is understood to mean "follow the directions on the page" which almost always calls for a written response in a blank or on a line.) But if the behavior is not clear to the students or was not fully thought out by the teacher ("What do we do, Mr. Jones?") then we could conclude "none" here. For example, "Do the next chapter in your book" may mean read and answer the questions at the end, read only, or read for the general idea, etc. Unless some routine has been established for what "reading a chapter" means, we could conclude this is "none" on "structuring behavior."

Procedures

Procedural moves set the details of who and how. For example, dividing a class into teams for a spelling bee, giving directions for a worksheet exercise, describing the procedure in a concept attainment game are all procedural planning moves. Included in this category are the negotiations, which may go on at some length, when students are given the opportunity to decide how they want to go about studying a given content area. Procedures may come from the teacher, from the students, or be negotiated. Which are the following?

> T: We are going to divide the class into three groups. John, Gary, and George will be in group 1.

> T: First we're going to do worksheets. Then I want you to write down the items that were difficult and when you've done that, we'll discuss those items.

> T: We're going to go round the circle here and each of you will tell us something you read about Hemingway and I'll write it on the board.

> T: How shall we do this? Shall everybody participate?

> T: John has suggested that we invite the editor of the newspaper to speak. Do you agree that this is a good way to begin our study of journalism?

[Joyce, *Teacher Innovator Interaction Analysis System, Training Manual*]

It may be that the teacher has some procedures in mind for the learning experience, but fails to state them. In that case, we have no structuring of procedures. "Work on your folders, boys and girls." If within each folder there is a structuring of procedures for each child in the form of a note ("Charlie, do the first two worksheets and then bring them to me for checking."), then we would score the procedures as structured by the teacher. But if it is unclear what the procedures are to be, because the teacher has either failed to state them or failed to think them out, and where she doesn't explicitly ask students to make decisions about procedures, then one might conclude "none."

Closure

How will the student know when the learning experience is over? The end point can be defined in terms of time, in terms of quantity of material completed, or in terms of a certain kind of product being produced. Who determines these limits: teacher, student, or negotiated?

For certain experiences closure is inherently determined by the student: e.g., a painting or creative writing (except where the teacher says, "Write a four-page story"). For others it is clearly teacher determined. ("Do the first three lines of problems.") But if closure is not inherently or explicitly delegated to the student, then failure to state it may lead us to conclude "none" on structuring of closure. The key questions are "Which ways does the teacher have for structuring closure to learning experiences?" and "Are they used appropriately?"

Teachers who hand out folders containing pages of new worksheets and expect students to just begin working are evidencing "none" for structuring of procedures and closure...and often experience the consequences of that lack of structuring.

Products

Who determines the form of the tangible products: teacher, student, or negotiated?

Teacher:	"I'll tally votes here on how many thought the Civil War represented progress versus setbacks." The tally is the product.
Student:	Any creative/expressive activity (painting, creative writing) makes a student responsible for the form of the product.
Negotiated:	"How shall we represent the data from our poll?" They negotiate a form, perhaps decide on bar graphs.

Which of the three ways to structure tangible form of product(s) does the teacher use across learning experiences?

Matching

Why would teachers treat students differently with regard to structure? One reason, obviously, would be learning effectiveness (see Colarusso, 1972). Jimmy may be capable of designing his own procedures for collecting data from his science experiment, whereas Fred needs the teacher to structure procedures to maximize the benefit he gets from the experience. A certain group of students may be quite capable of picking their own reading material, whereas another is not (content).

But another reason might have to do with long range goals. Some teachers have as a goal helping students to become more independent, self-motivated learners. This means moving gradually from high to progressively lower structure. Such a teacher takes students where they are and provides the degree of structure necessary for learning to proceed efficiently. If this happens to be high structure, so be it. Then, over time, the teacher introduces negotiation of certain sub-parameters, say procedures and closure, with some students. Over the course of the year, more and more students become involved in more and more decision-making about their learning as they show they are ready.

As a note of possible interest, we feel that understanding structuring (and accountability) is the key to understanding the erratic record of Open Classrooms in the 60s and 70s. Those that worked were in control of structuring and matched it to the students in the class. Those that didn't offered too much low structure to students who were unprepared to deal with it. The physical look and arrangement of the room, open versus traditional, is usually *no clue* about the level of structure and the degree of appropriateness for different students. Whole populations of students may be matched to a level of structure or structure may be differentiated across different individuals and groups within the same class. Few American visitors to British Infant Schools in the early 60s adequately perceived the high degree of structure and accountability built into students' working routines, despite the open, child-centered, and apparently effortless flow of constructive activity (Berlak, *et al.*, 1975).

A continuous line of research developed by David Hunt and his associates since 1966 has established the clear enhancement of learning that results when students experience a degree of imposed structure matched to their level of development. Numerous instruments are available for determining whether a student is suited to a high or low structure treatment (see Hunt, 1974, 1971; Rich and Bush, 1978). The possibilities we have sketched for who does the structuring—teacher, negotiated, or student—correspond to Hunt's ratings of high, moderate, and low degrees of imposed structure.

Grouping and Interpersonal Complexity

Definitions
Students may work alone, with a single peer, with a group of peers, with the total class, in a dyad with the teacher, with other adults (the principal, a visitor, a parent), or in a small group with the teacher. Any one or more of these six possible combinations may characterize learning experiences over the course of a day or week. Each individual learning experience may have its own grouping. First, one can simply count the number of groupings evidenced to index a teacher's range.

Significance

Characterizing the groupings in a teacher's teaching allows us to ask of the curriculum, "What kinds of interpersonal complexity are consistent with the objectives of the curriculum?" It also allows us to see how much congruence there is between intentions and reality.

Notice we have replaced the word "grouping" with "interpersonal complexity" in the above paragraph. This is because there is more to say about a group than how many people are in it. It is also important to know what kind of interaction they are having with one another. Six students and a teacher may be answering recitation questions in a small group. The students have no interaction with each other and only simple interactions with the teacher...giving direct factual answers. In that same group of six, however, the teacher may invite students to respond, extend, interpret or refute other students' answers. Students may begin speaking directly to one another without the teacher as intermediary between every student utterance. The teacher may still moderate the discussion and call on people, but the interpersonal complexity is now moderately complex and no longer simple. If the students are freely interacting with each other and create their own conversational rules and agendas as they go, then the interpersonal complexity, we would say, is high.

In a curriculum stressing social objectives, say cooperation, listening to each other, or mutual respect, we would expect to see learning experiences with groups of students, dyads, and other combinations that brought students together without exclusive teacher direction. Whatever the themes of the curriculum, the types of interpersonal complexity displayed enable us to describe an important and real part of the learning environment and ask questions about the effect of those patterns on students' learning. Taken from the perspective of curriculum-as-planning, interpersonal complexity is a design feature of learning experiences that a teacher can tailor to the nature of the objectives and the needs of the learners.

Matching Interpersonal Complexity

In studying a teacher's teaching we can determine whether or not the teacher discriminates between students in the kind of interpersonal complexity designed or allowed for in learning experiences (Colarusso, 1972). Jim works well in large groups, but tends to act out or be silly in small group instruction. He does have a few peers with whom he seems able to work effectively. He allows these students to help him and can work cooperatively with them when he has to deal with them only one at a time. So the teacher engineers teacher-Jimmy and peer-Jimmy learning situations as often as possible (while also working on his difficulties with being in groups) to maximize his productive learning time in the class. She has matched the interpersonal complexity in his learning experiences to observed characteristics of Jimmy.

A teacher observes that this class, in comparison with others she has had, attends very poorly in a large group. So, while making attention an objective for them, the teacher makes sure they have as many individual and small group work situations as possible. That is a decision to match the needs of this particular class.

Mrs. James notices her English class does not handle the high level of interpersonal complexity she encourages; they seem alternately to flounder or to attack each other when discussing the readings. She reduces the interpersonal complexity to moderate and increases her role as mediator. They prove quite capable of handling high level literary analysis, but require less interpersonal complexity than last year's class.

Where teachers show different patterns of grouping and interpersonal complexity for different children we can note "matching" on this attribute.

How about the possibility of a "mismatch" on this sub-parameter? What would it look like so that we could defend such a judgement? Probably the learning experience wouldn't be going very well. A "mismatch" means something is wrong, and when something is wrong we expect to see symptoms—disruptive behavior, or inattention most typically. Students are experiencing difficulty under these conditions and we must be able to attribute this difficulty to inappropriate grouping or interpersonal complexity rather than to other causes (students' emotional baggage, inappropriate work, poor transition). How can we distinguish such causes in an observation?

Repeated observations over a long period of time might enable an observer to see groupings that were consistently successful for a certain student and others that were consistently unsuccessful. If the students were frequently placed in these failure settings, the observer could attribute "mismatch" to the grouping or interpersonal complexity. This would put the observer in the position of knowing, through repeated observation, something the teacher did not. While such a situation is conceivable, a single observation is rarely enough to produce it. More likely the observer would be in a position to problem solve *with* the teacher, exploring what the cause of the problem might be, considering this sub-parameter as one of them.

Information Complexity

"Students who are low in conceptual level (CL) are less capable of processing information in a complex way and less capable of dealing with information in a responsible fashion; students higher in CL are more capable of processing information in a complex way" (Hunt, 1971).

Sound simplistic...obvious? It's not. The conceptual level of students is not the same as their intelligence or ability. We can often find two youngsters who are both quite "bright" but may be quite different in CL. What does it mean to process information in a complex way? We will define three levels of information complexity. One can look at learning experiences to see which is being demanded of students.

At level one, low complexity, information is *linear* and direct. One thing leads to another. Qualities of the learning tend to include remembering, sequence, performance, concepts, skills. Learners are not asked to consider alternatives or make distinctions between points of view or such things as people's feelings, orientations. They have difficulty developing concepts on their own, but can learn them receptively without difficulty.

At level two, the notion of *alternatives* appears. Students are asked to make distinctions, to differentiate sources, points of view, courses of action, possible explanations. The student can assimilate the idea that there is more than one possible explanation for a phenomenon. Comparison and contrast enter the picture. Students can develop their own concepts from data.

At level three, high complexity, students can consider several alternatives. Their ability to differentiate and distinguish increases and develops into the ability to see the *relationships* between different points of view or different explanations.

Significance

Clearly there is a developmental quality to these three levels. (Five-year-olds are usually not ready to describe the relationships between different points of view.) Thus, this sub-parameter reminds us to look at our students and to check if we are challenging them appropriately with the complexity of their tasks. It further challenges us to ask ourselves if they are ready for an increment up toward the next level. And finally it challenges us to differentiate among our students within a class (individualize, if you will) and adjust their work appropriately.

Hunt's developmental model (1971) considers what we have called separately Structuring, Grouping/Interpersonal Complexity, and Information Complexity all at once. These are three facets of "conceptual level." And they correlate with one another; that is, a student who is low in CL (as measured by Hunt's paragraph completion test) will function best with a high degree of imposed structure, simple dynamics in his groupings, and low information complexity. Conversely, a high-CL student learns best with low structure, more complex grouping interactions, and more complex information processing. The research supporting the effectiveness of this matching has really been quite striking and quite consistent. It has proven applicable for adults as well as children and has been used successfully as a way to form classroom and instructional groupings (Gower and Resnick, 1979; Rich and Bush, 1978).

Sensory Input; Motor Use; Student Output

Matching students' optimum input and output channels is often cited as one way to individualize learning experiences for different students. Dunn (1978) makes a strong case for it. To the degree to which this is taking place, we would expect to see similar or identical objectives being worked on by students through input/output channels adjusted for their characteristics.

A count can be made of how many of the following channels are used for input of information to students in learning experiences: visual, auditory, tactile/kinesthetic.

Regarding how students act in learning experiences ("student output"), the number of channels from among the following can be counted: talk, writing, performance of some kind (including drawing, building, manipulating, acting out motorically).

Regarding motor use, one can record how many of the following muscle groups are used by students: large motor, small motor, voice, passive (no motor).

One might use data about these three attributes of learning experiences to evaluate how active the learning was and how that level of physical activity fit one's goals for the learning program or for the needs of the students. But more likely the greatest significance of this data will be raising teachers' awareness of the range they can create and the potential for matching that range will offer.

Simply seeing a variety of perceptual channels operating differentially across students does not prove matching. To support a "yes" judgement there must be evidence that a particular mode is being used with a particular student or group of students and that there is not just random variety. Such evidence might be provided by a teacher remark or by a systematic assignment system for directing certain named students to a learning experience with a dominant perceptual mode different from other learning experiences being offered around the same objective to other students.

Scale

Definitions

Sometimes we see that the scale of objects, or of print, or of models used in learning experiences, has been adjusted in some way, enlarged or reduced (miniaturized). The scale of materials used can be either of these two, or it can be normal, that is, as normally found. This sub-parameter begins by a simple count of how many of these three possibilities are present.

Significance

Like all the other attributes, scale is an attribute of a learning experience that affects the interaction of the learner with the environment, and that environment is under the control of the curriculum designer and the teacher. It is something that can be controlled to effect. Examining this attribute of teaching brings it to consciousness and provokes questions about whether all the opportunities for scale manipulation in learning experiences have been taken. For example, by miniaturizing into models we can bring concepts from the abstract to the iconic level to good effect for students who don't function well abstractly. Whole outdoor physical environments (a stream, a town, a valley) can be captured in paint on giant 3' x 4' sheet boards and unfolded around the periphery of a classroom to simulate the environment of the stream. By enlarging worksheets or other standard school tasks onto giant plastic-covered boards, or using giant felt or plastic numbers, variety can be provided to the conduct of otherwise standard learning experiences.

Matching

When we see the scale of an object adjusted for use with a particular student or students, we can conclude "yes" on matching for scale. This can be particularly important for primary children for whom size of print and number of items on a page can be confusing.

Checking on Learning Experiences

1. Source of Information   conventional   constructed

2. Resources Used

text	observation
teacher	audio-visual
peers	reference books
parents	imagination
interviews	experiences

3. Personal Relevance   contrived   simulated   real

4. Competition   competitive   individualized   cooperative

5. Supervision

supervised	facilitated
independent	matched

6. Expressing the Self   no   yes   matched

7. Degree of Abstraction

concrete	representational
abstract	

8. Cognitive Level

   recall
   comprehension
   analysis
   application
   synthesis
   evaluation

9. Structuring

	none	teacher	student	negotiated
content				
behavior				
procedures				
products				
closure				

10. Grouping & Interpersonal Complexity

low	moderate
high	matching

11. Information Complexity

low	moderate
high	matching

12. Sensory Channels

Student Input	visual	tactile/kinesthetic
	auditory	matched

Student Motor Use	large motor	small motor
	voice	passive

Student Output	talk	writing
	performance	matched

13. Scale

	normal	miniaturized
	enlarged	matched

Source Materials on This Parameter

Anter, J. and Jenkins, J. "Differential Diagnosis-Prescription Teaching: A Critical Appraisal." *Review of Educational Research*, 49/4, Fall 1979, 517-555.

Aronson, E. *The Jigsaw Classroom*. Beverly Hills, CA: Sage Publications, 1978.

Bates, J. "Extrinsic Reward and Intrinsic Motivation: A Review with Implications for the Classroom." *Review of Educational Research*, 49/4, Fall 1979, 557-576

Berlak, A.; Bulah, H.; Tushnet-Baginotos, N. and Mikel, E.R. "Teaching and Learning in English Primary Schools." *School Review*, February 1975, 215-243.

Bloom, B. *Taxonomy of Educational Objectives, Handbook I*. New York: David McKay, 1956.

Bruner, J. *Toward A Theory of Instruction*. Cambridge, MA: Harvard University Press, 1966.

Bussis, A.M., Chittenden, E.A. and Amarel, M. *Beyond Surface Curriculum: An Interview Study of Teachers' Understandings*. Boulder, CO: Westview Press, 1976.

Colarusso, C. *Diagnostic Educational Grouping: Strategies for Teaching*. Bucks County (Pennsylvania) Public Schools, March 1972.

Dale, E. "Cone of Learning." University of Ohio, unpublished paper.

Davis, O.L. (*ed.*). *Perspectives on Curriculum Development*. Washington, D.C.: Association for Supervision and Curriculum Development, 1976.

Deutsch, M. "An Experimental Study of the Effects of Cooperation and Competition Upon Group Process. *Human Relations*, 2, 1949, 199-231.

Dunn, R. and Dunn, K. *Teaching Students Through Their Individualized Learning Styles: A Practical Approach*. Reston, VA: Reston Publishing Co., 1978.

Epstein, H. "Summary by Herman T. Epstein." Unpublished paper: Brandeis University, 1950.

Gehlbach, R.D. "Individual Differences: Implications for Instructional Theory, Research and Innovation." *Educational Researcher*, 8/4, April 1979, 8-14.

Gower, R.R. and Resnick, H. "Theory and Research: Evaluation Results." Project funded by Office of Career Education, U.S. Office of Education, August 1979.

Gregorc, A.P. "Learning Styles: Differences Which the Profession Must Address." *Reading Thru Content*.

Gregorc, A.F. and Ward, H.B. "A New Definition for Individual." *MASSP Bulletin*, February 1977.

Hunt, D.E. *Matching Models in Education*. Ontario, Canada: Ontario Institute for Studies in Education, Monograph No. 10, 1971.

Hunt, D.E. and Sullivan, E.V. *Between Psychology and Education*. Hinsdale, IL: The Dryden press, 1974.

Johnson, D.W. and Johnson, R.T. *Learning Together and Alone*. Englewood Cliffs, NJ: Prentice-Hall, 1975.

Johnson, D.W., Skon, L. and Johnson, R. "Effects of Cooperative, Competitive, and Individualistic Conditions on Children's Problem-Solving Performance." *American Educational Research Journal*, 17/1, Spring 1980, 83-94.

Joyce, B.R. *Selecting Learning Experiences*. Washington, D.C.: Association for Supervision and Curriculum Development, 1978.

Rich, H.L. and Bush, A.J. "The Effect of Congruent Teacher-Student Characteristics on Instructional Outcomes." *American Educational Research Journal*, 15/3, Summer 1978, 451-458.

Rosenholtz, S.J. and Wilson, B. "The Effect of Classroom Structure on Shared Perceptions of Ability." *American Educational Research Journal*, 17/1, Spring 1980, 75-82.

Sharam, S. "Cooperation Learning in Small Groups." *Review of Educational Research*, 50/2, Summer 1980, 241-272.

Slavin, R.E. "Cooperative Learning." *Review of Educational Research*, 50/2, Summer 1980, 315-342.

Toepfer, C.F., Jr. *Brain Growth Periodization Research*. Washington, D.C.: Association for Supervision and Curriculum Development, 1981.

Tyler, R. *Basic Principles of Curriculum and Instruction*. Chicago: University of Chicago Press, 1949.

Winne, P.H. "Experiments in Relating Teachers' Use of Higher-Level Cognitive Questions to Students' Achievement." *Review of Educational Research*, 49/1, Winter 1979.

Winne, P. "Aptitude-Treatment Interactions in an Experiment on Teacher Effectiveness." *American Educational Research Journal*, 14/4, Fall 1979, 389-410.

14

Dimensionality

What is my hidden curriculum?

Social
Personal
Moral
Political
Information Processing

DIMENSIONALITY

In the Learning Experiences parameter, we passed our gaze successively across numerous separate attributes of a student's experience, each with its own rather distinctive character. In this parameter, Dimensionality, we examine qualities of the learning environment that are less discrete, but equally real.

Gower and Scott (1977) have written about the nature of classroom reality in a way that has opened the eyes of many to new complexity and richness in teaching. They describe five realities that are present in any classroom (or for that matter, any human interaction) at all times: social, personal, moral, political, and information processing realities.

Classroom Realities

Social Reality

What is the social reality in a class at any given moment? Social reality has to do with the way people humanly interact. We can inquire into group dynamics, norms, roles, expectations, and interpersonal transactions from any one of a number of points of view. But the point remains that at every moment there is a social reality present, whether or not we attend to it. It has been constructed or allowed to develop, and can be described. And its form may or may not be a deliberate creation of the teaching. Students working together cooperatively on a group project constitutes a very different social reality with respect to norms, roles, and interpersonal transactions than the same group working with a teacher-as-director on a skill lesson.

Personal Reality

Every one of us has a personal reality at any moment that consists of how we are feeling and reacting. Our hopes, fears, dreams, and goals, which we carry with us at all times, are touched, to a greater or lesser degree, by the events of the moment. Each student in a classroom, at every moment, has a personal interior state of feeling. That state is complex, changeable, and real. Each individual's feelings at the moment are the personal reality for him. When we seek to understand or provide for personal reality in the classroom, we are examining the changeable, interior, personal world of individuals and their feelings of well-being.

Moral Reality

We enter the moral dimension in a classroom when we ask about the concepts of right and wrong, of duty and justice and obligation, that exist; that are embedded in curriculum materials, in teacher behavior, in class norms and procedures, in students' judgements and choices. Such concepts exist, they function, and they are describable and analyzable in any class, whether or not the teacher is aware of and deliberate about them. Sometimes in more modern curriculum packages moral considerations are taken up head-on in learning experiences (Shaftel and Shaftel, 1967; Lickona, 1972).

Political Reality

The political dimension of reality has to do with power, influence, and control. When we examine this dimension we ask questions like: Who has power? How is influence exerted? On whom, by whom? How are decisions made? Who influences the course of events and their form? How does one person (the teacher...a student) get another to behave in a certain way? Who decides what will be done next?

Information Processing Reality

The information processing reality in schools has to do with academics. How is information dealt with? How is it presented, acquired, received, manipulated, used? The answers are quite different when one contrasts a Discovery orientation with an Advance Organizer orientation, or a Socratic discussion with a laboratory experience, or programmed instruction with self-directed research.

In the Learning Experiences parameter, we scanned many facets of an instructional event from the student's point of view. In Dimensionality, when one looks at information-processing reality, a single facet is examined—a very big one—and it is asked how information is regarded and treated over a longer time frame. The general descriptors above are drawn upon to summarize the orientation as to how information shall be engaged, manipulated, acquired. The pattern of the multiple attributes from Learning Experiences comprises the event's profile, its picture. Likewise for an information processing reality labelled "laboratory experience," there are questions to be asked so that some meaning can be made of the general descriptor. Some of these questions emerged under the Models of Teaching parameter. Suffice it to say here that the orientation of information handling is a feature of the environment different from attributes of the learning experience, and of the same level as the other four realities considered in this parameter.

Variance Within Dimensions

By variance we mean the range of ways to be on one dimension, the number of different realities observable over time when the classroom is examined through a particular dimension's lens. The social reality of a class may remain constant, such as always one large teacher-directed group; or it may have two social realities: large teacher-directed group, and large democratic discussion group with emphasis on interpersonal transactions. (Note: This distinction is not one that would be picked up by the sub-parameter "Interpersonal Complexity" of Learning Experiences.) One may see a variety of social realities over a class day or week or year. The social reality within a small group changes if the teacher ceases being a direct skill lesson leader and becomes an equal participant and facilitator in a discussion of, say, states' rights.

Moral reality may be invariant: community norms and expectations that students do their work (the good, duty, obligation) are maintained and enforced by the teacher without discussion. Or, a different moral reality may be observed at different times as, for example, when children consider ethical issues as a learning activity or when groups are permitted to problem solve with the teacher acting as a mediator.

Emphasis Within Dimensions

The "hidden curriculum" can be taken to be those social, personal, moral, and political learnings which accrue to students as a result of the environment in which they function, both in the classroom and the broader school at large. These learnings may be built in unconsciously, or they may be deliberate and orchestrated by the teacher. Either way, they are happening and in all five dimensions.

When they are deliberate, we find teachers who can talk explicitly about their ideas of social curriculum, personal or psychological curriculum, and, less often, moral curriculum and political curriculum. This curriculum may evince itself in explicit learning experiences or, more subtly, in intentional aspects of the learning environment the teacher constructs or allows to exist (for reasons he attributes to social goals or moral goals, etc.). "Emphasis" in any dimension usually manifests in awareness, deliberateness, and objectives for that dimension. As we observe teaching and interview teachers about their teaching, dimensions can be identified that are being emphasized either in the design of the learning environment or in direct instructional activities. Such emphasis can be detected in zero, one, two, three, four, or five dimensions.

It is hard to conceive of a teacher who emphasizes no dimensions. Every teacher emphasizes at least one dimension—academics. "Emphasize" is taken to mean "has goals in a dimension." It has been said before that there is some describable reality on each dimension at all times, regardless of the teacher's awareness or deliberateness about what it is. When a dimension is "emphasized" though, even if it has only one form, it means that the dimensional reality figures prominently in learning experiences and one would expect the teacher to be able to say why. If we observe students in debate, stating and defending positions on issues with the teacher as facilitator and clarifier, we would expect the teacher to have something to say about getting students to be independent thinkers, or critical thinkers, or effective speakers, or some such goal.

Matching Dimensions to Needs

The dimension emphasized, or the particular form of dimensional reality shaped by a teacher at any given moment, may be a deliberate attempt to match characteristics of the group or of a student. If we can evidence that, we have matching.

Since observers cannot see "deliberateness" (at least not visually), they must look for what they can see; namely, different dimensional emphases for specific students, as distinct from the whole class. One can look for different treatments, different environments, or different patterns of interaction which could justify saying a particular dimension was being emphasized with a student or group apart from the main flow of the class day.

In interviews with teachers, we often find direct statements of intention and deliberateness about matching dimensions emphasized to groups and to individuals.

Source Materials on This Parameter

Gower, R.R. and Scott, M.B. *Five Essential Dimensions of Curriculum Design.* Dubuque, Iowa: Kendall Hunt, 1977.

Lickona, T. "A Strategy for Teaching Values." Pleasantville, NY: Guidance Associates, 1972.

Shaftel, G. and Shaftel, F. *Role Playing for Social Values.* Englewood Cliffs, NJ: Prentice Hall, 1967.

Stanford, G. *Developing Effective Classroom Groups.* New York: Hart Publishing Co., 1977.

15
Objectives

What should I teach, and how
should I frame my objectives?

Five Kinds of Teacher Thinking
Primary Sources
Secondary Sources
Level of Difficulty

OBJECTIVES

Introduction

What is the most important Parameter of Teaching? 80% of those polled in an early validation study of the parameters thought it was Objectives (Saphier, 1980). Why?

People gave us logical arguments such as, "If you don't know where you're going, you can't get there." "Objectives have to be the point of departure." "Everything you do is built on knowing what you want to accomplish."

All this seemed quite logical and convincing. (Eventually though, we stopped asking the question: we came to see that all the parameters are reciprocally important. Good objectives clearly can't get you anywhere without good instruction...and vice versa.) What was interesting about the responses was the contrast between stated values and known behavior. We know pretty convincingly that most teachers don't think in terms of objectives for student learning when they do their planning (Peterson, *et. al.*, 1978; Joyce, *et. al.*, 1981). They think in terms of activities. They plan what they will do and in what order, and also what activities students will do and in what order. Joyce, *et. al.*, (1981) explain this in terms of decisions made at the beginning of the year, like which text and what materials will be used.

The danger here is that it becomes easy to lose track of where you're going when you don't think or write in terms of student learning objectives. You can get tied to materials and activities, have students involved and liking their classes, but be achieving uncertain, erratic, and unpredictable results. Student involvement and enjoyment of school are great, but they do not, by themselves, make for effective teaching and learning.

Madeline Hunter tells a story that illuminates how fuzzy thinking about objectives can dilute learning. She finds a kindergarten teacher holding her head amidst a room that's a mess of paper and glue. There are mimeographed turkeys all around on which kids have been pasting squares of colored tissue paper to make Thanksgiving collages. Madeline asks what's been going on. "Well, it was an art experience for the kids," is the reply.

M. Why did you go to the trouble of mimeographing the turkeys? Why not just give them a piece of paper and the tissue and let them be creative, express themselves?

T. It really wasn't that. It was really a lesson in eye-hand coordination.

M. Well, then why didn't you have them outline the turkey? You can't tell whether they stayed within the line or not when they've got them pasted all over the turkey.

T. Well, it really wasn't that. It was a lesson in conservation.

M. Conservation!

T. Yes. The kids have really been very wasteful of paste. So I was trying to teach them to put just a tiny piece of paste on.

M. Then why didn't you give them a piece of paste, or a paper of paste, and see how much of their turkey they could finish before they ran out of paste? You can't tell if there's a cup of paste under some of these turkeys.

T. Oh, for cryin' out loud, can't kids just have fun?

M. Sure they can have fun. What do your kids like to do?

T. The thing they like to do best is just chase out on the school grounds.

M. Why didn't you take the last half-hour and go around, supervise them while they chased and you wouldn't have this mess to clean up?

Many of the differences we see in people's teaching can be traced back to their thinking about Objectives. The quality of that thinking is what makes the difference. When some teachers think Objectives, they are really thinking about what they want to cover. "My objective tomorrow is to get through the material on gas attacks in W.W.I." If I am thinking in terms of coverage, I am focused on getting through everything, and what's important is that the information gets said and that we get finished. This will influence my teaching. I tend to become wed to an agenda and a timetable and tend to do less checking, less intellectual exploration, and less integration with other learning. Instruction tends toward recitation.

Coverage Objectives

A Coverage objective means I'm thinking in terms of me, not the students. I am going to present, describe, explain, demonstrate, or cover the following information/events/procedures/processes. When I'm through my agenda, the lesson is done—I've "covered" it. I've taken it out of my head and put it "out there," but I'm not necessarily doing it in a way that is guided by what is in the students' heads before I started. I don't know if it passed through the nether regions of "out there" into students' heads.

Activity Objectives

At other times when teachers think about objectives, they mean what they want the students to do, what activities students will get through. They're going to do these workbook pages/answer these questions/solve these problems/do this experiment with these 6 steps/"discuss" the chapter/solve these problems/read this article/write a story. My objective, then, is really that they get the activity done. With such a focus it is possible that the activity is not teaching what should be taught...or that it can be done without students learning anything.

"Write a story," for example, may be the Activity objective for after lunch in this primary grade room. To get the kids involved (make the activity more fun, more attractive, more motivating) I have textured wallpaper pieces they can use to make covers for their "books." I'm helping them bind their books today. The quality of stories ranges from complete plots with beginnings, middles, and ends to random pictures with no text at all. As I bind each book, I ask the children about their stories; some make comments, some don't. I am focusing on the binding and keeping the flow of kids moving. As you watch you see no evidence that there is any particular feature I am looking for in children's stories. I make an effort to be positive about some aspect of what each child shows me, but appear to be looking for nothing in particular. My real objective is just that they produce stories...of any quality. Voila: an Activity objective! I might not admit that if you asked me. But judging by what I actually did, no other objective is supportable.

When teachers' objectives are to get the activities done, they miss opportunities to underline the critical learnings, to make connections between learnings for students, and to check and evaluate student learning. If I am thinking in terms of activities I am concerned with management. My focus is on giving directions and having everyone engaged. There may also be an emphasis on excitement, involvement, and debate in which case we also have an "involvement" objective.

Involvement Objectives

When teachers think about objectives in terms of student involvement, what they're really after is that students "get into it." "My objective tomorrow is to get all students to react personally...say what they'd do if they invented a horrible weapon. Would they turn it over to the government?"

We know from studies of teacher planning (conducted by having teachers think aloud) that activity objectives and involvement objectives dominate planning (Clark and Yinger, 1979). Involvement objectives are met if students appear to engage the activity with some absorption, enthusiasm, or intensity. The objective is really that the students be involved. Thus, it is met if the students like the activity and stick with it. There is nothing wrong with that state of affairs. In fact, it's wonderful. But it is possible to be absorbed in an activity that isn't teaching you much. You like to do it, perhaps, but fun does not necessarily equal learning. It doubtless enhances learning, but such activities may not be productive in and of themselves.

My students love to do word searches. So I make up one with their spelling words in it and they do it for seat work. I notice they are having fun. "Boy, they really got into that word search today!" But did it help them learn their spelling words? Did I, in fact, assign it because I thought it would help them learn to spell the words? No. I assigned it because I thought they'd like to do it; which they do. But as it turns out, there is noevidence that word searches actually improve students' ability to spell the words they find. It may improve their ability to scan complex data fields for visual information; they may (some of them) develop systematic searching strategies for finding the words more efficiently. But this was not my objective...and students who learn "systematic search" are learning it at random, and incidentally, not through any deliberate approach of mine.

Mastery (or Student Learning) Objectives

If my objective is mastery of the spelling words, then you will see me doing something which should increase the likelihood that the students will spell the words right. Perhaps I have them quiz each other in pairs. Then I have them make a list of the words they missed and go through a practice routine of seeing, saying, writing in the air, and retesting, over a 10-minute period. If you see that, then you can infer my objective is a Mastery objective for my students.

"My objective for tomorrow is for students to be able to distinguish between rational, amoral, and moral reasons for decisions from the list of positions we will generate in class." If I focus on student learning, there will be lots of checking to see what students' know, perceive, or can do. Timetables are flexible and what's important is that students learn well, even if less is covered.

To Summarize:

Student Learning objective: "When we're done they'll be able to..."

Involvement objective: "I want them to get involved in..."

Activity objective: "First they will...then they'll/we'll...then I want them to..."

Coverage objective: "What I'm going to do first is to give them…then I'll describe…then I'll ask them to…"

These four kinds of thinking are not mutually exclusive, and actually do tend to be cumulative. A teacher planning in terms of student learning still has to consider activities, involvement, and what will be covered. But it is possible to think in terms of either coverage or activities and not consciously about student learning.

This is an interesting lens for supervisors to use in reviewing events with teachers. Inquiring into the nature of thinking about objectives will often help us solve puzzles about why certain pieces of teaching are going awry or not living up fully to their promise. The quality of thinking about objectives accounts for much of what we see (or don't see) in classrooms.

Generic Thinking Objectives

Let's go back to the word search for a minute. Suppose I do want them to learn something about systematic search as a strategy. After all, that's useful in life. That's the kind of skill we use when we look through a collection of nuts and bolts for a particular size we need, or when we scan a map for Maple Street and we only know it's somewhere on the page. If I want my kids to learn strategies for systematic search, what would you be likely to see us doing? Certainly talking together about how different children were going about looking for the words…comparing approaches, strategies…perhaps giving names to the different strategies, perhaps listing them on the board, perhaps asking kids where else they could use these strategies, or what other kinds of tasks would be good places to try them out (transfer).

If you were to see some of the above, then you might infer I had a Generic Thinking objective for my kids, that is, an objective to develop a thinking skill apart from any particular content knowledge.

We are a 7th grade social studies class working on a chapter about Bedouins of the Arabian desert. There's a lot of information in this chapter, facts and concepts galore; but not only do I want you to learn them, I want you to learn about hierarchical relationships…not just relationships in Bedouin life, but the nature of hierarchical relationships in general, how to find them and represent them. So I add a little something to your assignment. I ask you to identify key terms from the chapter and make a diagram that shows their relationships to one another! Now something more is required. Figure 15-1 shows two different diagrams I may get.

Note the different kinds of thinking behind these two diagrams. The first has terms arranged subordinately according to size. The Murrah is one of many tribes.

Figure 15-1

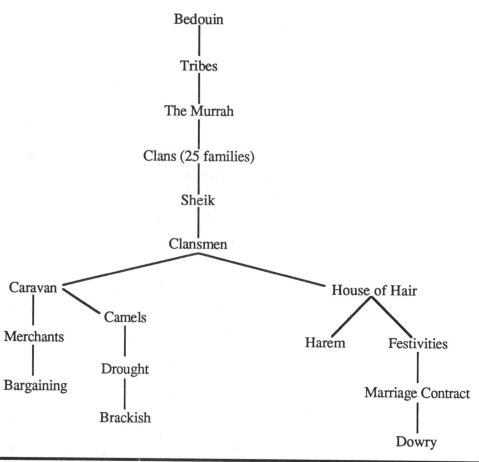

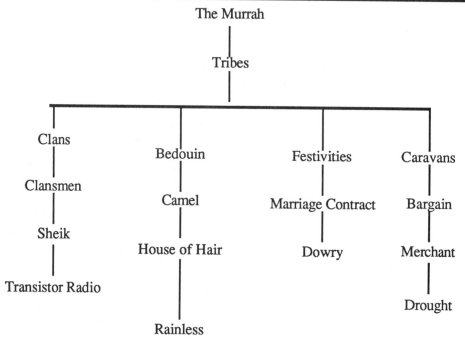

Each tribe (Murrah included), is composed of clans of about 25 families, and each clan is headed by a sheik. Each family is organized around a patriarch and inhabits a "house of hair" with a harem. Then the relationships shift to category groupings.

The second diagram shows relationships that are random and non-linear. The diagram seems to have been created by free association rather then consistent application of some particular kind of relationship.

Now I have students compare in small groups and explain the kind of relationships their connecting lines represent. I am getting them to talk to each other about their thinking, and later in a total class discussion will develop in particular what hierarchical or subordinated relationships mean, using their examples. I will use those words too (hierarchical, subordinated), because my objective for this and for the upcoming series of lessons is that they become able to do that kind of thinking, whether it's around Bedouins, sports, or computer programming. So I have an objective here that goes beyond mastery of content (though it includes that). I am also aiming to develop a particular thinking skill.

There are literally dozens of thinking skills that may be targeted and taught simultaneously with and through academic content. But for our purposes, the thing to note is if and when such an objective is present and how it alters the nature of assignments and of instruction.

Figure 15-2 summarizes the five kinds of thinking about Objectives we have described so far.

Questions About Objectives

This brings us, then, to the first of the questions we must ask about Objectives for a given lesson (or a given class).

Was There an Objective?

Was there a clear objective? When you reflect on the period, can you infer a clear statement of what students were supposed to be able to do at the end?

Let's pause here a minute and look at the notion of a "clear" objective. *A clear objective is one that creates an image of specifically what a student will know or be able to do* when the instruction is over. The image can be a picture in your mind, a sentence of inner speech you say to yourself, or a written statement; what's important is that the image is framed from the student's point of view. The objective is a clear picture of a student's performance that you, the teacher, have in your head. Thus, you can see that we are taking a position here about those five kinds of

Figure 15-2
Thinking About Objectives

Name	Language	Gist
Generic Thinking Skills*	"...diagram the relationship between key terms describing Bedouin life."	The objective is for students to express or develop a certain kind of thinking skill.

...thus these are student centered, centered on ways kids function intellectually.

Name	Language	Gist
Mastery Of Academic Knowledge or Skills	"...be able to describe to each other the principal causes of W.W.I." "...measure distance using scale on map."	The objective is for students to know or be able to do something specific.

...thus these are student centered, centered on what kids will learn in the way of information or skills.

Name	Language	Gist
Involvement	"After giving a dramatic reading of the story, I'll solicit their opinions and get them involved in a discussion."	The objective is for students to be visibly involved at least to participate actively and at best to be excited and have fun.

...student centered on how kids will react.

Name	Language	Gist
Activity	"They'll look at the filmstrip, then make a map of the South, then answer the questions at the end of the chapter."	The objective is for students to finish certain tasks.

...student centered on what kids will do.

Name	Language	Gist
Coverage	"First I'll discuss the heat of reaction, then I'll go over endothermic reactions, entropy, enthalpy, and then review valences."	The objective is to mention or get said pieces of information.

...thus a teacher centered objective, centered on what the teacher will do, what agenda to get through

* How would one know if a person had a thinking objective in mind? They'd explicitly call for and engineer a situation where that objective was expected of students. And they'd be likely to highlight it, talk about how to do it, and/or label it with students.

Objectives in the previous section: namely, that they're not all equally good. We would argue that there are *no objectives* that cannot be framed as a clear image of student performance, even objectives pertaining to "attitude" or "appreciation." Secondly, we argue that objectives that are not thought through in this way typically wind up as 1) Coverage objectives, 2) Activity objectives, or 3) Involvement objectives...and that all three of these are weaker than Student Learning objectives. Thirdly, we argue that thinking in terms of Student Learning objectives tends to improve teaching by leading us to do to more goal stating with students, more checking, more feedback according to criteria, better record keeping, and more diagnosis of individual student needs.

Let's return to the first point: no objectives cannot be framed as Student Learning objectives (i.e., creating a specific image of what a student will know or be able to do). How about attitude objectives?

Mr. Caswell wants students to develop a positive attitude toward classical music. How would we know if he'd accomplished that? What does he mean when he says, "I want my students to appreciate Beethoven." He might mean that he expects *knowledge* of the intricacy and subtlety of the design of a Beethoven symphony to generate *respect*. Further, he may believe that for some people, having to listen in a focused way to the symphony as they analyze its parts will lead to *aesthetic enjoyment*. All of that may be his concept of "appreciation": respect through knowledge, and liking through repeated experience. If that is his concept, it will lead him to do certain activities in class aimed at generating specific student performances—performances like being able to analyze parts of the symphony and label a score; like describing in words the principles by which Beethoven develops and restates themes; or like identifying the different symphonies. Now, all of these student performances he can picture because he's thought about what "appreciation" means. If he doesn't translate "appreciation" into some sort of student performance in his head, then what Mr. Caswell does with students in class may be random in its effect; he will not be looking inside *their* heads to create anything in a planful way. He will be operating outside their heads with "activities," "presentations" that may or may not contact anything inside students—who can tell? Without that image of the student performance he's aiming for, Mr. Caswell may do activities that lead to no performance or to an opposite student performance.

Objectives that say "students will be exposed to..." make us very nervous. If you're going to "introduce" students to an idea or "expose" them to an experience, do you expect anything to stick? If you do, you can say what it is and go for it specifically. If you don't, why are you exposing them to the idea to begin with? ("All you get from exposure is a cold."—Jim Kilroy, Tulane University.)

Here's another way of looking at this: If I don't have an image of the student performance I want, then I'm liable to pick activities that inadvertently get another performance...or no performance. If I don't specifically know where I'm going, why would you expect me to get there? If I do get there, it will be by accident, by luck, and certainly take a lot longer. If we look at the students who are along for the ride in such a class of 25 students, some may peel off and get to the destination on their own, despite the instruction. But others never arrive.

So again, the big question: *Was there a clear objective?* When you reflect on the period, can you infer a clear statement of what students were supposed to know or be able to do at the end?

Maybe the teacher stated the objective and the job is easy; or maybe the objective is written down somewhere in the book, on the worksheet, or in the packet. That is nice when it happens (and valuable for student learning—see Clarity: "goals"). But often it *isn't* stated. That might be OK, but can *you*, the observer (or self-observer), go back over the lesson from an outsider's point of view and say, "Well, clearly from what I saw and heard, the objective must have been for students to identify the six parts of a story (protagonist, antagonist, conflict, plot, climax, theme) and be able to find examples of them in the story read for homework." Maybe the teacher never said that in so many words, but clearly that is what students were supposed to learn how to do.

(By the way, if it's clear to you, it should also be clear to the students, and they should be able to make some such statement of objectives if you ask them at the end of the period.)

It should be noted, also, that the objectives we infer from observations may not be just cognitive. Pairs of students are coaching individuals on a certain bookkeeping procedure and we infer that there is an objective about cooperation and helping others in this room. Deirdre is excluded from the class meeting (first grade) and sitting near (though facing away from) a pile of blocks. We hear a few remarks and see some body language from the teacher that lead us to conclude she has an objective in mind for Deirdre, namely: cleanup; you can't get out of your responsibilities to others by pouting and stalling.

In our work, we have found that the question "Was there a clear objective?" can be answered by "yes", "no," or "yes, but fuzzy." The type of class most likely to look like a "no" or a "fuzzy" on Objectives is a rambling discussion that touches assigned material in an erratic way or not at all; or that covers course material without making relevant connections between items or making links to other course material. Another "no objectives" class has some students doing busy work, often on worksheets, about things they already know or have mastered. Calling this "reinforcement" won't wash. Practice has its place, of course, but let's be sure the practice is really strengthening a learning that needs it.

How About the Level of Difficulty?

"'Not too hot, not too cold, but ju-u-u-u-st right,' said Goldilocks. And she ate it all up."

Even before J. McVicker Hunt (1961) named it "the problem of the match," educators were striving to make the work we give students not too hard, not too easy, but just hard enough to stretch them toward optimum rate of learning. The problem of the match makes us look at where our students are now and ask, "How big a bite can I give them for the next increment of learning?" For example, judging the size of the bite for these six second graders may lead us to teach fractional notation and adding of fractions with common denominators in the same lesson. They can grasp that. It may lead us to have the 11th grade German History class not only assimilate the background and content of Bismarck's "Blood and Iron" speech, but also in the same class press them to *explain* it in terms of Bismarck's character.

If you think this sounds like individualizing, you're right. It is individualizing the number of learnings tackled at once and their pace—the size of the bites of learning—to individuals and to groups. There are many other variables that the term "individualizing" may include (see Chapter 13, Learning Experiences). Most of those variables are about "how" the learning shall proceed. Here we are talking about *what*, and *how much*, shall be aimed at for learning, regardless of the "how."

What might we see to convince us that the size of the bite was a good match for a group of students? Perhaps some evidence of initial struggling but then grasping of new ideas; perhaps moments of silence followed by student questions and clarification of difficult concepts; perhaps episodes of puzzlement culminating in "ah-hah" reactions; perhaps diligent notetaking. Negative evidence is easier to spot: confusion, dismay, frustration, or mute silence for work that's too hard (or inadequately presented); boredom as pencil-tapping, looking around, chatting, or sloppiness for work that is too easy. (Easy work is far from the only cause of the litany above, but it should be checked out when the behaviors occur.)

We must note that it is possible that none of those overt behaviors may be present, yet the objectives might still be mismatched to the students. Then, only a knowledge of the students' capacities in relation to the demands the teacher is making could help us make a judgement. Of all the sub-parameters of teaching, this one—matching the size of the bite—requires the most specific knowledge of the students and the context in order to make an accurate judgement.

Where Did the Objectives Come From?

The classic question of the curriculum field is, "What shall be taught?" The question overlays two critical issues: 1) *who will decide* what shall be taught/ learned; and 2) what kind of things are important and therefore will be *allowed on the menu*? We must look at the sources of the objectives we see in classrooms to answer those questions. The primary sources (the student, the teacher, an authority, or the group) tell us who is doing the deciding. The secondary sources will tell us what the program designers think it is important to learn. In more detail, the primary sources are as follows:

Primary Sources

The Student: A student is fascinated by frogs and toads and wants to learn everything about them. An eighth grade student is curious about movie special effects and wants to know how they're done. The teacher who legitimizes these learning objectives (maybe seeking ways to work in other ones from, say, math and language arts with what the student plans to do) makes available time and resources for the student to pursue them.

The Teacher: Things the teacher values may become objectives for no other reason than one's own idiosyncrasies, background, talents, experiences, or preferences. A teacher with particular knowledge and interest in whales may make that available to students through curriculum. A teacher with musical background may choose objectives relating to instruments in an orchestra. A teacher who values critical thinking as an important attribute of the "educated person" may make that a direct objective which they work on often.

An Authority: Many objectives come from outside authorities such as a text, a district curriculum guide, a system, a learning activity packet, or a teacher's manual. Suppose the teacher chose the text: Whom shall we say is the source of the objective, the teacher or the text? If the text is used regularly or methodically, the rule shall be "text" as source of objective, regardless of who chose it. If the teacher uses many texts and moves back and forth between them in some deliberate or purposeful way, or at any rate in a way that allows us to observe the teacher doing some thematic discrimination rather than the text, then we attribute the source of objective to the teacher.

The Group: The whole class as a group, or a subgroup of it, can be the source of an objective. Coalescing around some common interest, and usually in negotiation with the teacher, a learning objective may be developed by and for a particular group. "Let's make a movie!" The idea captivates six seventh graders and they organize a project, under the teacher's general supervision and guidance, to produce a film about their class. In the process a series of learning objectives about film production emerges (types of film: this will be a documentary which students can discriminate and describe as distinct from other types; planning a film: use of story-boards and formats, interviewing students, techniques, assemble-editing).

All Objectives can be attributed to one of these four primary sources. We can discriminate teachers whose objectives come from only one source, or from two, three, or four sources as we take an overview of their teaching. Knowing the primary sources different teachers use accounts for important differences between teachers and the experiences they offer students. Teachers who allow the group or the individual to choose some objectives have a very different climate and outcome from teachers who draw objectives exclusively from an authority. Teachers who allow (or are allowed to have) themselves as a source may have different amounts of energy and commitment to those objectives. It would be untenable to assert that any one of these four sources is any better than the others. Clearly all four have a place in schooling. To understand the experience students are having, however, and to be in a position to bring our own values to shaping those experiences, we all—parents, teachers, administrators, and school boards—need to know what stands behind the Objectives in curriculum. That goes also for the secondary sources.

Secondary Sources

Regardless of the primary source, any one or more of the following could be secondary sources or origins of Objectives. Which ones are, in fact, behind your curriculum objectives?—1) contemporary life; 2) the culture; 3) the community; 4) the academic disciplines; 5) the needs of the learners; 6) subject matter as bodies of information; 7) philosophy. The answer to this question tells what you think it is important to learn. Many of these have been developed previously by Tyler (1949).

Contemporary Life: Good examples recently have been ecology and pollution, the causes of inflation and how to protect oneself against it, marriage and divorce and the family. Objectives pertaining to these issues may or may not have been relevant in the past, and may not be in a future age, but are seen as important now because of contemporary problems. Curricula dealing with racial awareness and cultivating awareness and appreciation of differences in people, while universal in application and importance, may be particularly appropriate in integrated schools experiencing racial tensions, and thus have their secondary source in issues of contemporary life.

The Culture: Certain objectives may tacitly be mandated by local culture for consideration in the schools: correctly used terminology of weather in coastal fishing communities where weather affects livelihood directly day by day; a country's history for its inhabitants; understanding the cycle of plant growth for children in farm communities (though by no means limited to there).

The Community: Local resources may invite objectives that exploit these resources as objects of study: the ecology of pond life; the operation of the postal service (if there is a post office nearby); the life and thought of local author Henry David Thoreau (for residents in Concord, Massachusetts).

The Academic Disciplines: Learning how to think as a mathematician, a writer, a biologist, an historian, a geographer, an artist. Each discipline has a hierarchical structure to its knowledge, and when students enter this world, seeking either to acquire the knowledge in a hierarchical way or seeking to learn to think in the way of the discipline, then the secondary source of the objective is rooted in the discipline. We find many objectives in schools with a tie to the disciplines.

Needs of the Learners: Certain groups of students may have particular need for instruction in hygiene, for example. Curriculum will be designed or chosen for them around health, cleanliness, and perhaps nutrition, because the school (or the teacher) sees these students as lacking in these areas. Another group of students may fight a lot, not listen to each other, and "need" work on social problem-solving. Objectives with a source in the needs of the learners develop when someone judges that a deficiency exists: perhaps the teacher's judgement, or perhaps the administrators or the board of education. The deficiency may be with regard to present functioning (health and hygiene) or in anticipation of future needs. Most broadly construed, all Objectives are in anticipation of future needs, including instruction in basic skills. But needs of all learners will not be admitted as part of the meaning of this source of objective since that would include practically all objectives. By "needs of the learners," we mean a particular group of learners who, by virtue of a perceived deficiency or a special future need that is *not* general to all learners, are judged to need a particular piece of learning.

Subject Matter as Bodies of Information: Some objectives have as their secondary source the communication of a body of information related to a subject. Knowing the main products of the South American countries is information not from a discipline of hierarchical concepts; rather, it is a body of knowledge on a subject. We find objectives around such bodies of information throughout school at all levels. Who were the principal poets of 18th-century England? What are the math facts to 10? What is the profile of a patient going into shock?

Philosophy. Ideas about what should be—conceptions of the ideal—stand in back of some objectives. A vision of the "educated person" as one who thinks critically, listens to and reacts to others' positions while evaluating them objectively, stands up for his own positions...all these and many other conceptions of the "good" may be found behind certain objectives. Certain open classroom programs stress independence, decision-making, and creativity, because they reflect values of the program designers, or put another way, the program designers' visions of desirable characteristics to develop in learners. Objectives related to a vision of the good may be said to derive from "philosophy" as a secondary source.

The origin of Objectives tells us what is important to those in control of the educational program. Primary sources give us information about *who should choose what the objectives shall be.* Should the student have a role in the process? Should the teacher be allowed to bring some of himself directly and formally into the curriculum? How much shall the expertise of outside authorities influence the curriculum?

Secondary sources of Objectives tell us what the program directors think is *important to know.* What things should be known or learned by the students? What is important? What issues are related to contemporary life, local culture, the community? How much importance do the program designers place on the concepts from the disciplines? How much do they examine the learners and tailor objectives to their particular needs? How much and which ideas from philosophy enter the program through objectives? Answers to these questions give us important information about what is being taught and why. When we gather data about the sources of Objectives, we collect useful information for answering all these vital questions and can thus characterize a teacher's teaching in important and interesting ways.

Is the Type of Objective a Good Fit for the Content?

In the examples of types of Objectives above, the reader may have noticed particular kinds of content used. Mathematics was used with detailed behavioral objectives with criterion levels; high level reading comprehension was used to illustrate general behavioral objectives; social behavior (cooperation) was used to illustrate general patterns of behavior; and teaching management and curriculum development goals were used to illustrate teacher objectives. Particular kinds of content lend themselves well to very detailed behavioral objectives, typically, operational skills that can be observed at criterion levels of mastery (mathematical manipulations, decoding in reading, technical writing skills, etc.), but this same kind of objective may not serve instruction so well when one attempts to apply it to an area like "cooperation." How can we meaningfully specify a criterion level for mastery with respect to cooperation? We could have a student discriminate cooperative from non-cooperative behavior at a criterion level in stories read or filmstrips viewed, but how useful would that be?

Different types of objectives serve us best with different types of content. Thus, we expect teachers to use different kinds of objectives and to use the kind most suited for the content at hand. Two levels of performance can be discriminated here: teachers either *do*, or *do not*, match the type of objective they use to appropriate content. The use of detailed behavioral objectives for an art curriculum (or an oil painting course) might well trivialize that content.

There is one more issue, the "fuzzy match": What about the teacher who uses general behavioral objectives for material that *would* lend itself nicely to detailed behavioral objectives? Here's an example: Children will add 3-digit numbers with medial zeros competently." Well, what is competently? A criterion level for mastery would be nice here, *essential* Popham would argue, if one wants to really sharpen the delivery of skills and the evaluation of who knows what. Yet, use of general behavioral objectives here is better than using general patterns or topics as objective forms, which would be clearly inadequate and mismatched. We can say of this match, in effect, "It could have been better, but it could have been worse, too!" Rating degrees of matches that are not optimum in a good-better-best way brings us into the "fuzzy" area. It will be useful in feedback to teachers to discuss the optimum match and assess where the teacher is in relation to that optimum; how much "fuzziness" there is in the matching of types of objectives to content. A mismatch would occur if the form of the objective was inappropriate for the content; such a mismatch might distort the instruction-evaluation process by trivializing or overgeneralizing the learning targets.

Summary

Taken all together, this chapter offers five questions to ask about Objectives:

- Is there a clear objective that creates an image of specifically what students will know or be able to do?

- Is the level of difficulty appropriate?

- Where do the objectives come from (sources)?

- What types of objectives are used?

- Is the type of objective a good fit for the content?

Checking on Objectives

Circle the performance that applies to each question. Note any relevant details that support your observation.

1. Is there a clear objective that creates an image of specifically what students will know or be able to do?

    yes   no   fuzzy

2. Is the level of difficulty appropriate?

    too hard
       too easy
          appropriate
             stretches students with optimum match

3. Where do the objectives come from?

    student   community
    teacher   disciplines
    group   needs of learners
    authority   bodies of information
    contemporary life   philosophy
    culture

4. What types of objectives are used?

    generic thinking
    student learning (mastery)
    involvement
    activity
    coverage

5. Is the type of objective a good fit for the content?

    yes   no   fuzzy

Source Materials on This Parameter

Bussis, A.M., Chittenden, E.A. and Amarel, M. *Beyond Surface Curriculum: An Interview Study of Teachers' Understandings*. Boulder, Colorado: Westview Press 1966.

Clark, C.M. and Yinger, R.J. "Teachers Thinking." In Peterson, P.L. and Wahlberg, H.J. (*eds.*), *Research on Teaching*. Berkeley, CA: McCutchan, 1979.

Hunt, J.McV. *Intelligence and Experience*. New York: The Ronald Press Co., 1961.

Hunter, M. *Improving the Quality of Instruction*. Alexandria, VA: A.S.C.D., 1977.

Joyce, B.R., Clark, C. and Peck, L. *Flexibility in Teaching*. New York: Longmans, 1981.

Mager, R.R. *Preparing Instructional Objectives*. Palo Alto, CA: Fearson Publications, 1962.

Peterson, P.L., Marx, C.W. and Clark, C. "Teacher Planning, Teacher Behavior, and Student Achievement." *American Educational Research Journal*, 15/3, Summer 1978, 417-432.

Popham, W.J. and Baker, E.L. *Systematic Instruction*. Englewood Cliffs, NJ: Prentice Hall, 1970.

Saphier, J.D. "The Parameters of Teaching: An Empirical Study Using Observations and Interviews to Validate a Theory of Teaching by Linking Levels of Analysis, Levels of Knowing and Levels of Performance." Unpublished Doctoral Dissertation. Boston: Boston University, 1980.

Tyler, R.W. *Basic Principles of Curriculum and Instruction*. Chicago: University of Chicago Press, 1949.

Zahorik, J.A. "Learning Activities: Nature, Function, and Practice." *The Elementary School Journal*, 82/4, 309-317.

16
Evaluation

How do I know what students have really learned?

Purposes
Collecting Data
Eight Checkpoints
    for Implementation

EVALUATION

The Basic Questions

Teachers feel very good when students participate actively in class. In fact, they often judge the success of their lessons by how involved, interested, and active students get (Doyle, 1979; Clark and Peterson, 1981; Zahorik, 1982). "The kids really got into that one." "They were really there this afternoon." "It was great. Even Jerome got involved."

Most of us believe that interested students learn more and learn faster. That is certainly a reasonable belief. Involvement mediates learning—that is, it sits in the middle of the process of learning and helps it along. However, while we would never argue against working for high levels of student interest and involvement, we wish to point out that you can have that *without accomplishing your intended learnings*. If you measure involvement and use it as your criteria for successful learning experiences, you may or may not be getting the intended learnings. You just won't know.

Evaluation in education is irrevocably wed to Objectives. That is what Evaluation evaluates—the objectives. If this couple gets a divorce, or even a trial separation, the whole neighborhood is in jeopardy. So the first thing to look for in Evaluation is some direct way of asking if the objective has been met. "If students really knew their times tables, how would I know? What would I take as evidence that they did?" "If they really could take data and make inferences from observations, how would I know?" "If they really understood Turner's Frontier Thesis, how would I know?"

This is tantamount to the way we started the Objectives chapter. There, the first question was: "Is there a clear objective at all?" Here we are asking if Evaluation is happening at all. It's quite easy to let it slip through the cracks and have a smooth functioning classroom nonetheless.

From this global question, we can then proceed to address a series of specific issues essential to good Evaluation.

1.   What is the Purpose of Evaluation?

If Evaluation is occurring, we should next check to see if we are clear about the *purpose* of the evaluation, and that our students also know clearly what that purpose is. Strange as it may sound, students will often not know the purpose of a particular evaluation unless we tell them directly—and that rarely happens. We could count on one hand the number of teachers we've observed in any year who differentiate *for students* between summative tests and diagnostic tests. Telling students, "This test is just to see what you've learned so far" doesn't make the distinction—that doesn't tell students what you're going to do with the results (Group them for instruction? Make reports to parents about overall progress? Identify topics to reteach to the whole class?).

There are many legitimate reasons for doing Evaluation with students. Figure 16-1 on the following page summarizes a number of them. Teachers sometimes try to use tests for two or more purposes at the same time; for example, getting grades to rank students for honor roll and diagnosing student weaknesses for reteaching. Bloom, *et al.*, (1981) point out that mixed-purpose evaluation usually does not work too well, short-changing one of the purposes because of the different design demands of different kinds of evaluation. It is because of these differences in design that we need to be particularly clear about which purposes we have in mind.

In this chapter we are going to focus on Evaluation's role in making instructional decisions. Our orientation is toward teacher's evaluation of student learning for the purpose of improving that learning.

2.   Are You Testing What You Teach?

If Evaluation is aimed at instructional decision-making, the next thing to check is whether you're evaluating your objectives, or something else: Do you test exactly what you teach and what you really want students to be able to do? It's amazing how often this one is violated (content validity).

- We want third graders to be able to read for meaning, but we test them on sub-skills of word analysis that many *good* readers cannot do. (New York's Degrees of Reading Power test has attacked this problem by testing only reading, not sub-skills.)

- We want first graders to be able to decode words using initial consonant cues, but we test their ability to discriminate auditorily between

Figure 16-1
Purposes of Evaluation

1. to sort, rank or compare students
   — for honors and awards
   — for admissions into programs with limited enrollment

2. to norm students or groups of students
   — for comparitive achievement in relation to national groups
   — for comparative achievement in relation to other populations

3. to certify students
   — as competent in a field of knowledge
   — as competent in a field of practice
   — as eligible for "promotion"

4. to predict
   — success in a course
   — success in school
   — success in a job performance

5. for placement
   — in courses, in grades, in levels

6. to make summative statements
   — about how well students have done overall in meeting course or unit objectives

7. to make instructional decisions
   — about where to start students with instruction
   — about which skills are mastered
   — about which skills or sub-skills to reteach
   — ...to which students

   and give feedback to students
   — about students' strengths, weaknesses, interests, learning styles

   to give feedback to teachers
   — about the effectiveness of instruction
   — about the effectiveness of curriculum

three words with similar initial consonants. That becomes part of their global reading score. But that tests a *listening* skill, not a *reading* skill. They need not be, and in some children *are* not, the same (an error in construct validity, the construct of what reading is).

- We go over a large amount of information with 11th graders on the American Civil War in a series of recitation lessons. Then we give an essay test asking for comparisons and contrasts between military strategies of the North and South. Nothing we did in the lessons helped the students learn anything about how to do comparisons and contrasts.

In evaluating student learning (not diagnostic testing), we want to know what students have gotten out of the instruction. If we test for things that are not part of the instruction, it is difficult to make anything of the results. Right answers will probably reflect students' prior knowledge and wrong answers will not be their fault.

3. Are the Criteria for Success Clear to Teachers and Students?

The third crucial question in Evaluation is about criteria: What are your criteria for judging a student's performance as adequate? Our criteria get translated into many labels: "Mastery", "Pass", "C", "B", "75", "93%", "unsatisfactory", "satisfactory", "outstanding." If you can answer this third question, you can say what a student must demonstrate or be able to do, specifically, to earn any of the labels; i.e., you know what the labels mean in terms of student behavior. Knowing the times tables (mastery) may mean responding correctly to 60 random facts in two minutes; that's the criterion. Understanding Turner's Frontier Thesis may mean being able to explain it in your own words (orally or in writing), including the five key notions of American expansion, unsettled areas, challenge and entrepreneurial spirit, hope, and safety valve, and their relation to each other. It is very important that students know what the criteria for success are, because that knowledge guides the way they focus their attention and their effort.

4. Do Students Get Clear and Honest Feedback According to the Criteria?

There are a number of pitfalls to avoid so that students remain clear about criteria, and they crop up in the feedback we may see students receiving on their work.

...criteria for a worksheet are usually simple and objective, and the outcome is based on the number of problems solved correctly. As the task becomes more complex, the aspects of performance entailed increase, as do the potential number of evaluation criteria and the difficulty of ascertaining the purpose of the assignment. Grades on compositions may be based on numerous standards which are ambiguous to the child. Spelling, grammar, length, and penmanship may be considered, along with the nature and accuracy of the information mentioned or the originality of the ideas expressed.

> Teacher instructions and feedback are not always helpful in alleviating this confusion because often both are not clear or congruent with the learning goal of the lesson. Consider a reading comprehension assignment where students are asked to answer questions and draw a picture to depict the plot of a story. The teacher may focus on the form of the product as well as on its content, commenting on the quality of the drawing or neatness of coloration rather than, or in addition to, the match between the story read and the picture drawn. Students may infer that what really matters is, indeed, the artwork rather than the appropriateness of their illustrations for the story content....This belief may influence how the students spend time on subsequent tasks...to the extent that teacher feedback and students' understanding of what is important does not match the actual content learning goal of a task, students are likely to consider themselves successful, even though they are not learning essential skills. To the extent that students focus on the wrong dimensions and devote time to irrelevant aspects of the task, they are likely to fail to master required skills. [Blumenfeld, *et al.*, 1982, p. 408]

Consider the area of writing, where we may be concerned with fluency, content (good ideas), organization, and mechanics. Do the students really know which of these is the priority—the objective—of a particular writing assignment? Is their feedback based on that focus? If they are *all* priorities, then is feedback broken out into the four categories so that students know how well they did on each one? Some teachers will give four separate grades on this kind of an assignment, thus making clear to students their areas of strength and weakness.

Before leaving the topic of feedback, we should consider the possible ambivalence teachers may feel about delivering negative feedback in the face of their beliefs about encouragement and being positive. Summarizing a large amount of research on praise and criticism, Blumenfeld, *et al.*, conclude:

> ...feedback often is not well understood by students....Recall, too, that actual achievement is minimally reflected in children's self-perceptions, at least in the early grades, and only somewhat more in the later grades. Furthermore, the amount of negative feedback a student receives does not necessarily have debilitating effects on self-evaluation. Taken together, these findings mean that teachers need not worry excessively about possible adverse effects of negative feedback. Instead the results emphasize the importance of specifying the standards for success and making feedback clear, contingent, and helpful to students in terms of offering strategies which will lead to performance improvement and positive comments. Providing realistic feedback need not result in children's feeling badly about themselves, but in fact, may help motivate them to perform adequately in the not unlikely event that they fail to perceive that anything is amiss. [Blumenfeld, *et al.*, *op. cit.*, p. 413]

These findings do not challenge the large body of research about the role of students' self-image in school success. They simply point out that honest feedback about performance in relation to objectives and criteria does not damage students' self-image, and may help it grow when linked to helpful instruction. Teachers show they are caring people through feedback that is clear and honest and linked to supportive instruction.

There are four additional questions about Evaluation we should ask to have a more complete picture of the topic.

5. Are There Well Organized Records?

In some regular, organized way, we look to see the behavior of students recorded, categorized, and available in records.

6. Are Pre- and Post-Test Measures Taken?

Student behavior should be assessed before instruction begins to see if students already know the material or part of the material.

7. Is Evaluation Repeated at Some Future Date After the End of Instruction to Measure Permanence of the Learning?

8. Are the Technical Elements of the Evaluation Conducted Adequately?

- Is the *sample* of items big enough (enough questions on each area so chance error doesn't mask what students really know or can do)?

- Is the test administered *objectively*, without bias or distractions or confusion to individuals?

- Are tests scored/judged *accurately*?

- Is the test *reliable*?

Entire texts are devoted to those questions in #8. Matters such as test reliability are usually well covered in test and measurement courses given for educators, so we do not feel the need to go into them in depth here. They are, nevertheless, an important part of the picture in good Evaluation and should be part of what we check.

Variety in Evaluation Systems

These eight questions give us a framework for analyzing a teacher's Evaluation system. But some teachers have more than one system. Teachers' Evaluation systems vary according to how they get information on student performance, and there seem to be five basic ways to get it:

- observation
- work samples and products
- paper and pencil tests
- interviews, conferences, or oral tests
- student self-evaluations, self-reports, or surveys.

Let's take one, self-evaluation for example, and see what it might look like if we scan it with the eight questions.

Mrs. Arnold uses self-evaluation to collect data about eighth graders' ability to play different roles in discussion groups (e.g., summarizing, stating issues, breaking tension...). She has told the students she is collecting the self-evaluations to see whether they have increased their ability to play multiple roles and to identify students who need more help. Each role has been explained and modeled by the teacher, and practiced in structured exercises by students. Now students are asked to participate supportively in a new group discussion. In their self-evaluation, they are to record what role or roles they see themselves as having played, and the roles played by each other member of their group. They have succeeded when they can claim three or more different roles, and the majority of their group supports their claims. One instance of role-appropriate behavior is enough to claim that role. The teacher meets with students who play less than three roles and has them pick an additional one to try in the next discussion. Students who claim more roles than their group testifies to are asked to write examples of the unsupported roles, which the teacher may accept as evidence. In her grade book she keeps a checklist of students who meet the criteria. For comparative purposes she has her own observational records of which roles individuals played before instruction.

As an exercise, can you tell which of the eight questions about Evaluation have been handled adequately in the above description?

Try it!

If Mrs. Arnold uses observation to collect data about eighth graders' mastery of lab safety procedures, we should expect to be able to answer the same questions for that evaluation. Likewise, we could take each of the five methods of data collection and generate examples of what fully thought-out Evaluation systems would look like at any grade level and in any subject area. In practice, few teachers have fully developed systems for all five modes—nor do they need them. However, observation, interviews, and self-evaluation are often ignored and would be a useful addition to the repertoires of many teachers, especially those interested in measuring affective objectives.

Self-evaluation can also get the added dividends of more student involvement, more awareness of criteria, and better discrimination of quality. Waters (1980) has students periodically isolate their best work from the collections in their writing folders. As she explains,

> The making of this collection provides students with an on-going opportunity to:
>
> - review and analyze their best work
> - choose what best represents him/her
> - establish a sense of progress
> - establish a base line from which to move ahead.

It also creates the groundwork for individual teacher-student conferences around the collection. Such conferences are unmatched opportunities for involving students in goal-setting and helping them generate ownership for their own learning.

Our final set of questions pertains to how teachers adjust and match their Evaluation systems to the needs of students.

Matching Evaluation Systems

The first level at which matching can be seen is between the Evaluation system and the content. Rarely do we see a mismatch here, but it is conceivable. Anecdotal records are not as appropriate for tracking progress in mathematics as, say, checklists of skills with criteria for mastery clearly defined. (Primary teachers may, however, keep anecdotal records of students' use of mathematics-related materials, but they may do that for other purposes than tracking skill mastery.)

At another level we may see teachers adjust their Evaluations for characteristics of the class-as-group or for sub-groups. And at the final level, we may see adjustments being made for individuals.

Adjustments in the Evaluation system may occur in the way data is collected. For some students the teacher may use tests, while for selected others the teacher either modifies the language of the test or uses observation, personal questioning, or some other means of collecting data on the student. Students for whom the reading level of the test would obscure assessment of their real knowledge of, say, the causes of the Civil War, are candidates for this kind of adjustment. Teachers using a programmed approach to instruction may modify the level of difficulty of the program's test by altering its content to match particular students or groups. Certain test questions may be added or removed.

Evaluation is probably the least glamorous and most neglected Parameter of Teaching. It is also one of the most demanding and technical areas for teacher skill. To really get all eight questions answered for a given Evaluation system takes a good deal of thought and planning.

In addition, good Evaluation, being technically demanding, sounds anti-humanistic, or at least ahumanistic. The precision and clarity of competent Evaluation is in no way, however, at odds with humanistic goals. Teachers who really want students to cooperate with each other, to listen to each other, or to resolve conflicts will develop sound Evaluation systems.

Sound Evaluation makes you be clear about what you really want to accomplish and what it would look like if you did. It makes you and your students face it when an objective is not reached, and tells you with a high degree of certainty when it is reached. And finally, it makes you constantly examine your teaching to improve it, no matter how good it already is.

With dividends like that, an investment in good Evaluation is too good to pass up.

Checking on Evaluation

1. Which of these five methods is used to collect data on student performance? Circle any that apply.

   observation   interviews
   work samples   student self-evaluations
   tests

2. For each method, which of the following questions can be answered? Fill in appropriate details.

   a. Is the purpose of the evaluation clear to teacher and students?

   b. Do the tests test what is taught?

   c. Are the criteria for success clear to teacher and students?

   d. Do students get clear and honest feedback according to the criteria?

   e. Are there well-organized records?

   f. Are pre- and post-test measures taken?

   g. Is evaluation repeated at some future date to assess permanence of the learning?

   h. Does the evaluation provide for adequate sample, objectivity, accuracy, and reliability?

3. The evaluation is.... Circle the one that applies.

   absent
     mismatched to the content
       appropriate for the content
         adjusted for the group's needs
           adjusted for individuals' needs

Source Materials on This Parameter

Bloom, B.S., Hastings, J.T. and Madaus, G.F. *Handbook on Formation and Summation Evaluation of Student Learning.* New York: McGraw-Hill, 1971.

Bloom, B.S., Madaus, G.F. and Hastings, J.T. *Evaluation to Improve Learning.* New York: McGraw-Hill, 1981.

Blumenfeld, P.C.; Pintrich, P.R.; Meece, J. and Wessels, K. "The Formation and Role of Self Perceptions of Ability in Elementary Classrooms." *The Elementary School Journal*, 82/5, May 1982, 401-420.

Clark, C.M. and Peterson, P.L. "Stimulated Recall." In *Flexibility in Teaching: An Excursion into the Nature of Teaching and Training*, Joyce, B.R., Brown, C.C. and Peck, L. (*eds*.). New York: Longmans, 1981.

Doyle, W. "The Tasks of Teaching and Learning in the Classroom." Paper presented at the annual meeting of the American Educational Research Association, San Francisco, April 1979.

Engel, B.S. *Informal Evaluation.* Grand Forks, ND: University of North Dakota, March 1977.

Johnson, T.J. "The Development of Educational Products, A Theory of Curriculum: Initial Notions." "Instructional Content and Test Performance." Unpublished papers, Boston University, 1978.

Johnson, T.J., Driscoll, L.C. and Nolon, W.F. "Theoretic-Logical Foundations for the Assessment of Instruction." Paper presented at the annual meeting of the American Educational Research Association, San Francisco, April 1979.

Tyler, R.W. *Basic Principles of Curriculum and Instruction.* Chicago: University of Chicago Press, 1949.

Waters, F. "Waters' STEPS in Writing." Unpublished manuscript, Watertown, MA, 1980.

Zahorik, J.A. "Learning Activities: Nature, Function and Practice." *The Elementary School Journal*, 82/4, March 1984, 309-317.

17

Organization of Curriculum

How do I build/adjust curriculum for maximum effectiveness?

Continuity
Sequence
Integration

ORGANIZATION OF CURRICULUM

In the last several chapters, we covered parameters that are basic building blocks of curriculum—Objectives, Learning Experiences, and Evaluation. This chapter introduces the fourth, and the one least discussed in schools—the Organization of Curriculum.

Objectives tell you where you're going, what you're going to achieve. Learning Experiences tell you what you're going to do to get there. The Organization of Curriculum tells you how you're going to *arrange* Objectives and Learning Experiences for a *cumulative effect*.

OBJECTIVES + LEARNING EXPERIENCES + EVALUATION +
ORGANIZATION = CURRICULUM

The actual things that get organized in curriculum are objectives, content (meaning "information"), and learning experiences. However, skill at selecting objectives, isolating content, and picking appropriate learning experiences to go with them is not enough to insure good curriculum. The organization of those things in curriculum is important because it has a lot to do with making learning stick. It also has a lot to do with the quality, the breadth, and the depth of the things that are learned. Good organization has its own impact. And knowing what well organized curriculum looks like is something teachers need to know about directly.

As *consumers* of curriculum, teachers choose between competitors in the marketplace and need this knowledge to discriminate the poor from the good from the better.

Implementing a curriculum maximally requires an understanding of the design behind it, so that timing can be appropriate and choice points taken well.

Teachers are sometimes asked to *design* curriculum themselves, and often to *explain* what they are doing to such groups as parents and school committees. For all of these reasons, basic knowledge about curriculum organization has been included among the parameters of teaching.

Organization is the blueprint of the larger effort, the sum total of all the experiences the student has in a given curriculum. It is the broad pattern of instructional events and includes what we see students and teachers doing, their materials, and spatial arrangements. The effects of these patterns, when well constructed, are to achieve the higher level objectives of the curriculum, like "critical thinking." Individual learning experiences can achieve small, short-term objectives, like "understanding the traditions of the Puritans." The larger ones, however, like "understanding the role of traditions in society,"*only* get achieved if curriculum is organized well.

The following are key aspects of curriculum organization to be considered when reviewing, purchasing, or designing curriculum:

1. The *building blocks* of curriculum as learning experiences (described in Chapter 13; i.e., complex entities with many controllable attributes).

2. The *structuring* of curriculum through arranging entities of different size and duration (learning experiences, lessons, units, courses, programs).

3. The use of *key concepts* around which subordinate main ideas and specific facts or operations are developed (rather than organizing around topics).

4. Returning to, or recycling through, key concepts in spiral fashion again and again over time, so that each time they are dealt with students treat them with more abstractness, generality (applying in new contexts), and complexity. This we call the principle of *continuity*.

5. The organization of learning experiences in *sequence* so that each experience builds on previous learning and builds a basis for a subsequent one.

6. The principle of *integration*, by which students apply or see the knowledge from one area as it operates or relates in another area.

For a full set of examples of these principles in action, we refer readers to Ralph Tyler's classic 100-page book *Basic Principles of Curriculum and Instruction*. It is interesting how often one hears "the Tyler rationale" discussed by people who have not read this central work. It is one of the most cited and least read books in the business, and comprises a most useful part of our professional knowledge base.

Source Materials on This Parameter

Gagne, R.M. and Briggs, L.J. *Principles of Instructional Design.* New York: Holt, Rinehart and Winston, 1974.

Taba, H.; Durlin, M.C.; Prenhul, J.R. and McNaughton, A.A. *A Teacher's Handbook for Elementary Social Studies.* 2nd Edition. Reading, MA: Addison-Wesley, 1971.

Tyler, R. *Basic Principles of Curriculum and Instruction.* Chicago: University of Chicago Press, 1949.

18
Epilogue

EPILOGUE

Non-Parametric Variables
or
Why a Few Important Things Seem to Be Left Out of the Book

Readers have asked why there is no chapter in *The Skillful Teacher* on learning styles; how motivation fits into the framework; and why self-concept is hardly mentioned in the book. Surely these are areas of importance to successful teaching.

The answer to these questions is that all three of the above areas *are* in the book, only they are embedded within the parameters in ways that are, at first, not easy to see. One way to view the parameters of teaching is as a set of levers that teachers pull. To achieve a particular outcome we pull certain levers on each parameter. The levers, the moves, the Models of Teaching, are deliberate choices aimed at outcomes we want for our students.

The things that we do as teachers to effect student self-concept are already embedded in the Expectations parameter, the Personal Relationship Building parameter, the Objectives parameter, and Principles of Learning (especially Responses to Student Answers). Under Expectations, for example, the degree to which we communicate to students "You can do it," has a huge influence on their self-concept. Under Objectives, the degree to which we target work that is not too hard, not too easy, but doable with effort by students influences the degree to which they see themselves as successful, as does the explicitness of our feedback, and the way in which we vary Learning Experiences so that they are good matches for students. A teacher's goal to help students achieve maximum success has implications for how that teacher will pull levers throughout all the parameters.

A similar analysis applies to the idea of "motivation." Why do people do what they do? That's the basic question of motivation. There are multiple answers. Translating the question for school, we would ask,"What makes students study and learn?" Think of the range of answers we could give for that one!

They are afraid of what will happen to them if they don't.
They get tangible rewards if they do.
The material is inherently interesting.
They desire to excel and to receive recognition and credit for their excellence.
They are working in cooperative groups where their performance will affect the score or the rewards of other group members.

They feel some ownership and control of the way in which the learning is taking place.

They feel community and membership in the class and are thus invested in most of the things that are part of the operation.

Any one or a combination of the above reasons can account for why a given student is motivated in a given class (or, in their absence, why a student is not motivated). Every item in the above list is also one of those levers that teachers can pull, control, vary, shape. So once again we are saying that teachers do, indeed, greatly influence how motivated students are; but the way teachers influence motivation is through the levers they pull on one or more of the parameters, not by doing something separate, distinct, or different from the behaviors we have been studying. Thus, like self-concept, motivation is influenced by choices and moves teachers make from the parameters.

So far we have made the case that self-concept and motivation are both outcomes of levers skillfully pulled, not teacher skills themselves. The place of learning styles in the framework is slightly different. If we want to vary the learning environment so it matches a student's learning style, what is it that we vary? The things that we vary are Models of Teaching, the thirteen variables in the Learning Experiences parameter, characteristics of the physical environment (Space), the pacing and rhythm of events (Time), and whether or not we emphasize certain Clarity moves like Communicating Objectives (which is a must for quadrant one learners in both McCarthy's and Gregorc's frameworks). Readers will remember that "matching" has been a part of every parameter and the critical thing we look for in examining teaching decisions. What is it that teachers are matching? It is, of course, the student's learning style.

So these three areas then—self-concept, motivation, and matching learning styles—are not parameters. They are outcomes of teaching which are achieved through decisions we make in many of the parameters. And the knowledge base about how to effect them is embedded throughout the parameters. Far from being omitted from the book and from the framework, they are central to it and woven throughout it.

Strengthening School Culture

And so we come to the conclusion of this book...at least for the present. Lest that seem enigmatic, let us explain that for us this book is never finished. We are always learning more about teaching and revising and updating the book more often than most publishers would tolerate.

The unfinished nature of learning for all of us in the profession has been one of the themes of this book, struck in Chapter 1 when we quoted Joyce about the need to be "always a student of teaching." To stay professionally vital, we need to see ourselves as constant learners about our craft—and also contributors, for most of the moves in the repertoires we have examined here were developed by practicing teachers.

This attitude of being constant learners prompts us to look ahead with a particular cast to the era of reform and rejuvenation into which the flurry of national reports launched the teaching profession in the 80s. We believe strongly that improving the quality of life for adults in the workplace, specifically making schools more satisfying, growth-oriented workplaces for adults, is the key to improving schools. It is also the key to attracting bright, capable young people into the profession, and retaining quality veterans. Interview studies reveal that what teachers want for themselves, in addition to feeling they have made a difference for individual students, are:

- more time to prepare for and attend to individual student's unique learning needs and gifts
- more frequent, practical feedback—both affirmation and correction—on teaching technique and classroom organization and management
- immediate, constructive help for teaching problems
- more relevant and stimulating opportunities for professional improvement—from observations of each other's teaching within the school to instruction provided outside
- informal, continuing exchanges with other teachers about what they have learned from experience, as well as new information they have garnered, and about new materials or projects they can develop together for their own classrooms or for the whole school
- a voice in the school's organization, course of study, school day, schedule, budget, student policies, and plans for improvement (Devaney, 1986).

The notable absence of "higher salaries" from this list should not divert reformers from addressing that important issue; but Devaney's summary reminds us that money is not foremost in teachers' minds. Teachers want to do the best job for students that they can, and they know a great deal about the conditions it would take to maximize their efforts.

In a separate but related line of research several years earlier, Judith Warren Little (1982) found that effective schools identified by the classic measures (high test scores, low drop-out rate, and community satisfaction) had professional cultures among adults characterized by collegiality and experimentation. Collegiality had four observable elements:

- high frequency of concrete talk about teaching among teachers (in addition to talk about students, families, curriculum, and social topics)

- high frequency of teachers observing one another teaching (whether formally or informally)

- high incidence of teachers planning and making instructional materials together

- teachers teaching each other about the practice of teaching.

Experimentation meant freedom and encouragement to learn and try new things in one's teaching.

It is no small coincidence that Devaney's list of what teachers want most so closely overlaps the elements of collegiality that Little finds in effective schools. The implication is compelling: to improve schools for students we must improve the quality of life for adults, and to accomplish both means working directly on school culture and organization. That work will have to engineer the time, the structures, and the expectations for schools as workplaces so that the study of our craft becomes a permanent built-in feature of organizational life. We must create conditions for adults in schools where collegiality and experimentation are norms of behavior—along with appreciation and recognition, reaching out to the knowledge base, and involvement in decision-making (Saphier and King, 1985). Improving school organizations in these ways is the leadership challenge of the next decade.

How does this book fit in with efforts to strengthen school culture?

Conceiving this knowledge base about teaching in terms of Mission, Repertoire, and Matching instead of a list of "effective" teaching behaviors is a natural fit with efforts to strengthen school culture. To increase collegial exchanges and nourish attitudes of experimentation and constant learning among adults in a school, we need:

1. a conception of the knowledge base that respects and acknowledges what people already know

2. a range of options that shows even the most experienced and capable teachers that they can still learn new and useful teaching skills

3. a view of teaching itself that treats teachers as professionals because they are decision-makers

4.   an understanding of the ownership of the knowledge base (of the moves in the repertoires) by practitioners who developed them—for teachers, not researchers, are the creators and continuing inventors of most of the moves we know about in all the parameters.

One of our fondest hopes for this book is that the way we have framed the knowledge base opens the door for more concrete and productive exchanges among teachers and between teachers and administrators, exchanges aided by a common language and concept system and fueled by a desire for constant improvement.

Source Materials

Devaney, K. "The Lead Teacher: Ways to Begin." Report written for the Carnegie Forum on Education and the Economy. New York. January 1987.

Joyce, B.R., Clark, C. and Peck, L. *Flexibility in Teaching*. New York: Longmans, 1981.

Little, J.W. "Norms of Collegiality and Experimentation: Workplace Conditions for School Success." *American Educational Research Journal*, 19/3, Fall 1982, 325-340.

Saphier, J.D. and King, M. "Good Seeds Grow in Strong Cultures." *Educational Leadership*, March 1985, 67-74.

ORDER FORM

Please send _____ copy(s) of *The Skillful Teacher* by Saphier and Gower at
$21.95 each, to me at the address below:

_____ x $21.95 = _____ sub-total

plus shipping and handling (add $3.86
for single copies; $4.39 for 2 to 4 copies
or 5% of sub-total for order of 5 or more.)

_____ shipping

_____ Total

SEND BOOKS TO:

_____

_____

_____

MAIL TO:

Research for Better Teaching
56 Bellows Hill Road
Carlisle, MA 01741
508-369-8191

*When placing orders from overseas, please contact the Research for Better Teaching
office for specific price quotation on shipping and for documentation requirements.
Payment must be made in **US funds** and assigned through a specific US banking
institution.*